IMPERFECT UNION

A Father's Search for His Son in the Aftermath
of the Battle of Gettysburg

CHUCK RAASCH

STACKPOLE
BOOKS
Lanham • Boulder • New York • London

Published by Stackpole Books
An imprint of Globe Pequot
Trade Division of The Rowman & Littlefield Publishing Group, Inc.
4501 Forbes Boulevard, Suite 200, Lanham, Maryland 20706

Distributed by
NATIONAL BOOK NETWORK
800-462-6420

British Library Cataloguing in Publication Information available

Library of Congress Cataloging-in-Publication Data

Names: Raasch, Charles, author.
Title: Imperfect union : a father's search for his son in the aftermath of the Battle of Gettysburg / Charles Raasch.
Description: Lanham, Maryland : Stackpole Books, 2016. | Includes bibliographical references and index.
Identifiers: LCCN 2016012456 | ISBN 9780811718936 (hardcopy)
Subjects: LCSH: Wilkeson, Bayard, 1844–1863. | Wilkeson, Samuel, 1817–1889. | Gettysburg, Battle of, Gettysburg, Pa., 1863—Biography. | Fathers and sons—New York (State)—Buffalo—Biography. | War correspondents—New York (State)—Buffalo—Biography. | United States—History—Civil War, 1861–1865—Casualties. | Battle casualties—Pennsylvania—Gettysburg. | Buffalo (N.Y.)—Biography.
Classification: LCC E475.53 .R223 2016 | DDC 974.7/904092 [B] —dc23 LC record available at https://lccn.loc.gov/2016012456

♾™ The paper used in this publication meets the minimum requirements of American National Standard for Information Sciences—Permanence of Paper for Printed Library Materials, ANSI/NISO Z39.48-1992.

CONTENTS

INTRODUCTION

"The Probable Truth"

TWO YEARS AFTER THE BATTLE OF GETTYSBURG, *ATLANTIC MONTHLY* magazine correspondent J. T. Trowbridge visited the most famous battlefield in America. He had become an expert at picking through the great and terrible aftermath of the Civil War. Trowbridge spent that summer and fall of 1865 walking through the landscape where armies had clashed, passing through towns and fields scoured and scarred by four years of war. The next year, his book, *The South: A Tour of Its Battlefields and Ruined Cities*, gave voice to the scores upon scores still reeling in the war's wake.[1]

That aftermath is the truest legacy of war. Tales of heroism on the battlefields are told most vividly, and most often. But what is put back together from the pieces of shattered lives, after the guns go silent, becomes the forever.

This book is primarily about two people, a war correspondent and his son, in the great aftermath of the greatest battle on American soil. How they arrived there at that tumultuous rendezvous, and how they got caught up in the great tributaries of suffering that flowed from it, is the story of Gettysburg that still unfurls.

Correspondent Trowbridge was initially surprised at how quiet the town of Gettysburg was that summer of 1865, two years after the battle. He arrived on a "soft and peaceful summer day." Only the natural symphony of locusts and the "perpetual click of the stone cutters, at work on the granite headstones of the cemetery," interrupted the sultry summer tranquility. Yet there was an extra heaviness in the air, as if it was about to burst with "lively reminisces of those terrible times." Townsfolk were reticent to unleash one memory, lest it turn into two and then into too many, inflicting another fresh searing of souls and senses from the rages of three days of 1863.

Trowbridge arrived at the cemetery that Abraham Lincoln had dedicated with his famous speech four and a half months after the battle, the speech in which Lincoln lauded brave men for consecrating the fields with that final "full measure of devotion." The graves of more than 3,500 Union soldiers stretched out before Trowbridge on a plump knoll. They were spaced 2 feet apart sloping gently to the killing valleys around them, grave upon grave, story upon story, memory upon memory. New granite stones were still being installed to mark them, and as the monument workers dug into the rocky Pennsylvania ground to anchor fresh headstones, Trowbridge caught glimpses of coffins or remains of men buried just beneath the surface. It was as if the first layer of history was being peeled back and exposed again to the never-ending pain and loss of those three days, and to the questions the multitudes had left behind. The tranquility that Trowbridge first felt had simply masked a bottomless sense of loss. At that moment Trowbridge recognized that the aftermath of Gettysburg would last forever, and not in the way that history records winners and losers, or in the tales of old soldiers glorifying their actions.

"The spectacle of so large a field crowded with the graves of the slain brings home to the heart an overpowering sense of the horror and wickedness of war," Trowbridge thought.

A great weight of questions burdened him. Why did these men end up here, each of whom "had his interests, his loves, his darling hopes, the same as you or I. All were laid down with his life. It was no trifle to him, it was as great a thing to him as it would be to you, thus to be cut off from all the things dear in this world, and to drop at one into a vague eternity."

No trifle indeed, in these last, full measures of devotion. The toll their deaths exacted could not be counted just by the long casualty lists that ate up column after column in newspapers over the war's four long years. How had their families persisted and coped with that vague eternity that had stolen their loved ones? Had this man or that man died alone, or amidst the great wash of humanity that descended on Gettysburg in the days after the battle? Were they touched by the unknowable heroes of that second great invasion, those rivers of mercy that flowed over Gettysburg after the armies left their grim harvest behind? Or did they die alone in their own thoughts?

Why does war demand heroes? Is it because that believing the alternative—that people died on these fields because it was the only way to kill the arrogant and utter debasement of slavery—is unfathomable amid sacrifice and destruction on the Civil War's scale? Why is rationalization necessary at all when civilization has been shaped by conflict since its dawn?

"We indulge in pious commonplaces, 'They have gone onto a better world, they have their reward,' and the like," Trowbridge wrote. "No doubt this is true; if not, then life is a mockery, and hope a lie."

Hope a lie? Life a mockery? Questions left for the survivors. Irrelevant questions for the memory of the men lying in the ground at Trowbridge's feet. To Trowbridge, they "confronted for their country that awful uncertainty" of death.

"Did they believe in your better world?" he asked. "Whether they did or not, this world was a reality, and dear to them."

Volumes have been dedicated to the first three days of July 1863, to the hand-to-hand struggles on Little Round Top and Culp's Hill and Cemetery Ridge, to the point-blank slaughter in the peach orchard and railroad cut. They have been embedded in the history of America's seminal conflict. This book is not just about heroes on the battlefield. It is a story about the arduous, terrifying roads to the battle; about the reporters who were following the armies and the war correspondent profession they were inventing on the run; about the suffering that flowed from the battle for days, months, and in the years afterward; and about the struggles to find loved ones and peace in the eternal aftermath. When the soldiers left, a fresh civilian army numbering in the thousands descended upon the suddenly famous village—or infamous, depending on which direction you were looking upon it from. This second great invasion of Gettysburg, these legions of the aftermath, produced heroes and villains of a different kind—but just as meaningful, often just as courageous, as any sword-wielding hero on the field of fight.

In this aftermath was a nineteen-year-old soldier, a boy with the ambitions of youth that seek immediate fame and righteousness. A boy who became broken in body, struggling in spirit. His father, a staunch abolitionist and fearless journalist for *The New York Times*, was tasked with describing the battle and its aftermath while simultaneously searching for that oldest son. Ultimately, Bayard and Sam Wilkeson were just two ripples in those great rivers of the aftermath. But many heroes crossed their paths. We know the names of some, but others were lost forever.

The Wilkeson story is ultimately a love story, not only that of father to son and son to father, but that of the gentle mercies of those who stepped forward into the utter depravity and loss of three days of Gettysburg's savagery. As in battle, lives often intersected for only a few intense minutes. As in battle, those in the aftermath met challenges beyond anything they had previously thought themselves capable of doing.

The Civil War came amid a second American revolution. Before the guns opened on Fort Sumter in April of 1861, great currents of life-altering, age-defining changes were coursing through communications, transportation, and the social order of mid-nineteenth-century America.

The construction of new telegraph networks created expectations that news would be reported when it happened. In the twenty years since 1843, when Samuel Morse first transmitted "What Hath God Wrought" over the first telegraph line from the Supreme Court in Washington to a home of a friend in Baltimore, the United States had built more than 50,000 miles of telegraph lines.[2] (The invention's revolutionary impact on the news profession was foreshadowed with Morse's next transmission to his friend, Alfred Vail, when Morse asked: "Have You Any News?") The Union army alone built 8,000 miles of telegraph line during the war, and it transmitted 6.5 million messages over those four years, at an average cost of forty-one cents a message.[3] Sam Wilkeson and his intrepid war correspondent colleagues depended on that network to get dispatches back to their newspapers in what a few years earlier would have been unfathomable speed. War correspondents called the telegraph "the lightning" for its immediacy and its power.

The impact of the lightning on journalism and on all communications was every bit as revolutionary in the mid-nineteenth century as the

Internet was on citizens in the early twenty-first century. The embedded correspondents of twentieth- and twenty-first-century wars were merely following paths blazed by Sam Wilkeson, Lorenzo Crounse, Whitelaw Reid, Charlie Coffin, Francis Lawley, and a few score others who traveled with the armies of the Civil War.

By the Civil War, Americans were becoming more mobile, bursting the bubble of physical isolation that had defined the nation's first half century. Train trackage nationally had increased from 2,818 miles in 1840 to 33,170 by 1863.[4] It had more than doubled in the decade before the war, with roughly two-thirds of the track located in the more industrialized Northern states, factors in the North's eventual victory. Even during the first two years of the war, with governments North and South transfixed on building armies, roughly 2,000 new miles of railroad track still were built.[5] During the Civil War, a Congress devoid of Southern members passed laws establishing land-grant universities, transcontinental railroads, and the Homestead Act, all of which would feed one of the most significant migrations in the history of the world over the last third of the nineteenth century. It was on this expanding transportation grid that armies moved men and the material of war. But it was also on this grid upon which family members, friends, and fiancées of soldiers, along with aid givers and looters, descended upon Gettysburg from great distances and all points of the compass, even as the battle raged on.

In the lead-up to the Civil War, abolition and women's rights movements had exposed the false promises of a Constitution that was guaranteeing equality and freedom for less than half the population. Freedom of the mind and freedom of movement were simultaneously expanding. Just as the social movements of the mid-nineteenth century foreshadowed those of a century later, the great armies traversing the landscape foreshadowed the great westward migration that would follow.

"The war begot a spirit of independence and enterprise," Ulysses S. Grant wrote in his memoirs. "The feeling is that a youth must cut loose from his old surroundings to enable him to get up in the world."[6]

The American press was embedded in all these movements. Journalism was evolving, too, into an essential, flawed, pioneering, democratizing institution. Partisan and mistake-ridden, sometimes prone to comical oversubscription of hyperbole, and too frequently engaging in pure pro-paganda, it also time and again produced some of the most remarkable accounts of war ever written. War correspondents were adjusting to the pressures of daily deadlines in this new lightning communications age. Despite the flaws and growing pains, newspapers had become essen-tial to the growth of the nation. In 1863, the year of Gettysburg, U.S. Census Bureau superintendent Joseph G. C. Kennedy wrote that news-papers had played an integral role in spreading literacy and expanding the American middle class. The United States, Kennedy wrote, was "peculiarly a newspaper-reading nation."[7] The great debates that had once been the province of royal courts or elite societies were now taking place on the pages of newspapers that any American could pick up for a couple of pennies. As the stakes rose in the issues involved—slavery, equality, freedom, the eventual cleavage of two vastly different cultures and economies—newspaper consumption soared. There were 1,404 newspapers in the United States in 1840, when the population was just over 17 million. By 1860, with the total population around 31.4 million, the nation had 3,725.[8]

"The last decade in our civil history has been one of extraordinary political agitation," wrote the Census director Kennedy in classic bureau-cratic understatement, given that he wrote it in the third year of the Civil War. "Accordingly we find that there has been a very large increase in the number of political papers and periodicals."

Once staid and aimed at the literary elite, Kennedy observed, news-papers had become "popular educators.

"Instead of mere chronicles of formal proceedings or passing events they are vast depositories of discussion and information on all topics which engage the thoughts or enlist the activity of men in the figure of society," he wrote. "A free press has thus become the representative and, for the masses, the organ of that free speech, which is found indispens-able to the development of truth, either in the religions, the political, the literary, or the scientific world. In each and all these domains the news-paper and the periodical have accordingly become most efficient agents.

"And in no country has their influence been more sensibly witnessed, or more widely extended, than in the United States. The universal diffusion of education, combining with the moderate prices which the daily visits of the public press may be secured, has given newspapers a very great currency among us."[9]

Amid this, a new breed of journalist, the war correspondent, was ascending. Some of the most famous, like Coffin, Reid, Crounse, and Sam Wilkeson stood behind the ragged ribbons of waiting blue on Cemetery Ridge, took notes and dodged cannonballs, as George Pickett's Virginians charged into history on July 3, 1863. These war correspondents blazed journalistic trails through literal valleys of death.

By July of 1863, the correspondents had fully grasped the importance of their roles as recorders of the toll. Political intrigue in Richmond and the District of Columbia was widely covered and dispersed. The formation of the Associated Press cooperative in 1846 had opened the widespread sharing of stories over the telegraph. Home-front readers by the war's third summer had developed insatiable appetites for news from the actual battlefields. The war had touched virtually every American household. Roughly 10 percent of the American population served in the two armies, and 2.5 percent of all Americans died as a result of the war. Thousands of men, women, and children—spouses, escaped slaves, contractors, prostitutes, and preachers—followed them around the landscape. As a superb 1862 *Atlantic Monthly* piece by the father of a future Supreme Court justice would illustrate, hasty post-battle journeys of loved ones to the battlefields had become commonplace as the war dragged on. The whole country seemed to be on the move, and in distress, by the time of those three fateful days at Gettysburg.

Civil War journalists were trying to make sense of it all. They all had their shortcomings. But in their best hours they were ingenious, creative, courageous, and indispensable.

After the Battle of Antietam in the fall of 1862, the bloodiest single day of the war, the *Boston Journal*'s Charlie Coffin explained the war correspondent's challenge this way:

"When the soldiers are seeking rest, the work of the army correspondent begins. All through the day eyes and ears have been open. The note-book is scrawled with characters intelligible to him if read at once, but wholly meaningless a few hours later. He must grope his way along the lines in the darkness, visit the hospitals, hear the narratives of all, eliminate error, get at the probable truth, keeping ever in mind that each general thinks his brigade, each colonel thinks his regiment, every captain his company, did most of the fighting."

Some of America's best writers and poets—Walt Whitman, Ralph Waldo Emerson, and Harriet Beecher Stowe among them—wrote about the war. Emerson saw the Civil War as the ultimate definer of the nation and the character of its people. "Bad times have a scientific value," he wrote, and "civil war, national bankruptcy, or revolution, (are) more rich in the central tones than languid years of prosperity."[10]

Yet it was everyday Americans—the homesick nineteen-year-old in the ranks, or the young woman watching thousands like him march by her front door—that produced some of the Civil War's most powerful prose. They often wrote with bad grammar and sometimes could not spell a lick. But they exerted an innate honesty, a level of detail and description, often with endearingly noble guilelessness, that is too-often bleached from everyday communications in the ubiquity of the twenty-first century. The Civil War came at the dawn of visual mass communications, before words became throwaway objects. People in the mid-nineteenth century were forced to be more observant, perceptive, creative, and meaningful in their writing because the written word was still the primary canvass of communications, the most enduring record of memory. Everyday Americans were also essential chroniclers of the war's great aftermath.

Mary Bedinger Mitchell was eleven years old at the time of the battle of Antietam. She lived in Sharpsburg, the cloistered Maryland village 43 miles southwest of Gettysburg, where the battle of Antietam took place. Mary helped nurse wounded soldiers after the September 17, 1862 catastrophe. It was ten months before Gettysburg, and the struggles after the battle foreshadowed what would happen after Gettysburg. As an adult just after the war, Mary described her isolated town as "just nine miles from everywhere." She remembered her amazement at seeing the Town Hall turned into a hospital even as cannonballs arced over roofs and church steeples. "Somebody threw a few rough boards across the beams, placed piles of straw over them, laid down single planks to walk upon, and lo, it was a hospital at once," she observed a few years after the war. She described the suffering of the wounded, some of whom lingered for weeks on those rough planks, this way: "We were fond of calling them Spartans, and they were but too truly called upon to endure a Spartan system of neglect and privation."[11]

Charlie Coffin was right. Only the "probable truth" is possible in the first drafts. The war he and Sam Wilkeson reported on was so epic, with so many people on the move and so many political and social cross-currents flowing beneath them, that we will always be caught in its aftermath, always in search of its truth.

I became acutely aware of this reality on a visit to the battlefield at Gettysburg in 2013, just before the 150th anniversary. The Clark family from Addison, Vermont, had driven to the national monument to retrace the steps of an ancestor who had died there at the age of twenty-one, in the carnage at Culp's Hill, not far from where Bayard Wilkeson fought.

Pvt. Myron Clark, a beloved company clerk, kept a wartime diary that had been passed through generations of his descendants, from one coast of America to the other, through one century to the next, and then to another. The precious words were still held in reverence by the Clark family so many scores of years later, testament to the eternal stamp of Gettysburg on individuals and families. When I ran into the retired dairy farmers Erwin and Janet Clark, and their adult son, Bradley, they were using the diary to trace their relative's last hours in this world. Pvt. Myron Clark was killed, his head blown off by a cannonball, in a pre-dawn fight on July 3, 1863, on Culp's Hill.

Bradley Clark told me his family had always treated the diary as a what-if relic of life's great imponderables. They are the eternal unknowns that Trowbridge had raised in that peaceful visit two years after the battle. The Clark family thinks their ancestor is buried in one of the mass graves at Gettysburg, his body never identified or returned home, his remains literally now part of the soil of these historic fields. Myron's descendants often speculated about how different the family would have been had this promising young man survived the war. Myron's thoughts, so vivid on the pages of his diary, were so full of life and the wonderment of a young soul that his death, even after all these years, seems particularly cruel and sad.[12]

Myron's last diary entry was on July 1, when he wrote of changing to a clean shirt as his brigade of Vermonters double-timed to the battlefield. He threw away the old, dirty shirt he had been wearing to lighten his load. All around him, men were jogging in the morning's steamy heat to the rising sound of guns in the near distance. Lt. Bayard Wilkeson and the 120 or so men in his command would have been nearby. They, too, were throwing off the unnecessary, stripping down to battle weight, steeling nerves and mining memories for a comforting thought.

The final lines in Myron Clark's diary were written by a commanding officer. Private Clark "was a good boy and a good soldier," the captain wrote. "The whole Co. mourn his loss & Especially his Capt." Then, writing for Myron, his family, and for the ages, he declared: "Such are the fortunes of war. And they are deplorable."[13]

And so the aftermath continues.

CHAPTER I

Angels Above Him

HE LAY IN A PUDDLE OF HIS OWN BLOOD. THE BASEMENT WAS DARK AND dank. Frenzied soldiers, their wool uniforms soaked in sweat, carried freshly wounded men to any open space they could find. The world above exploded with sounds of whistling metal and pounding feet and the shouts of men in distress. All around him on the dirt floor wounded men moaned and cried out.[1]

He had just turned nineteen years old, but his dirty, bloodied blue jacket bore the stripes of a lieutenant. He was one of the youngest commanders of a six-cannon artillery battery in the Union army. His hair was black, and his skin bronzed and toughened by two years in the sun and heat and cold. He was handsome in the way of a boy just now shedding the softness of childhood for the firmer features of a man. He had tried so hard not to show his men how much he hurt. Bayard Wilkeson did not want to die.

That morning, July 1, 1863, he and his men had awakened 12 miles away in the steamy dawn of a Maryland field. There had been a frantic, four-hour march to Gettysburg in the heat and mud, the last of it on a forced trot, as guns in the distance boomed and crackled louder with each step. Now, he was lying in the basement of a poorhouse in a place called Gettysburg. He was frightened, but he did not want to show vulnerability to anyone.

It had been his wish to fight in a battle that mattered, to test his training and courage, to make a name. But on this day, there had not been a single second for contemplation. It had been an exhilarating, terrifying rush into the unknown for multitudes of men, including this young Bayard, this lieutenant of the Union army.

He drifted in and out of consciousness. When he was awake, the pain overcame him and he could not stop from crying out. The noise above him was becoming even louder and more chaotic. Men shouted, hooves pounded, the boom of cannon was so close it sounded as if it was coming from inside his head. Soon there came an earth-shaking crescendo of arms just overhead. Then the disturbance eased and moved into the distance, like thunder fading into the heavens. The young lieutenant's pain intensified. Cries and groans were now the primary sounds. This was his world now. He surrendered for a moment, crying out for his mother and father. But he had to be strong for the men. He went silent again.

Was this a dream? The faces of two women hovered above him. One face was black, the other ruddy white. Both were kind faces. One woman soothed him with a soft-Irish voice, wiping a dirty cool cloth on his forehead. The other held his hand. They kept coming and going, sometimes by themselves, sometimes together, angels to his call. He came and went, too, thinking of home, then thinking of nothing but the pain. The man next to him begged for water and he gave up his canteen for him. An aloneness came to him. He called again, and then again, for his mother and father. The angels reappeared with soothing voices and the cool cloth. They smiled and their gentle eyes made him unafraid. He tried to smile back. Another face appeared, this one a man's, and their eyes briefly met. All around him there were cries and quiet whimpers in the fading light.

He was only nineteen years old. He did not want to die.

CHAPTER 2

"Deathlike Stillness"

IN THE GATHERING HEAT OF LATE MORNING, A SOLITARY BIRD CHIRPED in a peach tree.[1] Sam Wilkeson fixated on it, as if it was a plea for normality. The battlefield south of Gettysburg this July 3, 1863, littered with the waste of three days of savage inhumanity, had gone ominously silent. Only an occasional zip of a stray shot, or the nearby clanging of metal equipment, or the low voices of soldiers along the ridgeline 300 yards up a slight slope to the west, competed with the bird's lonely call.

Its melody would only be a temporary respite. An unnatural fury was building. Everyone along the forebodingly named Cemetery Ridge and down its eastern, leeward slopes could feel it. One of Wilkeson's newspaper colleagues remembered it as an "ominous silence."[2] Across the divide, where thousands of men were also lying in wait, the sense of foreboding was just as strong. A. L. Long, a top aide to Confederate general Robert E. Lee, said it was as if a "deathlike stillness" had descended on the field.[3]

It was, Sam Wilkeson thought, a "silence as of deep sleep."[4]

Wilkeson, a veteran correspondent who had just joined *The New York Times* three months earlier from the rival *New York Tribune*, had sought shade along a whitewashed, 16-by-20-foot house, about 300 yards east of Cemetery Ridge, where thousands of blue-clad Union troops had held on for two blistering days. The tiny farmhouse, owned by the widow Lydia Leister, was the battlefield headquarters of George Gordon Meade's Army of the Potomac. As aides and orderlies swarmed about in the midday heat, Wilkeson had found relief in the shade with a cluster of war correspondents, some of them among the most well known of the great

American newspapers. A few of Meade's staff officers sat down with them. Veterans all, many carrying the psychological and physical wounds of previous battles, they intuitively knew by this third summer of the war that one took rest whenever, and wherever, possible.[5]

The house sat on the southern outskirts of the town, just a few yards from the rutted, muddy road connecting Taneytown to Gettysburg. About 300 yards to the northeast sprawled a cemetery occupied by Union troops and cannons, including artillery remnants of Maj. Gen. Oliver Otis Howard's crippled 11th Corps that had been pushed back to the cemetery and the ridge on the first day of the battle. The 11th was Lt. Bayard Wilkeson's corps, but he was not with it on this day.

Less than a mile to the west, tens of thousands of Rebel troops were shielded by trees along Seminary Ridge. Some were preparing, at this moment, for the climactic charge of the war.

Two days earlier, Meade had made this modest farmhouse the nerve center of an army of 93,000 men, of which thousands had already been killed or wounded or captured in two days of uncommonly brutal and efficient killing. The fighting had raged most furiously on the wings of the Union army's line, which was spread out over 3 miles of ridges east and south of Gettysburg. This center, behind which Wilkeson and his colleagues had situated themselves for the day, had not been as savagely hit. But that was about to change, and men in both armies could sense it. In the noontime pall, it was as if the two battered foes were taking one last breath before resuming the grim business that no one had been able to stop for more than two years.

Sam Wilkeson had slept on the grounds near these headquarters the night before with a fresh and heavy burden on his heart. He had been told that his son, Bayard Wilkeson, had been wounded and left behind by his 11th Corps companions on the battle's first day, and no one at headquarters or among the survivors in the cemetery knew his fate. Sam had arrived that first night of the battle, exhausted and mad at himself, to learn from one of Bayard's subordinates that his boy had been taken to a poorhouse basement on the north edge of Gettysburg minutes before it was overrun by thousands of Confederates. That was barely 2 miles from where Sam Wilkeson sat this morning, but a hostile Confederate army was not about to let him cross through, especially a war correspondent for a New York newspaper.

Sam had been awakened before dawn on this third day of the battle to the staccato sounds of rifles a few hundred yards to the northeast of Meade's headquarters. The smoke of that nasty fight on Culp's Hill, which had gone on for some time, had created a dreamy, gauzy haze over a rising sun. Some of that acrid battle smoke still hung in the sultry air as noon approached.[6] Rough-sounding action earlier in the morning had also been heard on the left flank of the Union lines less than a mile to the south, where a day earlier, gritty Mainers had beaten back Texans and Alabamians on Little Round Top. The whole expanse of the fields was littered with bodies and war detritus, and the air was ripe with the stench of dead flesh, human and animal.

That solitary bird soon got company. Unusually large flocks of pigeons and swallows flew overhead as the lull continued.[7] Could they sense the gathering, man-made storm? Still, that single bird kept warbling in the nearby peach tree. Wilkeson jotted the images in his notebook. A reporter never knew which normal-life detail would come in handy while trying to explain the unspeakable things that men were doing to one another to a reading public that could never fully grasp it.

The lean, long-faced Wilkeson had a brown, gray-streaked beard that flowed to his chest, a sharp nose, deep-set eyes, and angular features that conspired to make him look older than his forty-six years. He was a dean of the Civil War correspondents, older than almost all of the roughly four dozen reporters who had followed the two armies to Gettysburg. Given his age and reputation, most of his fellow correspondents, some of whom were barely into their twenties, naturally deferred to him. But there was greater deference than normal this morning. His colleagues could see that Wilkeson was weighted down by worries that would consume even the sturdiest war correspondent, or the heartiest man.

On top of that, Wilkeson knew he was behind in his reporting on the pivotal battle of the war. Some of his competitors had already filled their notebooks, and some had already headed out to file on the first two days of the fighting at this suddenly famous crossroads town. The fighting at Gettysburg was being described in blaring headlines, north and south.

Wilkeson took consolation in knowing that while those competitors were away in search of telegraph lines to file their stories, he was still on the field in anticipation of a climactic final eruption. There was plenty of correspondent work to be done. The first two days of battle had been a hellish draw, an orgy of killing so grandiose, yet so intimate and personal, that it defied description. And it was not over. More killing was necessary to render a final blood verdict on the field, and on history. Everybody could sense it.

Sam Wilkeson had taken a circuitous, frustrating journey to Gettysburg, fully anticipating the history that was about to be made somewhere in Pennsylvania, with the army of Robert E. Lee making its first full-on thrust into a Northern state. Like any war correspondent worth his words and witness, Wilkeson had desperately not wanted to miss any of it. But on battle's eve, he had taken a bad gamble on where he thought the Army of Northern Virginia and the Army of the Potomac would eventually clash, and he had headed in the wrong direction. He had arrived at Meade's headquarters in the overnight hours after the battle's first day, having missed the heavy fighting on the northern and western outskirts of the town. In that fighting, two corps of the Union army, around 20,000 men, had fought under the command of Maj. Gen. Oliver Otis Howard, a one-armed veteran of unquestioned bravery but dubious command authority. Howard's two corps had barely hung on, barely staved off another humiliating defeat to Lee's grizzled veterans, had barely held the high ground now occupied by the Union army. With the outcome of the battle still very much unresolved, Wilkeson had buttonholed every officer, soldier, and civilian who would talk to him to draw as accurate a portrait as he could of the history they were all caught up in.

Yet that far, far greater worry at times overwhelmed him. His flesh and blood was out there someplace on this ghastly, bloody landscape. All Sam knew was that Bayard's battery had been caught in a pincer of Rebel columns, that he and his men had fought heroically, but that Bayard had been badly wounded and taken by his men to a temporary medical aid station in the Adams County Almshouse. Sam did not even know if doctors, North or South, had reached his boy, who was one of several

6

thousand men wounded on the first day of the fighting at Gettysburg, and still unaccounted for.

Was Bayard even alive? Was he headed for a Confederate prison or had he been spirited into a Gettysburg home to hide from the Rebels, as scores of Union troops were doing at that very moment? There was no way to know. He tried to push those thoughts out of his mind. The outcome of the battle of Gettysburg, and all that it portended for the future of the United States of America, would have to play out first.

CHAPTER 3

"A Portable Battery of Nine Pistols"

A MONTH BEFORE THE BATTLE, GETTYSBURG WAS KNOWN PRIMARILY
as a carriage-manufacturing crossroads town of 2,400 residents. The seat
of Adams County was a prosperous hub where ten roads converged from
all directions. By nineteenth century standards, Gettysburg was a modern
community, with piped water and gas lights, the Lutheran Theological
Seminary, a college, seven churches, and two banks. It had rail connections, although they were temporarily cut four days before the battle
when Confederate soldiers burned a bridge east of town. Gettysburg also
had three newspapers.[1]

Swells of knolls and hills gave the countryside around it a comfortably gentle placidity. But while its geography and topography blessed it
with that pastoral serenity on normal days, on July 1, 1863, the landscape
became a devilishly inviting host for two veteran armies. High ground
was premium, and men paid dearly for it. Militarily, Gettysburg had
become a magnet, pulling in lethal columns of men down ten different
roads into a ripe host for slaughter. Within a 3-mile radius of the town
square, which itself became part of the battlefield, there was defensible
high ground on parallel ridges running north to south; woods and man-
made features that could hide movements of great numbers of men; and
open fields where commanders could organize frontal assaults or flanking
attacks, and where cannons could rip away at lines of exposed men with
sleeting bursts of canister. Gettysburg's narrow alleys and streets hosted
some of the deadliest street fighting of the war, and the steeples and
cupolas of its churches and homes became lookouts for commanders

trying to get a higher view of it all and for snipers picking out targets, one-by-one. These holy, pastoral peaks also became target references for cannoneers who would exhibit some of the most accurate shooting of the war to this point.

July 1, 1863, was not Gettysburg's first brush with Southern soldiers. Southern Pennsylvania's bucolic prosperity had been first interrupted in mid-June when bands of Lee's Confederates, having crossed the Potomac, passed through with Harrisburg, Philadelphia, and other important Northern cities in their sights. Some had more than the first invasion of a Northern state on their minds. Along the way, roving bands of Confederate cavalry and infantry sought out and captured blacks—both former slaves who had sought freedom north of the Mason-Dixon Line, and free blacks—to be sent south into slavery. They were terrifying and dangerous days for any black person in southern Pennsylvania in the early summer of 1863.

On Wednesday, July 1, leading elements of the armies of Lee and the newly promoted Union general George Gordon Meade stumbled into one another west and north of Gettysburg. The bloodiest battle of the Civil War ensued, a clash of such epic proportions that for the rest of his life Sam Wilkeson, a man of uncommon perception and a deep feeling for the gravitas of history he was witnessing, would feel inadequate in trying to describe it.

Sam Wilkeson's reputation preceded him, even in the colorful legion of correspondents who were essentially inventing a profession in the middle of a war. Their ranks included objective truth seekers, adventurers, daredevils, ideologues, heroes, men of high morality, at least in their own minds, politicians, ex-cons, and shirkers—the latter the label affixed to those who ran from the sound of the guns. Even among the intrepid and perpetually restless, Wilkeson stood out. Fearless, fiercely competitive, opinionated, confrontational, and sometimes reckless in action and quick to the temper, he had an eye for the most telling details, a flair for description, and a rare gift of being able to stitch chaotic events into a broad-meaning narrative in time for the next day's newspaper.

He came from a line of abolitionists, the son of a famous founder of the city of Buffalo, New York, and the husband of Catherine "Cate" Cady, younger sister of the suffragette Elizabeth Cady Stanton. As Washington bureau chief for Horace Greeley's *New York Tribune*, Wilkeson had by this third summer of the war arrived at the unassailable belief that only all-out war with a Northern victory could end the rebellion and slavery. As the war progressed, that underlying belief had seeped into his coverage, and it was more directly expressed in private correspondence with his boss and friend at the *New York Tribune*, Sidney Howard Gay.[2] Yet despite the distinct Republican nature of Greeley's *Tribune*, Wilkeson had not shied from criticizing Lincoln and his generals. In the weeks leading into the battle of Gettysburg, Wilkeson, who had just moved to the rival *New York Times* after a bitter separation from Greeley, had been conducting an unusually acrimonious public spat with a Union general who Wilkeson had accused, in print, of cowardice. The spat had resulted in a court-martial but eventual clearing of Maj. Gen. David Birney. But the case had become intensely personal to Sam Wilkeson, for it had involved the battlefield death of another Wilkeson soldier, Bayard's first cousin, John Wilkes Wilkeson, in the spring of 1862.

Sam Wilkeson had originally arrived in Washington in the late summer of 1861 to cover the exploding Washington war bureaucracy for Greeley. But by the spring of 1862, restless and hankering to get to the point of the sharpest action, Wilkeson embedded in the Union army during the Peninsula campaign, which ended as a costly and ultimately failed attempt to end the war quickly and decisively. Sam had gotten very sick after that campaign, and he had suffered soul-searing emotional stress at the death of his nephew. Wilkeson had spent much of the late summer and early fall of 1862 recovering at a farm near the upstate New York town of Canaan that he and Cate Cady Wilkeson had bought before the war.

While he had been the Washington bureau chief for the most-famous newspaper editor in America, Horace Greeley, Wilkeson had held considerable sway at the nexus of power and intrigue in the capital. Under Wilkeson, the *Tribune* office on 14th Street in Washington, DC, had become part saloon, part salon.

The sleepy, swampy capital had awakened to the business of war. Wilkeson's *Tribune* office was strategically located two blocks from the

Horace Greeley
LIBRARY OF CONGRESS

White House, just up the street from the famous Willard Hotel—also known then as Willard's—along the city's burgeoning newspaper row. Washington newspaper bureaus clustered around a Western Union office at 14th and H Streets Northwest, conveniently located near a string of taverns later known as Rum Row. The *Tribune* office became gossip central, a gathering place for fellow journalists, officers, bureaucrats, contractors, and various players of high and low motive in wartime Washington. That part of the city, which included the popular Ford's Theatre a ten-minute walk east, and the half-built marble obelisk monument to George Washington on the muddy, tent-festooned Mall that was a ten-minute walk south, was a warren of iniquity and intrigue, populated with prostitutes, profiteers, politicians, preachers, and pen-wielding journalists.[3]

Wilkeson wrote that the lobbies of the hotels Willard, National, and Metropolitan were full of agents peddling the latest war inventions, including a "man with a portable battery of nine pistols, to be worn as a girdle." Prostitutes in packs of a dozen or more wandered the boulevards, and on the second floors, above the newspaper offices and other buildings, were warrens of rotating games of roulette and poker. "Honest George" Adams of the *New York World* lamented that low-grade grog was served at "San Francisco prices."[4]

It was a journalist's dream, where the truth trumped any novelist's imagination. But it was not where the action was, and by July of 1863, Sam Wilkeson was well known among the Union officer corps, a nettlesome pain in the neck to some, a respected risk-taker to others. And he was about to take one of the biggest risks of his life.

CHAPTER 4

"You Should Have Seen Him"

SAM WILKESON WAS NOT PRONE TO SENTIMENTALITY, BUT HE SOMEtimes dreamed of his oldest boy in soft and tender ways. Bayard had joined the Union army at age seventeen in the first fall of the war. Sam's dreams seemed to come from a different lifetime. Like cool breezes on a summer night, the dreams and memories tempered the long war's burn.

A favorite memory was from a brisk September day three years before the war. It happened at the family's Hudson Valley farm, near Canaan. It was that splendid time of year when frosty dawns awakened the spirit and sunny afternoons warmed body and soul in the passing season. That morning was the first time that Sam realized that Bayard, although then just fourteen, was no longer a child. The gangly arms and legs and knobby knees of adolescence, the soft games and boyish interests of childhood, were beginning to surrender to a firmness of body and purpose. Bayard had always been a serious boy, in part because propriety and purpose was demanded from generation to generation of the Wilkeson and Cady clans. But Sam could see that day that the boy had become more driven, more disciplined. All that the boy had been taught about the freedom to act, about the discipline and fealty toward a useful life, about the need to leave a mark, had come together behind a team of burly oxen and a plow that glorious September morning.

Five years later, Bayard would summon those traits at a critical hour in the battle of Gettysburg.

That day at the farm, Sam Wilkeson remembered, the dark-eyed boy with an unruly shock of dark hair had arisen before sunrise while the rest of the family slept. Bayard quietly fixed himself breakfast. He walked out to the pasture to harness a pair of red oxen. By the time Sam had awakened, Bayard had already set furrow to field, plowing recently harvested ground, coaxing the oxen with firm commands and deftly pulled reins as he walked behind the two giant beasts.

For a long time, Sam watched and admired from a hidden distance the steadiness and skill Bayard displayed at the rein of the beasts. Bayard and his team kept going and going, unaware of Sam's gaze, coaxing and guiding with firmness and patience, preparing the ground for the next spring's planting. Rhythms of life had been learned and passed on. In every fresh furrow, the young man and his oxen released the redemptive, earthy, reassuring fragrance of freshly turned soil. It was a ritual of hope and rebirth, a handsome demonstration of honest toil and determination. Sam was so proud that he had written his brother, John, to declare that he felt that Bayard had grown up right in front of him.

"You should have seen him," Sam wrote.[1]

Now, on the first day of Gettysburg, that brother John, still reeling from the loss of his own son in battle the year before, was on his way to the suddenly famous Pennsylvania town to help Sam find Bayard. The people back home in Buffalo had gotten the news. A hometown paper in Buffalo reported on July 3 that Bayard had been wounded north of Gettysburg by Rebel guns "enfilading his position." "He is wished a speedy recovery," the Buffalo correspondent wrote, and "a brilliant career is before him."[2]

A telegram from Sam to John from Gettysburg only noted that Bayard "lost a leg."[3] Wilkeson's former paper, the *New York Tribune*, reported on Bayard's wounding on its front page.

"Lieut. Bayard Wilkeson, commanding Battery G, 4th Regular Artillery, son of Samuel Wilkeson, Washington correspondent of *The Times*, right leg shot off below the knee while gallantly fighting his battery against an eight gun battery of the enemy enfilading his position; believed to be a prisoner."[4]

Finding him would not be easy. Gettysburg's fields had been turned over, too, but not in the life-affirming manner that Bayard had displayed at the farm at Canaan. The orgy of killing had left the smell of decay and death. The bucolic had turned horrific. Maturing fields of wheat and knee-high corn, orchards of ripening fruit, and meadows of hay trampled and ground back into the earth. Windrows of dead and dying men in blue and gray striped the fields. The earth was being turned here, too, but to bury the dead by the scores. Homes became hospitals, gardens burial grounds, barns surgical centers that reaped harvests of arms and legs.

And now, as the final, climactic fighting of Gettysburg was about to commence, this is the aftermath that awaited Sam and John Wilkeson, and scores and scores of searchers for loved ones like them.

CHAPTER 5

"Jove! What a Dish!"

THE WILKESON FAMILY STORY EPITOMIZED THE RISK-TAKING EXPAN-siveness of eighteenth and nineteenth century America.

It began with two Irish immigrant families. John Wilkeson immigrated to the British colonies around 1760, and after the war for independence he was awarded land near Carlisle, Pennsylvania, for his service in the Revolutionary army. He married Jane Oram, whose family had emigrated to the United States with the Wilkesons. Their son, Samuel Sr., was born in Carlisle, in 1781, 35 miles from the knoll where his grandson, Bayard, would fight in the battle of Gettysburg eighty-two years later.[1]

Samuel Wilkeson Sr. was an early civic leader in Buffalo, New York, helping to turn a village on the shores of Lake Erie into a thriving and powerful nineteenth century shipping and manufacturing hub. Civic-minded, bold, and opportunistic, Sam Sr. was patriarch of a family that eventually owned iron mines, shipbuilding yards, and grain elevators in western New York and neighboring states. His wife, Sarah, the junior Sam Wilkeson's mother, died when the eventual war correspondent was just nineteen. Sarah was a religious educator and thought of as a "woman of great activity and benevolence."[2] Her war correspondent son got his curiosity and deep sense of equality and fairness from her. Sam got his wandering nature from his father.

By the time Sam Wilkeson Jr. was born in 1817, his father had built successful grist mills in Ohio, failed as a salt transporter, and had made a lot of money building ships for the U.S. Navy during the War of 1812. A neighbor across Niagara Square in Buffalo was future president Millard Fillmore. The senior Sam Wilkeson was one of Buffalo's first judges, a title he would carry for life. He also helped build the first iron foundry in Buffalo, owned a shipping line, and built factories that manufactured stoves and steam engines. The senior Sam Wilkeson was a tireless promoter of Buffalo as the terminus of the Erie Canal from Albany. He was a pioneer of big dreams, pushing the kind of broad-shouldered actions that defined the merchant and manufacturing class of the emerging America. There was virtually nothing Sam Sr. would not do, including entering politics, to advance his hometown's interests.

The elder Sam Wilkeson was widowed three times, served both as mayor of Buffalo and in the New York state Senate, and became one of the longest-serving judges in Buffalo's history. He was an uncompromising abolitionist and in his later years briefly moved to Washington, DC, to run the American Colonialization Society, formed to establish colonies for freed slaves in Liberia. Eulogizing his father at his funeral in 1848, the younger Sam Wilkeson credited him with paying the way to send 200 freed slaves to Liberia.[3]

Eight grandsons of Sam Wilkeson Sr. served in the Union army during the Civil War. Three, including Bayard and his younger brother, Frank, were under eighteen when they enlisted.[4]

The law, shipping, and commerce continued to be primary Wilkeson businesses into the mid-nineteenth century. But while his brother, John, continued the line of manufacturers and merchants, the junior Sam Wilkeson had diverged into other interests at an early age. While attending a grammar boarding school run by Amos Smith in New Haven, Connecticut, in the 1820s, Sam published a weekly paper, written in longhand, for his classmates.[5] He had been born at just the right time to mesh his interests and skills with a reading public's needs and desires, and with the technological advances of the age. The American newspaper industry was on the cusp of revolution. And in it, Sam Wilkeson saw ennobling, emancipating possibilities.

Cate Cady Wilkeson, whom he married in 1842, would have preferred that he'd farmed. Cate constantly worried about her husband's health while he was away from home during the war. She believed he was only feeling well when he was at home in Canaan. "Farming I hope will keep him in good health," she wrote her sister-in-law, Mary.[6]

Exactly a year before Gettysburg, Sam Wilkeson had nearly died after getting severely ill with dysentery while covering the Peninsula campaign in southern Virginia. On Independence Day of 1862, Sam was bedridden on the farm in upstate New York. Cate's cooking and nursing and farm work slowly brought him back to health. Writing his *Tribune* editor Sidney Howard Gay from the farm on July 29, 1862, Wilkeson said he was starting to feel better from a strange combination: Cate's creamed potatoes, and hard farm work.

"Jove! What a dish," he wrote Gay, describing Cate's potatoes. "My wife shall be canonized for instituting it. She shall go into the Calendar of the Blessed St. Catherine de Pomme du Terre."

"My dysentery declined into diarrhea," he went on, providing Gay more information than he probably desired. "This, chased with raspberries and garden vegetables and disturbed with hay forks and scythe swathes of deliberation has nearly comprised into an intermittent belly ache."

Then, a final word of advice: "May your bowels never be disturbed. This is the highest wish of good I can utter for my fellow man."[7]

Cate would have had him be at home on the farm, leaving the disturbances to others. She constantly worried about him, as she did Bayard after he enlisted in the army.

"You ask if it is necessary for Sam to go to the battlefields?" she wrote a sister-in-law in the second year of the war. "No, he only goes to gratify his curiosity. I greatly fear that he will be killed or wounded in some fight. How awful war is. If I had a good pair of legs, I would go in some hospital and help the poor fellows but my varicose veins trouble me a good deal, so I dare not use my feet much and I am a useless member of society."[8]

But in his soul Sam Wilkeson was not a farmer. Despite his physical maladies, he was always drawn back to the harsh living and coarse witness of the war.

When he first set out to cover the Peninsula campaign in southern Virginia in April of 1862, he lamented the role of "business of general agent" that the bureau chief of a major Republican newspaper had to assume in wartime Washington.

Samuel Wilkeson, photograph by Mathew Brady
COURTESY SMITHSONIAN AMERICAN ART MUSEUM

"For nine months I have borne its burdens," he wrote, "being afflicted during that long time with applications for about everything that the heart of man can desire out of a national capital in a time of peace or a time of war."

Since he had moved to Washington in mid-August of 1861, everyone from dreamers who thought they should be ambassadors to poor boys seeking work in army stables had darkened his doorstep, seeking his lobbying because of his perceived contacts in the Lincoln Administration. People had approached him with "requests to raise brigades down to the procurement of discharges from the ranks of boys, runaways from their mothers' homes." Soldiers seeking promotions thought he could put in a good word with his contacts in the administration and the army.

Going to the front was a relief after all that.[9]

"I give notice that the business of general charitable agent in the *Tribune* bureau at Washington is at an end," he wrote, grumpily. "The sign is taken down, and another slave is emancipated in the District of Columbia."[10]

He had seen the war become the ultimately indispensable avenue of change that he had come to believe was not possible in the more detached, plodding world of politics. Long before the battle of Gettysburg, Sam Wilkeson had decided that abolition would have to be won at the bayonet's point, no matter the cost.

Long before the heartaches and bellyaches of the Civil War, Sam Wilkeson could have been pardoned for living comfortably in the wake of his famous father. He could have continued his prewar abolition activism without going to the front lines of the war.

His marriage to Catherine Cady, the sister of the famous women's rights advocate Elizabeth Cady Stanton, fit his activism. Cate was more private than her famous sister, whose speeches and letters made Elizabeth Cady Stanton one of the most famous women in America. There is evidence Cate was more traditional in her views of marriage and relationships than her famous sister. But at important moments early in the women's rights and suffrage movement, Cate publicly and prominently supported her sister.

In 1848, Elizabeth Cady Stanton read the "Declaration of Rights and Sentiments" at the first women's rights convention in Seneca Falls, New York. Their older sister, Harriet, was one of sixty-eight women to sign it, although Cate was not. But two years later, Cate was among seventy-two signees of a September 6, 1850, call to a convention for women's rights that was held the following month in Worcester, Massachusetts. The call, published in newspapers, declared, "In every country, to this day, whether Christian or Pagan, woman has not been recognized or treated as the equal of her brother man, but has been subject to his tyrannical will, more or less absolutely."[11]

It was an historic document. Besides Cate Cady Wilkeson and Elizabeth Cady Stanton, signers included Lucy Stone and Lucretia Mott, and
the well-known abolitionist and suffragist editor of the *Boston Liberator*,
William Lloyd Garrison. Almost a third of the signers of the convention call were men, but Sam Wilkeson was not among them. He never
publicly disclosed whether he felt his journalism or his personal views
precluded him from doing so. But later in life, Elizabeth Cady Stanton
would proclaim her brother-in-law a "good man of progressive mind."
There is no evidence in the family of friction over Sam Wilkeson's views
on women's rights, and his public support of abolition, immigrant rights,
and the restoring of voting rights for felons after release from prison
suggested he would have been a supporter of gender equality.

In 1866, the year after the war, Cate Cady Wilkeson signed a petition
asking Congress to pass a constitutional amendment granting women
the right to vote. Her name appeared six lines below that of Susan B.
Anthony.[12]

The gender definitions, and restrictions, of the age were constantly
questioned in Cate's childhood, and she would have passed them on to
Bayard and his siblings. One of Elizabeth Cady Stanton's earliest recollections came when, as a child, she saw the disappointment on neighbors'
faces when another sister of Cate's and Elizabeth's was born. "What a
pity that it is a girl," the neighbor said. Elizabeth "did not understand at
that time that girls were considered an inferior order of beings."[13]

Although Cate held more traditional views of marriage than her sister did, there also is no evidence of any friction between Cate Wilkeson
and her more famous sister over their different private-public roles. There
was the usual ribbing of siblings. In late 1843, when Cate was pregnant
with Maggie, hers and Sam Wilkeson's first child, Daniel Cady, the father
of Elizabeth and Cate, wrote Elizabeth a letter imploring her to stop
scaring her sister with tales of childbirth. Defying Elizabeth's impressions, he was hoping for a granddaughter.

"I am anxious to hear from dear Cate," Daniel Cady wrote. "I hope
she will get thro her trials safely, then blessed with a stout, healthy daughter! You must not frighten her constantly what a horrid affair it is. You
must remind her of the royal courage of Victoria."[14] The reference was to

England's Queen Victoria, in her sixth year on the crown in 1843, a royal inspirer of scientists and innovators, who also gave birth to nine children.

Sam and Cate welcomed Bayard on May 17, 1844. Their second child and first son reveled in big family gatherings. In 1851, when Bayard was seven, Elizabeth Cady Stanton wrote lovingly of an extended Cady family gathering in Johnstown, New York, while they were stranded by a snowstorm. Cate had brought Bayard for the day. "We danced one evening in the great hall & played all sorts of pranks. We have had several sleigh rides as there is plenty of snow here."[15]

Educated in the prestigious Troy Female Seminary school for girls, later re-named after the women's rights activist Emma Willard, Cate Cady had received her secondary education degree in 1837. Her equal rights public pronouncements aside, she believed throughout her life that men should be primary breadwinners. In an alumni questionnaire from the Emma Willard School decades after she graduated, Cate responded to a query about her "professional life and work" by writing that she had had none. "My father supported his five daughters," she wrote.[16]

Cate, her famous sister, and two siblings were raised in modest privilege. Daniel Cady's family owned slaves until New York banished slavery in 1827; after that, one of the Cady's slaves, Peter Teabout, stayed on as a manservant. The Cady girls adored him, and later in life Elizabeth Cady Stanton recalled how the girls would sit with Peter in a segregated pew when Teabout worshiped at their Episcopal church. Peter was especially comforting to Cate and her sisters when their only surviving brother, Eleazar, died when Cate was about seven. For the Cady girls, it was a lesson in grieving, mourning, and gender roles in the mid-nineteenth century. [17]

"We early thought that this son filled a larger place in our father's affections and future plans than the five daughters together," Elizabeth Cady Stanton wrote of her father. She described long hours of the bedside vigil as Eleazar died. After her brother's passing, Daniel pulled Elizabeth onto his lap, and proclaimed: "Oh my daughter, I wish you were a boy!"[18]

Cate and her siblings viewed their father "with fear rather than affection," and it was a feeling handed down to his grandchildren, including

Bayard. Daniel Cady was most at home in the courtroom, but family was important in the strictest Puritanical sense. The Cady family was "as kind, indulgent and considerate as the Puritan ideas of those days permitted, but fear, rather than love, of God and parents alike, predominated," Elizabeth remembered.[19]

Cate grew up in a two-story white house with an ample garden that abutted the family of a Presbyterian pastor. The Cady children roamed the forests and streams of the Mohawk Valley. Barrels of hickory nuts, large maple sugar cakes, and spices were stored in the attic where Cate and her sisters often played. The cellar was packed with apples, vegetables, cider, and salt meat. Every September, Johnstown celebrated "Training Day." Farmers hauled in produce for sale and admiration, but mostly the day was about watching the local militia drill, and recounting stories of the Revolution.[20]

Bayard Wilkeson's family was deeply rooted in Revolutionary War tradition, and he would have heard their stories at an early age. His paternal great-grandfather had been awarded land for his service in the war. Bayard's maternal grandmother, Margaret Livingston, a "tall, queenly looking woman" and "courageous, self-reliant and at her ease under all circumstances and in all places," was the daughter of another important Revolutionary War officer, Col. Robert Livingston.[21] He had commanded a Continental Army regiment that helped capture the spy Benedict Arnold. By the time Bayard enlisted in the Union army, the legacy of military service was steeped in both sides of Bayard's family. His sister, Margaret, was named after her grandmother, the daughter of the famous Revolutionary War colonel.

Bayard's father, Sam, did not serve in the military. Sam came into adulthood studying at Williams College and Union College, where he studied the law. For a short time, before being admitted to the New York State Bar in 1842, Sam helped manage the Wilkeson family iron works in Buffalo.[22]

Later, after he left the law for journalism, Sam's modest salary for many years didn't top $3,000. It provided a comfortable middle-class life, but they were not ostentatious. Family correspondence hinted occasionally at money being tight.[23]

Sam and Cate could have lived far more comfortably if he had stayed in the law practice with Daniel Cady, who eventually would rise to the New York Supreme Court. After Sam and Cate were married in 1842, Sam had apprenticed under his father-in-law. But Wilkeson found the law lacking. Restless, he went into journalism. He could not stop moving. And it affected his family life. His work often took him far from home.

Besides Bayard and Maggie, Cate and Sam had two other children. Samuel Gansevoort was born in 1846, and Frank Wilkeson was born in 1848. Their father's letters revealed a parent who often longed to be home and who cherished news of his children's' accomplishments. But always, there was the pull of big causes.

During the same year that he was admitted to the bar, Sam Wilkeson unsuccessfully ran as an Abolitionist for the New York State Assembly. He lost in a landslide to a Whig incumbent, polling just 385 votes. Wilkeson framed his defeat as a first, necessary step, of a longer journey. In a November 1842 letter to a cousin, Sam predicted future success simply because the cause was just. Abolitionists, he said, were a sleeping majority, ready to be awakened.

"We have at least 1,500 Abolitionists in sentiment, and we will endeavor to make them acting Abolitionists before the next Congressional Election," he wrote the cousin. "We will organize the County thoroughly this winter upon the school-district system, and have lectures to the extent of our abilities. . . . I think Sir we can now throughout the north, see the pathway upon which our cause shall steadily glide to a triumph—we are destined to a political success, and to a moral success."[24]

Slavery would not end through the ballot box alone, although Lincoln's election and, more importantly, his re-election in 1864, would bring all the right political actors to the stage. Two decades later, Wilkeson would come to the grim belief that only the war, and its terrible toll, could end slavery.

Sam's 1842 letter to his cousin reflected the idealism and optimism of a young parent. Bayard's older sister, Maggie, had just been born; Bayard would follow eighteen months later. Then just twenty-five, Sam wrote in wonderment and delight about his daughter. Cate was already teaching Maggie "queen's English," Sam wrote. Sam was teaching her how to ride a horse. He joked that it was a great help that Maggie was "uncommonly compact."

"Prejudices apart," Sam wrote, Maggie was "about the finest child I ever saw." She looked "so matured in her face," Sam wrote, that "I perpetually wonder (if) she does not give advice."[25]

Maggie's unusual sagacity followed her into adulthood and a long and accomplished life. Twenty years later, Maggie would accompany her parents to a party at Secretary of State William Seward's home that would become a pivotal moment in Sam Wilkeson's wartime reporting.

CHAPTER 6

"To Conscientiously and Manfully Perform the Duties of a Journalist"

A SUCCESSION OF PRESIDENTS COULD NOT PREVENT THE CIVIL WAR. Long before the guns opened on Fort Sumter, Sam Wilkeson's youthful idealism and optimism that abolition would come through the ballot had been replaced by a world-weary realism. When he switched from law to journalism, he brought with him the edge of a crusader who had discovered how difficult the cause would be.

By 1848, with the nation at war in Mexico and trying to avoid Civil War at home, Sam's letters had harder edges. Idealism had turned into hard reality. In a letter that year to Cate's uncle, the staunch abolitionist Gerrit Smith, Sam noted that Cate had by then "squared" the family by giving birth to four children. By then Sam had given up the law and bought the *Buffalo Democracy*, which years later was folded into the *Courier Express*. In his letter to Smith, Sam complained about the "shavers" and "userers" at Buffalo banks who wanted 12 percent interest on a loan he sought. He wanted Smith's help in obtaining a loan with a bank in Peterboro, New York, and stressed that it would be backed by "our fathers [(sic)] endorsement . . . and it would be paid when it fell due. Of that there would be no doubt."

Then he segued to politics. Wilkeson told Smith he considered then-president James Polk—a supporter of the Missouri Compromise to allow expansion of slavery if approved by voters in new territories—a "heartless and base fellow" who "forgets favors." He asked Smith: "Are you Abolitionists again going to soil the chances of the next Whig candidacy for president?"

But Sam also closed with a more upbeat note that spoke to how his personal politics had invaded his journalism. He told Smith he was writing a speech advocating voting rights for new male immigrants and felons who had served their sentences. "I am going to lecture tomorrow night upon the 'Limitations to the right of Suffrage in the State of New York,' and shall maintain the apparently ultra and radical dogma that an immigrant is a citizen from the moment of his landing on our shores with the intention of making it his home forever—and should therefore be allowed to vote without delay," Wilkeson wrote Smith. "Also that excluding from the right of suffrage 'persons convicted of infamous crimes' and who have been discharged from imprisonment at the expiration of their terms, but have not been pardoned, is wholly unjustly and impolitic—that it is a violation of the inherent and inalienable rights of a citizen of a republic."[1]

In 1855, Sam Wilkeson bought the *Albany Evening Journal* from Thurlow Weed, a New York publisher, Whig Party insider, and principal adviser to Sen. William Seward, who would in a few years become Abraham Lincoln's secretary of state. The purchase of the *Journal* turned out to be one of Wilkeson's worst decisions in journalism and business. It also came at a time when Wilkeson was raising his national profile, in part by commingling politics and journalism.

In 1854, Wilkeson ghost-wrote a speech for Seward on a topic the senator knew little about: potential routes for the westward expansion of railroads.[2] It was an admission of ignorance for Seward, who as Lincoln's secretary of state would arrange for the purchase of Alaska from Russia. Neither Wilkeson nor Seward could foresee it at the time, but Wilkeson's ghostwriting for Seward would inspire both men's postwar years, and create a moment of supreme irony right after the war.

Upon taking the editorship of the *Journal*, Wilkeson was clear about his mission and goals. He would advance the "feelings and purposes of a great and progressive political party," the Whigs.

"I now enter upon the discharge of duties which my accession to the paper imposes on me," he wrote in the first edition under his editorship, on October 5, 1855. "I understand there to be labor for Freedom, for the culture and enlightenment of the People, for the growth of the State in material wealth, for the diminution of its social evils and the reform of its social errors—to conscientiously and manfully perform the duties of a journalist. These I dare undertake, and do freely possible."[3]

One could "manfully" pledge without penalty or pause, because journalism was overwhelmingly a man's profession in the mid-nineteenth century. Despite efforts by his sister-in-law and her allies, there were few women in journalism or public life in the mid-1850s. Women would not get the right to vote for another sixty-five years. The one big exception to the glacial place of social change in the nineteenth century would be abolition of slavery.

As war seemed more and more likely, Wilkeson always seemed primed for the next fight in the pages of his newspapers. He pushed for social reforms (abolition of slavery, immigrants' rights) and political reform (anti-machine). Yet he eventually became a consummate Washington insider. He pioneered a form of insider-advocacy journalism readily recognizable in later centuries in Washington, DC. He cultivated access to people in power not only to record events, but to try to shape them. He used that access to inform and contextualize his reporting, but also to protect and reward his sources and punish his enemies. He was not above appealing to editors to run stories praising a politician to boost that politician at the ballot box.

Wilkeson's editorship in Albany ended badly in 1859. In the gathering storm of war, he and Weed had a bitter public falling out. He left to join Greeley's *New York Tribune*, as its Albany correspondent, and turned the *Journal* back over to Weed.

The Wilkeson-Weed separation festered through Lincoln's unlikely victory in the presidential election of 1860, in which the powerful, deft Weed backed Seward for president but later became an adviser to the eventual winner, Lincoln. The politically connected, personally charming Weed claimed that Wilkeson had failed to make payments and had lowered the *Albany Evening Journal's* journalistic standards. Worse, Weed claimed, Wilkeson had been criticizing him behind his back. "No word of unkindness passed between us, nor, until recently, did we learn that he is our enemy," Weed wrote in the *Albany Journal* after taking back the editorship from Wilkeson.[4]

Wilkeson initially claimed he had given up the *Journal* because of failing health, but once attacked, he responded with a fury, painting Weed as a corrupt political boss in an article dripping with moralistic outrage in the *New York Tribune* in the spring of 1861. It was three weeks before the attack on Fort Sumter. "To your dictatorship I do confess myself hostile," Wilkeson wrote. "I think that the power you possess ought to be destroyed, and the office you have usurped ought to be abated. And as long as I shall remain in the profession of Journalism, I will improve timely opportunities to impress upon a free people, in a Free State, that they should deliberate in Convention without an engineer, and assemble for legislation without a director."[5]

But, while piously proclaiming his fealty to the public interest, Wilkeson was also not above playing the favor-trading insider political game he had thought so unsavory when Weed engaged in it. Wilkeson was unabashed in how he went about it. In a candid letter to his *Tribune* editor, Gay, in November 1862, Wilkeson described how he worked the access angle in Washington, DC.

Congress that summer had passed new income tax levies and was debating the National Bank Act that would set chartering standards for private banks. The Bank Act eventually passed in February of 1863, and it helped stabilize currency and the banking system as Lincoln's government struggled to finance the war. Wilkeson not only confessed to Gay that he had helped an unnamed politician write a speech on behalf of the act, but he submitted a story to the *Tribune* that backed that position as well.

"I am assisting, as the French say, in getting up the great speech of this session—whose points are foreshadowed in the dispatch," Wilkeson wrote Gay. With the nation's finances stabilized on the new taxes and the Bank Act, he wrote, the government could now keep fighting the necessary war, and "you and I will be in at the death of Slavery, either way."

Then, unabashedly, he wrote that trading access for favorable treatment in the paper was the best way to build sources and help the *Tribune* get the inside news before his competitors did. He would not wine and dine sources to get a story, he said. "I give no dinners, I go to no dinners. Consequently, I have no power of social influence," Wilkeson wrote Gay. "My only power here is the power of the paper. To obtain favors for the paper, and to strengthen this, I will explain to you and justify items personally commendatory of Congressmen."[6]

It was tit for tat, all around the great causes of the times. He could not have known it at the time, but it was all preparation for a coming storm greater than anyone imagined.

CHAPTER 7

"A Self-Made Man Who Worships His Creator"

MANY OF THE TWO SCORE OR SO REPORTERS[1] WHO COVERED GETTYS-
burg with Sam Wilkeson were part of a fraternity of New York journalists self-dubbed the "Bohemians" out of irreverence and the salon
society aspirations this group of intellectuals carried. They had become
accustomed to danger and privation with the armies, and to the suspicion
and hostility of officers and enlisted men. Wilkeson himself had somehow survived point-blank volleys and Confederate snipers a year earlier
at Seven Pines in Virginia, when he tried to help a Union officer rally a
routed brigade. He had also spent one night in a Union army brig, briefly
suspected as a spy, which could have gotten him hanged.

The Bohemians were reckless beyond reason, and the war would cost
some their health, their lives, or their freedom. The *New York Herald's*
principal naval correspondent, B. S. Osborn, was wounded seven times
in the twenty-eight battles he covered. Another *Herald* correspondent,
Finley Anderson, who like a few colleagues also served part of the war
on Union officers' staffs, was wounded in the arm at Spotsylvania Court-
house in 1864. But Anderson kept taking notes and after the battle rode
more than 60 miles to Washington to file his dispatch for the next day's
paper.

Two months before Gettysburg, correspondents Albert D. Richardson and Junius Henri Browne of Greeley's *New York Tribune*, along with
Richard Colburn of the *New York World*, were trying to get to Vicksburg,

which was about to be put under siege by Grant's Union Army of the Tennessee. Trying to cross the Mississippi River, the boat that the three correspondents were on was sunk by Confederate cannons. The correspondents were captured while floating on cotton bales in the river. They were held over the next twenty months in seven different Southern prisons.

Along with the *Cincinnati Gazette*'s William E. Davis, Richardson and Browne escaped from a Confederate prison near Salisbury, North Carolina, a week before Christmas, 1864. They spent weeks hiding and moving through forests, snow, and brush to elude captors, reaching Union lines near Knoxville, Tennessee, after a 340-mile journey. Their escape and harrowing journey back was one of the most compelling of a war filled with many hair-raising stories.

"War correspondents sought news as the brave soldier sought glory—at the cannon's mouth," declared a postwar feature on Civil War correspondents by the *Atlanta Constitution*'s J. Thomas Scharf. "No dangers daunted, no hardships discouraged them. They shared the perils, and the privations of the army and navy."[2]

Wartime competition was cutthroat and fierce among the Bohemians, and among the new ranks of competitors who signed up to cover the war for newspapers, North and South. Scharf declared that Civil War correspondents had a simple charge: "Obtain the most accurate information by personal observation and forward it with the utmost dispatch, regardless of expenses, labor or danger. Correspondents were told that to be beaten by any other papers was a crime; that to be up and even with them was not particularly worthy of commendation; but to beat them was a success that would not go unrewarded."

At Gettysburg, Francis E. Lawley of the *Times of London*, at the suggestion of Confederate corps commander James Longstreet, climbed a tree on Seminary Ridge on the second day of the battle to watch Longstreet's bloody assault on soon-to-be-famous slaughter pens at the wheat field, Devil's Den, and Little Round Top. With all the rifle and cannon shot whistling in the air, it was not the smartest or safest place to be, but Lawley survived.

New York Tribune Civil War reporter Albert Richardson estimated that about 200 full-time correspondents covered the Civil War, with another 300 doing part-time duty, some of them doing so on the side while holding public jobs.[3] Other estimates were as low as 150.[4]

They represented papers spread across the divided country, with war correspondents from Richmond, Atlanta, Chicago, Boston, Cincinnati, Philadelphia, New York, and Baltimore playing especially big roles in contributing to the growth of the profession. As was the case in the decades and centuries that followed, the center of the nation's media universe at the beginning of the war was in New York City, where the *Tribune, Times, Herald, Sun, World* and more than a dozen other newspapers and periodicals, most notably *Harper's Weekly* and *Frank Leslie's Illustrated Newspaper*, were published during the war.

A code of newspaper exchange existed along the armies' front lines. When the armies were close enough, pickets passed newspapers back and forth during fighting lulls. Besides giving relief to camp boredom, the papers became prime pieces of intelligence for officers on both sides. They also became the frequent targets of generals who saw them as nothing more than spy sheets.

For several years before the firing on Fort Sumter, New York–based reporters had begun referring to themselves as the "Bohemian Brigade" to denote an irreverent fraternity of reporters and editors who gathered to drink and gossip at The Cave, a New York bar owned by the plump and gregarious socialite, Charles Ignatius Pfaff. Among Pfaff's regular clientele was the poet-writer Walt Whitman. A leader of the group was the journalist Henry Clapp Jr., editor of the short-lived but influential journal, *Saturday Press.*[5]

Clapp had spent time in Paris in the mid-1850s, and his infatuation with the French writer Henri Merger's series of stories of 1840s and 1850s Parisian intellectuals in "Scenes de la Vie de Boheme," had led him to declare the regular crowd of journalists and writers who congregated at The Cave as "The Bohemians." They'd regularly gather around a single, long table. Whitman, a frequent participant, declared that "there was as good talk around that table as took place anywhere in the world."[6] Competition intensified within the fraternity as the business of daily journalism grew. Egos clashed as some gained fame or notoriety. Clapp uttered one of the great lines of Civil War–era journalism when he described Wilkeson's boss, Greeley, as a "self-made man who worships his creator."[7] Greeley did see himself in a part of the Bohemian code of questioner and contrarian. But when asked during the war if he was a poet, Greeley responded that he was not, although he allowed that he had been called many other things: "Aristocrat, communist, infidel, hypocrite, demagogue, disunionist, traitor, corruptionist, and so forth and so forth."[8]

Just before the war broke out, the *New York Illustrated News* described the Bohemians as "free-thinkers, and free-lovers, and jolly companions well met."[9] That their watering hole was called The Cave seemed fitting in a kind of self-important irreverence. Intellectuals, pronouncing on the evil and good of humankind, were going back to The Cave for their commentary.

But the Bohemians had to leave The Cave to cover the war. The age of mirth and frivolity and smug self-importance ended at Fort Sumter.

Sam Wilkeson was not much interested in that fraternity before the war, but he had become very much a part of it during the war. He had spent his early journalism career in Albany, outside the self-appointed corridors of power in New York, and he was not much interested in being on anyone's good side. But during the war many Bohemians became Wilkeson's friends and competitors. And his age, reputation, his connection to Greeley, and his unquestioned fearlessness on the battlefield gave him a certain status that caused other reporters to look up to him.

As pioneers, Civil War correspondents were hated, suspected, and occasionally welcomed by the commanders in the field, many of whom were political appointees who naturally viewed newspapers as one-sided political party organs, as almost all publications were in the nineteenth century.

Joseph C. G. Kennedy, the superintendent of the Census Bureau during the war, estimated that of the 3,700 newspapers in the country almost all of the daily papers and a majority of the weeklies were "political in their character."[10] Still, there was a strong desire to keep a distance from the politically powerful. In 1864, James Gordon Bennett's *New York Herald*, a bitter critic of Lincoln, conveniently throwing off its own Democratic Party allegiances, issued a blistering attack on papers that supported what it called "the party press."

"The party press is completely rotten with corruption and completely unreliable as the organ or as the leader of American public opinion," the *Herald* thundered, in an unsigned dispatch headlined, "The Corruption and Imbecility of the Party Press.[11]

But because the press in the North so favored one political party or the other, a correspondent could be viewed as an ally or enemy just by arriving in an army camp. Many, including Wilkeson, had been detained, mistaken as spies, and some were thrown into jail for sedition, or lesser trumped-up charges.

The crackdown began at the onset of the war, and while not instigated by Lincoln, this suppression of the press certainly took place with his tacit approval. He was complicit in not stopping the worst transgressions of those in his cabinet and in the military high command. It began soon after the war began. In the fall of 1861, federal troops had shut down and smashed property in the Alexandria, *Virginia Gazette* after its editor refused to print a notice of martial law in the community just across the river from the White House.[12] It was the first of many violent acts toward newspapers by soldiers and civilians during the war. Democratic or opposition papers from Baltimore to Chicago were shut down, attacked by mobs, or saw their editors tarred and feathered, or jailed, or run out of town.

Less than a week before Gettysburg, the publisher of the *Philadelphia Inquirer* was indicted by a federal grand jury for treason. His alleged crime: His paper had printed movements of the Northern army.[13]

Very few Civil War correspondents had experience being embedded with armies in previous wars. The *Times of London*'s William Howard Russell was a notable exception, and he generally looked down on all but a few American correspondents who had covered the Mexican War a decade and a half before the Civil War. The communications lines in that war were more primitive, the expectations of immediate news lower. There had been pioneers in that war, including the first American female war correspondent, the *New York Sun*'s Jane McManus Storm, who wrote under the pen name, "Montgomery." The *New Orleans Picayune* did good work during the Mexican War, in part because of its proximity to the war as compared to papers in New York, Boston, Chicago, and elsewhere.[14]

By 1863, pressured by the immediacy of the telegraph, mindful that photography was starting to bring actual images of the fighting's aftermath to the population, and confronting a war that had become more deadly and destructive than the naïve expectations of 1861, the rapid maturation of the war correspondent profession had become an invention of necessity.

News of previous wars had taken days, even weeks, to reach readers. News of the Battle of New Orleans, which launched Andrew Jackson to fame and the presidency, did not arrive in Washington until two weeks after the Treaty of Ghent was signed to end the War of 1812.

But by 1861, when the Civil War began, news from the battlefield was often just a short horse ride and few clicks of Morse code away, or at most a railroad ride to the next telegraph junction. Civilians in the North and the South lined up at the telegraph office or newspaper office to read casualty lists freshly delivered by the "lightning," the term the correspondents gave to the telegraph.[15] Newspapers sometimes bragged up the cutting-edge technology their correspondents used to file their stories by printing that the dispatches had come through "magnetic telegraph."[16]

Competition was cutthroat. Civil War armies strung miles of telegraph wire to communicate with Washington or Richmond, and correspondents would often have to fight through censorship to file dispatches on them. Censorship was heavy-handed and unevenly applied, and correspondents sometimes had entire dispatches spiked for no apparent reason.

"Our dispatches of all kinds are cut to pieces nightly," Wilkeson complained to his boss, Gay, early in the war. "No man can make a good paper here."[17]

War correspondents were also occasionally detained and banned from leaving after battles to file stories under the threat of arrest. Sometimes Civil War commanders went even further. Three months before Gettysburg, Union general Joe Hooker arrested the *New York Herald*'s Edwin F. Denyse for describing in his newspaper the "unmistakable preparations now being made for the movement of the army." Hooker ordered Denyse court-martialed, found him guilty, sentenced him to six months of hard labor, then commuted his sentence and banished him from Union army camps.[18]

As his army marched toward Gettysburg, "Fighting Joe" Hooker complained bitterly about details on his movements appearing in Northern newspapers. His gripe with the press originated in part with his nickname, stuck on him by a botched newspaper headline after the battle of Williamsburg the year before. Hooker had fought bravely and had a horse killed under him at Williamsburg, and a newspaper headline describing his actions was to have read: "Fighting—Joe Hooker." But the punctuation got dropped, and the nickname stuck. Hooker hated it, because he thought it made him out to be an unthinking brawler.[19]

By June of 1863, as his army cautiously moved north through Virginia to head off Lee somewhere north of the Potomac River, Hooker worried that the reporting from Northern newspapers was so much more accurate than the propaganda he saw in Southern papers smuggled through the lines that it gave the Confederate general Robert E. Lee a distinct intelligence advantage.

On June 18, less than two weeks before the battle of Gettysburg, Hooker sent a confidential message to the top newspaper editors warning them against reporting on his army's movements. The next day, a furious Hooker telegraphed Maj. Gen. Henry Halleck, the general in chief of Union armies, that he had just been supplied with an "extract" from the *New York Herald*, that described "the late movements of this army" in such detail that it took away any element of surprise in his movements against Lee.

"So long as the newspapers continue to give publicity to our movements, we must not expect to gain any advantage over our adversaries," Hooker complained. "Is there no way of stopping it? I can suppress the circulation of this paper within my lines, but I cannot prevent their reaching it to the enemy. We could well afford to give millions of money for like information of the enemy."

Halleck, nicknamed "Old Brains," responded that same day by suggesting Hooker ban the correspondents from following him.

"I appreciate as fully as yourself the injury resulting from the paper publication of the movements, but I see no way of preventing it as long as reporters are permitted in our camps," wrote Halleck, who had been a classmate of Sam Wilkeson's at Union College before going on to West

Point. "I expelled them from our lines in Mississippi. Every general must decide for himself what person he will permit in his camps."[20]

Hooker did not follow through with Halleck's suggestion to kick correspondents out of his army. But two days later he had Nathan G. Shepherd of the *Tribune* arrested for disclosing positions of the army and told him to leave and never come back. He also had arrested and charged with treason the editor of the *Washington Star* under allegations similar to those he put against Shepherd. But nothing came of either case, and they were eventually released after Hooker was removed from his command three days before the battle of Gettysburg.[21] And while Hooker was suddenly out of the loop, about forty-five reporters, including Sam Wilkeson, arrived with the two armies at that crossroads.

Sam Wilkeson had received special treatment to get around censorship soon after he arrived in Washington, but that dispensation eventually faded. A year before Gettysburg, with the war dragging on and Union losses piling up, the Lincoln Administration tried to clamp down more on news from the front, and the journalists fought back. Wilkeson complained to a congressional committee that "the general result of my observation since I have come into contact with this new institution of the censorship of the press, is that I am not permitted to send anything over the wires which, in the estimation of the censor, shall be damaging to the character of the administration, or any individual member of the Cabinet, or that would be injurious to the reputation of the officers charged with the prosecution of the war, and particularly those of the regular army."[22]

It was becoming harder and harder to do his job, and harder and harder to see the end of this war arriving any time soon.

CHAPTER 8

"If I Have Watermelons and Whiskey Ready"

By the battle of Gettysburg, Sam Wilkeson had become an adept, seasoned observer, and as Greeley's man in Washington, his dispatches would have been essential reads for Lincoln and the members of Lincoln's cabinet. Over the previous year, he had had plenty of official actions and general officer blunders to question, and he increasingly had grown to doubt the *Tribune's* famous editor Greeley's support for the war.

It had also been a deeply sorrowful year for Wilkeson, personally. Covering (and briefly involved in combat in) the battle of Seven Pines, Sam had the soul-searing task of walking the battlefield with burial parties to search for the body of his nephew, John Wilkes Wilkeson, who was killed there. That experience contributed to the physical and emotional problems he faced that summer. He almost certainly suffered from what more than a century later would be called post-traumatic stress disorder. The deplorable conditions in the swampy and desultory air of the Peninsula campaign and the experience of finding the bloated body of his nephew, John Wilkes Wilkeson, would have created PTSD in anyone.

By the time the cannons opened on Fort Sumter, Wilkeson's boss, Horace Greeley, had become one of the most famous Americans, respected for his up-from-the-bootstraps biography, but looked upon with wariness inside the Lincoln Administration as a loose cannon. Greeley also was reviled in the South as an Abolitionist whose editorials and articles had pushed the country into war. He needed a strong hand in Washington to cover the war.

Sam Wilkeson had turned out to be that man. He had the bulldog temperament to go get the story. He had a lyrical flair for composition. He could always see the big picture. But he was quick to the fight, and too judgmental, too unforgiving, to assume the more expansive public stature of editor of an influential newspaper, as Greeley had become by the dawn of the war.

They were very different men. Photographic portraits of Greeley and Wilkeson, employing cutting-edge mediums of the mid-nineteenth century, speak to the differences. The photographers who took them were the most famous of their age. Taken eight years apart—Greeley's in 1851 and Sam Wilkeson's in 1859—the images were made when both men were ascending in their journalism careers.[1]

The first image, called a daguerreotype, was taken of Greeley by the great Mathew Brady in 1851. It was made when Greeley's *Tribune* had just started national distribution by rail, and Greeley was using his *Tribune* as a platform for his expansionism and a vessel for his crusades for abolition, temperance, and the establishment of labor unions. Although it would take years before newspapers could develop the process of putting pictures on page, by 1851, the daguerreotype process—which involved printing a positive image in silver on copper sheets—was beginning to democratize and expand, in images rather than words, the depiction of events. Lifelike portraits were available to anyone who could afford them. During the Civil War, troops on both sides carried silver-tin images of their family or mailed home pictures of themselves in uniform. These images sometimes became important pieces of evidence to identify remains in the aftermath of battle. After Gettysburg, a dead Union soldier, Amos Humiston, was found clutching a photo of his children. Newspapers, yet unable to reprint the pictures, described the photo and Humiston's widow identified the body through those dispatches. The Humiston case demonstrated the power of social media in the mid-nineteenth century.[2]

In Brady's 1851 portrait of Greeley, Brady posed the editor as he often appeared: rumpled, a stovepipe hat tipped far back on his head, and a jacket too large for his frumpy frame. Cartoonists often satirized Greeley as disheveled yet always seeking to be noticed. Often, a mane of wispy chest hair poked through his collar; some mistook it for a fox pelt.

But in this photograph, some of those peculiarities were hidden. Brady posed Greeley sitting before a plain backdrop, focusing on the man, not his surroundings. A newspaper was tucked on his lap beneath calmly clasped hands. A sheaf of papers stuck out of Greeley's right coat pocket, as if to represent the absent-mindedness and always-at-work attributes that his friends laughed about and his critics panned. Greeley, who was forty at the time, appears approachable, a scribe of lofty aspirations but of everyman demeanor and physicality, more common sense than cerebral. Lincoln's biographer, Carl Sandburg, described Greeley as "pink-skinned, baby-faced, blue-eyed with a stare of innocence" who "shuffled rather than walked." Greeley had become known for lines like, "I never said all Democrats were saloon keepers. I said all saloon keepers were Democrats."[3] You could sense all of these attributes in this plain, straightforward pose for Mathew Brady.

Greeley had arrived in New York at age twenty with ten dollars in his pocket.[4] The crusading Greeley found a kindred political spirit in Sam Wilkeson. In the late summer of the first year of the war, Greeley sent Wilkeson to Washington, DC, to help direct the *Tribune*'s coverage of the war and to embed himself in official Washington, filing public stories and private correspondence to Greeley, who saw himself as a great influencer amid a great crisis.

Greeley used the pages of the *Tribune* to oppose slavery and engage in myriad causes, including those against alcohol abuse, capital punishment, and flogging in the Navy. Now the great cause was this war and its terrible aftermath, and he had his man in place in Washington. Wilkeson rewarded the mercurial Greeley with some of the best early reporting of the war, including a series of spectacular scoops and some of the most vivid correspondence of the fighting that, by 1863, had ascended to levels of death and maiming that few foresaw when the war began.

Greeley was in a constant struggle to find solid financial footing. Some parts of his business were profitable, but in 1854, while pushing to raise the daily street price from two to three cents, the *Tribune's* famous managing editor Charles A. Dana disclosed that the weekly *Tribune* edition was losing $15,000 a year because of the cost of newsprint.[5] Gathering the news, and paying correspondents who could write it with authority, did not come cheaply. And covering the war was a costly enterprise.

Early in the war, Greeley raised a ruckus over the creative writing in the expense account of a colorful Wilkeson colleague named Charlie Page. When Greeley balked at paying for some unusual expenses, an indignant Page wrote back to Greeley that he got the news he paid for.

"Early news is expensive news, Mr. Greeley," Page lectured. "If I have watermelons and whiskey ready when officers come along from a fight, I get the news without asking questions."[6]

And "early news" had been redefined in rapid fashion. The telegraph's revolutionary "lightning" speed, and other technological advances in the printing press and distribution networks (the railroad had the power to make provincial periodicals into national ones) made it so. The two portraits of Greeley and Wilkeson illustrated the change.

Brady had made his portrait of Greeley in 1851 in London at Queen Victoria's *Great Exhibition of the Works of Industry of All Nations*. Two years in the planning, the massive science exposition drew six million visitors and was a showcase of the scientific and technological breakthroughs of the age. Brady's daguerreotype was one of the new technologies on display. He had begun making a name by photographing such American luminaries as Henry Clay, Daniel Webster, and Dolley Madison. Brady was invited to London to make it a global phenomenon.[7]

Greeley went to the great London exhibition to cover it. The Americans were media pioneers, Greeley boasted. Brady won a medal for his photography. "It seem to be conceded that we beat the world, when excellence and cheapness are both considered—at all events England is no where in comparison—and our Daguerreotypes make a great show here," Greeley reported.[8]

It took his dispatch two weeks to arrive in New York by boat. A decade later, correspondents would file instantaneous dispatches from Civil War battlefields, and by the end of the war, a transatlantic telegraph brought the news in a day.

Sam Wilkeson's seminal portrait was taken the year he joined Greeley's *Tribune*, in 1859. The photographer was Brady's talented assistant Alexander Gardner, whose images of the battle of Antietam would shock the Northern public three years later.

Gardner posed Wilkeson with depth and position. In the portrait, Wilkeson is standing rigidly upright, his right hand resting on a table on which has been placed a book and an upturned hat, denoting scholarship, style, currency, and importance. Wilkeson's left arm is tucked in a "v" toward his body, his left fist against his ribs. He appears stiff and stern, as if cross at being interrupted from his work. Rich draperies cover a window, and an elegant chair sits to one side, suggesting sophistication and means; although he was not a rich man, there is a strong suggestion he mingled with the rich and powerful. Wilkeson's curly hair is swept neatly over his ears, its gray streaks lending an aura of maturity suggestive of someone older than his forty-two years. His clean-shaven face (during the war he grew a long, gray-streaked beard) hosts deep-set, discerning eyes, a prominent nose, and a mouth that seems eminently capable of sequestering emotion or unleashing it on cue. He seems to be taking as much measure of his viewers, as they of him.

Four years later, Wilkeson's portrait-maker Gardner, like Wilkeson himself, would also get swept up in the great aftermath of Gettysburg. When news of the battle broke out, Gardner and colleagues James Gibson and Timothy O'Sullivan loaded two wagons full of camera equipment and headed north from their office in Washington, DC. Joining a river of civilians flowing toward Gettysburg, they made Emmitsburg by July 5, the same town where Bayard Wilkeson and the Union army's 11th Corps camped the night before the battle. There, Gardner was briefly detained by Jeb Stuart's retreating Confederate cavalry. By midafternoon, the photographer was freed and he, Gibson, and O'Sullivan headed to the battlefield accompanied by a Christian Commission missionary, Charles Keener.

The party soon ran into the post-battle horror. They came upon a barn full of wounded men on the farm of an elderly man named Bentz, whose son had moved south sixteen years before, and had returned as a captain in Lee's army, only to be killed. The father "was so good a Union man," Keener said, "that he would not consent to look upon the corpse or the grave of his recreant son."[9]

As pillagers and mercy givers combed the battlefield in the aftermath, Gardner's party immersed itself in its work. Later scholarship would argue some of the images were staged, but its essence still served to shock and, if anything, the word portraits drawn of the scenes after the battle understated the horror. Gardner's "Harvest of Death" survived as one of the most recognizable photos of the war. It showed dead men at Gettysburg on a swath leading into a misty horizon, as if the battle was exacting its toll into the forever. A single body in the foreground is in focus, the man's mouth open, seemingly agape at his final witness. From then on, Gardner embedded photographers with the Union army as much as he could, making images of the aftermath of Cold Harbor, Belle Plaine, Petersburg, and Appomattox. In September of 1863, he began selling his Gettysburg imagery. His exhaustive, postwar "Photographic Sketches of the War" sold for $150, a year's salary for a soldier. It was sold as a limited edition; about 200 sets were sold.[10] The age of photojournalism had begun. It was a dynamic, expansive age.

At the beginning of the war, the *Tribune*'s weekly edition alone had a circulation of roughly 200,000 throughout the Northern states, and its multiple daily editions sold thousands more.[11] Given the country's population of just over thirty-one million in 1860, that was immense coverage, rivaling the domestic reach of any twenty-first century American news organization. James Gordon Bennett's *Herald* and Henry Raymond's *New York Times* were Greeley's leading competition.

At the *Tribune*, Wilkeson was one of many characters surrounding Greeley. The paper's managing editor, Charles A. Dana, who would, like Sam, eventually run into disagreement with Greeley over the course of the war, was quick-witted, ambitious, and skeptical. He suffered no fools. Early in the war, a green correspondent had begun a telegraph dispatch of a battle with, "To God Almighty be the glory! Mine eyes have seen the work of the Lord and the cause of the righteous hath triumphed." Dana shot back a one-sentence telegraphed response.

"Hereafter," Dana wrote, sarcasm dripping, "in sending your reports, please specify the number of the hymn and save telegraph expenses."[12]

The *Herald*'s Bennett had been an operative for the Democratic Party, and his paper was among Lincoln's biggest critics during the war. But when Bennett started his *Herald* in 1835, he had fancied the paper as an independent publication. He was a born skeptic and viewed most politicians, professional people, and clergy as craven and dishonest. In the *Herald*'s first edition a quarter century before the war, Bennett had declared that "we openly disclaim all steel-traps, all principle, as it is called—all politics. Our only guide shall be good, sound, practical, common life."[13] But despite his skepticism about politics and politicians, Bennett was also one of the first newspaper publishers to hire a Washington correspondent, and his was the only New York paper that had sent a correspondent to cover the Mexican War of 1846–1848.[14]

Yet Bennett also made no pretense about selling news as a commodity—and the more salacious the headlines the better. Prior to the war his pages were often filled with crime or sex news, some of it in first-person prose. One of his critics observed that Bennett "often denounced licentious books while quoting, at the same time, long passages from them." Unlike Greeley, who saw horse-racing and gambling as immoral, Bennett featured the horses in his pages, thereby creating the sports page as an enduring feature of American newspapers.[15]

Raymond's *Times* was first published only a decade before the war. Raymond had served as a Whig in the New York assembly and an ally of Whig political boss Thurlow Weed. For a time, Raymond edited Greeley's *Tribune*, but he left to run a paper for harder-line Whigs. He launched his paper in 1851 with $100,000 in loans.[16]

As the Civil War began, the competition among newspapers was fierce down to street corner news hawkers who sold papers for a penny or two. Newsboys were fixtures in American towns and cities. Weekly newspapers were popping up in villages and small cities all across the country. Afternoons and morning editions, special editions when the news warranted it—some in German or other foreign languages—were ubiquitous in cities awash in first-generation European immigrants. When Oliver Wendell Holmes Sr. traveled through New York on his way to search for his son after the battle of Antietam, he noted that newsboys on almost every street corner were selling the *Herald* with the unique cry of "'N'York Heddle."[17]

Although newspapers had yet to find a technological solution for printing actual photographs, wood-cut illustrations had become so sophisticated that newspapers and periodicals began using that technology to print depictions of battle scenes and maps of army movements. One New York paper spent $25,000 on engravings during the war, a significant investment. By the end of the war, the *Herald* correspondent Thomas Knox—whose vivid descriptions of the aftermath of Gettysburg would shock readers—invented a system to transmit descriptions of battle maps via telegraph that allowed engravers to depict battle movements within hours after a battle.[18]

Meanwhile, an exhibit by Mathew Brady and Alexander Gardner, called the "Dead of Antietam," had thrust photojournalism into the national consciousness. Shown in New York City in the fall of 1862, it was a newly crossed media threshold, bringing home images of the war in a way that challenged Americans to not look distantly, or disinterestedly, at the slaughter and the aftermath.

"The living that throng Broadway care little perhaps for the Dead at Antietam, but we fancy they would jostle less carelessly down the great thorough fare, saunter less at their ease, were a few dripping bodies, fresh from the field, laid along the pavement," the *Times* wrote on October 20, 1862, after the exhibit had opened. "There would be a gathering up of skirts and a careful picking of way, conversation would be less lively, and the general air of pedestrians more subdued. As it is, the dead of the battlefield come to us very rarely, even in dreams. We see the list in the morning paper at breakfast, but dismiss its recollection with the coffee."

But no more could the public afford that indifference, the newspaper went on. "If [Brady] has not brought bodies and laid them in our dooryards and along the streets, he has done something very like it."

The *Times* wrote that "hushed, reverent groups" lined up to view "these weird copies of carnage, bending down to look in the pale faces of the dead, chained by the strange spell that dwells in dead men's eyes."

The *Times* regretted what was omitted—the aftermath of battle. It lamented not being able to see "the background of widows and orphans, torn from the bosom of their natural protectors by the red remorseless hand of Battle." Traversing the contours of a theme that would become central to the word portraiture by Wilkeson and others after the battle of Gettysburg, the *Times's* review of "The Dead of Antietam" ended with the imagery of Christian rebirth and redemption. Mothers of dead men should not grieve, the *Times* said, for "this is not the last of your boy.

"With pealing of trumpets and beating of drums, these trenches shall open—the Son of Man comes. And then is reserved for him that crown which only heroes and martyrs are permitted to wear."

But pealing trumpets aside, there was no getting around the reality of what Brady and Gardner had brought forth. The pictures from Antietam had "terrible distinctness," and the "very features of the slain may be distinguished," the *Times* noted. Viewers of the photographs could put faces to the "men who have not hesitated to seal and stamp their convictions with their blood"—convictions that there are "wrongs and shame to be dreaded more than death."[19]

It was a pivotal moment in American media. Grandiose headlines and soaring prose were suddenly being challenged by a newfound grittiness, pushed by a relatively small but influential cadre of correspondents and photographers.

Civil War correspondents were relatively educated and young. One survey concluded that roughly half attended college. Two-thirds were in their twenties when the war broke out. Some correspondents had segued from politics to journalism. One had served time in New York's notorious Sing Sing prison, another had been a Shakespearean actor. Thomas Morris Chester, a well-known free black leader, returned from colonization efforts in Liberia to cover the war for the *Philadelphia Press*. Two years after Gettysburg, Chester was one of the first Northern correspondents to report from Richmond just before Lee's surrender at Appomattox.[20]

Some correspondents gained fame that outlasted the war and built postwar careers writing and lecturing about it. The *Boston Journal's* Charlie Coffin gave more than 2,000 speeches after the war and wrote several books about it. Almost always he featured the story of Bayard and Sam Wilkeson at Gettysburg.[21] Some war correspondents moved away from journalism when the war ended. One of Wilkeson's colleagues, Henry

Villard, who had arrived penniless as a German immigrant in 1855, rose to become president of the Northern Pacific Railroad (and Sam Wilkeson the railroad's secretary) after the war. Villard would become a great influence on Wilkeson, and Wilkeson on Villard, during and long after the Civil War.

CHAPTER 9

"A Fanatical, Impertinent, Revolutionary Fellow"

SAM WILKESON WAS A PROLIFIC, LIVELY, OPINIONATED WRITER, AND HIS outgoing, confrontational, daredevil personality was well suited for an era in which journalism and political activism were viewed as natural partners, when the public's insatiable interest in the war and the innovations of technology created a new market for the profession of war correspondent, and when its practitioners were making up the rules as they went along.

The best chronicler of Civil War correspondents, J. Cutler Andrews, described Sam as a "vigorous character of lusty humor with unnatural powers of story-telling and description."[1] His arrival in Washington in August of 1861 as Greeley's bureau chief was covered in the *Tribune*'s chief rival newspaper. Bennett's *New York Herald* in August of 1861 described Wilkeson as a "fanatical, impertinent, revolutionary fellow, who will bear watching." He was "deft and sometimes devious" to his colleagues and sources alike, the rival paper said.[2] The Wilkeson grapevine, flowing through and from his office near the White House, was one of the most active of the war.

One of his first colleagues was Harvard graduate Adams S. Hill, described by another reporter as a "sharp-witted and indefatigable collector of news." The office of Wilkeson and Hill, said their eventual *Tribune* colleague Villard, "was the resort of politicians, officials, and army officers, who frequented it, especially in the evening, to bring news or to hear and discuss it.

"This," the German-born Villard recalled wryly, "made it a very interesting place."[3]

Newspaper row in Washington, in between the White House and the Capitol, in the neighborhood of the whorehouses and watering holes that attracted officers, spies, and profiteers alike, was a constantly smoldering cauldron of intrigue, leaks, speculation, facts, and disinformation. Wilkeson was always scheming to get away from it, out with the cabinet members or the armies. He'd go to great lengths to do it.

Once, Wilkeson and fellow *Tribune* correspondent Francis C. Long tried to get to a vantage point on Pony Mountain, near Culpepper, Virginia, to see Confederates regrouping after they had been driven off the mountain by the Union army. Sentries were keeping journalists far behind the action. Wilkeson had forgotten his press pass, but Long had his. So they concocted a scheme: Wilkeson would pose as a member of the Christian Commission on a mission of mercy to preach to the battle-traumatized bluecoats up on the mountain. Once there, preacher would become reporter, and he'd have the scoop on the Union triumph.

The problem was that Wilkeson had been drinking to screw up his courage before the two men approached Union sentries. As they came upon the guards at the base of the mountain, Wilkeson tried to burnish his preacher's disguise by loudly proclaiming the evils of liquor. While the two correspondents were waiting for a skeptical corporal to get permission to let them through, Wilkeson's horse got nervous and reared. When Wilkeson began swearing at the animal, his Christian Commission cover was blown and the two correspondents were summarily turned back. They never made it to the top of Pony Mountain. They were lucky they weren't arrested and banned from the Army altogether.

If that false identity of a pious preacher failed, it was not because Wilkeson was uncomfortable in the role of taking sides or taking part in the action he was covering. Greeley had wanted someone to cover the war, but he also wanted in his Washington bureau chief a man who would be his eyes and ears in the capital, to dig into the intrigue and policy debates, to help Greeley influence Lincoln and his cabinet, which the editor thought did not conflict at all with his role as editor. Greeley wanted not only a reporter, but someone with opinions on the side, just so long as he did not overtly express them in the news columns. When he made him the chief of the *Tribune's* bureau, Greeley told Wilkeson that he wanted "a man in Washington to find out all that is going on or preparing, and calmly report it, writing Editorials separately, to be submitted to criticism and revision here, instead of embodying them in dispatches."[4]

Even though people at the highest level of government knew his opinions of the war and his willingness to reward sources, Sam Wilkeson never abandoned the perch of the outsider critically looking in. His war dispatches were factual, vivid, and analytical.

Wilkeson feuded with some colleagues, gained the respect of others, and dismissed those he felt were overblown or timid. Wilkeson did not get along with Charles Brigham, who gained notoriety for the *Tribune* for his courageous dispatches, filed anonymously under the threat of death at the beginning of the war from Charleston, South Carolina.[5] Even after Brigham's lengthy report on the historic 1862 naval battle between the pioneering ironclads, *Monitor* and *Merrimack*, Wilkeson and Brigham never hit it off, in part because Wilkeson suspected Brigham of sympathizing with the South. Sam told colleague Thomas Butler Gunn that he thought that Brigham was a "slaverer and a humbug generally." Some of Brigham's colleagues thought he had a propensity to jump their stories and claim them as his own.[6]

Gunn liked Sam Wilkeson, and the two men shared incredible privations covering the Union army early in the war. Gunn admired Sam for being willing to do almost anything to get a story, but he was not sure that Sam had the right temperament to head Greeley's Washington bureau. Wilkeson complained too much about the shortfalls and lack of courage of some of his colleagues. Wilkeson was a good man, Gunn thought, but he also saw how hard the war weighed on his colleague, how tightly the abolition cause had wound Wilkeson's soul. But unlike Brigham, Wilkeson never attempted to jump Gunn's stories.

"I don't think that Wilkeson was precisely the man for his place," Gunn wrote in his diary during the Peninsula campaign of 1862, when both men nearly died from illnesses while covering the Union army's movement through southern Virginia. "But I am equally sure that he was much more unselfish than the shrewd, exacting Brigham, who attempted to do the masterful towards me, once or twice, never succeeding. Wilkeson, on the contrary, was always kind and considerate."[7]

Irrespective of that outward kindness, Wilkeson had a steely, transactional, analytical approach to reporting. He also had that rare instinct of being in the right place at the most consequential times. That instinct would fail him for a time at Gettysburg, but also put him at precisely the place where the battle—and the war—would be decided.

Wilkeson's source-building and favor-trading began immediately upon his arrival as the *Tribune's* top Washington correspondent, and it would lead directly to one of the war's most controversial and enduring story lines: the sanity of Union major general William Tecumseh Sherman. Wilkeson got some of the most spectacular scoops of the war's opening year. He covered the news and, as illustrated in the case of Sherman, he occasionally created the news.

Shortly after arriving in August of 1861, Wilkeson wrote a very favorable feature—a "puff piece" in journalism parlance—on the embattled war secretary Simon Cameron, whose office was under attack for shady arms and war material deals. Wilkeson declared in one of his first *Tribune* dispatches from Washington that Cameron had been badly mischaracterized by his critics. "Secretary Cameron gives day and night to the service of his country," Wilkeson wrote. "The contracts made by him will defy the most unfriendly scrutiny."[8]

A grateful Cameron invited Wilkeson to his Pennsylvania farm, and Wilkeson accepted. After the visit Wilkeson wrote Sidney Howard Gay that his observations of Cameron in his home community further confirmed what he had written.

"Of Cameron after a close scrutiny, I say unhesitatingly that he is an honest man," Wilkeson wrote. "My prejudices against him I have fully dismissed. . . . There was no mistaking the sentiments of respect and gratitude which marked the approach of the many Pennsylvanians who came to greet him."[9]

But Wilkeson also confessed to Gay that he had had ulterior motives: source-building in order to catch up and surpass the *Tribune's* two big rivals, who had built big Washington bureaus and embedded more reporters with the Union armies than other papers. "Three of the [Cabinet] departments here are about secured to us," he wrote Gay, not naming the other two. "It will take me a week longer to finish the conquest. Then I shall advance on two others, and by detail & in time get them all. Then the *Herald* & the *Times* will be smilingly defied to a competition."[10]

For a time, Wilkeson got more than a foot in the door. Greeley's *Tribune* was the most prominent pro-Lincoln abolitionist organ in the country, so favorable coverage would be expected. But it would not last. By the battle of Gettysburg, Wilkeson would become such a critic of the administration that Lincoln would confront him on it in a meeting at the White House. And Wilkeson and Greeley would have a public falling out over what Wilkeson came to believe was Greeley's faltering belief that an unconditional Northern victory was the only way the war could end, no matter the terrible cost it was exacting on families.

A month after his visit to Cameron's farm in the fall of 1861, Wilkeson got an immediate payback for his cozying up to Cameron, when the war secretary signed a note to any potential government censor saying that "it is my wish that you neither suppress nor alter the telegrams of Mr. Samuel Wilkeson. Please send them as they are written and signed by him."[11] The letter and the order became moot when Cameron was replaced by Edwin Stanton three months later, and Sam's problem with censors would multiply during the war. But through that act of securing dispensation from the secretary of war, Wilkeson immediately demonstrated his insider skills to his editors in New York, and to official Washington. Although the reputation Wilkeson built with a series of scoops early in the war would not always win the argument with future censors, it would precede him wherever he went for the rest of the war.

The symbiotic relationships carried Cameron and Wilkeson early in the war, and they carried it a step further than source and journalist. Wilkeson, in a move that would have gotten him fired in subsequent journalism eras, boosted his income by writing pro-Union propaganda for Cameron aimed at European audiences. Sometimes members of the cabinet would drop by to offer suggestions for Wilkeson's weekly dispatch.[12]

It was totally antithetical to objective, detached journalism, and it is unclear if either the *Tribune* editor Greeley or Wilkeson's immediate boss, Sidney Howard Gay, knew about it. But it helped pay the bills, and it was important to the Northern war effort. Wilkeson's freelancing came as Britain and France were struggling with diplomatic responses to the South's succession. The South's cotton industry fed European factories, and the North's blockades of Southern ports were crippling Europe's textile industry. The freelance job ended when Stanton replaced Cameron as secretary of war the following January, but by then Wilkeson was becoming overwhelmed in his correspondence work for the *Tribune*, and he would spend too much time in the field and on the roads with the army to continue it anyway.

In the five months that Wilkeson and Cameron overlapped, the *Tribune* correspondent would shake Lincoln's cabinet and the Union army's high command in ways few correspondents would do during the war. Wilkeson did it through pluck, luck, and audacity. In the fall of 1861 and through the ensuing winter into 1862, as the nation confronted the reality that this war was turning from parades into endless casualty lists, Sam Wilkeson's scoops explained that changing reality. And his reporting was steadily leading him to an unassailable belief that the North needed to win the war, no matter the cost in life or material. Even if that cost, personally, could seem unbearable.

CHAPTER 10

"Now General Sherman, Tell Us Your Troubles"

IN MID-OCTOBER OF 1861, A FEW WEEKS AFTER VISITING CAMERON at his Pennsylvania farm, Wilkeson caught up with the secretary of war and top aides on their way to tour the Union army's Western command in Missouri and Kentucky. Wilkeson had smelled big news when he learned that the official party was headed to Tipton, Missouri, to inspect the condition of Union forces in the West and to meet with their commander, "The Pathfinder" John C. Fremont, the unsuccessful Republican candidate for president in 1856. Wilkeson's source-building spade work with Cameron paid prime dividends on this trip. The *Tribune* correspondent was in the room for one of the most controversial conversations of the war, and in the knowledge loop of another pivotal early moment.

The latter involved Fremont, who had been appointed to oversee scattered and disorganized Union forces in Missouri. The state was on fire with pro- and anti-slavery violence. Two months before Cameron's visit, Fremont had declared martial law. But there was widespread dissatisfaction in Washington over Major General Fremont's performance. The normally cautious, officious George McClellan, soon to be named the Union army's general-in-chief, charged that Fremont was presiding over "a system of reckless expenditure and fraud perhaps unheard of in the history of the world."[1]

Cameron was sent with orders to fire Fremont if he found conditions on the ground merited it. Wilkeson knew of the orders Cameron carried with him, most likely obtaining that juicy information from Cameron or a close aide. For the time being, Wilkeson was sharing it only with his bosses.

"Cameron has in his pocket a sealed order to Fremont, to surrender his command to the officer next to him in rank, and to report by letter to Washington," Wilkeson wrote Greeley from Indianapolis on October 15, 1861, where the official party had overnighted. "He was authorized and . . . directed to deliver this to Fremont, if after looking into the condition of affairs in Missouri, he should decide that the public interest required the Commander's removal."[2]

Ultimately, Cameron caved and temporarily kept Fremont in the job, but not before showing Fremont the letter and creating a scene that Wilkeson described in great detail in his letter to Greeley. It was not flattering of The Pathfinder's emotional health, nor to Cameron's ability to pull the trigger. Fremont "was overwhelmed" and "lost his mind" when Cameron told him he had been sent with the authority to sack him, Wilkeson wrote Greeley.[3]

"He could but utter expressions of grief and shame. He could not talk. His facilities were scattered. His misery pierced Cameron with a great pity," Wilkeson wrote. Cameron was "unable to resist this sentiment which as the Secretary of War he had no right to entertain. He came to the crushed Commander's relief with the suggestion that he might suspend the order. Fremont caught at the chance and begged to be permitted to fight a battle and win a victory."[4]

Finally, "overcome by Fremont's distress and his entreaties," Wilkeson wrote, the secretary of war gave in and "took back the order and placed it in his pocket."[5]

It was a consequential moment in the war's early events, and stunning access for a journalist. Within days, Wilkeson found a way to get Fremont's precarious position in Greeley's newspaper without divulging his sources at the highest level of the government, and in a way that ultimately helped push Fremont out the door after Cameron had flinched. Wilkeson obtained a copy of the official trip report and reprinted its unflattering portrait of Fremont in the *Tribune*.

Fremont was removed from command on November 2, 1861, three days after the *Tribune*'s report, in which Adjutant Gen. Lorenzo Thomas described Fremont as "more fond of the pomp than the realities of war," and unfit for command. Printed over much of page six of the *Tribune*, Thomas's report said Fremont's mismanagement and lack of military acumen threatened to throw Missouri over to the Confederates. It quoted, by name, a subordinate officer describing Fremont as "utterly incompetent."[6] Thomas, the report's author, would soon become a central figure in the career of the young artillery officer, Lt. Bayard Wilkeson.

But it was Wilkeson's reporting on another embattled general during that western swing with Cameron that would have a longer-lasting effect on the war. In another section of Thomas's official report, Willaim Tecumseh Sherman, whom Cameron also met with on the trip, was described as painting a "gloomy picture of affairs in Kentucky" and complaining that local militia had taken most of the supplies of rifles intended for his army. The report also disclosed Sherman's appeal for 200,000 more men to counter gathering Confederate forces and keep border-state Kentucky from tipping into full-scale rebellion.[7] Sherman's predictions would turn out to be right in the long war that would follow, but his appeal for previously unheard-of troop levels directly led to a narrative that Sherman had lost his mind.

Wilkeson's initial Fremont scoop got the immediate notice of Congress and prompted a First Amendment showdown between Wilkeson and a special House of Representatives investigating committee. It was then led by Rep. Charles Van Wyck, a New Yorker who a year earlier had survived an assassination attempt after he had delivered an anti-slavery speech on the floor of the House.

Subpoenaed to go before the committee, Wilkeson refused, telling Van Wyck he had no legal foundation to call him because he was not suspected of engaging in fraudulent contracts or making bad decisions on the battlefield. More importantly, he said, the public interest demanded that communications between journalists and informants should be privileged and confidential.[8]

On that trip west with Cameron in the fall of 1861, Wilkeson also had stunning access to a moment that, fair or not, created the narrative that Sherman lacked the mental stability to command troops. Although Sherman would maintain the support of Ulysses S. Grant and other superiors in the War Department, and although he would later command with great effect and eternal controversy in his march through the South in 1864 and 1865, a "crazy" tag applied to him after his short run-in with Wilkeson in 1861 would never entirely fade. Forever after that, Sherman distrusted his civilian overseers and despised the press, and his resentments culminated in one of the great public snubs of the war. When the victorious Union armies marched down Pennsylvania Avenue in a Grand Parade on May 18, 1865, Sherman refused to shake Secretary of War Stanton's hand. A general of the army refusing to acknowledge his civilian overseer at the army's triumphant moment created quite a stir. But Sherman had the best defender possible. In his memoirs Grant said he could not blame Sherman because of the "cruel and harsh treatment" inflicted on Sherman by his superiors and the press throughout the war.[9]

The Sherman-Wilkeson story went this way. During Cameron's official trip to the West to confront Fremont, the secretary of war and his party also passed through Louisville, where Sherman was in command of Union forces. Like Missouri, Kentucky was in turmoil. Sherman was being asked to hold the state with a few thousand green Union troops, many of them ninety-day signups whose time was running out.

Amazingly, despite Sherman's protestations, Cameron insisted that Wilkeson be allowed to sit in on the meeting between Sherman and Cameron and his aides. The gathering took place at Sherman's room at the Galt House, Louisville's grand hotel on the Ohio River. The proprietor, Silas Miller, set up a lunch for the official party. The lunch conversation, Sherman recalled later, was mostly about Fremont's "extravagant contracts and expenses." But what happened after lunch created the bombshell.[10]

Cameron—feeling ill—asked to lie down on Sherman's bed and with aides assembled, asked, "Now, General Sherman, tell us your troubles."

Sherman protested, saying he did not know everyone in the room. "I said I preferred not to discuss business with so many strangers present," Sherman wrote in his memoirs.

Cameron, taking affront, responded: "They are all friends, all members of my family, and you may speak your mind freely without restraint."[11]

Wilkeson stayed.

Sherman stepped to the door, closed and locked it, and then proceeded to unburden his worries, most strikingly his declaration that he felt "powerless for invasion." If the Confederate general Albert Sidney Johnston—then forming the Army of Central Kentucky—so chose, he could "march to Louisville any day."[12] The mention of Johnston forming with bad intentions alone would raise fears among a war secretary. Johnston, who five months later was killed at Shiloh, was considered the South's best general, better than Robert E. Lee. Sherman knew what he was up against.

Sherman told Cameron he needed 60,000 men initially, and ultimately 200,000 to do his job, and that at that moment he only had about 18,000 in his command. Some listeners thought he was saying he needed all 200,000 to just keep Kentucky from seceding, although Sherman would always claim he was referring to the vast area between the Allegheny Mountains and the Mississippi River. In his memoirs, Sherman wrote that he had even taken out a map to show the area he was referring to.

Either way, the numbers stunned Cameron, who, according to Sherman, proclaimed, "Great God, where are they going to come from?"[13]

Primarily from states in the "Northwest"—Iowa, Minnesota, Wisconsin, and Oregon, where men were ready to enlist but hadn't been deemed necessary, Sherman responded. Within days, one of those states, Oregon, would pay a heavy toll. One of its two U.S. senators, Edward Baker, a close friend of Lincoln's, and for whom Lincoln's son Eddy was named, would be killed commanding troops at Ball's Bluff overlooking the Potomac River in Virginia.

"I asserted that there were plenty of men at the North, ready and willing to come if he would only accept their services," Sherman recalled. "For it was notorious that regiments had been formed in the Northwestern States, whose services had been refused by the War Department, on the ground that they would not be needed."

Sherman left that meeting thinking he had Cameron on his side. "I thought I had aroused Mr. Cameron to a realization of the great war that was before us, and was in fact upon us," Sherman recalled.[14] In reality, he later learned that the official trip report referred to Sherman's request for 200,000 troops when he got back to Washington, and that Cameron and others thought it "insane." Less than three weeks after their meeting, Sherman resigned his command.

Sam did not write about the Louisville meeting with Sherman right away. But he did run into a competitor, Henry Villard, in the hotel lobby. Villard had been sent by his then-newspaper, the *Cincinnati Commercial*, to cover Sherman and the situation in Kentucky. He, like many correspondents, had been treated with, at best, indifference by the Union commander, whose hatred of the press was well known in newsrooms across the country. In his chance meeting with Wilkeson, a language barrier contributed to one of the most significant stories of the war. The two men commiserated on their impressions of Sherman, and at one point, Wilkeson recounted how Cameron thought Sherman's request for 200,000 men, "crazy." Wilkeson was using a colloquialism, but Villard, whose first language was German and who had lived in the country barely half a decade, took it as literal. On December 11, more than a month after Sherman resigned, Villard's paper headlined a story, "General Sherman Insane."[15]

It was about as blunt a lead paragraph as you could write. "The painful intelligence reaches us, in such form that we are not at liberty to disclose it, that Gen. William T. Sherman is insane," the *Commercial*'s account began. In it, Sherman is described as "stark mad" and suffering from "loss of mind."[16]

It was also unfair. Sherman never entirely shook that label, either among contemporaries or in the history books. And it was all based on an unidentified source, taken second-hand from a comment that Sherman always maintained was misconstrued, from a meeting he had reason to believe was off the record, given that Cameron had said that just friends would be present. Sherman was tempestuous and uncivil by nature. But this allegation that Sherman was "stark mad" at the beginning of the war was one of Civil War journalism's worst hours.

In his memoirs, Sherman said rumors about his mental health had circulated before that sensational Villard story and headline, and that he suspected Cameron or one of the members of his party, which included Wilkeson, had been the source. He hinted at it in a memorandum of

November 4, 1861, to McClellan, the newly appointed commander-in-chief of all Union armies.

"I am told that my estimate of troops needed for this line . . . two hundred thousand, has been construed to my prejudice, and therefore leave it for the future," Sherman wrote.[17]

Later, in his memoirs, Sherman said he finally had to confront the thought that many of his subordinates looked askance at him because of the rumors against him. Sherman was relieved by Don Carlos Buell. He said he initially viewed his removal as a "fulfillment" of him telling Cameron that he'd need hundreds of thousands of troops to do what the government was asking him to do. Upon reflection, however, Sherman knew that he could never overturn the perception that he was insane in bureaucratic infighting. It would take leading men in battle. He would get that opportunity five months later at Shiloh, where Sherman, initially surprised by Johnston's attack, assembled an orderly retreat that saved Grant's army from disaster.

"I saw and felt, and was of course deeply moved to observe, the manifest belief that there was more or less truth in the rumor that the cares, perplexities and anxieties of the situation had unbalanced my judgment and mind," he wrote in his memoirs. "It was, doubtless, an incident common to all civil wars, to which I could only submit with the best grace possible, trusting for an opportunity to redeem my fortune and good name. Of course I could not deny the fact, and had to submit to all its painful consequences for months; and moreover I could not hide from myself that many of the officers and soldiers subsequently placed under my command looked at me askance and with suspicion. Indeed, it was not until the following April that the battle of Shiloh gave me personally the chance to redeem my good name."[18]

Sherman was also ultimately proven right in his forecasts about the war in that Louisville meeting. It turned out to be a far, far longer war than Cameron envisioned in the fall of 1861, and it required troop levels way beyond what Sherman was talking about for his theater of the war. Eventually, more than 2.1 million men fought for the Union, more than 1 million for the Confederates—levels that war planners in Washington, DC, and Richmond were not dreaming necessary in the fall of 1861.

It's easy to understand why Sherman carried a grudge. He was furious that he had been left to hang by his superiors back in Washington, DC, amidst the sensational headlines. Describing his reason for stepping down from the command in Louisville, he wrote in his memoirs: "My position was therefore simply unbearable, and it is probable I resented the cruel insult with language of intense feeling." Sherman complained that he had received "no orders, not a word of encouragement or relief" from his superiors when his mental health was questioned, and that Cameron left him hanging, that he "never, to my knowledge, took pains to affirm or deny" all the allegations swirling around him.[19]

He was bitter that the "newspapers kept up their game, as though instigated by malice," and especially blamed Villard's editor, P. B. Ewing.[20]

But Sherman's observations at the Galt House about the long war ahead stayed with Sam Wilkeson, and informed his reporting that first winter of the war. It also led to a series of scoops that further intensified the *Tribune* correspondent's belief that the war would be a lot longer, and a lot costlier, than the public expected.

CHAPTER 11

"A Changed Man Was He!"

WILKESON'S REPORTING OUT OF THE TRIP WEST, DESPITE BEING unfairly hijacked by Villard, enhanced the *Tribune* correspondent's image as a dogged insider. And he kept getting scoops that not only beat the competition, but would within months be proven prophetic.

Two days before the *Tribune* printed the Thomas report on the state of affairs in the West, Wilkeson had come up with another impressive scoop that said that any major offensive by the Army of the Potomac under McClellan would not take place until the following spring of 1862. There were doubters, but his reporting was spot on. It was accurate, insightful, and informed reporting, and it flew directly in the face of the "On to Richmond" jingoism that many newspapers, especially Greeley's, had engaged in early in the war.

Wilkeson's *Tribune* report in late October 1861 concluded that the Northern armies were too undisciplined and too disorganized to carry any major offensive. The report echoed Sherman's central observation that the rag-tag short-timers called up by the various Northern states to put down the rebellion could not come close to doing the job. The war, scarcely six months old, would go on for "several years under the most favorable circumstances," Wilkeson predicted in his scoop.[1]

It was an about face from an "On to Richmond" crusade that had gotten Greeley's *Tribune* into big trouble in the spring of 1861, a few months before Greeley brought Wilkeson to Washington to anchor his war coverage. Some were still blaming the disastrous loss at the First Battle of Manassas on Greeley's newspaper. Wilkeson's predecessor Fitz

Henry Warren, had written a dispatch in late May exhorting the Union army to "unloose your chivalry" and "pierce the vitals of Virginia, and scourge the serpent seed of her rebellion on the crowning heights of Richmond."[2] A month later, as the new Confederate Congress prepared to gather in Richmond, Greeley's subordinate Charles Dana pushed headlines like: "THE NATION's WAR-CRY. Forward to Richmond! . . . The Rebel Congress must not be allowed to meet there on the 20th of July."[3]

After the disaster at Bull Run on July 21, other newspapers pushed back on the *Tribune*. Henry Raymond's *New York Times* decried the "insane clamor" of "certain reckless journalists" who had called for the movement on Richmond.[4]

This was the anti-*Tribune* atmosphere that greeted Sam Wilkeson when he took over Greeley's bureau in August. In the longer view of history, Wilkeson's cautionary report that followed six months later appears to be penance for that jingoism. But Wilkeson was reporting the truth: The Lincoln Administration was digging in for a long war. Phrases in the lengthy article betrayed Wilkeson's sources as either Cameron himself, or those very close to the secretary of war, or both.

"It is universally believed by well-informed men," Wilkeson wrote, "that the enemy is in larger force on the Potomac than we are," and that it had "better generalship" and better "rearward communications."

The only advantage the Union had at that point, Wilkeson wrote, was "the justness of our cause" and the "superior equipment" the North could bring to the fight. George McClellan, he wrote, was a "promising young general" who had simply not had the time to put an effective army in the field.

"There is not really one well-disciplined regiment in the country," Wilkeson went on, adding that "the whole army of the Potomac is yet much a mere mob than it is an army of soldiers."[5]

To illustrate, Wilkeson described in comedic detail a military funeral of an officer that he had just witnessed. The procession to the cemetery started an hour late because honor guards straggled in piecemeal. Men in dirty uniforms stood lackadaisically or squatted, "not a dignified attitude for a guard of honor," Wilkeson wrote. The soldiers wore "all sorts of irregularities of dress," Sam wrote, and "there was no evidence that any one had ever been properly cleansed since they were first worn."

Once the military procession finally started, it collided with a boisterous Irish funeral parade. Any remaining sense of military discipline dissipated. Part of the honor guard fell behind and got separated, and "recruits in dirty gray jackets and trowsers, and without a really clean-looking thing on them," got mixed up with the Irish funeral mourners.[6]

It took some courage to print it. Wilkeson's scathing dispatch appeared in the *Tribune* at a time when newspaper critics of the administration's prosecution of the war were being threatened by mobs or threatened with sedition, occasionally thrown into jail for months without charges. But Wilkeson held nothing back; his connections with Cameron at that moment made him untouchable. And in the piece, he made a broader assertion about the war preparedness of a civil society that had kept only a small peacetime army.

"It is impossible to state too strongly the unfitness and inadaptation to the business of a soldier which seventy years of peace have wrought in the habit of the people," Wilkeson wrote in the *Tribune*. "Neither among officers nor men do you yet see anything of the air and carriage which, when a traveler sees in Europe, he learns to say, 'there is a soldier.'"[7]

The rival press was unimpressed with Wilkeson's scoop about the offensive being put off until 1862, but it gave begrudging praise to his access. Henry Raymond's *New York Times* pointed out that "there might be something" to the claim that Union armies were woefully unprepared, but that the Confederates were in no better shape than the Northern armies. Therefore, better to fight now than wait for the Rebels to get stronger, too, the rival Republican paper claimed. "As they have to encounter soldiers no more used to war than they are themselves, the reasons urged for delay seem to us utterly inconclusive," the *Times* reported.[8]

But the *Times* also conceded it did not doubt that Wilkeson had reported the thoughts of Cameron himself. "The confidential relations which the *Tribune*'s Washington correspondent is understood to sustain to the Secretary of War give this letter more importance than it would otherwise possess," the *Times* wrote.[9] This, of course, was a reference to

Wilkeson, fresh off his visit to Cameron's farm and his front-row seat during Cameron's western meetings with Fremont and Sherman.

Still, the rival press was not convinced that public opinion would allow the Union armies to stay mostly idle until the spring. "The loyal people of this country will receive with 'astonishment and indignation,' any authentic announcement that this is to be the policy of the Administration," the *Times* went on, suggesting that Cameron did not speak for Lincoln. "For our own part, we do not give it a moment's credence."[10]

In retrospect, Wilkeson's piece, which he attributed to the beliefs of "well-informed men," has all the trappings of a Lincoln Administration trial balloon, as a way to prepare the public for the realities of what the president and his cabinet were confronting in the enormous task of putting the North on an all-out war footing. The stress and strain of building an army, navy, and a logistical infrastructure to fight and to win a war that had already gone on longer than the naïve expectations of spring would have tried any leader. And the "insane" prediction of a long and bloody conflict that Cameron had heard from Sherman may have begun looking more like reality as the first winter of the war arrived.

Wilkeson followed this story with other impressive scoops over that first winter of the war. He soon caught wind of big changes in Lincoln's cabinet.

The strain and stress were showing on Cameron, the secretary of war. Wilkeson observed it firsthand over dinner at a Washington restaurant with Cameron on a cold night in December of 1861. Also at the table were the British correspondent William Howard Russell, and John W. Forney, the editor of the rabidly pro-Lincoln *Philadelphia Press*. Forney had been awarded for his loyalty with an appointment as Secretary of the Senate, a lucrative job that helped augment his income at the newspaper and also gave him official access to Lincoln's allies and foes in the Senate. Vice President Hannibal Hamlin later dropped by Wilkeson's table, as did Owen Lovejoy, an Illinois abolitionist and minister who would be elected to Congress in 1863.[11]

Cameron, under increasing pressure as allegations of War Department profiteering continued to pile up, seemed to sense that he was nearing the end of his tenure in Lincoln's cabinet. Despite Wilkeson's favorable coverage, and the trial balloons that he had floated through the *Tribune*, Cameron was feeling the power of this new, immediate, competitive, ubiquitous newspaper industry.

"The press rules America," Cameron, a one-time printer who had gotten rich on railroad and canal construction and banking, told his dinner mates. "No one can face it and live."[12]

Later, Wilkeson, Russell, Cameron, and Hamlin dropped by a grand ball put on by the 5th U.S. Cavalry in their encampment in the city. If not impressed by their fighting prowess, the erudite Russell was taken by the pomp and celebration. The horse soldiers were living in wooden huts, but they'd set up a huge bonfire in the middle of the camp and had put "exceedingly pretty" decorations on the huts. The fire, "surrounded by soldiers, by the carriage drivers and by negro servants, afforded the most striking play of color and variety of light and shade I ever beheld," Russell wrote in his diary that night.[13]

A month later, at the start of 1862, Cameron was sacked for Stanton. Weeks after that, Wilkeson again observed the effects of the stress and strain on the faces of war planners. This time it was the face of McClellan. The pompous "Little Mac," revered by his troops but the source of eternal frustration to his superiors, had just turned thirty-six years old. But on one night in January of 1862, he looked much older.

It happened at one of those Washington dinner parties that Wilkeson had told his editor, Gay, that he rarely attended. In truth, Wilkeson had learned that such social gatherings often produced news and always built relationships. He also had learned that body language was a great tell of people in high places. Wilkeson's read of McClellan's body language at that party immediately led him down a reporting path toward another important scoop.

On Friday night, January 31, 1862, Sam, Cate, and their twenty-year-old daughter Maggie attended a party at the home of Secretary of State Seward, the man for whom Wilkeson had ghost-written speeches before the war.

It was a week after Wilkeson had testified against press censorship under Cameron's successor before the House Judiciary Committee, in which he had complained of heavy-handed censorship. "I am not allowed to send anything over the wires which, in the estimation of the censor, the Secretary of State, or the Assistant Secretary of State, shall be damaging to the character of the administration, or any individual member of the Cabinet," he had complained. He vowed to keep fighting it.

"Unless they go to the mails and search out my letters they cannot prevent the publication of what they suppress by telegraph," he told the congressional committee.[14]

With Cameron just dispatched from the cabinet, Wilkeson knew he would have increasing trouble getting his dispatches through censors. It could not hurt to make personal pleas, face-to-face, to the highest administration officials, to lay off his copy.

Some of the city's biggest political luminaries were at Seward's soiree. At 11:30 p.m., they all took note of McClellan's arrival. The days were long for "Little Mac," who, unbeknownst to many in the room, was embroiled in a fierce argument with Lincoln and the new war secretary, Stanton, over planning for the upcoming Peninsula campaign. If all went well, that campaign under McClellan's generalship would climax in the capture of Richmond and the crushing of the Southern rebellion. But McClellan believed he was not ready. He may have had an ally in Cameron, but no longer in Stanton.

Wilkeson cornered McClellan shortly after the general arrived. Six weeks earlier, McClellan had contracted typhoid fever while visiting Fitz John Porter's division at Hall's Hill in Virginia. By the time Wilkeson saw him at Seward's the next month, he looked to be physically on the mend. Emotionally, however, McClellan's body language said something different.[15]

"A changed man was he!" Wilkeson wrote Greeley the next day. "While he looked well, and while he told me he was stronger and more elastic than ever," McClellan also emanated "a mute appeal for empathy and forbearance that was too plainly legible.

"Any man with eye to note the contrast between the Commander in January and in December could see that he felt that his fame and his power had culminated . . . that he was standing on a slippery place," Wilkeson continued. "It's said that Stanton and he are already in a deadlock. If they are not, they inevitably will be. It is only a matter of time."[16]

Wilkeson's observations were dead on, a detection of a falling out between McClellan and Stanton that would have serious consequences for the Union military and practically end any prospect of a quick end to the war.

Just hours before Wilkeson ran into McClellan at Seward's party, Lincoln had issued "President's Special War Order Number One," directing McClellan to put "all the disposable forces of the Army of the Potomac, after providing safely for the defense of Washington," on the move within three weeks, with the "immediate object of seizing and occupying" rail line and territory south of Manassas, Virginia, near the site of the Union disaster the previous summer.[17]

It was a strategy Lincoln thought would both spur the Army of the Potomac into a decisive offensive that could perhaps just win the war, but at the least simultaneously strengthen the defenses of Washington by forcing Confederate armies threatening the capital to defend their own seat of government in Richmond. Days later, a furious McClellan wrote Stanton that he objected to Lincoln's plan, and McClellan laid out a far more ambitious course to move his army to the lower Chesapeake Bay, from there on to Richmond. It was a Hail Mary response to rising criticism of McClellan's unwillingness to move. McClellan blamed Lincoln for not supplying him sufficient numbers of troops to carry out a more ambitious plan. "I have not the force I asked for," he wrote.[18]

McClellan said he could not launch the Peninsula campaign until six weeks after Lincoln's February 22 deadline. And on February 3, he wrote Stanton a blistering letter, filled with self-pity and accusations. When he took control of the army the previous July, McClellan wrote, it was "a mere collection of regiments, cowering on the banks of the Potomac, some perfectly raw, others dispirited by the recent defeat" at Bull Run. Washington, DC, was so exposed when he took command, McClellan said, that "the city was almost in a condition to have been taken by a dash of a regiment of cavalry."[19]

He had begun whipping the army into shape, McClellan said, and the capital was now safe. But, he complained, "there is a vast difference between that and the efficiency required to enable troops to attack successfully and army elated by victory and intrenched in position long since selected, studied and fortified."[20]

Wilkeson pounced. Stanton was taking a firmer hold over Union war planning, and Wilkeson noted this shift in a *Tribune* dispatch less than a week after he ran into McClellan at Seward's party.

"Rumor grows into belief that Secretary of War Stanton will resume in fact, as he has commenced to do in form, the conduct of the war which usage and department law give him the right to do," Wilkeson's *Tribune* dispatch said. In later generations, "rumor grows into belief" would be simply, "sources said."

Wilkeson may not have gotten the scoop had he not run into McClellan at Seward's soiree. The cues from his observation of McClellan's body language, which he noted to Greeley the day after the party, sparked a more intense inquiry as to the relationship between Stanton and McClellan. His "hook" into the story was a subtle, but substantial, change in War Department official correspondence. Noting that the War Department had started issuing proclamations in Lincoln's name, where they had previously been issued in McClellan's, Wilkeson wrote: "The President is Commander-in-Chief of the Army and he, with his able and prodigiously magnetic War Secretary, will now lift this war out of mud and delay, and carry it to victory. General McClellan will be placed in command of the Army of the Potomac."[21]

Less than a week later, Wilkeson followed with another *Tribune* scoop that said that generals that heretofore reported directly to McClellan were now reporting to the War Department, leading to "communication and cooperation with one another, which Gen. McClellan had constantly refused or neglected to do." Stanton was exerting more power as war secretary, Wilkeson's *Tribune* reported, and "Gen. McClellan's changed and changing relations to the war will be developed to the whole country and made complete within two weeks."[22] It was the beginning of the end of McClellan's first tenure as Lincoln's top general.

McClellan never carried out Lincoln's plan to move on Manassas, but the Peninsula campaign he eventually embarked upon that spring and summer turned into a disaster that Sam Wilkeson chronicled in grim detail as an embedded correspondent in McClellan's army. In a campaign that stretched from March to July of 1862, Richmond was left intact, Washington was undisturbed, and the armies fought into a series of bloody stalemates or Union defeats. Union troops advanced close enough to Richmond to hear its church bells, but the war was not close to being over.

And in the midst of that Peninsula campaign, the Wilkeson family suffered a grievous personal loss, the death of John Wilkes Wilkeson at Seven Pines. A war that Sam Wilkeson had started to describe as a heavenly mission was about to become very personal for the entire Wilkeson family.

CHAPTER 12

"The Yeast Which Overflows in Many Columns"

THE DEPLORABLE CONDITION OF THE UNION ARMY IN THAT FIRST WIN-
ter of the war was a constant buzz among the press corps flocking to
the capital, which the *Times of London* correspondent Russell described
in his diary as "all suburb and no city."[1] Russell, accustomed to the
pomp and discipline of the permanent European armies that had protected barons and lords for centuries, was appalled at the condition of
the citizen army now assembling in the North. He had spent much of
that spring in the South, where he had been more impressed with the
preparations there.

Washington itself had the feeling of starting over, of growth and
danger and a future that the politicians were investing in, but no one
was sure of. Rumors of threats and plots abounded, and the thought of
a capture by columns of Confederates was never too far out of mind. It
was an exciting and scary time to be a correspondent in the capital. The
metaphors of a nation still under construction ran through it all.

The Capitol's dome was under construction, and the Treasury
Department was also being built, both buildings "surrounded by materials for their future and final development," Russell observed. The
Washington Monument would not be finished for a quarter century. The
"rather fantastic" red brick Smithsonian Institution's castle, open only six
years, was surrounded by "squalid little cottages," and muddy streets and
alleyways. The White House had seen better days, and with Lincoln now

living there, it was daily overrun with the calling and pleading of the privileged, the profiteers, and the down-and-out.

Henry Villard, Wilkeson's eventual colleague, described Washington during the war as "like a large village, with its preponderance of plain, low brick or wooden structures, wide, mostly unpaved streets, small shops, general lack of business activity, and a distinctly Southern air of insolence and sloth.

"Of its numerous hotels," he said, "some were spacious but all were poorly kept. It could not boast a single decent restaurant, but had no end of bar-rooms."[2] The Capitol itself was being used as barracks for soldiers.

Russell was put off by the boosterism of the early American war correspondents. A month before Wilkeson arrived, he lamented the "swarm of newspaper correspondents" that "has settled upon Washington, and great are the glorifications of the hightoned paymasters, gallant doctors, and subalterns accomplished in the art of war, who furnish minute items to my American brethren, and provide the yeast which overflows in many columns." The reporting by these rookie war correspondents, Russell harrumphed, primarily served as intelligence for the assembling Confederates across the river in Virginia.

But Russell took a liking to Sam Wilkeson, probably because the new *Tribune* correspondent seemed unafraid of telling the truth even if it ran counter to the Northern cause he knew Wilkeson favored. Throughout the war, Wilkeson would make no bones about which side he was on, and as the war progressed, he would become increasingly sold on the idea that only a total Union victory, no matter the cost, would truly end slavery and save the Union. Russell also respected that Sam Wilkeson could see what he could see: The Union army was not ready to win the war.

The correspondents "are grossly and utterly ignorant of what an army is or should be in the first place," Russell complained. That July of 1861, shortly before the first Manassas battle, he observed that "their artillery is miserably deficient" and made up of "different calibres, badly horsed, miserably equipped, and provided with the worst set of gunners and drivers which I, who have seen the Turkish field-guns, ever beheld.

"They have no cavalry, only a few scarecrow men, who would dissolve partnerships with their steeds at the first serious combined movement,"

Russell observed. The infantry, he thought, consisted of "some few regulars from the frontiers, who may be good for Indians, but who would go over like ninepins at a charge from Punjaubee irregulars."[3]

Sam Wilkeson was hearing the same from within his own family. One of his prime sources was his nephew, Samuel H. Wilkeson, John's oldest son, and Lt. John Wilkes Wilkeson's brother. A few months after his New York regiment's happy march to Washington, as it came to the end of its ninety-day enlistment, Samuel H. complained in a letter home that the 21st New York was "in a condition bordering on disorganization," and that within the regiment there was, "unanimously, almost, a desire to return home at the expiration of the three months." There were "so many hours idled away in camp life it is no wonder men become restless," he said.[4]

It was this military that Samuel H. Wilkeson's cousin, Bayard, joined two months later, and the one about which Sam Wilkeson so boldly reported that they would not be prepared for war at least until the spring of 1862.

As soon as he arrived as bureau chief for the *Tribune*, Sam Wilkeson had spent long days visiting the forts and the troops billeted around Washington. One was the 21st New York, in which Sam's nephew had enlisted. It had been a summer of dashed dreams and false pomp for Samuel H. Wilkeson. In June, John Wilkeson's oldest son had written home of a dreamy, parade-like journey his regiment had taken from New York to Washington. In town after town and at country crossroads along the way, appreciative elders and pretty girls had handed out fruit and drink and hosted picnics.

The early Wilkeson enlistees epitomized the cavalier attitude that spring and summer of 1861. Shortly after Samuel H. and John Wilkes Wilkeson had joined up in the spring of 1861, Samuel H. wrote their father that "I feel more than ever, when I am in a contemplative state, what a glorious contest this I have gone into is."[5]

The 21st New York was treated like a band of heroes in waiting as it marched southward through New York, Pennsylvania, and Maryland.

"Not only was the weather agreeable, but the hospitable manner in which the inhabitants all along the railroad in Pennsylvania greeted the regiment combined to give a holiday aspect to things," Samuel H. wrote. "Highly gratifying."[6]

In Williamsport, Pennsylvania, "the whole population turned out and conducted the different companies of the regiment to tables decked with beautiful bouquets and groaning under the choicest provender," he continued in the June 19, 1861, letter. "I shall never forget the scene presented as our men ranged themselves along the beautiful boards, surrounded as they were by fair women and smiling children."[7]

The correspondent Sam Wilkeson tried to look out for his nephew when the 21st New York encamped at Fort Runyon, one of the largest of the hastily built forts ringing Washington, DC. It was located across the Potomac in Virginia, a few miles west of what would in a later war become the Pentagon. "Uncle thought our location very unhealthy," Samuel H. Wilkeson wrote his father later that summer, "and told me he would try to get the regiment removed to a better place."[8]

His Uncle Sam could not move units, but he did have enough influence to try to move men. He told Samuel H. that he would try to get him transferred to the artillery "as he thinks that branch of the service will have the best chance to distinguish itself in the war, and will be more likely retained after the war than the infantry."[9] Sam's help led to an even better promotion. Samuel H. eventually got transferred to the "Scott's 900," an elite New York cavalry unit. By war's end, he would be promoted to major, assigning the cavalry escorts that went with Abraham Lincoln on his daily rides.[10]

Within weeks, Sam would pull the same strings for Bayard.

Chapter 13

"I Am Seventeen Years and Six Months of Age"

The penmanship is flowing but deliberate, the prose direct and respectful, the lines straight, the date on the letter noteworthy. It was written October 22, 1861, the day after the Union army's humiliating defeat at Ball's Bluff on the Potomac River scarcely 40 miles from Washington, DC. A seventeen-year-old was coming to join the Union army.

"I hereby accept the appointment of 2nd Lieutenant in the Fourth Regiment of Artillery made this day by the President of the United States," the young man wrote to Lorenzo Thomas, the adjutant general of the Union army, the same Lorenzo Thomas whose report Sam Wilkeson would days later use to scoop the world on Fremont's problems and Sherman's warnings.[1]

On the day Bayard joined, the Northern public was reading the first drafts of the Union army's humiliating defeat at Ball's Bluff, a battle in which some soldiers drowned after jumping off or being shot off the cliffs overlooking the Potomac River a scant 40 miles northwest of Washington. For weeks, bodies washed ashore as far south as occupied Alexandria, Virginia, a maudlin foreshadowing of how this war's rivers of suffering after battles would flow on and on.

Bayard Wilkeson betrayed none of his emotions in his letter to Thomas. He was matter-of-fact, straight to the point, and ready to serve.

"I was born in Albany in the State of New York," he wrote, continuing in neat, straight-lined penmanship.

"I am seventeen years and six months of age."

The soon-to-be commissioned lieutenant signed his letter, "Respectfully yours, Bayard Wilkeson."

It is the writing of a young man of privilege and education in 1861 America. Bayard was the kind of young man who—even though still a teenager—was filling the officer ranks of a rapidly growing and green Union army. The fiasco at Ball's Bluff led to a congressional committee on the conduct of the war, and further forced the Southern and Northern public to realize that this war had turned a corner to something much deadlier and costlier than the festive marches through the countryside that Bayard's cousin, Samuel H., had described just three months earlier.

Bayard Wilkeson had been itching to enlist even though his father still thought of him as a child, an "infant in the language of the law"[2] that Bayard was studying. He consented to the enlistment, but Sam Wilkeson's fatherly instincts occasionally interfered after Bayard put on the uniform. When the boy's 4th Artillery battery was detailed to southern Virginia during the Peninsula campaign the next spring, Bayard became so ill in camp that Sam thought he was going to die. Sam pleaded with Bayard's superiors for a short leave, most likely saving his life. Sam always carried a father's worry on his journalistic travels, an angst that intensified into personal loss after Bayard's cousin, John Wilkes Wilkeson, was killed at Seven Pines in the spring of 1862. Union officers said later that Sam carried John's death at Seven Pines as if it were his own son.

Cate Cady Wilkeson had no illusions about the dangers her oldest son faced when he enlisted. Writing to her sister-in-law, Mary, just eleven days after John Wilkes Wilkeson was killed the following spring, Cate confessed that the day Bayard left for the army that previous fall that she had made peace with the possibility that she would never see him again. "When my boy left me I gave him up to death," she wrote Mary, "and hope if a soldier he will prove a brave one, better to die than live a coward."[3]

Like his father, Bayard was lean and strapping, and he exhibited strains of discipline and industriousness not common in all teenagers. He was trusted with chores at an early age at the Wilkeson family farm near Canaan. Sam admired "his sturdiness and the skill with which he turned a furrow. He plowed all the day long, handsomely and thoroughly. That boy's future is assured."[4]

That, of course, was by design. Educated at a boarding school in Connecticut, grandson of a founder of Buffalo, New York, and nephew of the abolitionist and suffragette Elizabeth Cady Stanton, Bayard Wilkeson inherited an activist, educated pedigree. His maternal grandfather, Daniel Cady, the well-known lawyer and judge, was elected associate justice of the New York Supreme Court three years after Bayard was born.

There were clear expectations of responsibility, formality, and civic duty during his childhood. Writing in 1853 to his nephew John Wilkes Wilkeson when John was away at boarding school, his uncle Sam (and Bayard's father) referred to reports that had filtered back to the family that young John Wilkes, then eighteen, had been scolded for having dirty nails and a bad attitude. Sam opened his letter with stern admonitions on personal hygiene, then quickly segued into career advice, which, of course, meant journalism. Sam told John Wilkes Wilkeson, who would eventually become a lawyer before the Civil War, that the days of kings had passed, and that revolutions in literacy expression and in the pace of communications was forcing the change. An educated, civic- and fair-minded man who could communicate well would go far in this new world, Sam lectured John Wilkes.

"Bear in mind my recommendation to you to cultivate Composition," Sam wrote. "The time is gone by for the Orator to move masses of men. His day was in the infancy of Society, when the Press was feeble and immature. Hereafter the Writer is going to be the strong man. He will make opinion and lead the Social Movement. Write therefore—write clearly, simply, strongly. Give great attention to this art."[5]

In one final admonition, Sam Wilkeson closed by warning young John Wilkes Wilkeson to stay away from tobacco.

Sam Wilkeson was describing his own life's ambitions in that letter to nephew John. *Write clearly, simply, strongly. Give great attention to this art.*

Two years earlier, Sam had written his nephew, Samuel H. Wilkeson, after worrying that he'd fallen in with a bad crowd, and had been "running around a village at night" near his boarding school. The next generation of Wilkesons, Sam wrote to his nephew-namesake, must remember that there were certain responsibilities of being "born of a gentleman," and that "our associations make our characters." He warned against associating with "common, vulgar boys—with boys of low or vicious tastes."

Sam lectured on. "Acquire knowledge, get the materials in your head to talk well with & to write well with—and train yourself to think. The man that thinks correctly is the successful man."[6]

It was a lesson that had been drilled into Bayard, too. The evangelism about being able to write and communicate freely and directly had surrounded Bayard and his cousins throughout their childhoods. It was a strict upbringing, with one grandfather, in particular, an influence. Daniel Cady, the patriarch in Bayard's childhood, was the only grandfather present for much of it after the senior Samuel Wilkeson's death when Bayard was barely five. Daniel Cady was taciturn, proper, and a teetotaler. The first time he ran for a New York judgeship, he sat down at a campaign dinner in which champagne was served. When another guest noticed water in Cady's glass he asked why the candidate was not drinking. Daniel Cady responded that abstaining was the "best security for health." When another dinner companion opined that drink in moderation was not harmful, Cady shot back: "Sir, I don't barter my principles for popularity."[7]

From an early age, Bayard, his siblings, and his cousins received constantly reinforced messages about civic responsibility, action, honor, and upholding the family's reputation. The message from Bayard's grandfather came with history and pedigree. Early in his legal career, Daniel Cady had practiced law with Alexander Hamilton and Aaron Burr.

In an 1850 letter to Elizabeth Cady Stanton's oldest son and Bayard's first cousin, Daniel Cady spelled out what was expected of children of Cady lineage and Bayard's generation.

The eight-year-old boy's letters—he was named Daniel Cady Stanton, after his grandfather—must have contained spelling errors and sloppy penmanship. Daniel Cady told his grandson that he was "pleased that you write so well." But he would not barter principle for popularity with a grandchild, either.

"In order that you may learn to write and spell correctly I advise you to never send a letter to the Post Office until you have taken a dictionary and ascertained that every word in your letter is spelled correctly," Daniel Cady lectured. "After you have done this, then make a fair copy of your letter (so) that there are no blot or erasure on it."[8]

Eight years later, writing to the same grandson while he was away at boarding school, Daniel Cady pleaded to his namesake: "I hope you may become a man distinguished for learning, talent and honesty. Without honesty no man can be truly great. There is no book which you can study so important as the Bible."[9]

So it came as no surprise that Bayard Wilkeson's enlistment letter was precise, grammatical, and adorned with flawless penmanship. Or that he carried his grandfather's piety against strong drink. Bayard would eventually complain in letters to his father, no teetotaler himself, that many of the officers he served with liked the bottle too much. Many fellow officers who served in the 11th Corps at Gettysburg under Oliver Otis Howard derided the Bible-quoting Howard's piety behind his back, but not Bayard. His grandfather, Daniel Cady, had drilled biblical canons into his grandchildren.

"Your body can live but a few years, but your soul will never die," Daniel Cady wrote his teenaged grandson. "The great and important business of the present life is so to employ it that never-ending happiness of the soul shall be secured."

He signed it with formality, "yours truly."[10]

There are no known surviving letters from his grandfather to Bayard, but given Grandpa Cady's profligacy in writing, it is a fair assumption Bayard received similar written homilies. And not just from the Cady side.

On the Wilkeson side, high expectations of military service and honor followed the eight grandsons of Samuel Wilkeson Sr. into the Union army. "The honor of your native town, and that of your family is in your keeping," the senior John Wilkeson wrote Samuel H., on May 21, 1861, as Samuel's regiment embarked on that lark of a march to Washington, DC.

"It will be hard at first, but come easy soon," the father went on. "It would disgrace all of you to quit the service because of hardships."[11]

The family name and personal honor must be upheld—there was no other way. Come what cost it would exact.

In the letter, the senior John Wilkeson said he'd spoken to Samuel H.'s regimental commander before the Buffalo boys had headed south to the war. The commander told him that "We hope and believe duty will sanctify the families that they represent, and the City whose children they are."

"Brave, noble words," John Wilkeson wrote. "You see what is expected of you."[12]

There was no question about the Wilkeson boys enlisting, and the place of honor that battle hero Bayard's and John Wilkes Wilkeson's portraits held at the family home on Buffalo's Niagara Square home after the war attested to the value that the family put in service to country. But anti-war strains emerged in the family, too. Bayard's free-spirited younger brother, Frank, came out of the war believing that service for many men in the Union army fell woefully short of the patriotic hype and the idealization of upright, selfless service for country. After the war Frank wrote a highly personal book in which he concluded that many Union army enlistees were simply bounty hunters, just another form of war profiteer.

His older brother, Bayard, was named after Cate's brother-in-law, Edward Bayard, another law partner of her father's. But Cate and Sam Wilkeson also liked the name because it was that of a heroic fifteenth century French soldier, Chevalier de Bayard, one of the last chivalrous knights.[13] By virtue of the name Bayard carried, what he had been taught about honor and service, and the fear and fervor over saving the Union, the pull of duty to fight in the Union army would have been irresistible for any seventeen-year-old.

He grew up, physically, after enlisting. By the time he was nineteen at Gettysburg, Lieutenant Wilkeson was a sturdy 175 pounds and around 6 feet tall. His father's friends described him as bright, sunny, and open. He had a naturally receding hairline, but the shock of black on his crown spilled over onto his forehead and swept back over his ears. He let dark whiskers grow under his chin, but the rest of his face was clean-shaven. Rosy cheeks most prominently betrayed his youth.[14]

Bayard was, like his father, strong-minded but also self-controlled, drawn to action, naturally disposed to lead others. His family nicknamed him "Bay" or "Bye." Like his father, he craved independent authority within a larger mission, and he had no tolerance for fools or slackers. He could also be a scold.

So when the seventeen-year-old Bayard wanted to join the army, the only question was where he would serve. A short, unsigned biography of the boy's early years, possibly written by his father, described Bayard coming to his parent with an ultimatum. "In the first year of our civil war, the lad, seventeen years old, smilingly gave his father the choice of seeing him a private in a battery of heavy artillery, or getting for him a commission as second lieutenant in one of the five regiments of United States artillery," the biography read. "Experience from his babyhood of the unconquerable will of the sunny-tempered and exemplary boy, impelled the father to a quick choice of the best of the two evils."[15]

Bayard, the account read, "was commissioned in the 4th Artillery before the sun set on the announcement of his purpose to fight for the Union."[16]

Sam's string-pulling got the young man commissioned as a second lieutenant in Battery K of that 4th U.S. Artillery. Shortly thereafter Bayard was transferred to Battery G, where he started as second in command and eventually rose to its leadership. He was promoted to first lieutenant and given command of the company less than three months after his eighteenth birthday. At Gettysburg he was one of the youngest artillery officers in the Union army.[17]

Bayard had taken de facto command of his battery by Thanksgiving, 1861. He wrote his cousin, Samuel H., still billeted in Washington, DC, that in the artillery, much of the drilling and parade duties fell on second lieutenants, like himself.

"For a boy that has not handled a sword or musket over a month it is quite rapid promotion," Bayard's cousin wrote shortly thereafter. "Bay has the stuff in him to make a good soldier."[18]

That first winter of the war, still just seventeen, Lt. Bayard Wilkeson was stationed at Fort Monroe near Hampton Roads, Virginia, a staging ground for the fighting the next spring in the Peninsula, a major Union outpost during the Civil War. Bayard built a house near Suffolk and told his father and uncle, John, that it was big enough to host them should they want to visit.[19] It was his way of saying he was homesick.

It would be some time, however, before Lieutenant Wilkeson saw any serious battle action. Eventually, he was singled out for leadership in a minor battle in Virginia early in 1863. But although his battery saw minor action at Fredericksburg in December of 1862 and at Chancellorsville just weeks before Gettysburg, heading into that battle he lamented his and his men's lack of fighting experience. He wrote his father that he longed to prove himself, to make a name.

Although it was not uncommon for boys younger than Bayard to serve in the Union army in 1863, the average age of a federal soldier during the Civil War was just under twenty-six.[20] It was likely that most of the 120 or so men under Bayard's command were older, some much older. Lieutenant Wilkeson made up for the age difference with a stern, outward confidence and a reputation as a commander who was concerned about his men's creature comforts. As a commander, Lieutenant Wilkeson "commanded the confidence and love of his men (that) enabled him to maintain a discipline which made his battery a model to which not a few Volunteer artillery captains were sent by angry generals to see better methods," one anonymous biographer wrote.[21]

Bayard literally took older Union artillery commanders to school. Maj. Gen. John Peck, one of Bayard's superiors, who would help Sam find John Wilkes Wilkeson's body at Seven Pines, said Bayard's battery had "a reputation for discipline and efficiency which virtually made it a school to which incompetent or negligent artillery officers were sent by irritated commanders to learn their business." The young lieutenant could be a nag about his men's diets, Peck said, and he would "force them to be comfortable and cleanly." Bayard Wilkeson loved horses, and he made sure his men spent long hours caring for the battery's animals. Lieutenant Wilkeson was known for "never having sick or disabled horses," Peck said.[22]

Bayard's battery also developed a reputation for thrift and self-sufficiency. He was especially adept at mending feed bags and horse blankets. General Peck later said Bayard was renowned for "never making a requisition for artillery property that could be made to do service by mending or patching." Bayard was "as conscientious as he was brave."[23] He became known as a superior horseman, a product of spending summers on the family's farm near Canaan. Ultimately, all of these characteristics—a demand for discipline and performance from his men, a fealty to training and order, self-sufficiency and the gung-ho drive to get to the action—contributed to a stand that Lieutenant Wilkeson and his men would make at Gettysburg, in one of the war's pivotal hours.

He almost didn't get to the field at Gettysburg. Disease in camp for a Civil War soldier could be as dangerous as a bullet in combat. In July of 1862, while the 99th New York regiment he was attached to was camped near Norfolk, Virginia, Lieutenant Wilkeson came down with cholera. He lost 35 pounds, and was laid up for days with cramps, diarrhea, and vomiting. "I did not eat any for three days," he complained. His weight loss, he said, felt like he was "throwing ballast overboard."[24]

Even while ill, he was worried about his men, worried that the disease infiltrating the camp would decimate his battery. "At last this place is beginning to tell on the soldiers of the 99th and on my men," he wrote his father. "Very few are yet sick enough to be off duty—but soon will be."[25]

Worried and ill from the dysentery he had gotten on the campaign himself, Sam wrote Brig. Gen. Egbert L. Viele, military commander of the Union forces at Norfolk, to plead for a medical furlough for his son. "He joined his regiment in October last and has not been absent from it an hour since," Sam wrote. "He does not ask for sick-leave, and would not if he were to die on the spot—but to save him from another attack I do."[26]

Nine days later Sam went straight to the top. Writing from the farm in Canaan, New York, Sam wrote to General Thomas, who had just finished a stint as chairman of the War Board: "My boy will die down in that marsh back of Norfolk. He has been awfully sick." He enclosed excerpts that he had copied from Bayard's letter, and a copy of his letter to Viele.

"Mr. Thomas give me sixty days leave for the boy—otherwise I may lose him," Sam wrote.[27]

It's unclear whether the second bold plea from the father turned into a sixty-day furlough, but Bayard eventually recovered his health. By December, his battery of six 12-pound Napoleon guns saw action at the

Union's defeat at Fredericksburg, although it was placed away from the heaviest action.

Roughly 40 percent of the artillery weapons in both armies were Napoleons. The six in Bayard's command were smoothbores, not as accurate as rifled guns, but still deadly up to 1,600 yards in the right hands, most dangerous within 1,200, and capable of shooting spherical or solid shot or the murderous anti-personnel canister and grapeshot that hurled shotgun-like blasts of metal into infantry formations.[28]

At Fredericksburg, Lt. Bayard Wilkeson's Company G, then under the command of Lt. Marcus P. Miller, was placed near what was then known as the Lacy House, where the nurse Clara Barton set up an aid station for wounded federal troops. The injured were hauled by the dozens into the house and surrounding ground, the byproducts of Union assaults on Marye's Heights and other dug-in Confederate positions. Union army artillery bombarded Confederate lines trying to cover doomed crossings of the Rappahannock River and the infantry assaults on the heights, and their retreat across temporary barge-bridges placed across the river by Union engineers.[29]

Eight months later at Gettysburg, the tables would be reversed. The Confederates would attack uphill on Cemetery Ridge and in the first-day action on the knoll north of town that Bayard Wilkeson occupied. Many Union generals who commanded the doomed assaults at Fredericksburg—including John Reynolds and George Meade—would recognize the crucial need to hold the heights at Gettysburg and wait for Lee's men to come to them.

At Fredericksburg, the Union army suffered more than 13,000 casualties, the Confederates a third of that total. Like the aftermath of Antietam, personal letters of civilians who came looking for loved ones and the war correspondents' reporting out of Fredericksburg struggled to describe an incomprehensible aftermath. No letters from Bayard over that period survived; perhaps it was too much to write down.

A prominent member of the army of the aftermath at Fredericksburg was the poet Walt Whitman, he of the prewar Bohemians of New York's Cave. Whitman's "Leaves of Grass," first published seven years earlier, had included a plea to avoid the war now dividing and consuming the nation. One of its stanzas must have especially seemed out of touch in the hell at Fredericksburg: "We thought our Union grand and our Constitution grand," Whitman had written. "I did not say they are not grand and good for they are. I am this day just as much in love with them as you; but I am eternally in love with you and all my fellows upon the earth."

Whitman had set out from New York City to Fredericksburg immediately after seeing the name of his brother, George Washington Whitman, on the *New York Herald*'s casualty list. On the way he was pickpocketed, arriving penniless at Fredericksburg. For two weeks Whitman wandered through temporary hospitals in barns, homes, and tents before he found his brother, who had survived the deadly assault on Marye's Heights. Whitman became a volunteer orderly.[30] The grim work of those two weeks was a foreshadowing of the aftermath of Gettysburg. People were becoming famous in these armies of mercy.

At the Lacy House when Whitman arrived, Clara Barton and scores of army surgeons were still dealing with overwhelming numbers of wounded men. Barton had nearly died herself, a Confederate shell shredding her dress as she stepped off a pontoon boat during the battle. At the Lacy House, wounded men were stuffed in cupboards, under tables, "covered every foot of the floors and porticos," she wrote in her diary.[31]

Once a regal plantation home, the Lacy House—also known as Chatham—had through the years hosted George Washington, Thomas Jefferson, and Robert E. Lee. At Fredericksburg, it was anything but regal. "Outdoors, at the foot of a tree, within ten yards of the front of the house . . . I noticed a heap of amputated feet, legs, arms, hands, etc.—about a load for a one-horse cart," Whitman wrote. "Several dead bodies lie near, each covered with its brown woolen blanket. In the dooryard, toward the river, are fresh graves, mostly of officers, their names on pieces of barrel staves or broken board, stuck in the dirt."[32]

And the leaves of grass were bloody.

CHAPTER 14

"He Was Pure in Thought, and Word"

THE BATTLE OF SEVEN PINES, AND THE ENTIRE FAILED PENINSULA campaign for the Union army in the spring of 1862, fundamentally changed Sam Wilkeson, hardening him to the costs of the war, and firming him in the belief that winning the war would be costly. Following George McClellan's army through a boggy, disease-infested landscape, at times accompanied by his brother, John, Sam nearly died, physically. Part of his soul did die.

In the aftermath of the fighting at Seven Pines, Sam faced the same grim challenge he would confront almost a year later with his son, Bayard. At Seven Pines, when the fighting died down, he headed out to find what happened to his nephew, John Wilkes Wilkeson.

Seven Pines was one of several battles of the Peninsula campaign and is generally overlooked in the great set-piece accounts of the war. But it provided many predicates to Gettysburg a little over a year later. At a mistake-ridden, muddy, bloody stalemate near the tiny village of Seven Pines, 6 miles from Richmond, Sam became more than a journalist observer. His actions that day drew official Army commendation, raised his profile among fellow correspondents, and gave him notoriety—good and bad—among commanders of the Army of the Potomac. It also shook him in body and spirit as it did Cate Cady Wilkeson. Right after Seven Pines, reflecting on John Wilkes Wilkeson's death there, Cate revealed how she had resigned herself to giving up her own Bayard to fate the moment he had enlisted in the Union army.

On May 31, 1862, Sam Wilkeson was embedded with Union major general Sam Heintzelman's III and IV Corps south of the Chickahominy River in southern Virginia. McClellan's prolonged campaign down the Chesapeake Bay to a long peninsula formed between the James and York Rivers had not been going well. It was the first major eastern offensive of the war, and McClellan's army struggled in the marshes, swamps, and woodlands between the two rivers.

A violent rainstorm the night before the Seven Pines battle was an eerie foreshadowing of the lightning and thunder of the following day. The downpour turned the camps of two opposing armies along the Chickahominy into vast mud fields.[1] Seeing an opportunity to smash two Union corps separated by a river from the rest of McClellan's army, Confederate general Joe Johnston ordered a direct assault on Heintzelman's position.

Under the sound of the Rebel yell and a frontal assault, some Union lines broke and fell back from the assault. When Heintzelman arrived on the battlefield late in the afternoon to rally Brig. Gen. Silas Casey's cracking lines, one of the first men he recognized was Sam Wilkeson. The two men, on horseback, together tried to rally fleeing troops, including those of the shattered 1st Long Island regiment, whose colonel, Julius Adams, had been badly wounded.

Heintzelman designated Wilkeson as a temporary aide de camp. In his official report, Heintzelman noted of Wilkeson: "I wish to bear testimony to his gallantry and coolness under fire. When rebel reinforcements arrived about 5 p.m., and our troops commenced to give way, he was conspicuously in the throng aiding in rallying the men."[2] Another Union commander, Gen. John J. Peck, wrote that Wilkeson had "been constantly employed in the transmission and execution of orders, involving great personal risk."[3]

Wilkeson briefly mentioned his role in the fighting at Seven Pines in a letter to his *Tribune* editor, Sidney Howard Gay, a week later. "T'is said that a *Tribune* editor who volunteered as an aide to Heintzelman and then to [General John J.] Peck, all through the battle, will receive honorable mention in the Reports of those generals," he boasted. "The colonel of the 1st Long Island might also thank him for rallying his broken regiment."[4]

Seven Pines, also known as Fair Oaks, produced multiple story lines that led directly to Gettysburg for Sam Wilkeson and Bayard Wilkeson, and for the war as a whole. Many key actors at Gettysburg had seminal moments at Seven Pines.

Confederate general Joe Johnston's poorly coordinated assaults on the two isolated Union corps helped stymie McClellan's advance on Richmond, and produced a combined casualty count exceeding 13,000. Johnston was seriously wounded, and soon relieved of command of the Army of Northern Virginia and replaced by the aggressive, offensive-minded Robert E. Lee, whose invasion of Pennsylvania climaxed at Gettysburg thirteen months later. The assault on Heintzelman's corps included men under the command of Confederate general James Longstreet, an ambitious, rising officer, who struggled to coordinate his attack, but two months later redeemed himself, and gained the notice of Lee, at fighting at Glendale and Malvern Hill, Virginia. A year later at Gettysburg, Longstreet reluctantly triggered the war's climactic assault when he passed on Lee's orders for Pickett's Charge that Sam Wilkeson described with one of the best battlefield accounts ever written.

At Seven Pines, Union major general Oliver O. Howard—who thirteen months later would command Bayard Wilkeson and the 11th Corps at Gettysburg—was shot twice and severely wounded in the right arm, necessitating its removal. Howard, known as "the Christian general" after he had become an openly devout evangelical Christian during U.S. Army fighting with Florida's Seminoles four years before the war, was developing a reputation as a courageous but tactically lackluster leader. At Gettysburg, that reputation would precede him, and the lives and fates of Howard and Sam Wilkeson would be intertwined for the rest of their days.[5]

One of Howard's colonels, the hard-charging, boyish-faced Francis Channing Barlow, distinguished himself with courage at Seven Pines, leading the 61st New York regiment in some of the fiercest fighting of the battle, which cost him more than a fourth of his 417 men in a few chaotic minutes. He had ordered his men forward to relieve endangered and decimated Union regiments that were being hard pressed by Johnston's men in front and on the flanks. A little over a year later, Barlow

Oliver O. Howard

would issue the orders that placed Bayard Wilkeson and his battery at one of the most controversial, consequential positions of the entire war.

The battle of Seven Pines was a pivot point for Sam and Cate Wilkeson in multiple ways. It escalated the *Tribune* correspondent's professional criticism of the Lincoln Administration and Union military leaders. It intensified Sam and Cate's personal stake in the war with the death of their nephew, John. Cate Wilkeson had had a premonition about John's death. "I was afraid John was killed when I read the papers of the rout of Casey's brigade, for I knew he would never run from the enemy. John was as good a young man as ever lived," she wrote a sister-in-law, Mary.[6]

Cate had become close to her nephew, and they had "talked much" the summer John Wilkes enlisted, when he was in New York studying the law, and ostensibly visiting his aunt and uncle's farm in Canaan.

"He said, 'Aunty, my life is utterly useless.'" Cate told Mary, who was married to another of Sam's brothers, Will. "I said, 'John, you can never know what your correct moral life has done for those around you.' . . . He was pure in thought, and word, and he has gone to his reward."[7]

John Wilkes, too, had a premonition of his own death. In a letter to his brother, Samuel H., nine days before his death, written as his regiment was encamped 11 miles from Richmond, Lt. John Wilkes Wilkeson wrote about the deaths of mutual friends in battle. The reality of life on the front lines of the fighting had become searing and wearying, and a deep sense of fatalism had set in. John Wilkes had just been visited in camp by his father, John, and his Uncle Sam, the famous correspondent, and he told his brother that he feared that might have been the last time he would see both.

"All our best friends have gone before, or are fast going, and what matters it how soon for us or them?" John Wilkes Wilkeson asked his brother. "It will be right since it will be God's will, and if I don't see you here, we must meet in the spirit world. Pa I have often seen, and Uncle Sam, who rides with the army, and often comes to our camp."[8]

He concluded the letter with a heartbreaking prediction: "We shall have fought hard before this reaches you, and perhaps from the Hundredth my name will be dropped. I hope so, rather than I shall fail to show pluck and marked bravery. Pray I may not fail."[9]

Lt. John Wilkes Wilkeson was more worried about fighting well than dying. If he would die, he prayed it would be a good death.

On the day he was killed, John Wilkes Wilkeson mailed a letter to his sister, Louise, to tell her that he had seen his Uncle Sam, the *Tribune* man, just the evening before. They discussed the need to win the war, despite the terrible death toll it had already exacted. "I don't want to leave this till we whip them," John wrote his sister. "They are very strong and know the land but our boys have northern valor."[10]

He was tired, though. "We go on picket every other day, and fatigue every other day, so we sleep but 3 nights in the week," he wrote. There was skirmish firing going on as he wrote, and men all around him were digging entrenchments. He needed to go help six men under his command dig deeper trenches. It was important, as a commanding officer "to encourage the men & render service equal to what any order requires and duty calls for," the young lieutenant wrote Louise.[11]

His last night on earth was marked by that monstrous thunderstorm. "I never heard such thunder resembling artillery 1,000 times in . . . force magnified," he wrote his sister. He would find a moment to mail the letter when "there is a lull."[12] Hours later, the letter mailed, he was dead.

Young John's death crushed the extended Wilkeson clan. Sam Wilkeson faced the sorrowful duty of locating the body. In the smoldering stench of Seven Pines, he set off in search of John Wilkes.

It was macabre duty. After staying up until 3:00 a.m. the night after the battle to write his dispatch by candlelight, with all his personal effects having been taken by the Confederates who had overrun Union positions, Sam set out at dawn the next morning to find John Wilkes. He turned over or looked into the faces of at least twenty bodies piled in front of what was left of Casey's brigade before he recognized what he thought was his nephew's brown hair. Even before he looked at the face he felt as if this "was the blood of my blood and the kith of my kin."[13] But the bloated features did not look like the John he had seen two nights before, and he left the body there, unattended and unclaimed. Sam continued his search along the line of Casey's dead, Rebel pickets shooting at him, their insolent fire only angering him. Soon he came across John J. Peck, the brigadier general who had taken over Casey's shattered brigade after McClellan had removed Casey from command. Peck, the officer who would laud Sam Wilkeson's bravery in the previous day's fighting in later official reports, was struck by the hard-boiled correspondent's fragile state.

The *Tribune* correspondent was in tears, torn between utter dismay and fury at the Confederate snipers trying to kill him. Peck ordered eight men to grab shovels and join Sam for a second search. Soon a man that Sam had hired to help him told him he had located John Wilkes Wilkeson's body. It was the body Sam had initially thought was John's. By then John Wilkes had been temporarily buried, wrapped in a tent, under a wooden headboard, crudely etched with his name and regiment, the 100th New York. And the date of his death: May 31, 1862.

John Wilkes Wilkeson' pockets had been turned out, but the plunderers had missed a ten-dollar and five-dollar note, which were wrapped around a button. Sam gathered that to send to John's parents, and he borrowed a surgeon's scalpel to cut locks of John's hair, which he also sent home to his brother and sister-in-law, Maria. Sam found an abandoned Confederate stretcher nearby, and he and the men Peck had ordered to help him hauled John on a somber procession through a field littered with sixty-five dead artillery horses and twenty dead Confederates. There, surrounded by about one hundred Union soldiers standing in silence, they buried John under an oak tree, where he remained until his father was able to arrange for the boy to be returned to Buffalo to be buried. Sam noted with pride where his nephew had fallen. "John was way ahead of all the dead of his Regiment where a brave man should lay," the Tribune correspondent wrote his brother, Will.[14]

Sam was consumed with grief and a burn for revenge. "I conceived a great desire to enter the army and fight these damned villains," he wrote Will. He only now had time to consider what he'd done at Seven Pines. It was as if he was living outside his body. "I did rally broken regiments—did drive stragglers and skulkers back under fire," he said of his attempts to help Heintzelman rally fleeing troops. His horse "was terrified by the dead falling under his legs. And yet I was unconscious of doing anything more than it was natural and inevitable that every man who respected himself, and had a positive nature, should do."

He added: "I am worn out with the main excitements of the day and must lie down, and sleep."[15] In that weariness, the correspondent's work became a burden almost too deep to bear. But Sam did file to his newspapers in coming weeks, struggling as he did with sorrow and, eventually, dysentery. A year later, in the horrific aftermath of Gettysburg, Peck would harken back to Sam's deep emotional reaction to John's death at Seven Pines and worry anew about Sam's ability to cope with the fate of his own son, Bayard.

Cate worried about him always. "I fear his sad search for John has, when the excitement was over, made him sick," she wrote her sister-in-law,

Mary, less than two weeks after John Wilkes was killed. "He is weak and with that sore ought to be leading a more quiet life. When peace comes I hope he can get his property in a condition to be able to live without working sick or well."[16]

John's death eviscerated all memories of that gallant march to war the previous year for his brother, Samuel H. Wilkeson. The cavalry officer described confronting an emptiness so vast it seemed impossible to fill. It captured what the entire family must have been going through.

"I feel as if a portion of my life had gone," Samuel H. wrote his father a few weeks after John Wilkes's death. "Never will life appear to me as formerly, I so lived in the life of John that, now that he has gone, I am shattered as by tempest I shall never cease to mourn his death and if I can by my efforts avenge his death I will do it."[17]

Months later, Samuel H. again wrote his sister, this time saying that he feared he would always suffer from "never to be obliterated grief."[18]

If there was any saving grace, it was that both John Wilkes's father and uncle had spent a lot of time with him in his final weeks of life. Typical of the long tails of the armies traversing the landscape, the two elder Wilkeson brothers had been embedded with the 100th New York for about a month in the spring of 1862.

Sam had invited, John, eleven years his senior, to travel with him as Sam reported on McClellan's Peninsula offensive. The older Wilkesons frequently camped near John Wilkes Wilkeson's regiment.

The senior John Wilkeson, fifty-six years old when his son was killed at Seven Pines, still ran the family iron works in Ohio and Pennsylvania and ship and grain elevator operations in Buffalo. He was unabashed and charismatic and, like his younger brother, always moving. As a young man John Wilkeson had run a mercantile exchange in Tabasco, Mexico, then in the early 1840s, worked as his father's secretary when the senior Samuel Wilkeson ran the American Colonization Society. After John Wilkes's death at Seven Pines, John Wilkeson became increasingly eccentric; he began frequently appearing in public in a long white beard, black frock coat, and with a parrot perched on his shoulder.[19]

Like his brother Sam, the elder John Wilkeson did not hide his hawkish views on the war. Shortly after his two sons joined the Army,

Samuel H. wrote a family member that he wished that "Pa will go down to Washington and see what he has always 'hankered' after: war on a large scale."[20]

It was a "father's and patriot's interest" that had brought the elder John Wilkeson to the Peninsula.[21] He had his correspondent brother's instinct for detail and expression, and his diary is rich in both.

On April 16, 1862, six weeks before his son was killed, John and Sam caught up with the 100th New York at a tiny outpost called Youngs Mills, Virginia. The older Wilkeson brothers were riding army-issued horses. Sam talked of his pride in Bayard's rise in rank in his artillery company. Moving along with the column on the march, they discussed how proud they were that their boys had become leaders at such young ages.

"Johnny and his regiment were moving along in the first brigade and doing as well as any, though their drunken colonel had them marching on the 'double quick,' in great heat," the senior John Wilkeson recorded of the march to Youngs Mills. "Thermometer at 80 degrees in the shade. Johnny was actually carrying a lame, fagged-out soldier's musket—one of his men—and declined his Uncle Sam's offer to take it and carry it for him."[22]

On May 8, 1862, near Hampton Roads, Virginia, the senior John Wilkeson witnessed a second brief encounter between the Confederate ironclad, *Merrimack*, and the Union ironclad *Monitor*, which had famously fought it out in that same vicinity two months before. The Union ironclad was shelling Confederate positions at a place called Sewell's Point, a peninsula in the city of Norfolk near where the James River and other streams converge into the Chesapeake Bay. The *Merrimack* approached but soon backed off and retreated. "It struck me that this was the end of the Confederacy on the sea forever, as well as an end of their famous ironclad," John Wilkeson wrote in his diary. Three days later, sleeping at Union headquarters at Fort Monroe, the Union stronghold near Hampton Roads that would accept freed slaves throughout the war, the Wilkeson brothers were awakened by an explosion at 4:30 a.m. They later learned that it was the sound of retreating Confederates blowing up the *Merrimack* to keep it out of federal hands.

This "new system of naval warfare," John wrote, "is another evidence of our influence upon the world's progress. Perhaps this is an error, but I think not."[23]

On May 14, 1862, the senior John Wilkeson said good-bye to John Wilkes, and to his brother, and headed back north to see his other soldier son, Samuel H. The parting between John Wilkes and his father was difficult, and emotional. "I hope to never have another day like this in all my life," the senior John wrote in his diary. "It almost broke my heart to part with dear Johnny, and he doubtless felt as heartsick as I did. He looked firm and determined, but so sad, when he said good bye."[24]

Sadness, perhaps, from the powerful sense of fatalism that had already descended on the young soldier. Three days before the two parted, for good, Lt. John Wilkeson had asked his father, "Why are you so anxious about me? When a man sends his son to the army, he should give him up and never expect to see him again. I will go through this—live or die."[25] Twenty days later, John Wilkes Wilkeson died on a muddy field at Seven Pines.

CHAPTER 15

"True, Steadfast and Gentle"

THE PENINSULA CAMPAIGN ACCELERATED WAR-WARINESS IN THE North, raising serious doubts about the commanders if not the cause. On the way home from his time with Sam on the Peninsula, days before his son was killed, the senior John Wilkeson recorded a harsh assessment of officers in the Union army, especially its overall commander. "Everything I see, more and more convinces me of McClellan's unfitness for the command of a great army," he wrote on May 16. "So slow, so dilatory, such a want of dash or vigor."[1]

His brother Sam did not come to that conclusion about McClellan quite so quickly, at least publicly, even amidst the sorrow of his nephew John's death at Seven Pines. The muzzle came from the top. The *Tribune*, still smarting from criticism of its "On to Richmond" jingoism of the previous year, was editorially tamping down criticism of tactics and actions in the midst of a Union offensive on Richmond. It was, after all, a Republican newspaper, and its editor Greeley, though showing occasional signs of wavering in the cause or in his own emotional health, tied Northern victory with the cause of abolition of slavery he had long thundered for. The paper's reporters were chafing at a go-soft on McClellan approach. It was the beginning of a fallout between Wilkeson and Greeley that would come to a head a few weeks before Gettysburg.

In a diary entry of May 4, 1862, Wilkeson's *Tribune* colleague Gunn complained that his observations and reporting about McClellan were "suppressed" because the *Tribune* was "trying to ignore its past wholesome denunciation of the little humbug."[2]

The *Tribune* had been badly damaged by its jingoistic "Forward To Richmond" reporting before Wilkeson had arrived. Fair or not, many had held the paper responsible for the Union army's defeat at the First Battle of Manassas.

Some readers dropped the *Tribune* in the months following the first Bull Run defeat. In the war's early months Greeley's paper had suffered a circulation drop from about 215,000 to 189,000 by about the time Wilkeson arrived in Washington later in 1861.[3] He sent Wilkeson to Washington to try to fix things. Things were so dire. Greeley wrote Wilkeson on November 17, 1861, that "I don't see how we are going to live through the war as times go."[4] He claimed the paper was losing money. Part of it was from his own doing. In the weeks following the Confederate attack on Fort Sumter, Greeley's *Tribune* had demanded that the Union army act immediately to prevent the Confederate Congress from organizing on July 20, 1861.

When the federal army was badly beaten at First Manassas that month, politicians and rival newspapers blamed the *Tribune* for pushing a premature battle on an unprepared army. The *Tribune* made matters worse by initially falsely reporting a smashing Union victory. The rival *Herald* accused Greeley's paper of bringing on "war by headlines." Greeley, who had two months earlier severely cut a leg while chopping wood, went into a deep funk. He retired for a time to his bed for what he called "brain fever"[5]—possibly depression.

Nine days after the battle of First Manassas, at midnight on July 29, 1861, Greeley wrote Lincoln a letter full of self-pity and an apology to a "great president." Greeley, describing himself as heartsick over the Union defeat, told Lincoln that he had not slept for seven consecutive nights, and "yet I think I shall not die, because I have no right to die." He was "hopelessly broken" after the defeat, worried that "our recent disaster is fatal." He might have been referring to both the Union and the newspaper at that point. Greeley urged Lincoln to seek an armistice and a "peaceful adjustment" if the president determined "that our union is gone."[6] Lincoln, of course, did no such thing, and the war lasted another four brutal years. Lincoln kept the letter to himself for nearly three years, bringing it out to his young secretaries, John Nicolay and John Hay, in April of 1864 after Greeley had written a favorable *Tribune* editorial.

In that brief encounter, Hay read the letter out loud, proclaiming at the end it to be "the most insane specimen of pusillanimity that I have ever read." Nicolay jokingly said Lincoln should sell it to Greeley's bitter rival Bennett for $10,000. Lincoln responded that while he could have used the $10,000, Bennett "could not have it for many times that."[7]

For a time after the *Tribune's* "Forward To Richmond," debacle, Greeley, having backed out of his self-pitying funk, vowed to keep his correspondents from criticizing Union army actions in print, the move that Gunn had chafed about in his diary during the Peninsula campaign. Sam Wilkeson's reporting about the lack of discipline and preparedness of the previous winter had given way to a more favorable reporting when the army finally hit the Peninsula in the spring of 1862. As Gunn had complained in his diary, the order had come from the top to go lightly on McClellan.

But if the *Tribune* was purposely sparing McClellan and Lincoln of criticism while the campaign was underway, Wilkeson was not so lenient on other Union commanders, one in particular. In the wake of John Wilkes's death, his spar with a Union officer became bitterly personal and public, and would play out for nearly a year in the nation's most powerful newspapers.

In the days after Seven Pines, tired and sick, Wilkeson increasingly wondered if Heintzelman's corps had been left to its destruction by the timidity of another Union officer. His grief over John Wilkes's death intensified. "He was as pure as he was brave, and true, steadfast and gentle."[8]

For a few weeks, Sam rose above his anger, grief, and weariness, to forge on. Despite his grief and his illness, his day-to-day reporting during the Peninsula campaign had already been some of the best of the war to that point. Wilkeson's *Tribune* dispatch after the battle of Williamsburg on May 5, 1862, had been so rich in the detail of how Northern and Southern boys were killing one another it transfixed and horrified at the same time. He deftly wove together descriptions of the battle, analysis of commanders' tactical moves and errors, and anticipation of the dilatory effect on Northern morale once the casualty rolls would hit hometown newspapers. The cost of victory, he warned, would be great.

"The thousands who unnecessarily wear mourning in the North and West, for our victory at Williamsburg, will now understand the causes of the terrible mortality which accompanied the cause of demonstration of our superiority to these Barbarians," he wrote.[9]

In truth, Wilkeson was so worn out, so wrought up in the calamitous fighting, that it took great effort to keep going. The morning after the fighting at Williamsburg, as he composed his notes for the dispatch, his colleague, Thomas Butler Gunn, who had arrived too late to the battle-field to be of much help, ran into Wilkeson in a decrepit house where Wilkeson and other correspondents had congregated to write their dispatches.

Gunn worried that Wilkeson seemed "mired" and had "lost his nerve" after witnessing the carnage of the day. Gunn bucked up his colleague with a hot breakfast of hotcakes and ham he had bought from a black cook, one of the many stragglers following the army. Gunn and Wilkeson washed down the meal with what Gunn described as "dirty water."[10]

Gunn was supremely sympathetic with Sam that morning because he had had an epiphany of his own the night before, a realization of his own mortality and limits. Lying on the hard floor of a small cabin filled with weary officers fresh from battle, wet to the core, and using his reporter's shoulder bag as his pillow, Gunn was suddenly overwhelmed with "a profound sense of my utter helplessness as to any danger that might be impending—a sort of quiet fatalism." Events had entered a stage too large to be under his control.[11]

But the best war correspondents soldiered on. Despite all that was afflicting him, Sam Wilkeson's Williamsburg battle dispatch was inspired, insightful, and heartbreaking.[12]

To his *Tribune* readers, Wilkeson described one captured Union officer as "too brave and too proud to run." The trees where two armies had clashed, he said, were "checkered white with musket balls and grape." The fighting had been "hand to hand, bayonet to bayonet, musket-butt to musket-butt." He described a charge of the 38th and 40th New York as "swarming" with "savage tatterdemalions." Their assault, he said, became a test of "the comparative Manhood of Northern and Southern men." The fighting, which took place in marshes and swamps and murky forests, claimed nearly 4,000 casualties. The aftermath was ghastly.

"Sixty-three Rebels lay in a heap in one section of the rifle pits," Wilkeson wrote, "fury and the outlay of the last and best powers of their savage natures met with iron hardness by death upon their coarse and brutal faces."

Although he was getting sicker by the day, Wilkeson kept up his exceptional reporting. A month after John's death at Seven Pines, he described McClellan's retreat through the White Oak Swamp at the end of June 1862, as "a Napoleonic conception of the only salvation of his army from annihilation by fire, or loss by capture." In the dispatch, which came at the end of the Seven Days Battle, Wilkeson had escalated his criticism of Lincoln to such a degree that Greeley and Gay attached an editor's note disclaiming the piece as Wilkeson's thoughts alone. He datelined his *Tribune* dispatch, "On the March Through White Oak Swamp."

Wilkeson's article was a tour de force of wartime reporting, but, in retrospect, not without its flaws. McClellan's escape through the swamp, he wrote, was a "masterly stroke of genius" though "its trail will be bloody." Some 30,000 men were retreating along the James River 10 miles southeast of Richmond, and they were being pursued by columns of Confederates under Generals Jackson, Longstreet, and Hill, among others. The predicament was not McClellan's fault, Wilkeson wrote, buying into the Little Napoleon's dubious claims that Lee's armies badly outnumbered him and that Washington had refused his pleas for reinforcement.

"The politicians and statesmen who left us here to be outnumbered and cut off from our supplies and the possibility of retreat are doomed men," Wilkeson raged.[13]

His editors back at the *Tribune* were not in agreement. But they also deferred to his eyewitness perspective and decided to print his scalding piece. It was a testament to Wilkeson's stature; other correspondents later in the war, including Wilkeson's eventual colleague Henry Villard, would see their tougher pieces toned down by editors back in the home offices.

"We print the above letter unaltered, presuming our readers would like to judge of themselves the views of an intelligent observer on the field of operations," the paper said in an editor's note, probably written by Greeley or Gay, or perhaps both. "But we do not hold ourselves responsible for his opinions, or even agree with him in his strictures upon the government, which we believe has done all in its power to reenforce [(sic)] from time to time, and as speedily a possible, the Army of the Potomac, so far as it could to safety with other exposed points."[14]

The prominent disclaimer marked the beginning of the end of Wilkeson's first stint with the *New York Tribune*. Sam was so ill and exhausted after the Peninsula campaign that he took months to recover. But editor's note or not, he was on record with criticism as harsh and deliberate as any from any battlefield. In retrospect, it is stunning in its condemnation of an administration his newspaper supported.

Wilkeson claimed that Lincoln's alleged refusal to send adequate reinforcements for McClellan "came within a hair's breadth of ruining the nation." "I don't care about the question—which legislators, soldiers, and politicians have debated—of this General's fitness to command. The York and James River Peninsula were not the place for that discussion. . . . When loyal New York regiments, lifted from their feet by the fire of Rebel brigades, cry out of their wounds and death for help; when the choicest of New-England and Michigan and Pennsylvania troops, out-numbered . . . by whole divisions of the enemy, beg for re-enforcements, I say that the blackest crime that Power can commit is to stalk upon the field of peril and say, 'Soldiers, I have no faith in your commander. Let your martyrdom proceed!' And so says this Army of the Potomac."[15]

In the next day's *Tribune*, on July 4, 1862, exactly a year before he would work his way through the detritus after the battle of Gettysburg in search of his own son, Sam followed with a Napoleonic description of McClellan's struggle to fight off Lee through the hip-deep swamps and marshy trails of White Oak Swamp. Greeley reprinted it in *The American Conflict*, his 1864 book on the Civil War, as an example of the finest wartime reporting. Wilkeson had described the tattered tail of the army as 10,000 mostly wounded soldiers, but also most certainly including the aftermath of freedom-seeking slaves, relatives, and profiteers that often followed along. They were "wounded, sick or utterly exhausted," Wilkeson wrote, and some were left behind in the marsh as the army struggled to avoid a Confederate trap.

He wrote: "The confusion of this herd of men and mules, wagons and wounded, men on horses, men on foot, men by the road-side, men perched on wagons, men searching for water, men with ghostly eyes, looking out between bloody bandages that hid the face—turn to some vivid account of the most pitiful part of Napoleon's retreat from Russia, and fill out the picture—the grim, gaunt, bloody picture of war in its most terrible features."

Wilkeson had marched out of the swamp with Brig. Gen. Albion P. Howe's 4th U.S. Artillery brigade. They marched all night of June 30, "dark and fearful" hours under a threatening canopy of thunderclouds. They were surrounded by Rebels looking for them in a landscape occasionally lit by flashes of lightning. "We were forbidden to speak aloud; and, lest the light of a cigar should present a target for an ambushed rifle, we were cautious not to smoke." At dawn, they emerged into a "magnificent wheat field," and he fell asleep "on a couch of newly cut wheat."[16]

In truth, McClellan's army of more than 100,000 men during the Peninsula campaign was slightly larger than Lee's forces, although exact numbers on both sides have always been roughly estimated.[17] Although there was bungling of command on both sides, Lee's audacious, sometimes risky, but almost always offensive strategy kept McClellan on the defensive, even though both sides suffered terribly, with a combined casualty rate exceeding 20 percent during the campaign. After McClellan's failure on the Peninsula, Lee felt he'd thwarted the threat to Richmond sufficiently enough to take the war north, and the two armies would again clash in the bloody cornfields and sunken lanes and bridges of Antietam in September 1862. In November, frustrated again at McClellan's slow pace in pursuing Lee after Antietam, Lincoln sacked "Little Mac" for good. Two years later, McClellan would unsuccessfully challenge Lincoln as the Democrats' presidential nominee.

The Peninsula campaign drained Sam Wilkeson, left him ill and in mourning for his nephew. Still recovering from his Peninsula illnesses,

Sam missed the battle of Antietam in September, which gave Lincoln the military cover to release the Emancipation Proclamation. But if there were leftover hard feelings about the editor's note attached to his scathing file out of White Oak Swamp, he was not letting on to his managing editor Gay.

"Sufficient time has elapsed in your premiership commenced to enable your friends to pronounce judgment upon your management of the *Tribune*," Sam wrote Gay late summer from the Canaan farm. "I say that the *New York Tribune* is the best edited paper in America—in all respects the most carefully, ably and interestingly edited."[18]

Later that month, though, Wilkeson was not so sanguine. He wrote Gay complaining about a story the paper had run that alleged that a Union colonel had been given horses by an Army contractor. Wilkeson told Gay the colonel had been an invaluable source throughout the Peninsula campaign, and that running the story would damage his future access to this particular colonel.

Wilkeson worried that his source would see him as an "ungrateful, penny-a-line screech. Let me tell you I know Washington thoroughly—and I assure you that the publication of rumors of official misconduct is chock full of injustice and chock full of peril. If these rumors shall be foolishly placed on the wires at Washington they should be flung from them in New York."[19]

Despite Gunn's complaints of editorial restraint and Wilkeson's worries that the paper was burning some of his sources, he soon let loose on Union major general David Birney, a Philadelphia lawyer who had joined the army right after Fort Sumter and raised the 23rd Pennsylvania Volunteer Regiment largely with his own money.

Wilkeson accused Birney of cowardice in not coming to the aid of Heintzelman's overrun positions at Seven Pines, where John Wilkes had been killed. Wilkeson's criticism in print was so harsh it led to Birney's arrest and court-martial. Birney was eventually acquitted, his judges deciding he had done the right thing under confusing circumstances and conflicting orders. But the Wilkeson-Birney saga dragged out in public for months, and the two men hurled charges back and forth in the pages of the *Tribune* and *The New York Times*. "If you fight, Sir, as stupidly as you write, I pity for your brigade," Wilkeson wrote in the *Times* in March 1863, barely two months before the battle of Gettysburg.[20]

Irrespective of Birney's claims that he was following orders to the best of his abilities, Sam had argued that Birney should have seen the rout and come to the aid of the fleeing men that Heintzelman and Wilkeson had tried to rally at Seven Pines. Sam argued that if a journalist was willing to step into the breach, certainly a man in uniform could have ignored orders, especially confusing ones, to reinforce comrades he knew were in trouble. The spat got grandiose at times. In one dispatch, Wilkeson invoked the memory of England's Lord Nelson, the Royal Navy legend who lost an arm, then an eye, and eventually was killed during the Napoleonic Wars some forty-eight years before.

"My creed in military affairs justified me as a journalist in these strictures," Sam wrote. "For I believe with Nelson, sainted by a musket ball at Trafalgar, in the solemn duty of blindness in at least one eye, to signals to keep out of battles, in which a Commander ought to get, and ought to stay."[21]

In another rejoinder to Birney, Wilkeson preached his personal code of military conduct. "I believe in the contract made by the act of enlistment, and the acceptance of a commission, that the soldier and officers shall face death and fall forward, crown to the foe," he said. "He is bargained away his life, and is morally and legally bound to die for his country on call."[22]

Sam wrote this ten months after describing, proudly, how John Wilkes Wilkeson had fallen, facing the enemy at Seven Pines, ahead of his men, and two months before his son, Bayard, marched into the fury of Gettysburg's opening salvos.

At Seven Pines, Sam Wilkeson raged, Birney spent the battle in "comfortable but obedient submission to an order" while an "unequal fight was piling the arena in front of you with the corpses of your comrades in arms."[23]

Left unsaid was that John Wilkes Wilkeson was one of those corpses.

But in a court-martial that concluded with Birney being cleared barely a week before the battle of Gettysburg, his commanding general Phil Kearny had testified on Birney's behalf just weeks before Kearny, himself, was killed at the battle of Chantilly. Kearny said that by standing firm on the ground he was assigned to occupy, Birney's brigade at Seven Pines had helped stem an even bigger rout the next day for the Union army.

Birney did not let the accusations against him die quickly. He said Wilkeson was the sole source of the "fulmination of the charge against me." He wondered how a civilian—albeit a war correspondent with Wilkeson's reputation—could force court-martial proceedings on a general of the army.

"I have the honor to submit whether the code that governs our army is not defective in not providing redress for injuries of this kind," Birney wrote. "In this case a general officer is placed temporarily before the country in a pillory of disgrace, arrested by daybreak on the battlefield, these facts sent over the country by a newspaper correspondent acting as volunteer aide-de-camp."

In his official report on the battle, Birney escalated his counterattack on Wilkeson to his superior officers. "I must also complain that one Samuel Wilkeson, a volunteer aide-de-camp of Gen. Heintzelman, was permitted, as a correspondent of the *Tribune*, to spread far and near, through his own paper and others, these wretched stories as to myself. His semi-official position as an aide-de-camp on the General commanding the corps's staff gave his insinuations weight unwarranted by his own character for veracity."[24]

Wilkeson had just moved from the *New York Tribune* to the *Times* after his falling out with Greeley. He responded in his new newspaper with a barrage of renewed accusations. "You have disfigured a false report of a battle in which you did not participate," he mocked Birney.[25]

Wilkeson then went on: "I reaffirm that you halted your brigade in sight and sound of the battle, in direct violation of your Corps Commander's orders to go forward. Two such orders were sent to you—one at 3 o'clock, the other at 5 (on the afternoon of the Battle of Seven Pines). The last one found you squatted where the first one found you squatted. I leave to you the benefit of the justification for your disobedience which you have had the stolidity to publish—that Gen. Kearny ordered you 'not to forward your command in obedience to orders not from himself.' Not a teamster in the army can be made to believe that."[26]

In his final letter on the subject to the *Times*, published on April 2, 1863, Birney broached what many may have suspected—that Wilkeson was carrying on a public vendetta against him because of John Wilkes Wilkeson's death at Seven Pines.

"I claim no reputation for bravery than the private in my ranks," Birney wrote. "Mere bravery is the smallest requisite of the general officer; the enlisted man who rushes to the front, amid the volley, expecting to die unheralded and unknown, can speak of bravery—the true article. However, I simply wish you to contrast the opinions of Samuel Wilkeson, uttered by him under feelings of personal animosity and hereditary hatred, with the opinions expressed by my immediate commander."[27]

Wilkeson, furious, got the last word. He responded in that April 2, 1863 report in the *Times* with a declaration that he was too weary to continue the fight with Birney. "The misstatements of this report of yours, which are its warp and woof, I did intend now to ventilate," he wrote of Birney. "But the game is not worth the candle. I have written myself at once into weariness, and the consciousness that an imputation put by you on a gentleman's veracity ought not to disturb him."[28]

Birney, who would go on to temporarily command Dan Sickles' shattered 3rd Corps during Gettysburg's second day, would be dead within fifteen months. He would fall ill with either malaria or dysentery during the siege of Petersburg and die in a Philadelphia hospital.

In retrospect, Wilkeson was likely suffering from PTSD in that summer of 1862. His letters to his editor, Gay, during 1862 and early 1863, provided glimpses of a correspondent under severe stress. Wilkeson begged for time off. He complained in one that "my health is going to the grave."

"I shall go manfully through the next fight and write the *Tribune* handsomely into Richmond and through a week after I get there," he wrote Gay. "Then Sidney, you must relieve me—or I shall break down."[29]

His expectations about the capture of Richmond were optimistic and wrong. It took almost three years for Union forces to capture the Confederate capital. The stress and strain on Wilkeson and the country would only deepen.

CHAPTER 16

"They String You Up to a Tree Damned Quick"

"WE PIONEERS WERE CREATING THE PROFESSION OF THE WAR CORRE-spondent in America," wrote Sam Wilkeson's friend, twenty-seven-year-old Edmund Clarence Stedman of the *New York World* after the first Battle of Manassas, "and this was prentice work."[1]

It was dirty, dangerous and unappreciated work. At the *Tribune*—and later, for a brief time, at the *Times*—Wilkeson often felt outmanned by the *New York Herald*, whose editor, James Gordon Bennett, had hired a strong contingent of war correspondents, often numbering twenty at any one time. The competition for news from the front was fierce. And the news from the North was not good.

During the Peninsula campaign, Wilkeson began to see his own declining health as a metaphor for the war itself.

Writing to his editor, Sidney Howard Gay, from 4 miles south of Cumberland Landing, Virginia, nineteen days before the death of John Wilkes Wilkeson, Sam complained: "I have been 'night' sick as these Ruffians say. For nearly three days I have maintained my anchorage under the lee of a privy—and have dieted on black tea and blasphemy. I never took such clear views of the wicked & brainless mismanagement of this war as have been vouchsafed to me here in the mud."[2]

By then in his mid-forties, he was writing about a war where non-combat disease took five lives for every three killed in battle.[3] Less than a year after Gettysburg, Wilkeson got deathly ill again covering the prolonged brutality at the Wilderness in Virginia in 1864. The conditions there would have made the healthiest man ill. Fires raged and burned wounded men to death, and soldiers on both sides tromped over the bones of comrades killed a year before at the battle of Chancellorsville. Rainstorms turned the landscape into a ghastly sea of mud and corpses. Writing to Gay on May 1, 1864, from near Union army headquarters in Belle Plaine, Virginia, Wilkeson said he had slept on "water-soaked earth" that had set off another severe bout of rheumatism, which he called "nature's executioner against me."[4]

Besides the physical challenges, Wilkeson often felt outmanned by competitive newspapers, especially by the feisty, irreverent, crime- and sex-steeped *Herald*. Wilkeson also often complained about colleagues who disappeared when the battles began. Writing to Gay again shortly after Seven Pines in 1862, Wilkeson said that two of his *Tribune* colleagues had stayed in the rear and left him as the paper's sole witness to the battle.

"I was in the field, constantly under fire, and saw most of the fighting," he wrote Gay, but "no one man can see the battlefield which is covered with extensive woods and is a mile and a half deep & two miles wide."[5]

Wilkeson complained that one *Tribune* colleague "had seen nothing of the fighting" and was useful only to copy surgeon's lists. Another was "whining forever about his poor diet, and the hardship he undergoes and, tardy and timid and slow, he is not worth a curse for this business. I can't get him to go to the front or center."[6]

Six weeks later, still embedded in McClellan's army in Virginia, Wilkeson erupted in scorn about a colleague who had just received a box of summer clothing from his wife. Wilkeson, who had been wearing the same clothes for over a month, thought that dressing in fresh clothes sent the exact wrong signal for a correspondent. He told Gay that a reporter embedded with soldiers should suffer the same daily depravities as the soldiers, so as to better understand what they were going through. And it did the paper no good to have a correspondent constantly better off than the men they were covering, Wilkeson told Gay.

"He has no more right to (clean clothes) than private soldiers have," Wilkeson wrote. "His insisting upon them is. . . . out of place and out of harmony.

"I wear four shirts a week when I am home," Sam told Gay. "The flannel shirt I have on I have worn five weeks. It is abominable, certainly. But it is not unendurable—and I never should think of whining out a claim to reward or admiration, based in my submission to nasty necessity. Rails make my bed and sleep comes up through them only as the followment of exhaustion. My jackknife is my spoon, knife, fork . . . the rebels got everything else I had under the Seven Pines. There is no martyrdom in being obliged to hold meat with the finger of one hand while the other uses the toothpick-fork-spoon knife."[7]

Wilkeson confessed to Gay that he had broken into stores or barns to get corn for his horse, which he had named Bayard.[8]

"A fragmentary, migratory, broken up life this is of mine—with a world of petty cares and duties which leave a man no time for the better things," he said in one letter to Gay.[9]

Wilkeson and Gay were quite a pairing. Wilkeson was strapping, direct, and confrontational. Gay was slightly built, witty, and quiet. They had a mutual interest in the law and equally deep commitments to abolition of slavery. Gay, who like Wilkeson had been a lawyer before turning to journalism, refused to swear an oath to the Constitution because it had not banned slavery.[10]

Even during his later falling-out with Greeley, Wilkeson remained close to Gay, to the point where he tried to enlist Gay into open insubordination and a coup against Greeley's editorship of the *Tribune*.

As roving correspondents do, Wilkeson frequently complained about the treatment of his copy by editors sitting safely and comfortably in New York. In a letter to Gay shortly after he took over the Washington correspondent's job, Wilkeson complained that one of his stories had been so badly edited and trivialized that it made him ashamed to read it in his own newspaper. Wilkeson implored Gay to study how the *Herald* handled its correspondents.

"Study the telegraphic arrangement in the *Herald*. See how always not casually, but inevitably, the important items are placed first, and the minor gradually go last," Wilkeson wrote, underlining "always" and "inevitably" with a heavy scratch. "I have to wend the matter as I get it. Your duty is that of arrangement. Endeavor to beat an improvement into the Night Editor's head."[11]

During the Peninsula campaign of 1862, Wilkeson fretted to Gay that his reporting and writing from the field was "unorganized—I deeply regret it—but I could not help it. I shall do my best for the paper—but I cannot alone collect and transmit news as fast and thoroughly as the 16 men of the *Herald* can do."[12]

From the other side of the notebook, military leaders also were making up the rules as they went along. Ulysses S. Grant ultimately viewed the correspondents in his armies with bemusement but mostly with suspicion. He viewed the Southern newspapers passed through his lines as half propaganda, half intelligence briefs. He viewed Northern papers as constantly flirting with sedition.

Lee, too, used newspapers for intelligence and satirized editors as a class. Lee sarcastically told a Confederate senator early in the war that the South had made a "fatal mistake" in how it chose generals.

"In the beginning," Lee proclaimed, "we appointed all our worst generals to command the armies, and all our best generals to edit the newspapers.

"As you know, I have planned some campaigns and quite a number of battles," Lee went on. "I have given the work all the care and thought I could, and sometimes, when my plans were completed, as far as I could see, they seemed to be perfect. But when I have fought them through, I have covered defects, and occasionally wondered (why) I did not see some of the defects in advance. When it was all over, I found by reading a newspaper that these best editor generals saw all the defects plainly from the start. Unfortunately, they did not communicate their knowledge to me until it was too late. . . . I am willing to yield my place to these best generals, and I will do my best for the cause of editing a newspaper."[13]

Grant frequently found it necessary to tamp down Lincoln's worries about the impact of newspaper reporting on the Northern morale and public opinion. Grant also blamed Northern correspondents for questioning the fighting capability of Union soldiers, for overstating Union battle losses and overplaying Confederate victories and, most of all, for building up Lee's reputation to mythical proportions. Such reporting, Grant said after the war, had intimidated Union army leaders.

"To be extolled by the entire press of the South after every engagement, and by a portion of the press North with equal vehemence, was calculated to give him the entire confidence of his troops and to make him feared by his antagonists," Grant wrote after the war. "It was not an uncommon thing for my staff-officers (when he was commander in the West) to hear from Eastern officers, 'Well, Grant has never met Bobby Lee yet.'"[14]

Grant came to believe that the press in the North was vastly more hostile to the Union cause than the South's press was toward its military and political leader because of the chasms between the two region's economics and politics. Grant was especially hard on the Northern Copperhead press, the organs of the Democratic Party who favored a peaceful settlement with the rebellious states. He thought of the Copperhead press as "an auxiliary to the Confederate army."[15]

"The press of the South, like the people who remained at home, were loyal to the Southern cause," Grant wrote. Unquestionably loyal Southern correspondents, Grant thought, were offshoots of the reality that "the whole South was a military camp," while the Northern states kept up a more normal footing that was naturally more conducive to disagreement and dissent.

"In the North, " Grant said, "the press was free up to the point of open treason."[16]

Sherman, with whom Wilkeson had become entangled early in the war, was even more critical. War correspondents "are the world's gossips" that "pick and retail the camp scandal, and gradually drift to the headquarters of some general, who finds it easier to make reputation at home than with his own corps or division," he wrote.[17]

"They are also tempted to prophesy events and state facts which, to an enemy, reveal a purpose in time to guard against it," Sherman complained. "Moreover, they are always bound to see facts colored by the partisan or political character of their own patrons, and thus bring army officers into the political controversies of the day, which are always mischievous and wrong. Yet, so greedy are the people at large for war news, that it is doubtful whether any army commander can exclude all reporters, without bringing down on himself a clamor that may imperil his own safety. Time and moderation must bring a just solution to this modern difficulty."[18]

Sherman's observation about generals being pulled into politics is disingenuous. He was plenty adept at pulling himself into political controversies. He opposed enlisting black men in his army, a position he had to have known was sure to create enemies within the Lincoln Administration and invite press scrutiny. But Sherman's broad observations about the public's thirst for news in time of war, and of the inherent tension between the aims of the commanders and of the correspondents covering them, were spot on.

A tectonic shift was under way. The Civil War, Sidney Kobre observed, "signified the emergence of the reporter as the dominant person on the staff," a transformation "accelerated by the news sent in by reporters on the warfront and by Washington correspondents."[19]

Correspondents, North and South, tailed the armies using every conceivable means of transportation. Wilkeson took the train, walked, rode on hastily bought or borrowed horses, took steamships, or hitched rides on Army wagons across hundreds of miles of the American landscape. Like the troops, the correspondents slept in the open, in small tents or under trees, good weather and bad.

Correspondents generally earned thirty to thirty-five dollars a week, about twice what Union army privates got. Wilkeson, as a chief correspondent of one of the nation's most prominent newspapers, pointed out to Gay when he left the *Tribune* for the *Times* in 1863 that he was earning less than $3,000 annually, a decent wage, but not enough to make him wealthy.[20]

But the costs of covering the war went far beyond the correspondent's modest salaries. It was a vagabond's life of constant movement and adaptation, and it required a good deal of walking around money, as illustrated by an expense account that Wilkeson filed to Greeley after the battle of Spotsylvania in Virginia in 1864.

Wilkeson charged the paper one dollar for a "portfolio"—a tablet—and forty cents for a new canteen. It cost him three dollars to hire a carriage to get to a military steamer that would take him near the battlefield, and $2.25 for meals while on board, including $1.25 for "breakfast with soldiers." One of the biggest costs was the four dollars he paid for passage for his horse on the steamer. While at Spotsylvania, Wilkeson forked over ten dollars to the quartermaster of the 11th New York Artillery for 5 pounds of feed a day for all the horses of the *Tribune* correspondents covering the battle.[21]

At the beginning of the war, Wilkeson carried his press pass in a small pouch engraved with his name and "*Tribune* Editor Washington" on it. Inside was a letter signed by then–secretary of war Simon Cameron and dated August 29, 1861. More valuable than anything else he could have carried, it read: "The bearer Samuel Wilkeson will be permitted to pass to and from any military works or camp of the troops of the United States, within the lines of the Army, and is recommended to the protection of our forces and to the courtesy and hospitality of our officers."[22]

Correspondents were constantly in search of food, and often dependent upon hostile commanders for a bite to eat from a company mess. Alfred Waud, the illustrator whose illustrations and woodcuts would famously adorn papers and other printed works throughout the war, and who would eventually make Lt. Bayard Wilkeson famous, went almost an entire week covering the Seven Days' battles at the end of the Peninsula campaign without finding anything to eat except a chicken he stole from a farmer.[23]

Embedding with an army could be, like it was for the soldiers, tedious and frustrating and, in disease-ridden times, life-threatening. One of Wilkeson's colleagues covering the Peninsula campaign, the British reporter Thomas Butler Gunn, described one typical day between battles this way: "Hither and thither, sometimes in camp, sometimes about in the wet, muddy fields, with (an officer) to the House (headquarters), reading, scribbling, dozing. Dined at 4. The rain presently flooded our tent, necessitating vigorous operations in the way of trenching and digging."[24]

Pushed out of that tent, Gunn ended up sheltering in a regimental doctor's tent and slept that night in a bunk with another man. The next day, a soldier no more than sixteen was brought to that tent suffering with fever and chills, which he had caught by sleeping on the wet, cold ground. The boy died within an hour. Another young soldier infected with smallpox was brought in. His fellow soldiers, fearing infection, had hauled him out of their camp and left him lying in the rain in a crude shelter beneath hastily erected fence rails.[25]

On top of those appalling physical positions, early in the war Gunn, Wilkeson, and the other handful of *Tribune* reporters embedded with the Union army during the Peninsula campaign felt they were badly treated by McClellan, who they thought favored *New York Herald* reporters because of the favorable treatment the Little Napoleon got from Bennett's paper.

The *Herald* was a bitter critic of Lincoln and its pages were riddled with racist comments. The editor, Bennett, was often accused of favoring appeasement with the South. Wilkeson and his colleague continuously complained that McClellan's inner circle was shutting them out in favor of the *Herald*'s reporters. "We who belonged to the paper, were snubbed and cold shouldered by the partisans of the bogus little Napoleon on every possible occasion," Gunn wrote in his diary three days before the battle of Seven Pines.[26]

But there were times that reporters and soldiers respected their different roles. Two days before the battle of Seven Pines, Wilkeson and Gunn were denied supper by a young Union officer, but for reasons that both reporters could understand and respect, and that spoke to McClellan's favoritism.

The officer "said that he thought that the whole system on which the army correspondence was done was mischievous and partial, there being an inevitable tendency on the part of a correspondent to blow the trumpet for those who awarded him hospitality and that he knew of flagrant misrepresentations in consequence," Gunn wrote in his diary. "I couldn't help agreeing with his sentiments."[27]

The *Tribune* correspondents caught it from both sides. Greeley's notoriety—his high profile, his hot-and-cold support for the war, his crusading abolitionism—preceded any *Tribune* reporter into camp. Soldiers on both sides blamed Greeley's on-to-Richmond jingoism in the early months of the war for jacking up war fever. After Seven Pines, placed in a hospital tent with three wounded Confederates, an ill Gunn soon found out how unpopular his boss was. When the Confederates discovered he worked for the *Tribune*, a "truculent" Louisiana soldier told Gunn he'd be hung if Gunn was ever captured by Confederate troops. "Oh, Greeley, eh?" he said. "They string you up to a tree damned quick."[28]

That night, Gunn got so ill from diarrhea that when he left his tent on one of his many frequent trips to relieve himself he fell face-first into the dirt and needed several minutes to muster the energy to get up.[29]

During the Peninsula campaign and ensuing battles in the spring of 1862, Gunn and Wilkeson frequently shared tents or slept nearly side-by-side outdoors or in private homes commandeered by Union troops. The experiences of May 25, 1862, typified their situation. Gunn had procured a bottle of whiskey, which he'd shared with officers who had granted him interviews, keeping enough to try to soothe an ailing gut. But the horrific living conditions continued to take tolls. Over the course of the next week, he would also twice be prescribed opium by Union doctors treating his serious stomach pains and diarrhea.

One night, Gunn and Wilkeson shared a beaten-up bed in a beaten-down cabin procured as temporary headquarters for Union brigadier general John J. Peck, whom Wilkeson had long courted as a source. Wilkeson spent most of the evening interviewing officers and was "approbative and friendly" when Gunn joined him. Not so much the next morning. The mattress they had shared was so bad that "in spite of my fatigue I tumbled and tossed considerably, as Wilkeson told me in the morning," Gunn said.[30]

After Seven Pines, Gunn became so ill that Gay and Wilkeson ordered him back to New York. He arrived via train on June 5, 1862, looking like a walking skeleton in rags. "I was gaunt, wretchedly thin with a sunburned hollow face, my hair long," he wrote later. "My hat an old felt one, without a band, in which I had often fed my mule; my heavy coat, threadbare in places, and all stained from the rain, the earth and the resinous guns against which I had leant; my waistcoat was almost buttonless, my trousers tucked into rusty old boots, and one thickness of the seat worn into rags from friction on the saddle."[31]

To make matters worse, his editors immediately began lambasting him about the access that the rival *Herald* was getting and, by implication, the stories the *Tribune* was not getting. During a dinner with several editors, one of them told Gunn—who had almost died covering the war for his paper—that he admired the "tact of Bennett of the *Herald* in championing (McClellan)—thus procuring favors and facilities for its correspondents."[32]

Even pushing yourself to the threshold of death's door to get the story was not enough to please editors in this hyper-competitive new world of the war correspondent.

CHAPTER 17

"A Country Redeemed, Saved, Baptized"

THE COMPETITION TO GET THE NEWS OUT OF GETTYSBURG WOULD BE among the fiercest of the war. And it was dangerous work. Lorenzo Crounse, one of Sam Wilkeson's *Times* colleagues, had a horse shot out from under him. And V. A. S. Parks, one of three reporters there for the Savannah, Georgia, *Republican*, was killed during the second day of the fighting.[1] He had been embedded in John B. Hood's division of James Longstreet's corps.

Sam Wilkeson's eventual dispatch would be the most famous, and would come after he, himself, dodged death in the cannon bombardment before Pickett's Charge. Others went to heroic lengths to be first. By then, correspondents had become veterans themselves, had moved beyond the mistakes and the delayed accounts of First Manassas, into a more professional and more urgent pursuit. As the war progressed, there was greater emphasis on accuracy, and a more sophisticated reporting of tactics and effects of the fighting. As Sam Wilkeson rushed to the battlefield on July 1, 1863, his colleague Crounse, who had started his career with the Milwaukee *Free Democrat*, had already filed a dispatch for the next day's paper that accurately described the opening day's action as "very severe, and attended with heavy losses" and involving the "forces of Longstreet and Hill" for the Confederates versus the Union's 1st and 11th Corps, the latter Bayard Wilkeson's corps.[2]

The four dozen or so correspondents at Gettysburg—about three-fourths of them with the Union army—knew they were witnessing something extraordinary, something to be remembered for all times. The

New York Herald had managed to get ten reporters to cover the battle. Wilkeson's old paper, the *Tribune*, had nine. Wilkeson and Crounse were half of the four-man *Times* contingent at Gettysburg. The Associated Press and a smattering of national and local papers had one reporter each. Inside the Confederate army, two Richmond *Enquirer* reporters were embedded, as were Parks and two colleagues from the Savannah *Republican*, along with correspondents from Charleston, South Carolina, and other Richmond papers.[3]

But none could match, in flair and reputation and controversy, the swashbuckling Francis Lawley of the *Times of London*, whose reputation was built partly in his status as a fugitive from scandal in the British Parliament. A gambler professionally and personally, Lawley watched the fighting at Devil's Den and the wheat field high up in a tree. His reputation had been burnished after he slipped through a Union blockade to get to Richmond. The fact that Lawley looked very much like the portraits of George Washington, a Virginian, helped him in the Confederate army, too.

Lawley had angered the good Northern residents of Chambersburg, Pennsylvania, a couple days before the battle of Gettysburg when, at breakfast, he held up a Confederate twenty-dollar note and declared loudly that within a month it would be worth more than all the money in the North combined. He had also recorded one of the memorable lines of the days leading into Gettysburg when, writing from east of Chambersburg, Lawley described a young woman standing in front of a house with a small Union flag stuck in her blouse as the grizzled Hood's division marched past. The Southerners marched by without comment, Lawley wrote, until one called from the ranks: "You had better lower that flag, madam—our boys are tigers at breast works, especially when they mount the Yankee colours."

At Gettysburg, getting reports to the world was an especially difficult challenge. Jeb Stuart's Rebel cavalry cut telegraph lines and Confederates destroyed railroad lines leading into the town. Reporters went to ingenious lengths to work around it.

Like Sam Wilkeson, his former colleague, the *New York Tribune*'s A. Homer Byington arrived at Gettysburg after the fighting began.[4] But his ill fortune had sent him on a detour of good luck. With rail lines cut and roads clogged or cut off by armies rushing to the field, Byington took a circular route of a couple hundred miles to Gettysburg, getting as far as Harpers Ferry, West Virginia, then retreating back to Baltimore, where he headed north through Philadelphia and then west on rail and horseback through York and Hanover, Pennsylvania. There, Byington discovered little fighting but evidence of great movements of armies, and he ran into legions of civilians fleeing the battlefield. Byington learned that Stuart—who had by then drawn Lee's ire by losing contact with the main army while plundering the Maryland and Pennsylvania countryside—had cut all the telegraph wires for 10 miles in any direction of Hanover. Knowing that he was already behind other correspondents in actual reporting on the battle itself, Byington took a few hours to set up an advantage once it was time to transmit dispatches.

In Hanover, as the fighting erupted 15 miles west, Byington found a telegraph operator, named Trone, asleep on a hotel bench, the telegraph's battery hidden from marauding Confederates at home under his bed. The man agreed to send Byington's dispatches if Byington fixed the wires that had been slashed outside the town. Byington rounded up some men and a hand car and they headed out to patch the lines. By the end of the first day of the battle, the "lightning" to Baltimore and the world beyond was re-established. Byington was in business, and he ensured it would be a temporary monopoly. In exchange for fixing the lines, the operator granted Byington two days' exclusive use among newspaper correspondents.

Byington's luck continued. He raced to the battlefield overnight and almost as soon as he arrived early on the second day, Byington ran into Oliver Otis Howard, commander of the Union 11th Corps. Howard gave Byington a detailed account of the first day's fighting, including the desperate stand on a freshly scorched rise called Barlow's Knoll where Lieutenant Wilkeson had been wounded. Byington, who had recently been plucked from a small-town paper by the *Tribune* and was unknown to the more veteran correspondents at Gettysburg, had a significant scoop. He and colleague Josiah Sypher hurried back to Hanover, where they dispatched their story on the telegraph line that Byington had fixed.

About 65,000 copies of his exclusive were sold on the streets of New York on July 3, as the battle still raged.

Helping Byington was Lincoln himself. As usual, Lincoln was sitting in the government's telegraph office back in Washington waiting for fresh bolts on the "lightning," and the president saw Byington's signed dispatch come across the telegraph wire. "Who is Byington?" Lincoln said, in a return message to the reporter. "Ask Daddy Welles," Byington fired back, referring to Navy Secretary Gideon Welles. Roused from his bed in the middle of the night, Welles vouched for Byington. Once it became known that Byington himself, not the army, had repaired the line, the correspondent and the War Department cut a deal where Meade could use the line to communicate with Washington as long as the government sent Byington's dispatches, uncensored, on to the *Tribune* in New York.[5]

The competition responded with equal ingenuity. After the battle Frank Chapman of the *New York Herald* raced to Baltimore and arrived in the pre-dawn darkness of July 4, hours before the telegraph office normally opened. Chapman found an operator and roused him from his sleep, and he immediately began sending lengthy dispatches describing the three days of action to Bennett's editors back in New York. Having exhausted everything in his notebook, he came up with a devious plot to monopolize the line for the rest of the day and keep his competition at bay.

Chapman was about to leave the office and do more reporting when a competitor, former Sam Wilkeson colleague T. C. Gray of the *New York Tribune*, arrived, expecting to have his copy sent as soon as Chapman's was finished. Upon seeing Gray approach the office, Chapman pulled out his pocket Bible, and he instructed the operator to begin transmitting the first chapter of Genesis. Throughout the day, as the telegraph operator kept clicking through Genesis, Exodus, and Leviticus, Chapman kept coming back with new snippets of information garnered from wounded soldiers and civilians returning from Gettysburg. He'd have them transmitted and order the operator to take up where he had left off in the Bible. Gray and other furious competitors had to scramble elsewhere to transmit their stories.[6]

Whitelaw Reid and Charlie Coffin were with Sam Wilkeson on Cemetery Ridge on Day Three, where they rode out the heaviest artillery bombardment of the war to that point at Union headquarters along the Taneytown Road.

Reid was typical of the new breed trying to make sense of it all. Just then twenty-five years old, he, like Sam Wilkeson, was fearless under fire, a prolific and lively writer, always in search of the next story. Like many correspondents on the field that day, he used his experiences during the war for greater roles later in life. After the war, Reid edited the *New York Tribune*, served as ambassador to France, and ran as Benjamin Harrison's vice presidential running mate in 1892.

Reid's editor had hastily telegraphed him to cover Lee's invasion of Pennsylvania, pulling him from an assignment covering the Ohio state Democratic Convention in Columbus, the hottest political story of the year. The convention had just nominated in abstention a Copperhead peace candidate for governor named Clement Vallandigham, who was arrested for treason and banished to Canada. Vallandigham, who that November would lose the election while watching it from across the border, was the primary target of Ambrose Burnside's General Order 38, eleven weeks before Gettysburg. That order had threatened arrest and prosecution for anyone declaring sympathy for the Confederates.

It had been a tough story to give up, but Reid sensed something even bigger was brewing.

"Equip yourself with a horse and outfit," Reid's editor had telegraphed him, and join the Union army "in time for the fighting." And so he did. His journey to file his story after the battle was every bit as urgent and adventurous.[7]

At dawn on July 4, 1863, the morning after the battle, Reid and Coffin set out by horse to Westminster, Maryland, hoping to catch a train to Baltimore to file. It took them less than three hours to make the 28-mile ride. Halfway there, it began raining, soaking the correspondents to the skin. Along with Gray of the *Tribune*, they caught a train from Westminster to Baltimore. Along the way, the train was frequently forced to sidings to allow empty hospital trains to pass by on their way to Gettysburg. At Baltimore, the exhausted Coffin finally got access to a telegraph line for enough time to file a brief report for the next day's paper to his editors back in Boston. He then caught the next train north, writing as he rode on the bumpy trip, arriving in Boston on the night of July 5, where two waiting editors rushed Coffin and his half-completed copy to the *Journal* office. Hundreds of people were crowded outside and poring over bulletin boards that contained the latest telegraph snippets from Gettysburg, as people would congregate around televisions during big events a century and a half later. In a locked room accessible only to a few editors, the coffee-fortified Coffin sorted through his soggy notes and wrote one of the most comprehensive and descriptive reports of the great battle.[8]

Coffin, like Sam Wilkeson, had sensed that Gettysburg had turned the war inexorably in the Union's favor. Like Sam Wilkeson, Coffin embroidered his descriptions of Gettysburg with the language of rebirth and redemption.

"The invasion of the North was over, the power of the Southern Confederacy broken," Coffin wrote. "There at the sunset hour, I could discern the future; no longer an overcast sky, but the clear unclouded starlight—a country redeemed, saved, baptized, consecrated anew to the coming ages."[9]

He added: "They have not fought in vain, they have not died for nought," and "for Christ and for God they have given themselves a willing sacrifice."[10]

Coffin had had good training for this kind of exhausting work, and he was no stranger to danger. About to turn forty at Gettysburg, he had been a surveyor on a road crew in his twenties when a man felling trees accidentally chopped deeply into his left ankle. The old injury had prevented him from entering the Union army, but it had not prevented him from embedding himself with the armies during the war. Self-taught in music and engineering, he'd helped develop the first electronically transmitted fire alarm. Patriotic and full of energy, he also was one of the closest correspondents in age and disposition to Sam Wilkeson.

"No man liveth to himself alone," Coffin wrote in the *Boston Journal* on the same day Sam Wilkeson's famous Gettysburg dispatch would appear in *The New York Times*. "Not for themselves, but for their children;

for those who may never hear of them in their nameless graves how they yielded life; for the future, for all that is good, pure, holy, just, true."[11]

Charlie Coffin's reporting at Gettysburg would also be integral to understanding Bayard Wilkeson's actions, and fate, in the Civil War's most pivotal hours.

CHAPTER 18

"My Hunt After the Captain"

By the time of the Battle of Gettysburg, tributaries of suffering had flowed into every community, North and South, from the accumulated slaughter. The aftermath of the battles was becoming as big of a story as the fighting itself. The scores, sometimes thousands, of freed slaves that were following Union armies had been joined on the war roads by armies of civilians—parents, wives, siblings, friends, ministers, looters, photographers—descending on battlefields after the fighting to search for loved ones or simply to ease the suffering of the aftermath.

One of the war's greatest pieces of journalism described one man's such journey after the battle of Antietam in September of 1862. Its author was no ordinary citizen.

Ten months before Gettysburg, the slaughter at Antietam, uncommonly vicious and intimate even by Civil War standards, had turned the nearby town of Frederick, Maryland, and surrounding villages and farms into one vast hospital. As they would at Gettysburg the following year, civilians from all over the country descended on Sharpsburg, Maryland, and in surrounding communities.

One of them was Oliver Wendell Holmes Sr. His son Oliver Wendell Holmes Jr., the future justice of the Supreme Court, had been "shot through the neck thought not mortal at Keedysville," the telegram of September 17, 1862, had said.

No one could tell the father where the son had been taken. The telegram reporting his wounds was not reassuring. "Not mortal" was not a naturally believable diagnosis in Civil War medicine. Men with grievous injuries survived Antietam; others with untreated minor wounds marched on and died of gangrene or sepsis in a few days.

The senior Holmes's 18,750-word *Atlantic Monthly* piece, about his furtive search for his badly wounded boy, was a stunning account of what happened after the armies retreated. Entitled "My Hunt After the Captain," it described a two-week drama by train, horseback, and on foot. It oozed despair and loss, although it ended on a hopeful note. It encapsulated, in one man's journey, the heartaches of a divided nation and the wounds that the war was leaving behind.[1]

Holmes adorned his story with soaring references to Wordsworth and Hawthorne, yet his prose was so finely grained in detail and unflinching observation that it forced readers to confront the sad and absurd brokenness that the war had become. Holmes recognized redemption and hope where he saw it, but mostly he gave voice to the utter emptiness and suffering of the people who were left to deal with the aftermath.

The senior Holmes was no ordinary correspondent. Considered one of the best writers of his age, he and other famous American men of letters—William Cullen Bryant, Henry Wadsworth Longfellow, James Russell Lowell, and John Greenleaf Whittier—had been dubbed the "Fireside Poets" for their popularity and style. Moralistic and preachy at times, their work also had a political astuteness and approachability that accompanied the rising literacy and emerging questions about nationalism and national identity that arrived with the Civil War.

Holmes began "My Hunt After the Captain" in the *Atlantic* of December 1862 with a confession, one very similar to the one that Sam Wilkeson would make in *The New York Times* after Gettysburg ten months later. Holmes said he felt inadequate to describe what he had seen. Holmes had started his journey consumed by worry for his son and overwhelmed by the level of destruction in the wake of a great battle. "I set out with a full and heavy heart," the senior Holmes wrote. At Gettysburg, Sam Wilkeson would speak of his "heavy pen."

Over the next two weeks Holmes became so consumed in finding his son that he frequently forgot to eat, drink, and sleep. He compared his experience to what it must have been like for his son to go off to war. Pursuing a wounded loved one "is almost as hard in certain circumstances as for one of our young fellows to leave his sweetheart and go into a Peninsular campaign," Holmes thought. He felt "a worrying ache and inward tremor underlying all the outward play of the sense and the mind."

Describing a circuitous and frustrating journey by train, carriage, horse, and on foot, Holmes was struck by how the expansive, sparsely populated American landscape—so inviting and so celebrated in the frontier ethos—was an especially cruelly open and inviting host for this war of massed armies. As he was leaving Philadelphia on a train headed toward Frederick, Maryland, the senior Holmes fixated on a solitary soldier guarding a railroad bridge, a lonesome sentry to the vast destruction they knew was down the tracks.

"It was the first evidence that we were approaching the perilous borders, the marches where the North and South mingle their angry hosts, where the extremes of our so-called civilization meet in conflict, and the fierce slave-driver of the Lower Mississippi stares into the stern eyes of the forest-feller from the banks of the Aroostock," the senior Holmes wrote. "All along the way the bridges were guarded more or less strongly. In a vast country like ours, communications play a far more complex part than in Europe, where the whole territory available for strategic purposes is so comparatively limited. Belgium, for instance, has long been the bowling alley where kings roll cannon-balls at each other's armies; but here we are playing the game of live ninepins without any alley."

Soon the senior Holmes saw evidence of the mass movements that had swept through Frederick and over South Mountain and through Crompton's Gap to the deadly clash on the banks of Antietam Creek. That brook had days earlier run scarlet with the blood of the dead and wounded. Holmes said the landscape reminded him of "one of those tornadoes which tear their path through our fields and villages," but with greater human cost.

On horseback, he and a small party of companions rode against long files of the wounded from both sides. Some of the injured soldiers walked in a stupor in search of a hospital; some were lying feverishly along the road. Their fragile states had no allegiance to uniform color, and their vulnerability was immediately apparent. They were "delicate boys with more spirit than strength," Holmes thought.

Arriving on the actual battlefield, Holmes and his companions ran into roving civilians scavenging for souvenirs and material. Holmes momentarily joined them but soon turned away in disgust at his own actions.

"I picked up a Rebel canteen and one of our own—but there was something repulsive about the trodden and stained relics of the stale battlefield," he wrote. "It was like the table of some hideous orgy left un-cleared, and one turned away disgusted from its broken fragments and muddy heeltaps." He decided to do penance by promising to mail a blood-stained letter written by a dead North Carolina soldier that he had picked up on the field.

Holmes and a companion he called "The Philanthropist" searched one makeshift hospital after another, including a church whose pews were covered with planks on which wounded men lay, blood staining the sanctuary floor. The stains lasted into the twenty-first century.

Men who had days before been willing to kill one another had forged bonds in mutual suffering. The senior Holmes's first encounter with a wounded Southern soldier was with a lieutenant from North Carolina, an "educated, pleasant, gentle, intelligent" young man. In saner times this young man's temperament and education might have made him natural friends with his own son, Holmes thought. But there, in the aftermath of a great battle, the journalist also found moral clarity in the young North Carolinian's suffering.

"One moment's intercourse with such an enemy, lying helpless and wounded among strangers, takes away all personal bitterness towards those with whom we or our children have been but a few hours before in deadly strife," the senior Holmes wrote.

"The basest lie in which the murderous contrivers of this Rebellion have told is that which tries to make out a difference of race in the men of the North and South. It would be worth a year of battles to abolish this delusion, though the great sponge of war that wiped it out were moistened with the best blood of the land. . . . It made my heart ache to see (the wounded Confederate officer), a man finished in humanities and Christian culture, whom the sin of his forefathers and the crime of his rulers had set in barbarous conflict against others of like training with his own—a man who, but for the curse which our generation is called on to expiate, would have taken his part in the beneficent task of shaping the intelligence and lifting the moral standard of a peaceful and united people."

Standing on a railroad platform in Baltimore waiting for a train to Frederick, where thousands of wounded men were being cared for, another of Holmes's companions—who also was searching for his son—was handed a telegram. The boy had died, the message said. The father was instructed to wait for the next train from Frederick; his boy's body would be on it. Holmes could not think of a thing to say, and his small group simply stood in stunned silence.

"It was no time for empty words of consolation," Holmes thought. "I knew what he had lost, and that now was not the time to intrude upon a grief borne as men bear it, felt as women feel it."

Holmes spent increasingly worrisome days chasing down leads of his son's whereabouts, from Sharpsburg to Harrisburg, Pennsylvania, a distance of 90 miles, and points in between. He doubled back on crowded trains more than once, stopping to tromp through chaotic temporary hospitals. At one point, he was told young Oliver was dead, so he began searching for a body. The nights were the most unsettling, and he often shared beds in rented rooms or in the homes of strangers. The only comfort was in numbers. Across a broad swath of Maryland, the railroads and highways and inns and homes were filled with people on the same sad journeys.

Holmes and his companions ran into a man he had known from Philadelphia who was bringing the body of his son home. Holmes had known the boy as a child, and he remembered him as a dreamer, dark-haired and slim, "always with a trance-like remoteness, a mystic dreaminess of manner, such as I never saw in any other youth." The boy had shown great promise as a Latin scholar, and Holmes could not at all picture him as a soldier. Holmes reached for a sliver of redemptive meaning from the boy's death, a rationalization that elevated the boy's sacrifice, and that of his father's, with generous speculation on a future the boy would never have. "Had he lived, I doubt not that he would have redeemed the rare promise of his earlier years," Holmes wrote. "He has done better, for he has died that unborn generations may attain the hopes held out to our nation and to mankind."

Eventually, Holmes found Oliver Jr., who was in serious condition, but he would survive. His father brought young Oliver home to recover, the journey of the aftermath complete. The senior Holmes's *Atlantic* piece ended with an image of the father talking his son to sleep in the boy's childhood bed. He would "sleep off his aches and weariness." He would rejuvenate for a life-long journey that took Oliver Wendell Holmes Jr. to the pinnacle of American justice.

"So comes down another night over this household," the grateful Holmes Sr. concluded, "unbroken by any messenger of evil tiding, a night of peaceful rest and grateful thoughts; for this our son and brother was dead and is alive again, and was lost and is found."

In the broken remains of Gettysburg ten months later, Sam Wilkeson would also employ the biblical language of rebirth and redemption to describe how he found his own son, Bayard.

CHAPTER 19

"He Believed That I Was Aiming
to Tell the Truth"

SAM WILKESON MISSED THE BATTLE OF ANTIETAM WHILE RECOVERING
on Cate's potatoes and farm work in upstate New York. But by December
of 1862, he was feeling better and back in Washington, and his frus-
trations were boiling over. One episode especially illustrated his rising
belief that the war was going badly and that his paper was going wobbly.
It came after one of the most important meetings between Abraham
Lincoln and a reporter during the Civil War. The meeting took place in
December 1862.

While Wilkeson spent most of that early winter of 1862 covering
Lincoln and his cabinet, one of his colleagues, Henry Villard, whom the
Tribune had hired away from the *Cincinnati Commercial*, had been sent
to cover the battle of Fredericksburg, 55 miles southwest of Washington,
DC. Eventually, Villard would make one of the war's most exhausting
and dangerous journeys to file his report, only to be undermined by nervous editors in New York. But in doing so, in fighting so hard to get the
truth out, Villard was able to make an impression on the most important
reader in America.

Villard witnessed the appalling slaughter of unsuccessful Union
assaults on the heights of Fredericksburg. Fearing public reaction to
a resounding Union defeat, the Army of the Potomac's commander at
Fredericksburg, Maj. Gen. Ambrose Burnside, initially forbade reporting from the battlefield. To tighten the information clamp even further,

Burnside required special permits for correspondents to even leave the Union army camps. That temporarily cut off any independent news from the battlefield. It was understandable. Burnside was still smarting from criticism of his tactics on the Union left wing at Antietam, where he had ordered repeated assaults on a bridge that would bear his name, and where much of the blood spilled into the creek that day had come from.

Villard defied Burnside's orders and headed out of camp for the long journey to the *Tribune*'s Washington, DC, office to file his story.[1] At 3:00 a.m. on Sunday, December 14, after his exhausted tent mate, Charlie Coffin of the *Boston Journal*, had fallen asleep, Villard quietly snuck away. It was cold and dark. Villard and his horse often stumbled in the dark on muddy roads. He fell headlong into a mud hole. Arriving covered with mud at Aquia Creek north of the battlefield, Villard—a German immigrant with legendary drive—was horrified to see that Charlie Coffin, fighting the same horrific conditions, had caught up with him. But they were both initially stymied when a Union quartermaster refused their request to board the next boat to Washington.

Villard was about to give up when he spotted two men in a rowboat coming down the river. Villard never determined if they were free black men or escaped slaves, but he enlisted them to help his journey north, loudly proclaiming for the quartermaster's deniability that he wanted to go fishing. And Villard was able to go it alone; Coffin had fallen asleep once again. Once they got to the middle of the river, Villard paid his boat mates five dollars each to continue downstream, where he hoped to board a steamer heading up the Potomac River toward Washington.

Villard was able to do that, but only after grabbing a rope dangling from the steamer and crawling aboard, then bribing the jittery captain fifty dollars to take him along. Villard wrote his story and took a nap as the steamer chugged north on the Potomac. But when he arrived in DC, he discovered that censors had locked down all telegraph transmissions. Villard sent his dispatch on the next train to New York. Even after all that effort, Villard was censored by his own editors. They were nervous that their correspondent was the only one reporting a Union disaster at Fredericksburg, and they toned down his description.

"I had stated it as strongly as possible that the Army of the Potomac had suffered another great, general defeat," Villard recalled in his memoirs years later. The battle was nothing more than an "inexcusable, murderous blunder" by Burnside, he wrote. Unfortunately for Villard, Greeley "would not let the *Tribune* solely assume the responsibility for what would no doubt prove a great shock to a loyal public," and his dispatch was "modified."[2] But he had given it his best shot, and he was not finished delivering the message.

Eating a late dinner at the Willard Hotel, across the street from the *Tribune* office, with his dispatch on its way on a late train to New York, Villard ran into Sen. Henry Wilson of Massachusetts, "the most persistent news hunter in Washington." When Wilson inquired of the news from Fredericksburg, Villard gave it unvarnished, as he had done in his dispatch to Greeley.

Villard told Wilson that Burnside, who after the war became a Rhode Island senator and governor and the first president of the National Rifle Association, had been badly defeated. The defeat was so crushing and costly, Villard told Wilson, that he believed it would be impossible for the general to command an army again. A visibly troubled Wilson listened, and then left. Senator Wilson then returned at 10:00 p.m. and asked the young reporter to accompany him to the White House. Still in his dirty battlefield clothes, the exhausted Villard complied. The president was calling and the recent German immigrant could not say no to the president of his new country.

At the White House, Villard and Wilson met Lincoln in a second floor reception room. Incredibly, the news hawk Lincoln had heard very little from his own military command out of Fredericksburg. He shook Villard's hand and declared: "We are very anxious and have heard very little." The three men talked for half an hour and Villard felt he was providing Lincoln the necessary truth by describing the utter destruction of the repetitive Union assaults that he had seen at Fredericksburg. "The questions and expressions on his face showed that he believed I was aiming to tell the truth, and that he felt growing anxiety," Villard remembered. After momentarily mulling whether a reporter should have the audacity to give unsolicited advice to the president of the United

States, Villard told Lincoln that the president could not "render a greater service to the country" than to order Burnside to retreat, to abandon the deadly frontal attacks.

"I hope it is not as bad as all that," a melancholy Lincoln responded. Mercifully, Burnside's subordinate officers had by then talked the general out of personally leading one final assault on Marye's Heights, and the Union army was making plans to withdraw. Burnside, whose mutton-chop facial hair style later became known as sideburns, would be replaced by Fighting Joe Hooker within a month.

"I felt thankful myself that I had been thus permitted to make an effort in the highest quarter for the salvation of the army, and I walked away with a sense of having dispensed a patriotic duty," Villard wrote of his encounter with Lincoln.[3]

But the night was not over. To cap off what had to have been the longest and strangest twenty-four hours of his life, when Villard returned to the *Tribune* office after seeing Lincoln, he turned in his expense account. It was quite a document, filled as it was with cash payments to rowboaters and bribes to steamer captains. Wilkeson, still at work, perhaps tired himself and having had too much to drink, took a look at the report and then took a swing at Villard. Their colleague Albert Richardson witnessed the brief fistfight.[4] Wilkeson later apologized and he and Villard made up, and after the war Villard became Sam Wilkeson's boss at the Northern Pacific Railroad.

Villard's experience at Fredericksburg demonstrated all the pressures on Civil War correspondents. Many of them never thought twice about defying censorship at any personal cost. Who determines what information is detrimental to a country's war efforts? Were correspondents strictly observers or participants? Should they offer advice? And what if your editors don't believe you, or believe, as Greeley may have after Fredericksburg, that the North couldn't handle the truth out of Fredericksburg?

Villard actions were his answers to all those questions. In the end, he concluded that honest witness was worth the risk to personal safety and standing.

CHAPTER 20

"An Unusually Gauzy Mystery of Enchantment"

SIX WEEKS AFTER THE UNION ARMY'S HORRIFIC DEFEAT AT FREDER-icksburg, Lt. Bayard Wilkeson's artillery battery was involved in one of those obscure skirmishes that did not make many Civil War history books, but typified the war's wasted effort and life. The reporting on it, both journalistically and by the officers of both armies engaged, illustrated how events were viewed very differently in the North and South. Both sides claimed victory after a nasty little fight in the night.

At a place called Deserted House near Suffolk, Virginia, the battle had virtually no effect on the outcome of the war except to add a few score names to its long casualty list. It was a crucial moment for Bayard Wilkeson, however. The young lieutenant's notoriety and stock rose among the Union army's artillery brass as a result of his actions at Deserted House, directly leading to his battery's placement at Gettysburg.

Union army after-action reports didn't even refer to it as a battle. It was the "Engagement at Deserted House, or Kelly's Store, near Suffolk, Va." The troops just called it "Deserted House" or "Deserted Farm." The bumbling affair took place on January 30, 1863, 190 miles south of Washington, DC.

The roughly 120 men in Company G of the 4th Artillery and the six Napoleons they serviced were part of a force of about 4,800 cavalry, infantry, and artillery soldiers and officers engaged there. The Union infantry with them were mostly from Pennsylvania, New York, and Indiana. They were ordered to attack a smaller Confederate force that scouts had discovered foraging about 15 miles away near an obscure junction called Holland Corners. It was a misty and cool Virginia winter night, but not overly cold, and a robust moon gave the landscape a mystical, dreamlike feel.

"The scene at this time was remarkably interesting," a private from the 167th Pennsylvania wrote home to the *Berks and Schuylkill Journal*. "The moon shone brightly and all nature—the broad fields and the vernal woods—seemed tricked out in an unusually gauzy mystery of enchantment, strange peculiarities and oddities of every kind, of course imaginary ones."[1]

As often happened, the two small armies stumbled into one another in that gauzy scene along the Blackwater River. Fighting erupted at 3:20 a.m. between cavalry skirmishers, followed by artillery duels set off when the batteries of the 4th U.S. Artillery, including Wilkeson's, set up in a clearing, fixing their guns on enemy campfires. The Confederates were pushed back, but a pre-dawn Union infantry follow-up attack fell apart when a green Pennsylvania unit got lost in the forest. The Pennsylvanians turned into what Gen. John Peck described as a "confused mass" that blocked other units from attacking or flanking the Confederate force of roughly 2,500 men.

It was chaotic, muddy, and bloody, and would have been comical had men not died. Some green soldiers showed their fear. "The priest was with us at the battle's start and we kneeled down and he blessed us," Sgt. George Tipping of the 155th New York Volunteers wrote home. "There was terror in all hearts. Our Colonel showed the coward some—there was nothing seen of him for three hours in the morning. It was called the Battle of the Deserted Farm. We lay flat on our faces in the mud to escape the shells. Two men were killed next to me and one lost his arm at the shoulder. At any rate, we made the rebs to start their boats across the Blackwater."[2]

Although the Confederates retreated from the field and were briefly pursued by the disorganized federals, the outcome of the battle was essentially a draw with neither army gaining permanent advantage over the other. The number of dead on both sides numbered in the dozens, and both sides claimed victory and inflated the casualty lists of the other.

In his official report, the Union side's General Peck said that had his forces been able to carry out a planned successful flanking move, the battle would have been "decisive, the victory full and complete." Peck reasoned that "under all the circumstances it was a handsome affair, and the enemy will long remember his losses, disappointment, and narrow escape from capture." He recorded the Union dead at 25, wounded at 102, missing at 9, but supposed "the Rebel loss must have been more than ours" judging from the 1,140 artillery shells Wilkeson's guns and other Union batteries had shot toward the campfires.[3]

The New York Times two weeks later printed a post-battle report from a Richmond paper that had been smuggled through the lines. No surprise, for hearts and minds needed to be won, the Confederates also declared the affair at Deserted House a fine victory. Gen. Roger A. Pryor said his side sustained only "slight loss" while inflicting 300 casualties on the Yankees. "When the disparity of force between the parties is considered," General Pryor wrote, "with the proximity of the enemy to his stronghold, and his facilities of reinforcements by railway, the result of the action . . . will be accepted as a splendid illustration of your courage and good conduct."[4] In Pryor's rationale, his army won because his men were more courageous. It was pure spin. The papers were full of it, generals turning draws or defeats into moral or actual victories, editors both North and South both fighting the spin or engaging in it. Hearts and minds were at stake.

Two years later, Pryor, a newspaper editor and secessionist politician before the war, was captured trying to exchange newspapers through the lines during the Union siege at Petersburg.[5]

Despite the battle of Deserted House's relatively minor status and comparatively light casualties, one important result came from it. Lt. Bayard Wilkeson had gotten the notice of his superiors and a big vote of confidence in the Union command hierarchy. In Peck's official report, he singled out Lieutenant Wilkeson and a handful of other officers for "zeal, gallantry and good conduct."[6]

CHAPTER 21

"Mr. Wilkeson Has Been Constantly Attacking the Administration"

IN MARCH OF 1863, SAM WILKESON TOOK AN UNNAMED "POWERFUL man" to the White House for a private meeting with Lincoln, just days before Wilkeson left the *New York Tribune* for the rival *Times*. The president greeted Wilkeson with a barb disguised as a compliment. With a laugh, Lincoln told Wilkeson's companion that "Mr. Wilkeson has been constantly attacking the administration. We understand he has attacked or criticized or found fault with Cameron, Hooker, McClellan, Burnside, and the way in which the war is carried on, and everything."[1]

Wilkeson attributed some of Lincoln's irritation with him to Greeley's peripatetic and what seemed to Wilkeson as increasingly soft support for Lincoln and the war. Wilkeson had just written his editor, Sidney Howard Gay, that "the course of the *Tribune* has so constantly been made the theme of wonder and reproach in the White House that every editor connected with it, suffers with it."[2]

For a time after the *Tribune's* "Forward To Richmond" debacle, Greeley had vowed to keep his correspondents from criticizing the war effort in print. But in fact, Wilkeson's scoops and aggressive war reporting that exposed failure along with acknowledging success had helped put the paper on better journalistic footing, and by late summer of 1862, Greeley was back regularly chiding Lincoln in editorials for not declaring the abolition of slavery as the war's central purpose.

Greeley's "The Prayer of Twenty Millions" appeared August 20, 1862, in the *Tribune* and provoked one of the most significant declarations of Lincoln's presidency. The number was a reference to the population of the Northern states. Greeley ostensibly was speaking for them all. In the editorial, he pleaded for Lincoln to more vigorously push to free slaves, specifically by stepping up enforcement of congressional acts that approved the seizing of slaves as war contraband. In a stunningly bold challenge to a commander-in-chief in the midst of the Civil War, Greeley accused Lincoln of having a "mistaken deference to Rebel slavery."[3]

Lincoln responded evenly with a message designed to cut the difference between the rabid abolitionists who sought a Union victory, no matter the cost, and pro-Unionists who wanted to end the war even if slavery survived. But as a slap back at Greeley for such an open challenge, Lincoln—one of the most adept presidential press strategists in U.S. history—gave his response to the *Washington Intelligencer*, an establishment Whig paper. The *Tribune* published Lincoln's response two days after the *Intelligencer*, on August 25, 1862. In it, Lincoln told his "old friend" Greeley that while he personally abhorred slavery, saving the Union was his primary objective.

"If I could save the Union without freeing any slave I would do it, and if I could save it by freeing all the slaves I would do it," Lincoln wrote, "and if I could save it by freeing some and leaving others alone I would also do that." He concluded: "I intend no modification of my oft-expressed personal wish that all men every where could be free."[4]

What Greeley did not know at the time was that Lincoln already had the Emancipation Proclamation in a drawer in the White House and was awaiting a military victory to issue it. James Roberts Gilmore, who in 1862 had founded the *Continental Monthly* as an abolitionist organ with the help of Greeley, had for eighteen months been a secret emissary between Lincoln and Greeley, in essence detouring around his primary eyes and ears in Washington, Sam Wilkeson.

Gilmore had been in the White House the day before Greeley issued his "Prayer." Gilmore knew both that Greeley's "Prayer" was coming and that Lincoln was waiting for the right time to issue the Emancipation

Proclamation. But he was too late to get back to New York to alert Greeley of the pending proclamation and talk him out of issuing the "Prayer."

When Gilmore told Greeley of Lincoln's plans, too late, Greeley responded: "If Mr. Lincoln were not so very cautious and reticent we should get along much better together; but I could forgive him all and everything, if he would infuse a little energy into affairs; he seems to forget there is a possibility of exhausting the patience as well as the resources of the country."[5]

When Gilmore saw Lincoln a few days later, the president was irritated. "What's he so wrathy about?" Lincoln asked Gilmore, referring to Greeley.

Gilmore responded: "The slow progress of the war—what he regards as the useless destruction of life and property, and especially your neglect to make a direct attack upon slavery."

Lincoln asked Gilmore why Greeley simply didn't come to see him. Gilmore responded that the feisty editor "objected to allowing the President to act as advisory editor of the *Tribune*."

Lincoln shot back: "I have no such desire. I certainly have enough now on my hands to satisfy any man's ambition."[6]

Throughout 1862 and into 1863, Wilkeson shared with Greeley and Gay his frustration over Lincoln and the course of the war, yet he increasingly felt restrained by their editorial caution. In one undated letter he begged Gay and Greeley to let him "write with ripping pen" a piece condemning prisoners thrown into a notorious Washington prison without charges or the right to a speedy trial, the result of Lincoln's suspension of habeas corpus. Wilkeson began calling the prison "Stanton's Bastille"—a rip at the secretary of war—and he decried the idea of large numbers of "unaccused" languishing "immersed dark and lonely without trial, for weeks and months."[7]

Sam never got to that exposé of "Stanton's Bastille." There were too many battles to cover, too much political intrigue elsewhere to track and decipher. Leading up to Gettysburg, the war was going badly, and the military situation demanded full-time attention. Lee was outgeneraling any Union commander thrown against him, and opposition to the draft was simmering in Northern cities.

The stress of keeping up kept weighing on Wilkeson, and he increasingly soured on Lincoln and on his own newspaper. In late summer of 1862, still recovering from his illness from the Peninsula campaign and his sorrow over Lt. John Wilkeson's death at Seven Pines, Sam wrote Gay an angry letter about the defeat of a Union army under John Pope by Confederates under Stonewall Jackson and A. P. Hill at Cedar Mountain, Virginia. Sounding disconsolate and depressed, Wilkeson called the battle a "Mountain of slaughter" and Lincoln "the border-State Joking Machine," the latter a reference to Lincoln's Kentucky origins and propensity to tell jokes as illustrative points.

Of this "afflictive president," Wilkeson wrote, "May his shadow shorten!!!"[8]

A little over a month later, at Antietam, Lincoln got enough of a military victory to issue the Emancipation Proclamation.

But then the Union army suffered another bad defeat at Fredericksburg. In December, after Burnside sent those waves after waves of Union men to be cut down like wheat before scythes on the heights at Fredericksburg, fresh doubts erupted over Lincoln's leadership and the Northern public's willingness to endure such a brutal war. As news of the defeat slowly trickled out despite Burnside's extreme censorship orders and the *Tribune*'s toning down of Henry Villard's account, Wilkeson ran into one angry senator after another on Capitol Hill. As the wounded and dead were still being hauled off the field at Fredericksburg, Wilkeson wrote Gay that Sen. William Fessendon of Maine, a staunch abolitionist, was barely restrained by "his patriotic prejudice from denouncing the administration in the Senate yesterday and demanding a resignation of the entire Cabinet." Of Lincoln, Wilkeson lamented: "What a huge untimely joke the man and his administration are."[9]

In January, Wilkeson's fears that the North was going wobbly, and that a negotiated settlement with the slave-holding Confederates might be better than continuing this bloody and inconclusive war, began a falling out between him and Greeley. It would be temporary, but significant.

Reports began circulating in Washington that Greeley had met with French foreign minister Henri Mercier about the possibility of a brokered peace. Publicly, Greeley acknowledged that he and Mercier had met, but he claimed it was merely to ascertain how the French felt about Lincoln's administration. Anyone who construed that he was proposing or supporting a French-brokered peace, Greeley responded, "must be strangely ignorant or utterly demented."[10]

But about that same time, Greeley's *Tribune* published a series of principles about how Greeley thought the war should be prosecuted from that point on. Taken as a whole, the principles could logically have been construed that Greeley believed that a brokered peace by the French or British was inevitable, if not advisable. It was a confusing declaration. Greeley began his great principles by asserting that Union armies were on the verge of great victories that could end the rebellion. But he also predicted that the "Great Powers of Europe" would eventually feel compelled to "mediate—not by blows, nor by menaces, but by representations—against a continuance of the struggle, as fruitless, wasteful butchery, and urge a settlement in the interests of Humanity and Commerce."[11]

Wilkeson was incredulous and furious. Even before the *Tribune* published Greeley's thoughts on prosecuting the war, he had received another barrage of negative responses from Republicans in Congress when news of Greeley's meeting with the French ambassador leaked out. The editor with so much influence appeared to be conducting his own foreign policy, one that undermined confidence in the administration and the war effort, and one that went against Wilkeson's own belief that only an all-out Union victory would stamp out slavery.

In a January 28, 1863, letter to Greeley, which he copied to Gay, Wilkeson wrote that "you are escaping great peril," suggesting that Greeley might have been arrested for treason had Wilkeson not intervened with the right people.

"Your visit to the French minister was industriously published in Republican circles yesterday by Secretary Seward," Wilkeson wrote. "Your conversations with [the French minister] on the subject of Mediation" was interpreted as "an initiation of foreign intervention between the Government and its endeavors to suppress the rebellion."

Furthermore, Wilkeson wrote Greeley, the reports of the meeting had seriously damaged the *Tribune's* influence among its readers and supporters.

"I took hold of the matter this morning," he wrote. "In my conversations with Senators of the extremist Republican sentiment, I found the irritation against you to be profound and almost implacable. They charge you with an endeavor to end the war against the sentiment, and interests, & honor of the Loyal States."

Wilkeson wrote his bosses that Republicans on Capitol Hill were accusing Greeley "of using tremendous power of the *Tribune* to introduce foreign intervention" in a way that would "separate yourself and the followers of the *Tribune* from the administration and the war." Such actions, Wilkeson continued, would "weaken our cause everywhere and . . . strengthen the enemy." Wilkeson said he may only have temporarily saved Greeley from prosecution on treason charges, and he urged his editor to respond with a declaration that the *Tribune* still favored conducting the war with nothing but ultimate capitulation of the rebellious states as a goal.

"I of course stopped" the talk of arrest, he wrote Greeley. "But I can't stop Seward's talk against you and I can't stop the social criticism of . . . the *Tribune* among Republican members of Congress. The only way to stop this is for you to put the paper on the warpath, and keep it on the warpath, to the bitter end—cost what of life and what of treasure it may be." Just in case Greeley and Gay didn't get his admonition to go all-in, in lives and treasure, Wilkeson underlined the last eleven words of that final sentence.[12]

Greeley gave the final snip to their relationship two days later by publishing the principles that seemed to want it both ways—the principles that had both the Union on the verge of winning while alluding to the inevitability of a European-brokered peace. That did it for Wilkeson. He was on his way out the *Tribune* door, but he did not leave without suggesting a coup to topple Greeley. In a letter to Gay, Wilkeson broached the possibility of outright *Tribune* editorial mutiny, even extortion. "I propose the majority of the stockholders of the paper resolve to put the *Tribune* on the warpath until the last dollar is spent and the last man drafted—that they require (Greeley) to accept this as the editorial programme he is to follow or to offer his stock for sale. The money to buy it can be raised in 24 hours."[13]

That uprising never materialized. On March 7, 1863, a Saturday, Wilkeson wrote Gay that he would resign effective the following Monday, March 9, after which he would "never again [work] for it under Greeley's leadership an hour while I live."[14] That would turn into false prophecy when Wilkeson returned to the *Tribune* later in the war. But the next major battle that Sam Wilkeson would cover, the most important battle of the war, would be under the banner of *The New York Times*. The stage was set for Sam Wilkeson's emotional, transformational, hours at Gettysburg, four months later.

The Greeley-Wilkeson falling out was big news in journalism circles. While Greeley's support in Lincoln's cabinet and among hawkish Republicans in the Senate suffered, Sam Wilkeson's resignation placed him more firmly in the bitter-end camp at a time when people across the North were engaged in an emotional debate over the war's escalating costs in lives and treasure.

Two months after Wilkeson quit the *Tribune* and joined Henry Raymond's *New York Times*, the Union's humiliating defeat at Chancellorsville in Virginia shook up Northern support for war even more. Anti-draft sentiment was building. The casualty lists were never-ending and the post-battle rivers of suffering were getting larger and larger. Then Lee crossed the Potomac into Pennsylvania. The summer of 1863 opened in restless, worrisome days for the Union.

Sam's stern admonition to Greeley about the need to be steadfast "to the bitter end—cost what of life and what of treasure it may be," was about to get intensely personal one more time for the Wilkeson family. Sam and Bayard Wilkeson were about to go on separate roads to a fateful rendezvous at Gettysburg.

CHAPTER 22

"Howard's Cowards"

IN THE SPRING OF 1863, LT. BAYARD WILKESON'S SIX-CANNON BATTERY was shifted to the widely derided 11th Corps, just after the 11th had been smashed by Stonewall Jackson's audacious surprise flank attack on the Union right wing at Chancellorsville. The transfer was part of Fighting Joe Hooker's reorganization of the Army of the Potomac, a reshuffling that transformed the artillery from its own brigade command to units attached to the various Union army corps. As the Army of the Potomac marched north toward Pennsylvania to confront Lee, there was much grumbling and confusion in the ranks about how this new chain of command would work out in the next battle.

Bayard was mighty unhappy to be a part of it.

Even before the Union defeat at Chancellorsville, the 11th Corps was held in low regard throughout the Army of the Potomac. Made up largely of first-generation German immigrants, many of its soldiers could not speak English. Fair or not, they were looked down upon as unprofessional, unruly, and cowardly by English-speaking officers. Adding to its dubious reputation, the 11th had missed some of the Army of the Potomac's biggest fights, including Antietam.

Then in early May 1863, at Chancellorsville, the 11th Corps, assigned to hold the Union's right flank, was caught by surprise, shattered and driven back 2 miles by Stonewall Jackson's corps. Only deadly artillery fire by Union cannons prevented an even worse rout. One of Bayard's new fellow battery officers in the reconfigured 11th Corps, the German-born Capt. Hubert Dilger, later received the Medal of Honor for actions at Chancellorsville. Dilger's horse was shot from under him and he was trapped for a moment, but he recovered in time to save five of his six guns. His cannons, firing point blank into charging Confederates under Robert Rodes, blunted Jackson's assault enough to prevent the total destruction of Hooker's right wing.

Oliver Otis Howard, commander of the 11th Corps, had tried to rally his fleeing men by placing a battle flag in the crook of the stump of the right arm he had lost at Seven Pines the year before. Some of his men retreated in an orderly fashion, but others turned into a "dense mass of beings who had lost their reasoning facilities, and were flying from a thousand fancied dangers," the *New York Herald's* Thomas Cook wrote. Cook observed "battery wagons, ambulances, horses, men, cannon, caissons, all jumbled and tangled together in an apparently inextricable mass, and that murderous fire still pouring upon them."[1]

Afterward, the nicknames of "Howard's Cowards" and the "Flying Dutchmen," the latter a derisive reference to Germans, stuck to the 11th even more.

In the ranks and up the chain of command of the 11th, there were substantial worries. After Chancellorsville, twenty-year-old Capt. Theodore Ayrault Dodge of the 119th New York, barely older than Bayard Wilkeson, complained in a letter to a friend that press reports of the entire 11th Corps capitulating and running at Chancellorsville were inaccurate.

"We were surprised through the fault of the Generals," Dodge, who would just weeks later lose a leg at Gettysburg, wrote, "and therefore it was not our fault that we were driven back; but I never saw men run as did those Dutchmen. Our boys stood—all American Regiments did— but the panic among the Dutch was fearful."[2]

Even some of the 11th's top officers spoke privately of the corps's shortcomings. After Chancellorsville, where he had distinguished himself in another corps, Maj. Thomas Osborn was among those, along with Bayard Wilkeson, transferred to the 11th Corps to shape up its artillery. On June 11, less than three weeks before Gettysburg, Osborn wrote his brother that the 11th Corps was in "the most deplorable condition and in a state of complete demoralization."

"I left the best artillery in the army when I left the Third Corps, and when I came here I took the worst," Osborn complained.[3] Perhaps he could have the men shaped up in three months, he told his brother. He would not get three weeks.

In the ranks, Howard was ridiculed as a religious zealot, and the debacle at Chancellorsville had hurt his standing even more. He "does not now stand by many pegs as high in my estimation as before the beginning of this month," Dodge wrote a friend less than a week after Chancellorsville. "Not only, as he himself says, has he not got confidence in the men, but the men, who are almost entirely Germans, have no confidence in him."[4] At Gettysburg, Dodge's regiment would be positioned near the county poorhouse, the location where a badly wounded Bayard Wilkeson would be taken on July 1.

The young Lieutenant Wilkeson did not disguise his unhappiness about being detached to this humiliated corps so soon after its defeat at Chancellorsville. Bayard told his father that he feared the 11th's reputation would preclude it from ever getting into another real fight. Impatient and unhappy, Bayard nonetheless continued to build chits and raise notice in the Union high command. Two weeks before Gettysburg, he was commended after a drill while officers of other artillery companies were "raked over the coals," Bayard wrote his father.[5]

The nineteen-year-old by-the-book lieutenant belittled the language of the German-Americans in the corps. He thought many of the officers were drunkards. He complained about them in a lengthy June 22, 1863, letter to his father from near Leesburg, Virginia, where the 11th was temporarily bivouacked. By then, the bulk of Lee's army was already in Pennsylvania.

"At the present time there is no chance for a fight," Bayard wrote to Sam. "Two or three Corps have been sent ahead but there is no danger of the 11th having anything to do."[6]

How wrong the young lieutenant would be.

Bayard's obsession to get into the action was what you would expect of a nineteen-year-old with illusions of invincibility and a desire for fame. The letter to his father, 35 miles away in his Washington office, dripped in sarcasm and impatience.

In the letter Bayard was so critical of the 11th that he declared that John Wilkes Wilkeson was better off having been killed at Seven Pines than assigned to the 11th Corps. After the maudlin joke, he pleaded with his father to call in chits all the way to Lincoln, if necessary. "Please speak to General Thomas and 'Uncle Abe,'" Bayard wrote. Referring to the war secretary, he declared: "Stanton will surely give in if you have those two on your side. . . . I will get out of this Corps some day. Do please help me to get out."[7]

He was very worried that alcohol abuse was hurting preparedness in the ranks. An officer in another company was a "great drunkard," Bayard complained, and "most all of the officers of this Corps are so, and I am tired of them. No order—no method—much confusion, and whisky." The pleas continued: "Please get me and my Battery out of the Corps. . . . I would rather fight every day than remain in this Corps."[8]

He was not alone in his worries as the 11th Corps marched north through Virginia. Osborn, the 11th Corps's new artillery commander, worried about "deplorable condition" of his batteries. The stern and taciturn Brig. Gen. Francis Barlow, a hero of Seven Pines, was now commanding Bayard's First Division. Barlow had served in Dan Sickles's 3rd Corps at Chancellorsville and had not been involved in the 11th Corps rout, but he had had plenty to say about his new corps. Barlow wondered if Fighting Joe Hooker would ever send the 11th into a fight again.

"You can imagine my indignation & disgust at the miserable behavior of the 11th Corps," Barlow wrote his mother and brothers shortly after Chancellorsville. But he also said it was unfair to just blame the German immigrants in the corps.[9]

"You know I have always been down on the 'Dutch' & I do not abate my contempt now, but it is not fair to charge it all to them," he wrote. "Some of the Yankee Regts behaved just as badly & I think that Hooker's failure thus far has been solely from the bad fighting of the men."[10]

Howard, Barlow wrote, "is full of mortification & disgust and I really pity him." Showing self-confidence that fellow officers often saw as arrogance, Barlow lamented that had he and his brigade been on that routed right flank at Chancellorsville, "we could have done a good deal towards checking the rout."[11]

Francis Barlow
LIBRARY OF CONGRESS

Barlow had already developed a reputation as one of the toughest disciplinarians and most ardent abolitionists in the Union army. Though approaching thirty, he appeared to be barely out of his teens, looking not that much older than the nineteen-year-old Lieutenant Wilkeson. Barlow was slightly built, probably weighing no more than 135 pounds. His wife, Arabella, was a prominent member of the legions of civilians following Hooker's armies. She followed him wherever he went, and she was well known throughout the Army of the Potomac for nursing her gung-ho husband back to health after the battle of Antietam. Union officers never forgot the sight of Arabella Barlow arriving on the battlefield at Antietam as the fighting was winding down, wearing a flowing dress and accompanied by a man she had hired to carry all her belongings in a wheelbarrow. They had walked 13 miles from a train station in Hagerstown, Maryland, to get to her badly wounded husband.

Barlow had been a lawyer in New York before the war, where each day he commuted on the steamboat *Edwin* from Yonkers to the city with a group of young professionals. On one evening commute home, a conversation on slavery got heated. Barlow sat quietly for a long time, then interjected: "You may talk politics until you are deaf and dumb, but slavery in this country can only be ended by war, and war is sure to come, and all of you must be prepared to enlist."[12]

Twelve days after the cannons opened on Fort Sumter, Frank Barlow and his friend, James Scrymser, visited several regimental recruiting stations in New York before joining the 12th New York. Barlow chose it because he liked that its newly recruited chaplain told him that the 12th was "a damn good regiment." Barlow told Scrymser that any regiment whose chaplain cussed like that was his kind of regiment. Barlow joined on the spot, married Arabella that night, and left for war the next day.[13]

Barlow rose steadily in rank. Spurred by his heroism at Seven Pines and Antietam, he was a logical choice to help Howard shape up the beleaguered 11th Corps after Chancellorsville. Its 12,000-man ranks had been reduced by 20 percent casualties at Chancellorsville. Replacements were green and trickling in too slowly to bring it back to strength. North of Gettysburg on July 1, because of losses, stragglers, and units deployed elsewhere, barely half that Chancellorsville strength would try to hold the Union right wing against Confederate columns more than twice their numbers.

Besides the alcohol abuse, Bayard Wilkeson constantly worried about his battery's lack of real battle experience. His men had not seen the close-up fighting that Dilger's guns had seen at Chancellorsville. They looked good in drills, but he was trepidatious about how they would perform under fire. On top of that morale was suffering throughout the 11th. He also felt miscast. Bayard asked Sam to get him moved to a command of the more accurate Parrot rifled guns. Unlike the smoothbores he now had, he reasoned that Parrots were more likely to be deployed where it counted most in the next fight.

"With that Battery and my men I can do good service to the cause," Bayard wrote his father. "A light 12 Pdr. Battery in the 11th Corps will never see fighting after this, and I want to get out of the Corps and see some hot work."[14]

The very same day Bayard wrote that, Robert E. Lee sent J. E. B. Stuart's cavalry on a slashing arc through Maryland. Stuart foraged, disrupted commerce, and cut telegraph lines for the ensuing ten days. But Stuart's marauding also left Lee to travel more blindly in Pennsylvania than he liked. The first major decision of the battle of Gettysburg had occurred. The accidental clash of more than 90,000 federals and 70,000 rebels had been set in motion.

As Bayard Wilkeson marched toward that crossroads town, he had a singular goal in mind.

"I want to have a name at the end of this war," he wrote his father.[15]

CHAPTER 23

"They Are Just Like Our People"

THE COUNTRY THAT BAYARD AND SAM WILKESON PASSED THROUGH IN late June of 1863 was teeming with armies on the move, refugees fleeing ahead of them, and camp followers stringing along in the armies' wakes. Some 160,000 men in arms fanned out over a 100-mile swath from northern Virginia to central Pennsylvania. Lee's divided army alone stretched over 50 miles as it fed and clothed itself with fresh provender of southern Pennsylvania's breadbasket. The Union's Army of the Potomac, about to get yet another new commanding general, was desperately trying to catch up and soon found itself spread out almost as much. On the eve of the battle of Gettysburg, Union corps were encamped from north of Emmitsburg, Maryland, where Bayard Wilkeson and his 11th Corps overnighted, to near Manchester, Maryland, where the 6th Corps of John Sedgwick had set in for the night. More than 90,000 men were spread over 30 miles.

For almost a month, as Lee moved north through the protective screen of the Shenandoah Valley and Hooker—and then Meade—tried to intercept him, civilians were disrupted and dislodged. Many went to great lengths to hide cattle, food, and grain. Men of the 61st Georgia were some of the first Confederates to march through Chambersburg, Pennsylvania, on June 15. The reaction they got was a far cry from the picnic spreads laid out for Samuel H. Wilkeson's New Yorkers when they had marched south after enlistment two years earlier.

Pvt. G. W. Nicols of the 61st Georgia saw a young girl standing on the front step of a Chambersburg home with her mother as dusty gray columns marched past. Nicols thought the little girl was about eight years old. "Mama, are these men Rebels?" she asked. Yes, they were, the mother responded. "Why mama, they haven't got horns," the little girl replied. "They are just like our people."[1]

That was not always true. Renegade units in Lee's Army had begun rounding up every black person they ran across—man, woman, and child, free or escaped slave—to be sent south into slavery. It was not Lee's order per se, but it was happening, and it was terrorizing blacks throughout southern Pennsylvania.

Lee had tried to minimize the effect of his army's movements on civilians with an order issued from Chambersburg on June 27. He lamented "instances of forgetfulness" he was hearing about, and urged his men to remember that "the duties exacted of us by civilization and Christianity are not less obligatory in the country of the enemy than in our own."[2]

Pleas for Christian behavior aside, the word of the capture of blacks had spread with the armies. An estimated 200–300 free blacks were in Gettysburg and the surrounding countryside. Many of them went into hiding as the Confederates approached.[3] One did not, and her life would soon intersect with Bayard Wilkeson's in an act of courage and compassion that defied the reality of what had been happening to blacks over the previous two weeks.

In Chambersburg on June 15, a white woman, Rachel Cormany, watched in horror as a long train of refugees that included several large black families passed through town ahead of the invading Confederates. Their eyes, Rachel recorded in her diary, "fairly protruded with fear." The panic abated somewhat that night after the first waves of refugees passed, but it turned out to be "the calm before a great storm," she observed. More desperate streams of refugees, many of them blacks eluding capture, hurried through the town in ensuing days.[4]

At Mercersburg, 41 miles west of Gettysburg, residents were so shaken by refugees trying to stay ahead of Rebel cavalry that they suspended classes at the local seminary and urged students to join a home-guard militia called up by Pennsylvania governor Andrew Curtin. "These rumors of war are actually worse than war itself," the Reverend Phillip

Schaff wrote in his diary on June 18, 1863. "The sight of Rebels was actually a relief from painful anxiety."[5]

He did not feel that way for long. Sights of "the flight of poor contraband Negroes to the mountains from fear of being captured by the Rebels and dragged to the South" stayed with him forever. The next day, he wrote, a Rebel cavalry force came through Mercersburg with 200 head of cattle, 120 horses, "and two or three Negro boys." Gathering in the town square and ordering his men to draw pistols and sabers, an especially loud captain named Crawford dared the citizens to fight. The cavalry commander, a colonel named Ferguson, then stepped forward to lecture the Mercersburg citizens on the evils of Lincoln's suspension of habeas corpus, a stunning display of moral relativism given that his men were at that moment holding people they intended to enslave. "You live under despotism," Ferguson lectured the gathered citizens of Mercersburg. It was the South, he said, that had the courage to defend "rights." He vowed that the war would not end until "you must either acknowledge our Confederacy, or there is no one else left to fight."[6]

In the days that followed, marauding Confederates kept coming through on "regular slave hunts," threatening to burn the homes of any Mercersburg resident even suspected of harboring them, Schaff wrote. Risking his own freedom, Schaff hid a black cook named Eliza and her child in his cellar overnight and secreted them to a nearby grain field to hide during the day.

Three days before the battle of Gettysburg, another band of Rebel guerillas came through Mercersburg with twenty-one black prisoners, mostly women and children. The sight was "sad and mournful," all the more because Reverend Schaff recognized several free black neighbors, including Sam Brooks, who "had split many a cord of wood for me."

Schaff approached one of the Rebels guarding the wagons and asked him if he felt "bad and mean in such an occupation." The man replied that he felt "very comfortable" because he was merely "reclaiming their property which we had stolen and harbored."[7]

Confederate lieutenant general John B. Gordon, whose men would charge Lt. Bayard Wilkeson's battery north of Gettysburg on the battle's first day, wrote his wife that en route to Gettysburg he was "mortified . . .

to see how much afraid of us these people were."[8] They had good reason to be.

The night before the battle of Gettysburg, a Confederate officer named Imboden led a force through Mercersburg and declared his pleasure in seeing the citizens of Pennsylvania experiencing what Southern civilians had felt for two long years. "Your army destroyed all the fences, burnt towns, turned poor women out of house and home, broke pianos, furniture, old family pictures, and committed every act of vandalism," Imboden lectured. "I thank God that the hour has come that this war will be fought out on Pennsylvania soil." If true, Schaff wrote in his diary that he agreed with the Confederate general on that point. "If this charge is true, I must confess that we deserve punishment in the North."[9]

On July 1, as the battle was erupting in full fury at Gettysburg, another "lawless band" of Confederate mercenaries came through Mercersburg, also with captive blacks, and the guerillas left behind June 24 editions of Richmond newspapers. The broadsheets were "shabby and mean, full of information from Northern papers of the rebel invasion," Reverend Schaff recalled, and "full of hatred and bitterness for the North, urging the Southern army to unmitigated plunder and merciless retaliation."[10]

Mercersburg suffered terribly in the aftermath of the battle of Gettysburg. On July 5, a miles-long train of Confederate ambulances coursed through, and 600 Rebel wounded were unloaded at the seminary. By July 7, the "filth and foul odors" emanating from the Mercersburg Seminary would push citizens "beyond endurance." Confederate wounded stayed in Mercersburg until July 21, and some, including a captain named Williams who Schaff befriended, were cared for by their wives, who had hurried north after learning their spouses had been wounded.[11] The armies of the aftermath had shared a single credo: To get to a loved one as fast as possible, and hope and pray for the best on the way there.

In Gettysburg itself, some blacks who were surprised and didn't have time to flee the oncoming Confederates hid for days in homes or under porches. Some traded freedom for work for the occupying Southerners. Some escaped. On July 1, a white boy named Albertus McCreary said he saw several black Gettysburg residents rounded up and marched out of the borough, some "crying and moaning" as they were pushed along. Among them was Liz, who did the McCreary's laundry. "Good bye, we are going back into slavery," Liz called out to Albertus. But she escaped as she passed by a Lutheran church, and she hid for three days in the belfry without food and water.[12]

Lincoln's administration was fully aware of the terror that Lee's army was spreading. Headlines warning of impending doom from Northern newspapers added to the uncertainty and panic among civilians. Correspondents were doing the best they could to describe the situation, but events were fluid. Censorship and snipped telegraph lines made filing difficult, and the scale of Lee's invasion and Hooker's response made it impossible to draw a full picture. On June 18, Lincoln's general-in-chief Henry Halleck telegraphed Hooker with a plea born of frustration. Halleck wanted better intelligence from Hooker: "Rumors from Pennsylvania are too confused and too contradictory to be relied upon. Officers and citizens are on a big stampede." Hooker responded with a request to beef up signal-officer stations on South Mountain, 10 miles northwest of Frederick, Maryland.[13]

As June ended, Lee had decided to concentrate his forces near Cashtown, Pennsylvania, 8 miles northwest of Gettysburg. That same day, June 30, Meade was hoping to lure him into a trap along Pipe Creek, some 20 miles southeast of Gettysburg, on the border between Pennsylvania and Maryland.

Instead, the two armies were hours from blundering into one another for the most important battle of the Civil War.

CHAPTER 24

"The Sun Shining on a Piece of Hot Iron"

ON THE NIGHT OF JUNE 30, 1863, LT. BAYARD WILKESON AND HIS
father, Sam, were 23 miles apart. Sam, the recently named *New York
Times* correspondent, had made it to Frederick, Maryland, and Bayard
was camped just south of the Pennsylvania border. Each must have wondered where the other was in this massive movement of soldiers, stragglers, refugees, and journalists. Each had had a long, exhausting journey.

Bayard's weary 11th Corps was camped on the outskirts of Emmitsburg, Maryland, a town of roughly 1,000 people about 12 miles south of
Gettysburg. His Company G Battery had broken camp at Goose Creek,
Virginia, six days before, where they and the rest of the 11th Corps had
taken a short rest after steadily moving north from Chancellorsville, more
than 120 miles south of Gettysburg, on June 11. Since breaking camp at
Goose Creek, the 11th Corps had gone on a meandering march of more
than 50 miles to get to Emmitsburg.[1] Orders kept changing from Union
commanders trying to determine Lee's whereabouts and lure him into a
fight.

Until mid-June of 1863, Emmitsburg had been a tidy village best
known as the home of Mount St. Mary's College and Sister Elizabeth
Ann Seton, the first native-born American citizen to be canonized by the
Catholic Church. But on June 15, in a fire that started in a stable near
the town center, more than fifty buildings had been destroyed. Although
a local man was immediately arrested for starting it, some locals thought
the fire had been set by Rebel spies or that the town had been burned by a
Union sympathizer desiring to keep supplies away from Lee's advancing

army. Piles of smoldering ash greeted elements of the 11th Corps when they camped along Toms Creek east of the town two weeks later.[2] In retrospect, those ashes were a foreboding resting place for men who were spending their last night alive.

Before camping at Emmitsburg, Bayard's battery and the rest of the 11th Corps had passed through Frederick, which was still recovering from the aftermath of 10,000 wounded men hospitalized there after Antietam less than ten months earlier.

As the two giant armies moved north, piecemeal, that June, it was as if nature itself was recoiling from the man-made violence of the previous two years. A smothering heat wave and throat-choking drought had blistered the East Coast in the late spring. By mid-June, the drought broke and roads in Virginia, Maryland, and Pennsylvania turned to mire. Spectacular thunderstorms lit up several nights on the march, and rain intermingled with the fighting and the aftermath at Gettysburg itself. In fact, extreme weather had marked the campaigns of late 1862 and well into 1863. The previous fall had been warmer than normal; the winter of 1862–63 had more snow and lasted longer than normal. A heavy snowstorm along the Atlantic Seaboard on the last day of March had delayed farmers' planting.[3]

Between Chancellorsville and Gettysburg, the 11th Corps covered 20 miles on some days, and men rejoiced at the cooler weather and overcast skies that came with the drought-breaking rains. Captain Dodge, the New Yorker who had expressed so little faith in Howard, constantly tried to keep a wet sponge in his hat. To beat the heat, some marches began with a 3:00 a.m. wakeup. Men in both armies wore out their shoes and had to try to keep up the march with ugly and dangerous blisters.

But it was not all suffering. The New Yorkers in Bayard's 11th Corps marveled at the marble columns and plantation houses and the majestic old oaks that lined Virginia roadsides. "In this lovely country it is impossible to turn any way without beholding something pleasing to one's sense of beauty," Dodge wrote before a 20-mile march to Catlett's Station on June 13.[4]

But the heat occasionally came down like a heavy blanket, and officers worried about its effect on the fighting capabilities of their units.

On June 18, as the 11th Corps camped at Goose Creek, near Leesburg, Virginia, its commander Howard wrote in his journal that it was "almost too hot for campaigning."[5] His men had just marched 54 miles in five days to reach that temporary billet near Leesburg. The night before, some of his men had slaughtered an entire flock of a farmer's sheep and many in the 11th Corps feasted on mutton.[6]

On dry days, the 11th Corps created dust clouds that could be seen for miles across the Virginia and Maryland countryside. Men suffering from heat exhaustion were left behind to fend for themselves.

One private in the 11th Corps, Reuben Ruch of Company F of the 153rd Pennsylvania, a regiment whose fate would soon be forever intertwined with Bayard Wilkeson's, had just returned to duty after being hospitalized for typhoid fever for four months. The march north from Falmouth, Virginia, on June 12, almost killed Ruch.[7]

"The dust was from two to three inches deep, and one could see the heat waves curl up from the dry roads about 25 feet," he recalled of that day's march. The scene had "the appearance of the sun shining on a piece of hot iron. The wells and springs were about all dry, and the creeks very low. The clouds of dust would rise about 100 feet above us, and I was informed that these clouds of dust could be seen for miles."[8]

The next morning, awakened by bugles, they were on the road before dawn. "The dust is very plenty and we have to walk right in a cloud of it," said Pvt. John McMahon of the 136th New York, a farm boy who had wanted to be a preacher before the war. The previous day, while his regiment was resting near a place called Hartwood Church, he'd spent nearly an hour crossing dry creek bed after dry creek bed in search of fresh water. The heat was oppressive. "I never sweat so much in my life," McMahon wrote in his diary.[9]

Some collapsed or died of heat exhaustion along the way. On June 20, a private in the 1st Minnesota Regiment of the Union army's 2nd Corps wrote his hometown newspaper that "there have been no less than 70 men who fell dead out of this corps" from "hard marching and excessive heat."[10] Eleven days later, the Minnesota regiment's reward for that hard marching was to be placed in some of the battle of Gettysburg's toughest fighting; it suffered more than 50 percent casualties among its 420 men.[11]

At one brief stop outside of Goose Creek, Ruch pulled off his boots and socks and a patch of skin the size of "an old fashion copper cent" came off in one. To make the march more miserable, the men also carried heavy packs, a hint of what was to come. Men were ordered to carry three days' food rations and one hundred rounds of ammunition; Ruch sardonically noted that the people in charge always made sure ammunition was more plentiful than the food. As the 11th Corps snaked north, day after day, he was so ill and suffering from the heavy heat that he often straggled late into camp late at night, long after his companions had settled in for a short night's rest.[12]

Spies hung on the fringes and deserters were rounded up and executed. Near the tiny crossroads of Greenwich, Virginia, the 75th Ohio, commanded by Andrew Harris, a future governor of the Buckeye State, was ordered to temporarily halt. A wagon with three men in gray uniforms and three crude coffins was brought up. Men were ordered to dig three graves while the prisoners in the wagon hauled their caskets to edges of the freshly dug holes. The three had deserted the Union army and had been captured while wearing Confederate uniforms. They were shot and buried. "In ten minutes it was all over and the wagon drove away," said Pvt. William B. Southerton, of the 75th.[13]

At Goose Creek, engineers built bridges so the 11th Corps artillery could cross. The creek ran high and fast again after heavy rains before the corps broke camp there on June 19.

On June 24, the 11th Corps changed course. At 10:00 a.m. the head of the column headed out under orders to move toward Harpers Ferry, where a Union garrison was trying to hold out against part of Lee's army. But the next day, Howard was ordered to double back toward Sandy Hook, Maryland, east of Harpers Ferry, and Bayard's battery and the rest of the corps moved out at 4:00 a.m.

Bayard's 11th Corps cut a wide swath but civilians welcomed them, even as they, too, suffered. The corps crossed the Potomac at Edwards Ferry on the morning of June 25, and on one of the longest marches on the way to Gettysburg, they passed Poolesville, Maryland, where women and children stood on front steps and waved flags and handkerchiefs. It was the first time many of the men had ever seen such support on the march.[14]

Camped near Jefferson, Maryland, that night of June 25 after a 24-mile march, Wilkeson's battery and the rest of the 11th Corps ended up in a farmer's field. As Ruch recounted, the farmer, hearing of the approach of thousands of men, tried to preempt their scavenging for wood for cooking fires by hauling three wagon loads of logs into a field where scouts had marked the camp for that night. But the farmer was too late and far too short in his offerings. By the time he arrived, the 11th Corps had torn down a quarter mile of his fences.[15]

More frequent rains by then had turned the dirt roads from dust into 4–6 inches of mud. But spirits were sometimes lifted by civilian hospitality. Bayard's battery got another heroes' welcome as they passed through Jefferson, 8 miles southwest of Frederick. "The band struck up a jig, the boys gave a cheer, and the ladies waved their handkerchiefs," Private Ruch said. "And the remarks made were, 'who wouldn't be a soldier?'"[16]

Other Union corps were boosted by similar scenes. Approaching the Potomac, the 1st Corps, which included the famous Iron Brigade, was met by farm families lining the road with loaves of bread, fresh milk, and cherries. A farm wife, in tears, yelled out as they passed: "You poor boys don't know what's ahead of you. I'm afraid many of ye'all be dead or mangled soon." Someone yelled back, "God bless you, old lady."[17]

On the night of Saturday June 26, still in the narrow Middletown Valley, the 11th Corps camped near the farm of a family named Cookerly. Rows upon rows of dirty-white tents from the 11th, 1st, and 3rd Corps covered the fields on both sides of the road to Boonsboro. The sight reminded one observer of "a hundred circling camps." Some men from the 1st Corps visited the South Mountain battleground at Turner's Gap where the Iron Brigade had gotten its nickname in a nasty fight leading to the battle of Antietam the previous September. The graves of many men they knew were by then overgrown with grass, and the crude wooden headboards marking them had been worn by the weather.[18]

The 141st Pennsylvania, which would be virtually wiped out in fighting at Gettysburg's famous peach orchard five days later, was treated to a feast brought by nearby farm families. They sang patriotic songs as night fell.[19]

On the 26th, Bayard and the 11th Corps passed over previous battlefields near South Mountain and Burkittsville, Maryland, where a field
was pocked with scores of fresh graves of New Jersey troops. Undeterred
by the sight, the men broke out of column to pick cherries from nearby
groves. Blackberries and raspberries were ripening in the heat, and the
men gorged on them, too. On the night of the 27th, a brigade of Union
cavalry arrived in their camp. The 11th Corps rank and file—filled with
many men far from teetotalers themselves—thought these horse soldiers
were the drunkest group of soldiers they had ever seen. "I saw two privates trying to keep an officer in the saddle," Ruch remembered. "I also
saw officers trying to keep a private in the saddle. . . . I was informed
they had struck a distillery, but I think the distillery must have struck
them."[20]

By then, Howard—fighting more and more with the War Department back in Washington, where his superiors seemed unsure and
uneasy—was ordered to take his corps on a more easterly course toward
Middletown, Maryland. Hooker, too, was fighting with his superiors. He
and Halleck, in charge of all Union forces, had disagreed on Hooker's
original intention to send part of his army to Harpers Ferry to confront
Lee after receiving reports of parts of Lee's army crossing there. As those
disagreements mounted, Hooker's relationship with Lincoln soured.
The disagreement over Harpers Ferry was one too many. Hooker was
removed from command.

Fresh rain came down with the news of Hooker's removal on June
28. After crossing a swollen Potomac into Maryland near Sandy Hook,
the 11th Corps camped in a clover field. It rained so hard "I thought we
would drown in the fields," said Private Southerton of the 75th Ohio,
whose regiment would fight near Bayard Wilkeson's battery on the
deadly afternoon of July 1 at Gettysburg.[21]

The next day, while eating fresh bread and butter supplied to their
regiment by two local women, the men of the 75th heard cries of "spy"
ring out through adjacent units. A man posing as a Quaker who had
been following the army had been discovered to have Confederate orders
hidden in the heels of a boot. A rope was strung over a large walnut tree
and soon the suddenly barefoot man was hanging, "his long black coat

flapping in the wind." Men fought over souvenir buttons and pieces of cloth from the black coat.[22]

That Sunday, June 28, a day of worship was overwhelmed by a sense of foreboding and some decidedly unholy work. Church bells rang continuously as spread out Union columns passed through northern Maryland towns and villages. Roughly 50 miles away on the other side of Gettysburg, Dick Ewell's Confederate corps—including the divisions of Robert Rodes and the irascible Jubal Early—also heard the peal of bells.[23] At York, Pennsylvania, any sense of holiness did not stop Early from demanding a ransom of $100,000 (although he received less than $30,000), three days' rations, 2,000 pairs of boots, 1,000 felt hats, and 1,000 pairs of socks from the good citizens.[24]

The Confederates then converging toward Cashtown were plumped up with fresh Pennsylvania provisions and filled with the cockiness of recently victorious invaders. Henry Heth's division camped roughly a dozen miles northwest of Gettysburg on June 28, less than thirty-six hours before it would run into Buford's Union cavalry and light the battle flame for good. Heth's men were luxuriating in the spoils.

"We are getting up all the horses and feeding our army with their beef and flour, etc., but there are strict orders about the interruption of any private property by individual soldiers," Virginia's Col. William Christian of Heth's division, a doctor in civilian life, wrote that day, in a letter discovered on the Gettysburg battlefield at week's end. "Though with these orders pigs and fowl don't stand much chance."[25]

Christian, who had been slightly wounded at Chancellorsville, said his corps was rumored to be heading to Gettysburg the next day. "We are paying back these people for some of the damage they have done to us, though we are not doing them half as bad as they done us," Christian wrote.

Yet Christian also had a fit of conscience on this Sabbath. He concluded he could not exact the revenge he desired because of the fear he saw in the eyes of the Northern civilians. Furthermore, he could not participate in the slave-hunting that other men in his division were doing.

"We took a lot of negroes yesterday," Christian wrote. "I was offered my choice, but as I could not get them back home I would not take them.

In fact, my humanity revolted at taking the poor devils away from their homes. They were so scared that I turned them all loose."[26]

He knew the stakes. "A defeat here would be ruinous," he wrote in the unsent letter to his wife. "This army has never done such fighting as it will do now, and if we can whip the armies that are now gathering to oppose us, we will have every thing in our own hands. We must conquer a peace. If we can come out of this country triumphant and victorious, having established a peace, we will bring back to our own land the greatest joy that ever crowned a people. We will show the Yankees this time how we can fight." He was captured eleven days after the battle.[27]

In Carlisle that Sunday, Confederate general Dick Ewell's staff presided over a flag-raising ceremony which replaced the flag of the United States with that of a North Carolina regiment. After it was over many men got passes to attend churches in the town. Some ended up at the Presbyterian church, where the minister did not mention the war but did ask for God's help for everyone in authority. Some of Ewell's men recognized the minister from a previous appointment in Alabama.[28]

That same Sabbath, Bayard Wilkeson's 11th Corps camped outside of Frederick. The men got the same heroes' welcome in Frederick that they had received in Jefferson two days earlier. "People (were) on balconies, in open door-ways, in side streets, throngs cheering and waving flags," Private Southerton recalled. "We felt proud and important."[29]

Frederick was overwhelmed again. Its population of 8,000 would end up hosting wounded men continuously for almost the entire duration of the war. Shopkeeper Jacob Engelbrecht watched for hours as men of the 11th Corps and other corps marched past his storefront. He talked with many of the young men as they passed. Many called out the battles they had fought in. "The streets are chucked full of wagons & cavalry and infantry," Engelbrecht wrote in his diary at 10:30 a.m. on Monday, June 29. He estimated that along with thousands of men marching through, that 300–400 cannons, and 1,000 wagons had passed by, "and still they are passing the door."[30]

Two days later, just as Henry Heth's Southerners and John Buford's Northerners fired the first shots at Gettysburg, Engelbrecht wrote that "all Pennsylvania & Maryland are in a general commotion," and that "we rub along in these revolutionary times." He hoped that "the day of retribution will speedily overtake the commencers of this wicked Rebellion."[31]

The 11th Corps kept moving. On the march north of Frederick to Emmitsburg on June 29, some 11th Corps men again broke ranks to pluck ripening cherries from a farmer's grove. "Was that a hot, humid day," Private Southerton remembered. "Miles and miles, with so little rest."[32] They marched almost 40 miles in twenty-four hours, stopping only for a midday meal, arriving in Emmitsburg late in the afternoon of the 29th.

The 11th, many of them New Yorkers and New Englanders, marveled again at the country as they approached Pennsylvania. Ripening wheat fields stretched like amber-colored oceans on both sides of the muddy roads. "The country here is the best I have ever seen," McMahon, of the 136th New York, wrote in his diary on the night of June 29. "It will beat our land at home." He had been sick on and off for days, but that long march, although making his feet terribly sore, seemed to invigorate him.[33]

In the 11th Corps ranks, the changing directions and monotonous marching in the heat were confusing and frustrating, but nothing new to the veterans. The urgency of movement had raised expectations of an imminent fight, but as the march grew longer, morale suffered. On the 28th, of June, word came down that Lincoln had replaced Hooker with Meade.

While his men were preparing to camp at Emmitsburg, Howard was ordered to a meeting with the new commanding general of the Union army in Frederick. Some commanders of other Union corps rolled their eyes when the devout Howard offered a pre-meeting prayer.[34]

Meade, nicknamed "The Old Snapping Turtle" for his stern look, sharp nose, and balding head, laid out a plan that included orders for Howard's 11th Corps to support John Reynolds's 1st Corps as both marched north into Pennsylvania. The ultimate goal of seven converging Union corps was to lure Lee into a trap at Pipe Creek, just south of the Mason-Dixon Line. Roughly 20 miles southeast of Gettysburg, Pipe Creek was near a vital rail supply head at Westminster, Maryland. The Pipe Creek Circular, as the battle plan was called, would ultimately prove to be Meade's pipe dream.

Meade and Howard, both products of the army's engineering corps, were no strangers. They had traveled together before the war when Meade directed U.S. Army engineering and topographical work in New York's Finger Lakes. Going into the council on June 28 in Frederick, Howard worried whether this new commander was up to the task, but Howard came away feeling more assured. Meade, he said, "looked tall and spare, weary, and a little flushed, but I knew him to be a good, honest soldier, and gathered confidence and hope from his honest face."[35]

To many of his fellow commanding officers, Howard came across as more interested in religion than in soldiering. His troops called him "Old Prayer Book" behind his back.[36] He was undeterred. The important thing was "not how people see me, but I wonder how God sees me," he often said.[37]

No one questioned Howard's personal courage. Although outgeneraled and caught by surprise by Jackson at Chancellorsville, he had courageously stood in the sleet of Confederate fire raking his lines and tried to rally his men. At Seven Pines the year before, as Howard was hauled off the battlefield with a shredded arm, he had run into Union general Phil Kearny, who had lost his left arm in the Mexican War. "Well General, I will buy gloves with you now," Howard joked.[38]

Perhaps in part because of his heroism at Seven Pines, Howard was kept in command of the 11th Corps despite the debacle at Chancellorsville. Now on June 30, Howard could sense that his corps was about to get a chance to redeem itself.

One of Howard's new division commanders was Barlow, and the two men had a history. Barlow had taken over Howard's command at Seven Pines when Howard had gone down. Howard recommended Barlow as a "worthy man" and "a most excellent disciplinarian and tactician."[39]

Premonitions abounded on the 11th Corps's march to Gettysburg. Two days after the June 28 council with Meade, as Bayard's Battery G and the rest of the 11th Corps camped at Emmitsburg, the 1st Corps commander John Reynolds summoned Howard to Reynolds's headquarters 3 miles north of the town. There, in a sparse room in what Howard described as a small cottage along Marsh Run, the two generals went over Meade's latest communique. In it, Howard felt that Meade had urged "every patriotic sentiment which he felt assured would arouse to enthusiasm and action his whole army, now on the threshold of the battlefield—a field which he felt might decide the fate of the Republic."[40]

But Meade's intelligence of Lee's intentions was "abundant and conflicting," forcing Howard to the uneasy conclusion that "Lee's infantry and artillery in great force were in our neighborhood."[41] Exactly where was anyone's guess. Howard and Reynolds talked until 11:00 p.m., and both men had a sense that history was about to play big before them. The two men were "discussing the probabilities of a great battle, and talking about the part our wing would play in a great battle," Howard recounted in his memoirs.

Reynolds, Howard wrote, "seemed depressed, almost as if he had a presentiment of his death so near at hand."[42]

Howard's brother and aide, Capt. Charles H. Howard, had come along. He described Reynolds as "a tall, vigorous man of quick motion and nervous temperament." On this night, though, Howard seemed "paler than usual" and "keenly alive to the responsibility resting upon him."[43]

Such premonitions were widespread throughout the war, and all the way up to the commander-in-chief. Ten days before his assassination in 1865, Abraham Lincoln would dream about hovering over his body as it was lying in state. The dream was so vivid—he described "pitiful sobbing" by mourners lining up to see him—that it left Lincoln shaken. He told friends that a "deathlike stillness" had descended over him.[44]

"Deathlike stillness" was the precise phrase that Robert E. Lee's aide, A. L. Long, would use to describe the calm that came over the battlefield at Gettysburg just before Pickett's Charge.

The deeply religious Oliver Otis Howard had no bad premonitions, perhaps because he had received a boost in spirit and flesh on the eve of the battle of Gettysburg. Another brother, the Reverend R. B. Howard, a member of the Christian Commission, a by then very active aid organization that followed the armies around to give comfort in camp and after battles, joined his brother at Emmitsburg after a 45-mile ride that included several close calls with marauding bushwhackers.[45] Besides its calming effect on Howard, his minister-brother's arrival was evidence of how private aid organizations were pre-positioning for the aftermath of the killing that seemed imminent.

What was left of Emmitsburg had already been stirred up by Reynolds's 1st Corps by the time Bayard's battery passed through. On the battle's eve, some brigades of Reynolds's corps had delayed their march to Marsh Run to wait for paymasters to come with their thirteen-dollar monthly pay. A minor ruckus broke out when paymasters for some units were delayed. Throughout the 11th Corps's stay at Emmitsburg, activity in the town kept building. Although Meade had shifted shipments of supplies to Westminster in anticipation of a fight closer to Pipe Creek, Emmitsburg had also become a major supply nexus of the Union army. Tons of food, ammunition, and other material were being assembled there. On the evening of June 30, Lt. Bayard Wilkeson and the rest of the 11th Corps settled in for a second night with the ash of burned-out buildings still in the air, and the sounds of teamsters, creaking supply wagons, ambulances, and herds of mooing beef cattle.[46]

The people of Emmitsburg did their best to be hospitable. By 1863, Emmitsburg was a well-known charitable and religious center, anchored by the St. Joseph's and St. Mary's Catholic churches. It had the first Catholic school in the nation, founded by the Sisters of Charity of St. Joseph. For two nights, Howard slept in a bed at Mount St. Mary's College, a welcome respite from the hot tents of his headquarters.

It had been raining when the 11th Corps arrived at Emmitsburg on the evening of the 29th, but that did not stop a large welcoming party from assembling. Some of the young men from the college marched along with the arriving troops. Some men in the 11th Corps had marched so long and so hard they had taken their shoes off because their swollen and blistered feet would no longer fit in them.[47]

On the night of the 30th, there was unusual tension in the 11th Corps ranks. Some men tried to calm their nerves by feasting on fresh onions pulled from a town garden.[48] The evening was cloudy, leading to the tension and sense of foreboding. Guards were trigger happy. Lt. Clyde Miller of the 153rd Pennsylvania was ordered to send out pickets as night fell. It was a "murky and misty night," and after sitting for hours he thought he saw Rebels creeping toward him in the cornfield in his front. He left to scout, telling his pickets that he would whistle "Yankee Doodle" upon his return so they would not shoot him. He found nothing on his brief scouting mission, but before he got back within whistle range a few of his pickets fired a volley of musket shots. There was stirring as men braced for a reaction, but silence persisted, the threat deemed false. At sunrise, Miller's pickets saw the harvest of their volley: dead sheep littering the field in front of them. It was the last moment of levity for the day. Within hours, these men, Wilkeson's shells screaming overhead so closely they could feel the heat, would be shooting at Rebel-yelling men much closer and in far greater numbers than the harmless animals heaped in front of them.[49]

On the morning of July 1, Howard, who had been so gloomy about the fitness of his corps after their devastating defeat at Chancellorsville, tried to buck up his own confidence. On the march north, he had become slowly more encouraged by the better discipline his corps was showing. Like a snake shedding old skin for new, he hoped the 11th was letting loose the humiliation of Chancellorsville the farther it moved toward Maryland and Pennsylvania. It certainly had marched on as a more disciplined unit, covering more than 120 miles in eighteen days. "This corps has marched in very orderly style and all my orders are obeyed with great alacrity," Howard wrote in his diary shortly before arriving at Emmitsburg.[50]

But in the ranks the men were not nearly as optimistic. Lt. Bayard Wilkeson fretted that his largely untested battery was demoralized by false alarms and confusion at the top. His battery had been ordered to prepare for an imminent fight twice on the march from Chancellorsville to Goose Creek and once while encamped there. His men were excited at the prospect of those fights, but when they were proven to be false alarms, men began going "around with faces a yard long," Bayard wrote his father, admitting that his own morale had suffered. "My lieutenants and I are just as badly off, and the whole Company is in a very dissatisfied state," he fretted.[51]

CHAPTER 25

"Pandemonium!"

By the evening of June 30, Frederick, Maryland, had the appearance of one large bar fight. Bayard's 11th Corps had passed through it five days earlier. Now his father arrived, and what he and fellow war correspondents who converged there saw appalled them. The numbers of stragglers and looters was staggering. Maj. Gen. Henry Slocum, whose 12th Corps had passed through Frederick two days before, was shocked at what he had seen. "There were a great many men of every corps around the army lying about the streets, beastly drunk," he wrote Meade shortly after Meade had taken overall command of the army. Slocum urged Meade to send cavalry units to the town to move the stragglers along.[1] Meade would have been excused for wondering what he'd gotten himself into.

"Pandemonium!" was how the colorful correspondent Whitelaw Reid described Frederick when he, Sam Wilkeson, and Uriah Painter of the *Philadelphia Inquirer* arrived together on the night of June 30. If anything, the debauchery of stragglers and army camp followers had become worse than Slocum had described it just forty-eight hours before. Mere drunkenness had moved into larceny and worse. Frederick had not yet recovered from the economic and human disaster of Antietam of the previous fall. Besides the burden of caring for 10,000 wounded soldiers, some of them who had languished in makeshift hospitals for months, the two armies had also swept through in the fall of 1862 on their way to Antietam, just as crops of grain and fruit were being harvested. The armies tried to pay for some of what they took, the Confederates offering largely worthless script, but the economic shock on Frederick and the surrounding countryside had been immeasurable. Now Union columns passing through Frederick to head off Lee were once again leaving destruction in their wake.[2]

"Somebody has blundered frightfully," Reid wrote in his dispatch from Frederick. "Scores of drunken soldiers are making night hideous; all over the town they are trying to steal horses, or sneak into unwatched private residences, or are filling the air with the blasphemy of their drunken brawls. The worst elements of a great army are here in their worst condition; its cowards, its thieves, its sneaks, its bullying vagabonds, all inflamed with whiskey, and drunk as well with their freedom from accustomed restraint."[3]

This was what Charlie Coffin, the hard-charging *Boston Journal* correspondent, called the "driftwood" of the Civil War armies. Some soldiers straggled because they could not keep up, others straggled to take advantage of the chaos of the aftermath, some straggled to stay away from the fighting. The latter group was "reliant at the mess table, brave in the story around the bivouac fire, but faint of heart when the battle begins," Coffin wrote.[4]

And the Union army's record-keeping left something to be desired. After the battle, when Mrs. Sara J. Ackerman of Rochester, New York, wrote the commander of her husband's 108th New York about his whereabouts—he had been listed as missing—Lt. Col. F. E. Pierce responded on July 28.

"I do not know where he is," Pierce wrote. "He fell out near Frederick, when we were advancing against Lee, and is probably working for some farmer in Md. or snugly stowed in some hospital. You may be certain of one thing—that your husband will never be killed by a rebel shell or bullet, as he was never yet in a fight and probably will never get near enough to be badly injured."[5]

But the chaos that Reid was describing at Frederick was unsettling. This was the tail of the army that was going to meet Lee and save the capital and the Union? It was a scary, treacherous, vulnerable moment for the North, and the correspondents had tried to capture the mood.

Reid's dispatch from Washington the day before had been full of foreboding. On the streets and in the salons of the second guessers, there was searing criticism of the timing of Lincoln's removal of Hooker in favor of Meade as a great battle loomed. Reid lit into Army chief Henry Halleck's role in Hooker's axing, over what his sources were saying was the cause—high command tactical contretemps over whether or not Hooker should have gone after Lee's tail at Harpers Ferry.

"Washington was all abuzz with the removal," Reid wrote. "A few idol-worshipers hissed their exultation at the constructive disgrace; but for the most part there was astonishment at the unprecedented act and indignation at the one cause to which all attributed it."[6]

Reid reported that when news of the firing hit, Washington "for once forgot its blasé air, and through a few hours, there was genuine excitement. The two or three Congressmen who were in town were indignant (over Hooker's removal) and scarcely tried to conceal it; the crowds talked over the strange affairs in all its phases; a thousand false stories were put in circulation, the basest of which was that Hooker had been relieved for a fortnight's continuous drunkenness; rumors of other changes, as usual, came darkening the very air."[7]

Reid concluded that Hooker was the victim of a rash and ill-advised decision by a "parlor chieftain, in his quiet study, three score miles from the hourly changing field."[8]

The worry about the threat on Washington, DC, and other major eastern cities had hit a crescendo just as the 11th Corps approached Frederick. On June 27, a *Chicago Journal* correspondent reported out of Washington that "the news from the front . . . Is more threatening today," that "things look bad," and that "the destination of Lee is Washington, not Philadelphia." In the days leading into Gettysburg, Wilkeson and his colleagues in the press had been clear about what would happen if Lee won a victory in Pennsylvania. Washington, DC, the *Chicago Journal* correspondent wrote, was in an "unusual state of alarm." Harrisburg, Philadelphia, and Baltimore all braced for invasion.[9]

At least twenty war correspondents had planted themselves in Harrisburg under the belief that Pennsylvania's capital was Lee's eventual target. Wilkeson's intrepid *New York Times* colleague, Lorenzo Crounse, was one of them. Mocking the fantastical estimates of the size of Lee's army, Crounse added up the reports of all his colleagues and wrote that, if true, Lee had 500,000 men and 4,000 cannons about to descend on the Pennsylvania seat of government.[10] It was seven times the amount of men and roughly fifteen times the number of cannons Lee eventually brought to Gettysburg.

Government officials were taking no chances. On June 30, Secretary of War Stanton requested that Halleck place "batteries at the avenues of approach and at different points in" Washington, DC, and to "see that every possible means of security is adopted against any sudden raid or incursion, by day or by night."[11]

But Lee had no immediate intentions of heading back south, and even as the battle of Gettysburg approached, there was a sense that other Pennsylvania cities had been temporarily spared. A Wilkeson colleague at *The New York Times* sensed it at Harrisburg as the armies were inexorably congregating toward Gettysburg.

"The day has passed, and the enemy has not made an attempt to capture this city," the *Times* correspondent wrote from the Pennsylvania capital. "The present quiet state of affairs was certainly not looked for by the inhabitants this morning. Everyone expected to hear the sound of musketry and the roar of cannon sometime during the day."

The best he could tell, the correspondent wrote, was that the advance elements of Lee's army were 18 miles away, at Carlisle. "Perhaps, after all, the rebels do not intend to occupy Harrisburg," he wrote.[12] By the time this dispatch was printed in the paper, Lee's army was fighting at Gettysburg.

A correspondent for the *Baltimore American* reported that Meade's decision to continue moving some of his army corps north had also lessened the fear of an attack on Baltimore or Washington.

"Gen. Meade, as soon as he took command, issued orders for a general movement, and in a few hours relieved both Baltimore and Washington of all present fear of rebel invasion," the *American* reported. "We apprehend that there is not a rebel in arms within thirty miles of Baltimore, and none on this side of the Potomac within a similar distance of Washington." The paper speculated: "There is a probability that a great battle will be fought in the course of the present week in the neighborhood probably of Hanover or Gettysburg."[13]

The dispatch also said that damage to the Baltimore and Ohio Railroad and to telegraph lines by marauding Confederate cavalry had been repaired, that a damaged rail bridge over Piney Run had been fixed, and that "the train which left this morning for Frederick and Harpers Ferry has gone through without interruption."[14]

Reid, Sam Wilkeson, and Painter, the chief Washington correspondent for the *Inquirer*, all were on that train. They had left Washington, DC, in the morning that Tuesday, June 30, switched trains at Baltimore, and then caught an express to Frederick, hoping to catch up to Meade. They were quite the trio, all well known through all ranks of the Army of the Potomac.

Reid was daring, prolific, a talented and entertaining writer, with a love of adventure. For his part, Reid described Wilkeson as "well-known and brilliant," and Painter as "a miracle of energy."[15] Painter was a lobbyist as well as a journalist, but he had had a few big scoops of his own, being among the first to report the truth of the disastrous Union loss at First Manassas. In later life he would befriend both Thomas Edison and Alexander Graham Bell.[16] Charles Carleton Coffin, the *Boston Journal* correspondent, another reporter who liked to be in the middle of the action, had telegraphed Reid asking to "meet me in the army."[17] Some of the greatest correspondents of the war, sensing that a pivotal battle of history was about to break out at any time, were desperately trying to get to the fighting before it began.

But where and when would it happen, and how best could they get there in time? Civil War armies on the eve of battle were festering hosts of rumor and disinformation, fringed with spies and know-it-alls and speculators for whom the truth was an accidental occurrence or some educated approximation of it.

By the time they arrived in Frederick on the night of June 30, Reid, Wilkeson, and Painter had already had a frustrating week of second-guessing, of tracing and retracing their steps through teeming, anxious Maryland. Hearing reports in Washington of a great battle about to break out somewhere along the Mason-Dixon Line, the three war correspondents had tried to reach Frederick by rail on Monday the 29th, the same day that Reid reported the signs of panic in the capital. The three men left Washington early that morning and arrived at Baltimore at 11:00 a.m., where they had expected to transfer to an afternoon train to Frederick. But the Baltimore agent Prescott Smith told them: "Am very sorry, gentlemen, would get you out at once if I could, would gladly run an extra train for you, but the rebels cut our road last night this side of Frederick, and we have no idea when we can run again."[18]

Returning to Washington that night, Reid recorded the palpable fear in the nation's capital. "Troops were marching; orderlies with clanking sabers clattering along the streets; trains of wagons grinding over the bouldered avenue; the commissaries were hurrying up their supplies; the quartermaster's department was like a bee-hive; every thing was motion and hurry."[19]

Amidst that nervous activity, the correspondents spent another restless night in the capital, then set out for Frederick again the next day. This time they made it, but not without more great adventure. Leaving Washington early Tuesday morning, June 30, Painter, Reid, and Sam Wilkeson caught another train to Baltimore. On the way to the station they passed a New England regiment whose nine months' enlistment had expired. The regiment was going home. Reid was appalled that the regiment was mustering out with the army on the brink of a potentially climactic battle, and after Lincoln had called for 100,000 militia—50,000 from Pennsylvania, 30,000 from Ohio, and 10,000 each from Maryland and pro-Union "Western Virginia"—to help turn back Lee.

Reid let rip his pen. He described the embarking New England regiment as a "blistering sight that should blacken every name concerned" because it came amid "cries for reinforcements from the weakened front, with calls for volunteers and raw militia to step into the imminent breach and defend the invaded North." But the regiment was going home. "Would that Stuart could capture the train that bears them," Reid wrote, disdainfully.[20]

The adventures and sights continued on their trip to Frederick. Upon reaching Baltimore midday of the battle's eve, Wilkeson, Reid, and Painter were told that the rail line to Frederick had been repaired from the damage inflicted by Stuart's cavalry. While awaiting transfer in Baltimore, the three correspondents jotted in their notebooks scenes of a city still in the throes of war panic, despite the local newspaper's report that the danger had passed. Baltimore was being overrun with what Reid described as "improvised soldierly" of regular troops, militia, and citizens. The correspondent interviewed residents who told them that reports of Rebel cavalry passing near the city the night before had set off a fresh panic. "Frightened persons had rushed in with the story that great squadrons of horse were just ready to charge down the streets," Reid reported.[21]

As they waited for the train to Frederick, Wilkeson, Reid, and Painter came across a small boy throwing pebbles at a pig running wild in the street. The boy was mostly missing the pig, but he was hitting freshly erected barricades of empty tar and sugar barrels that volunteers had filed with sand and topped with fence rails to slow down any attacking Confederates.

Ever the wit, Wilkeson called out to the child. "Small boy," Wilkeson chided the urchin, "you must stop that, sir! You are destroying the defenses of Baltimore."[22]

Later, as the train to Frederick pulled out of town, they noticed more substantial earthworks that had been built around the city overnight.

Although the train to Frederick was supposed to be a special for war correspondents heading toward Meade's army, it soon filled with people of all interests and pursuits, also hoping to intersect with whatever was about to happen. Along the way, the correspondents soaked up every bit of information and rumor they could hear. Some travelers had heard Lee had already reached York (parts of his army had), that the Union army had left Frederick far behind and was fanning out on all available roads to head him off (largely true), that this general was seen here or that Confederate regiment reported there (unsubstantiated in the fog of war). It was uncorroborated and raw, and in the end, each correspondent had only his intuition and gut to rely on. On a human level, though, it ought to have made the correspondents more sympathetic to Meade and to Lee, who were then commanding vast movements of men toward unknowable fates and certain fury on the muddy roads of Maryland and Pennsylvania.

CHAPTER 26

"Hard Times at Gettysburg"

AFTER SPENDING THE NIGHT IN FREDERICKSBURG AMIDST THE PANDE-
monium, Whitelaw Reid decided to break off from Sam Wilkeson and
Uriah Painter the next morning, July 1, 1863. He got lucky. Reid procured a horse and caught up with the tail of the Union army as it moved
north. Wilkeson and Painter took a gamble that the battle would be east
or southeast of where it was even then breaking out without their knowledge. Although the sounds of the guns at Gettysburg were eventually
heard dozens of miles away, Frederick—35 miles south of the Pennsylvania town—was a little too far that sultry July morning for them to hear
thunder in the distance.

Acting on rumors of Meade's Pipe Creek trap plans, Wilkeson
and Painter doubled back to Westminster, about 20 miles northwest of
Frederick. It had become an important railroad junction for Meade's
supplies and, had his original battle plans gone the way he wanted them,
Wilkeson and Painter would have been perfectly situated for the climactic battle of the war. But Reid was the lucky one. While it took Sam
Wilkeson the entire day to get to the battlefield at Gettysburg, Reid was
almost immediately caught up in the great rush of action at Gettysburg
on July 1.

Bayard Wilkeson's second in command, Eugene Bancroft, said he ran
into Sam Wilkeson at Gettysburg on the night of July 1.[1] Most likely,
Sam arrived around midnight or in the early overnight hours as the battle's first day concluded in anxious preparation for a second. While Reid's
gamble to head north out of Gettysburg paid off, allowing him to almost

immediately catch up with the 11th and 1st Corps at Gettysburg, Sam Wilkeson's and Painter's gamble on Pipe Creek put them behind from the beginning.

Although Reid made the best choice, his day was no picnic. Riding hard, he eventually caught up with the lead elements of Meade's army that ended up doing the bulk of the fighting that day. One of those was Bayard Wilkeson's Battery G of the 11th Corps's First Division.

Sam never publicly described how he got to the field, nor did it show up in known correspondence to family, and for good reason. Events of far greater importance to him and the country were unfolding faster than he could keep track, and the importance of what would follow overwhelmed any details of his own journey to Gettysburg. But if Reid's trip to the battlefield was any indication, Sam's road to Gettysburg was arduous and exhausting, begun by rail but almost certainly finished on horseback or on foot.

While Sam and Painter took the train back to Westminster, Reid, on a freshly procured horse, quickly overtook Union stragglers streaming out of Frederick. Soon, he ran across a messenger for another newspaper, and together, they steadily gained on the stream of federal stragglers heading north toward Emmitsburg and into Pennsylvania. Reid heaped scorn on these "skulkers" and "skeedaddlers" of a great army.

"Take a worthless vagabond who has enlisted for thirteen dollars a month instead of patriotism, who falls out of ranks because he is a coward and wants to avoid the battle, or because he is lazy and wants to steal a horse to ride on instead of marching, or because he is rapacious and wants to sneak about farm-houses and frighten and wheedle timid countrywomen into giving him better goods and lodging than camp-life affords—make this armed coward or sneak or thief drunk on bad whisky, give him scores and hundreds of armed companions as desperate and drunken as himself—turn loose this motley crew, muskets and revolvers in hand, into a rich country, with quiet, peaceful inhabitants, all unfamiliar with armies and army ways—let them swagger and bully as cowards and vagabonds always do, steal or openly plunder as such thieves always will—and then, if you can imagine the state of things this would produce, you have the condition of the country in the rear of our own army, on our own soil, today."[2]

From this flotsam, Reid had picked up intelligence that Meade had set up his headquarters at Taneytown, east of the main columns of federals. Reid and his messenger-companion rode cross-country to find the newly installed commanding general of the Army of the Potomac in a cluster of tents roughly 14 miles southeast of Gettysburg. Meade was seated on a camp stool inside the open flap of a tent, bent over a map. The camp seemed pulled between furtive movement and contemplative repose and always seemed on the verge of picking up and moving, although Meade spent most of the battle's first day here. "Slender baggage is all packed, every body is ready to take to the saddle at a moment's notice," Reid noted. "Engineers are busy with their maps; couriers are coming in with reports, the trustiest counselors on the staff are with the general." Yet Meade, in grizzled beard, struck Reid at that moment "rather as a thoughtful student than as a dashing soldier."

Moments after Reid and his companion arrived in camp, up rode Crounse, Sam Wilkeson's *New York Times* colleague. Crounse, who had mocked the rumors about the size of Lee's army, was mighty excited at finally seeing it in Pennsylvania. He had found Lee's army, he said, where hard fighting at a "little post village" an hour's hard ride up the road was at that moment raging.[3]

Crounse later was one of the first reporters to get the crushing news of the death of the revered Reynolds, the 1st Corps commander.[4] As he had headed out of Gettysburg toward Meade's headquarters, Crounse had run into 11th Corps soldiers on a trot headed the opposite direction toward the sound of the guns. The 11th Corps was pushing north on the double quick along the Emmitsburg Road and on fields on either side, and Bayard's battery was near the lead of the column. That was a march that no man forgot.

Bayard Wilkeson's 11th Corps—down to roughly 8,700 men fit for duty on the morning of the battle[5]—had been aroused for breakfast at dawn in Emmitsburg. But in the heavy air it took time to shake off the lethargy and the weariness of three weeks of marching. Bayard's battery and most of the corps did not get on the road until well after sunrise. Tensions were rising, and while many men in the ranks still found it hard to believe that Rebels were that far north, the officers could sense from the higher command that a big fight was coming that day. And the significance of the ground was becoming very apparent, and heartfelt. At 9:00 a.m., as the 153rd Pennsylvania fell in line to begin the march, a captain, tears streaming down his cheeks, silently went down the line and shook the hand of every man in his command.[6] Later, intermittent rain showers along the march felt as if the heavens were weeping, too. Those showers turned the morning air into a sauna, and they further muddied the roads for thousands of trampling feet.

Howard had gotten Meade's orders to join Reynolds's 1st Corps and head toward Gettysburg by messenger in the middle of the night. The general had just fallen asleep after his late-night meeting with Reynolds, and was savoring the bed at the Emmitsburg seminary. But now urgency came upon him. Be prepared to move to Gettysburg early in the morning, he was told.

At daybreak, Howard ordered Francis Channing Barlow's 1st Division of the 11th Corps to take the most direct route to Gettysburg, on the Emmitsburg Road. This was Bayard Wilkeson's division, and the road they were ordered to march on turned out to be one of the most difficult paths to the battlefield that day. It was ankle-deep in caking mud and clogged with stuck, broken, or barely moving 1st Corps supply wagons. Bayard's battery, according to his second in command, Lt. Eugene Bancroft, did not get moving until about 9:00 a.m. Creased and scarred by the wagons and caissons of Reynolds's 1st Corps and the thousands of pairs of feet that had already marched over it, softened by the humidity and previous days' rains, the Emmitsburg Road was a "road full of ruts and stone," Howard later complained. It took Barlow, normally "vigorous and pushing" in Howard's judgment, the rest of the morning to move his division to Gettysburg.[7]

Some men found beauty amid chaos on the march north that morning. Pvt. William A. Clark of the 17th Connecticut said that a rain that had fallen "like the old cat all night" on the night of the 29th had turned all roads around Emmitsburg into a gumbo-like soup. His regiment was up by 5:00 a.m., but did not cross into Pennsylvania until mid-morning. As the 17th crossed the border, the men saw a field of flax in full bloom, its gorgeous blue blossoms giving the impression of a gentle sea amidst the man-made chaos passing by.[8]

"The weather was hot, the main road obstructed and the men loaded with rations and ammunition," Howard wrote of his 11th Corps after the war. "Yet (Barlow's) 1st Division at the rate of two and a half miles an hour could complete its journey before 1 p.m. without fatigue."[9]

The 17th was given just one water stop on the 12-mile march. It arrived in Gettysburg just after noon, with Bayard's battery moving as fast as it could in the snaking columns of infantry and artillery right behind it. "Double quicked through the city. The first corps opened the fight we were sent off at the right and then the ball opened for us," Clark wrote.[10]

The 75th Ohio also was given a brief break on its march, and "the boys dropped to the ground almost like dead men, so terrific was the heat and humidity, and our heavy woolen uniforms so unbearable," said Pvt. William Southerton.[11]

As they moved north, news of Reynolds's death filtered through the ranks of the arriving 11th Corps, setting off a pique of sadness and fury. But the men barely had time to digest that bad news before it was ordered to pick up their pace. More men kept falling behind in the heat. Rickety ambulances kept pace, stopping to pick up those falling from heat exhaustion. Approaching the town, the men of the 11th Corps began discarding anything weighting them down. "Blanket, blouse, any article that could be disposed of was thrown away," Private Southerton said. "Fields along the way were dotted with the discard."[12]

For an army accustomed to the earth, the mud on the march to Gettysburg seemed especially nettlesome and cloying. Pvt. Stephen Romig, of Company F of the 153rd Pennsylvania Volunteers, described it as "the most particular sort of clay, being of a very sticky nature."

He found out how sticky it really was a few days later. Lying in a hospital tent after being shot in the knee on the battle's first day, Romig watched as an orderly struggled to remove his shoes. Mud and leather had coagulated into an indistinguishable, hard mass around his feet. Parts of his shoes had worn completely through from the hard marching. The dried clay mud from the July 1 march had filled the holes in the shoes, and it had been caked and baked in hard layers around it. At Romig's urging, the orderly cut away the mud and leather, but he did not have time to wash Romig's feet. The dirt was so embedded in Romig's skin that it took literally months for the earth of Gettysburg to wear and wash off.[13]

Men could hear what was in store for miles leading into the field. As men of the 1st Corps had moved north first, their first sounds of the battle sounded to cannoneer Augustus Buell like a pounding "boom boom boom" with intermittent crackles, like the "snapping of a dry brush-heap when you first set it on fire."[14] The fire, indeed, was starting.

The anticipation built all morning. 11th Corps private Reuben Ruch said the men were ordered to clean their guns as breakfast was being prepared, "as we might expect a skirmish before night." It was a "cloudy, close morning," he remembered. Captain Theodore Dodge felt his 119th New York appeared more "taciturny" than he ever remembered that morning, and to him the march to Gettysburg was one of the hardest of the war.

"The marching is wretched and the atmosphere so oppressively close that the men scarcely make any way at all," he wrote in his diary at a short break at 10:00 a.m. "If we march ten miles today we shall do well."[15] They would do 12 miles by midday, and then they would fight in close-in combat at the end of it. Dodge estimated that his regiment arrived in the battlefield around 2:00 p.m., roughly the time Bayard's battery had been able to push through Gettysburg. Approaching Gettysburg from the south, the "booming" that had gone on "sullenly" for miles on their approach became increasingly sharper, the lethality of war turning from a distant echo to an immediate challenge.[16]

Men on the march soon showed a change in attitude. Captain Dodge paid attention to make sure none of his soldiers were losing their nerve. But two years into the war, he also knew that those showing the most fear often became the fiercest fighters.

"Here one whose face may be a shade paler, but his eye is none the less lustrous, nor his lips less firmly knit, as he weighs his inclination with his duty," Dodge remembered about men on that march to Gettysburg.

"Beside him lags a dead-beat, who five minutes hence will complain of sore feet, and make every excuse, and look for every chance to drop out and straggle; not far off, the bragging fellow, whom you would dub a lion from his words and a hare from his deeds; who will talk loud, and vent his gasconade on every side, but who will be as far to the rear in the coming broil as he can get, by sneaking or deliberately running away.

"The boy, fair-faced and small, scarce eighteen years old that trudges behind him, whistling to keep his courage up and drown the remembrance of mother's kiss or sister's smile left far behind at home." This frail-looking boy, probably bullied in camp and on the march, was "an unconscious hero," Dodge said. "He will be in line when the braggart is skulking in the rear. . . . He will stick to the ranks until he is shot down and crippled."[17]

Shortly after arriving at Gettysburg, Dodge was shot in the ankle. Languishing as a prisoner for several days, he eventually had his foot amputated.[18]

Mid-morning, when Bayard's battery passed the border into Pennsylvania, the Pennsylvanians in regiments ahead and behind him gave out a cheer. But soon, they were held up by Reynolds's 1st Corps supply wagons that were mired on the muddy roads, and the men were ordered to fan out through adjacent, soggy fields of corn and wheat. Within minutes those fields were trampled into a pulp. Men in the 11th's lead columns soon saw what appeared to be a man on a white horse coming at them on a gallop. It was a messenger from Reynolds—carrying one of the last he gave—to 11th Corps officers, and they soon learned that the horse was actually a dark-colored bay. The animal had become so lathered from galloping at full effort in the heat that it had looked white from a distance. Five or six more messengers and lathered horses arrived to urge the 11th to push harder as they approached Gettysburg.[19]

"We had had hard marching in this campaign before but this was the worst," Ruch, the 153rd Pennsylvania private, remembered.[20]

To hurry his corps to the field, Otis Howard had ordered two divisions to take a less clogged but slightly longer Taneytown Road to Gettysburg, which intersected with the Emmitsburg Road just south of the town. One division was commanded by Maj. Gen. Carl Schurz, a Prussian-born, self-taught officer, ardent abolitionist, and a tireless campaigner for Lincoln in the 1860 election. As Schurz and his column approached Gettysburg on the double-quick, they ran into what the general described as "fugitives from Gettysburg, men, women and children, who seemed to be in great terror" and heading in the opposite direction. One middle-aged woman, holding a child's hand and bent over from a bundle of belongings on her back, reached for Schurz in the saddle and tried to stop him from going forward. "Hard times at Gettysburg," she cried out. "They are shooting and killing. What will become of us?"[21]

Within three hours, Schurz would pass on orders that would result in Lieutenant Wilkeson's battery being placed in the middle of that shooting and killing.

Approaching Gettysburg, Wilkeson's battery and the infantry regiments accompanying it were ordered into double time, a "dog trot" that robbed wind from the fittest man. They had had only "short breathing intermissions," according to Lt. Louis Fischer, of the 11th Corps's third division. But as soon as Gettysburg came into view, the breathing breaks stopped, and the adrenaline kicked in.

"As soon as we passed the Round Tops [referring to the Little and Big Round Tops at the south end of the eventual battlefield], part of the First Corps' fighting came in to view due north, Gettysburg being visible north-northeast," Lieutenant Fischer remembered. "For quite a distance we had heard the crackling of fire of the infantry, and seeing the First Corps heavily engaged, our men struck the long-winded dog trot, and went in that style through the town, emerging on the Mummasburg Road."[22]

By then men of the 11th Corps had "met a thousand or more citizens, fleeing from their homes, as from the wrath to come," according to Pvt. Levi E. Walter, Company E, 153rd Pennsylvania.[23]

The 119th New York's Dodge, whose regiment would eventually join the line not far behind Wilkeson's guns north of town, said an adrenaline rush wiped out "any symptoms of fatigue.

"Every one's blood flows quicker, every pulse beats louder, every nerve is more sensitive, and every one feels he is living faster than he was half an hour since," Dodge recalled.[24]

Later, when the correspondent Reid approached the battlefield on a double back from Meade's headquarters, wounded men of the 1st Corps were being hauled back in the midst of an anxious refugee stream. Some painted pictures of heroic action north and west of the town from both Union corps engaged. "Everything looks favorable," one man told Reid. But a few 1st Corps men were already cursing their 11th Corps companions. "Damned Dutchman of the 11th Corps broke and ran like sheep," one said, using the common slur for German immigrants, "just as they did at Chancellorsville, and it's going to be another disaster of the same sort."[25]

Not if Bayard Wilkeson could help it. About 2 miles south of town, he pushed his men to an even faster trot.[26] By then, the distant boom-boom of artillery had turned into overhead thunder, the distant crackling of rifle fire into the lethal buzz of sudden death. His second in command, Bancroft, a bookkeeper in civilian life, remembered arriving at Gettysburg around 11:00 a.m., but in actuality it was more likely early afternoon, according to the preponderance of the accounts. Bancroft's confusion can be excused given the chaos that the 120 men of Battery G found in the town itself. It took agonizing minutes to maneuver men, horses, and machines up Washington and adjacent streets crowded with men trying to get to the battlefield, all the while running upstream of the 1st Corps wounded being carried back from the front and civilians fleeing their homes. Some men were so parched they were begging for water, and Gettysburg residents began setting out water in any containers they could find. As men broke ranks to quench thirsts, the march further slowed.

Even as the boom of cannon and waves of massed musket fire crescendoed to the north and west, some Gettysburg residents refused to leave. Mary McAllister's store was on Chambersburg Street. As a continuous line of Union boys passed by, many panted and called out "Give us water, give us water!" Mary and two neighbor boys filled tin tubs with water and handed out tin cup after tin cup; grateful soldiers drank and tossed the cups back over their shoulders for a refill for the next parched throat.[27]

Fourteen-year-old Albertus McCreary was one of the boys dipping water. As he did so a drummer boy younger than he stepped out of ranks, handed over his drum and drumsticks, and asked McCreary to hide them for him until after the battle. The drum had the drummer boy's name and regiment painted on it and after the battle, McCreary wrote to the boy in care of the regiment. McCreary never heard back. "I suppose he had been killed," he said. "He looked to be about twelve years old."[28]

Near the town square on Baltimore Street, a beautiful young woman and her middle-aged father dipped ladles of water into tin cups of soldiers passing by. It was the coolest water some men would remember ever drinking. Private Walter was overwhelmed by her "white dress, and an apron and bib representing the stars and stripes." Going into battle, he remembered, the men around him "were as eager for the sight of a pretty girl as for the refreshing water she dipped with almost provoking impartiality."

As he passed by, Walter called out to the young woman, "This is no place for you."

"Oh that's all right, I think," she replied.[29]

The young woman became legendary in the 11th Corps. In a speech more than forty years later, Howard, the 11th Corps commander, described her almost identically as Walter had. "She was very brave and she gave us great cheer," he said.[30]

Sallie Myers, a young schoolteacher who lived in Gettysburg, also spent July 1 passing out cups of water to soldiers rushing by her house on West High Street. Over the coming chaotic days and weeks, Sallie would nurse a half dozen wounded soldiers in her home, and she would marry the brother of one of them. As she ladled cup after cup she became horrified at the sight of 1st Corps wounded men and animals being carried or walked back from the fighting just outside the northwest outskirts of the town. "A horse was led by, blood streaming from his head, which was covered," she recalled. "The sight sickened me. Then a man was led by, supported by two comrades. His head had been hastily bandaged and blood was visible. I turned away, faint with horror, for I never could stand the sight of blood." For someone with that condition, she worked heroically through her fears in the coming hours and days.[31]

In Bayard's battery, moving the one-ton cannons and their loaded ammunition caissons through the narrow streets in ankle-deep mud strained the strongest men and horses. What they saw when they emerged out of the town and onto the battlefield added to their psychological burdens.

Upon reaching the northwestern outskirts of Gettysburg, the 11th Corps band near the head of the column stopped playing and stepped to the side as the infantrymen and artillery units kept moving into the open landscape. Band members watched with silent, somber countenance, focusing on one face after another as ranks moved inexorably onto the fighting fields. As soon as the infantry and artillery passed by the band onto the unusually open ground north of the town, "we received yet another reception," Ruch recalled, "but this one was in the shape of solid shells and shot . . . and everything that could be shot out of a cannon."[32]

When Lieutenant Wilkeson's battery arrived at Gettysburg, the battle had already ebbed and flowed for several hours. The fighting ranged from long-range artillery duels to hand-to-hand combat along McPherson's Ridge, with similar actions on a rise called Oak Hill, in small woods and farm fields, and in an unfinished railroad bed along Chambersburg Pike that became a death trap for both armies. Dismounted cavalry and early-arriving infantry units of Reynolds's 1st Corps had temporarily checked the advance elements of a Confederate corps under A. P. Hill. That Rebel forward advance was commanded by the able Henry Heth. Other Rebel corps under James Longstreet and Dick Ewell were pushing hard toward Gettysburg from the north and northeast, and Union officers knew they were out there. But their exact location and the full scope of their threat remained unknown to the Union high command when Bayard and his men emerged onto the field north of town. They'd soon find out the threat was imminent, and crushing.

Many of the decisions made on the first day of Gettysburg were based on little more than educated guesses. Lee was still without Stuart's eyes. And the Yankees were partially blind because one usual source of intelligence—Southern newspapers—was not available. Although Meade had gotten valuable and timely intelligence from observers in Pennsylvania who passed their information to the War Department, who then telegraphed it to Meade, the few correspondents traveling with

Lee's army had had trouble getting their dispatches back to their papers or had lost contact with Lee after he crossed the Potomac.

Even when they had gotten information from Northern correspondents' dispatches, Southern newspapers were skeptical of reports coming out of the Northern press. The *Charleston Mercury* pronounced that it would not believe "the systematic lying of the Yankee Government." On July 10, that paper would report a "brilliant and crushing victory" at Gettysburg. The *Richmond Enquirer*, too, cautioned its readers to not believe everything reported Up North as the armies moved toward a certain clash. The paper blamed the new medium—the telegraph—which it said had put so much time pressure on correspondents that it led to half-baked and inaccurate reports. The paper said the "infernal invention of the electric telegraph" was "one of the worst plagues and curses that has ever befallen this human race."[33]

Such pronouncements would not have registered with the soldiers at Gettysburg, who knew the reality all too well. While the fighting had gone reasonably well for the Yankees early, newly arriving units of Confederates began tipping the tide by the time Lieutenant Wilkeson and the rest of the 11th Corps arrived. With scouts telling him that Confederate forces were bearing down on his front, rear, and right flank, Reynolds had sent messengers back to Howard and other Union corps commanders asking them to come quickly. He needed all he could get of Meade's army or he would be overrun, surrounded, or both, before the bulk of the Army of the Potomac could arrive in force.

Upon approaching Gettysburg late in the morning, Howard ordered two brigades of his corps to dig in on a prominent ridge south of town on which the cemetery was located, while he sent the rest of the 11th through the town to hook up with the embattled 1st Corps's right flank.

By then Reynolds's premonition of death that Howard had so vividly felt from his fellow corps commander the night before had been proven true. Reynolds had been mortally shot while trying to place the fabled Iron Brigade into furious action at Herbst's Woods. With Reynolds's death, Howard, the discredited commander from Chancellorsville, was now in charge of all Union forces on the field at Gettysburg. The one-armed general would hold that responsibility until the late-afternoon arrival of Winfield Scott Hancock. But much fighting and killing would happen before then.

All urgency was required. Lieutenant Wilkeson's artillery commander, Maj. Thomas W. Osborn, was ordered by Howard to "move the artillery to the front as rapidly as possible."[34] Pressure was building on the weak and exposed Union right flank. Gettysburg was threatening to turn into a disastrous repeat of the rout at Chancellorsville.

Upon orders by Schurz to position his men on the right flank of 1st Corps's wavering line, Barlow ordered Lt. Bayard Wilkeson's battery and a supporting infantry brigade forward to a gentle knoll about a mile north of town. It was one of the war's most controversial decisions. There, on the extreme right of the Union army, the heat that the teenaged lieutenant had so desperately sought was descending on him in a cloak of destruction and death.

CHAPTER 27

"The War Devil Is in Him"

SAM WILKESON HAD A NAME FOR WHAT BURNED IN HIS SON'S SOUL IN that summer of 1863. "The war devil is in him," he'd say about both his boys' soldierly impulses.[1] On the afternoon of July 1, 1863, the war devil had led nineteen-year-old Lt. Bayard Wilkeson and the men of his battery into hellfire north of Gettysburg.

Bayard's reputation as a disciplinarian and leader of one of the beleaguered 11th Corps's best batteries preceded him. Those expectations almost certainly influenced Barlow's decision to place Lieutenant Wilkeson and his men on the most dangerous promontory of the first day at Gettysburg. It was called Blocher's Knoll, an exposed and gentle rise roughly a half mile north of the town. After this day, it would be known as Barlow's Knoll, for obvious reasons.

After pushing through Gettysburg, Wilkeson and his battery, along with about 2,450 infantrymen in brigades under the commands of the Prussian-born Col. Leopold von Gilsa and Maine-born Brig. Gen. Adelbert Ames, were ordered by Barlow to drive scattered Confederate troops off the knoll, place the big guns at the highest point, and set up defensive positions in the open fields to the rear of the knoll, and along a narrow creek that meandered past it to the northeast and east. It was approaching 2:00 p.m. Blocher's Knoll, named for the family that owned it, overlooked Rock Creek and offered a good view of the field, but not commanding heights from which to control it. If the right flank of the existing Union lines already fighting on the field when Wilkeson arrived had been stronger and closer to the knoll, it would have been solid ground to anchor the Yankee right wing and hold off Dick Ewell's onrushing Rebels then crashing down the Harrisburg Road from the northeast. But on this day, the knoll was detached by several hundred yards from any other concentration from 1st or 11th Corps troops. With not enough men to fill in the gaps, Wilkeson's guns were in a badly exposed salient, vulnerable to cannon and rifle fire from three directions of columns under the command of generals Jubal Early and Robert Rodes, and even Henry Heth's division that had first run into Buford's Union cavalry that morning on the west side of town. The roads from Mummasburg and Harrisburg upon which the Rebels were approaching snaked through woods and other natural features that provided cover and offered the opportunity for surprise, and were angled in a way that provided textbook conditions for simultaneous frontal and flanking attacks on hastily forming defensive positions on the extreme right of the Union lines.

It was a death trap.

Eventually, Wilkeson's battery was outgunned by Confederate cannons by a ratio of 3–1 from murderous in-close distances in his immediate front and flanks. He and his men also were within range of more cannon fire from other Confederate batteries farther to his left and rear. The Union infantry brigade sent to defend the knoll with Wilkeson would within minutes be outnumbered on their front by 2–1, with pressure building on both flanks.

Barlow's Knoll in 1863 was a relatively barren 50-foot rise overlooking meadows and crop fields. It had no natural defensive features. But in Barlow's defense, it was the last high ground on the field within his grasp, and the entire day so far had been defined by races to any heights commanders could find. A later student of the battlefield described the knoll as a "gentle breast isolated in open fields," and "geographically lonely."[2]

It certainly would have seemed lonely to Lieutenant Wilkeson. While not massively outnumbered on the total battlefield when Bayard's battery arrived, the federals on the extreme right were too spread out to hold off the combination of Confederates already pressing them and those, under Jubal Early, about to descend down the Harrisburg road from the northeast. Barlow's decision to hold the rise had exposed and isolated almost a third of the men of the 11th Corps now engaged. In military parlance, when Bayard's battery arrived on the battlefield the Union right was in the air, and there were few brigades of either army who could have done much to hold off the rout that was about to ensue.

What they could do, and what they did do, was to stand and fight long enough, to help delay long enough that they were able to stave off total disaster and the total destruction of two Union corps. Some men ran, but some—including Wilkeson's battery—held out as long as they could. Had Wilkeson and the outnumbered infantry regiments not held their ground so long, the battle of Gettysburg might not have become imprinted on history as the high-water mark of the Confederacy and the start of the South's slide toward Appomattox.

Soldiers who fought north of Gettysburg on July 1 and civilians caught in the middle of it described the panorama that day as one of the most open battlefields of the war, a prime host for all the staples of nineteenth century infantry tactics: massed frontal assaults, enfilading fire from rifle and cannon, flank movements, long-range artillery duels, and the ghastly, close-range slaughter of canister and grapeshot from retreating cannons.

On normal days, it was pretty country. Earlier in the war, fourteen-year old Amelia Harmon had been sent to a farm west of Gettysburg to live with her aunt because Amelia's father was worried their home in Baltimore was not a safe place for a young girl during the war. Suddenly, on that July 1 morning, the war surrounded her. She and her aunt watched from the farmhouse cupola as Confederates descended, locust-like, on a field of grain adjacent to the farmyard. When Rebel officers and sharpshooters occupied the house—they would eventually set it on fire—Amelia and her aunt fled toward the rear of the Confederate lines.[3] But not before witnessing a scene that was simultaneously frightening and impressive.

"The whole landscape for miles around unrolled like a panorama below us," Amelia recalled. "What a spectacle! It seemed as though the fields and woods had been sown with dragon's teeth, for everywhere had sprung up armed men, where but an hour ago only grass and flowers grew." She and her aunt escaped by running for 2 miles against the dragon's teeth, where they finally came across a cluster of newspaper correspondents and Confederate officers conversing under a tree. "The officers looked attentive, the newspaper men attentive," Amelia remembered. A *Times of London* correspondent took notice and helped arrange for them to be placed under guard in a nearby cottage.[4]

Amelia and her aunt made their dangerous escape about the time that Bayard Wilkeson's battery was rushing forward into danger. Pushing his men and horses hard through the heat, the men of Wilkeson's Battery G traversed through a once-bucolic tableau of rolling hills, farmhouses, red barns, orchards, fields of ripening wheat and timothy, and meadows of clover and grass. It would have been a beautiful stroll had it not been for the metal flying through the air. To their left, as they approached the knoll, the higher Oak Hill, named after the cap of timber at its top, stood most prominently north of the road to Mummasburg. By the time Bayard and the six cannons under his command emerged onto the field, that hill and its base were swarming with Confederates. A big red barn owned by Moses McLean along the Mummasburg Road near the base of Oak Hill stood out in almost comical normality compared to all the deadly activity around it. Rock Creek, flowing north and east of Barlow's Knoll, was narrow but had steep banks, which would provide temporary kill zones when the Confederates crossed it. Rock Creek was also flanked by woods directly in front of Ames's and von Gilsa's assembling brigades and the four cannons that Wilkeson eventually deployed on Barlow's Knoll.[5]

Throughout the day, accurate and intense Yankee artillery fire had helped slow the Confederates for precious minutes, then hours. But momentum was inexorably turning against the Union as the 11th Corps came upon the field. Every man in blue could sense it as they emerged out of Gettysburg.

Barlow's Knoll was about a quarter mile north of the county poorhouse. Formally known as the Adams County Almshouse, it consisted of a large, barracks-style house and about a dozen barns and outbuildings. It housed not only the indigent, but those declared mentally ill or disabled. On the afternoon of July 1, 1863, the almshouse became one of the most prominent features on the battlefield.

By the time Wilkeson's six big guns and the brigades of von Gilsa and Ames approached the Almshouse in the early afternoon, the challenge facing them and other 11th Corps troops deploying elsewhere on the field would have been obvious to the lowliest private.

"The rebel infantry was coming down the Mummasburg road at a run, about 600 yards from me, and taking shelter on the southwest side of the road in the ditch behind the fence, (and) fired into the exposed ranks of the 13th Massachusetts and 104th New York, who stood in an open meadow," said Lt. Louis Fischer, of the 11th Corps's Third Division, who led a fence-cutting crew ahead of arriving artillery and infantry. "I could see every man fall as he was hit by the enemy (who lost hardly any in this unequal contest), until of the original line of blue was left only a thin line, with great gaps at that. My heart bounded with joy when the skirmishers of the 157th and 45th New York of my division, drove the enemy out of the road and took those of them prisoners that had taken shelter in McLean's red barn."[6]

Barlow never saw his occupation of the knoll as the mistake that some of his superiors, and historians through the years, would portray it. He could have reasonably believed the 11th was arriving in sufficient numbers to close the gap with the 1st Corps's right wing. But as it played out, by ordering Bayard Wilkeson's guns and supporting infantry regiments to seize and control the knoll, Barlow created the perfect opportunity for the pincer of two large Confederate forces coming to the field simultaneously. And the Rebels did not miss a second opportunity to roll up the right wing of an 11th Corps that they had routed just two months earlier at Chancellorsville.

Over the next frantic minutes, attempts were made by the new, temporary 11th Corps commander Carl Schurz to tighten the Union right wing and call in reinforcements. Schurz had had a battlefield promotion to command of the 11th Corps after Reynolds was killed and Howard took control of all Union forces on the field. The woman who had warned of "hard times" at Gettysburg had been right. The boys from Ohio, New York, Pennsylvania, and Connecticut were stretched too thin for the ground they were being asked to defend. But the fearless and battle-tested Barlow had made his decision. He would try to hold on with what he had. Wilkeson's battery was all the artillery he had to spare for his badly exposed right wing. It would have to do.

CHAPTER 28

"The Most Fortunate Hazard of the Day"

THE FIGHTING HAD BEGUN WEST OF GETTYSBURG AROUND 7:30 A.M. AS Bayard's battery was eating breakfast in Emmitsburg. All morning long, in a battle that neither Meade nor Lee had wanted to start the way it did, the Union 1st Corps infantry and a battalion of dismounted cavalry under Gen. John Buford had held back piecemeal advances of 7,500 Confederates under Heth. But the arrival of Dorsey Pender's 6,700 Rebels and Rodes's 8,000 men steadily gave the Rebels superiority in men and artillery pieces. Some of Gettysburg's deadliest close-quarters fighting took place along McPherson's Ridge, another rise west of the town. More than 5,000 men under Jubal Early that crashed into Barlow's division on the knoll would add to the Confederates' Day One advantage.

Infantry volleys along the line of fighting in the woods and on the rises of McPherson's Ridge west of Gettysburg had come at point-blank range. Along the railroad cut and the farm fields around it, wounded and dead men were lying in lines as organized as they had marched. One North Carolina company of ninety-one officers and men, which had exchanged volleys with federals at no more than twenty paces, saw every last man either wounded or killed. A Michigan regiment lost nine color bearers.[1] Artillery on both sides had been appallingly effective.

The death of the respected, highly competent Reynolds had been a devastating morale blow for the Yankees, and Wilkeson's men knew it when they arrived. But word also filtered through the ranks that 1st Corps Yankees had captured Confederate general David Archer, and driven back Heth's men while inflicting heavy losses. Gettysburg would have been a draw had both armies withdrawn from the fight midday. But amidst the confusion of the day, with the rest of both armies now rushing to this crossroads, events were now out of control of any one commander.

When all the pieces of the three-day battle came together, Meade's Army of the Potomac outnumbered Lee's Army of Virginia, 93,000 to 70,000. But on the first day the Union got roughly 23,000 men to the eventual battlefield against 28,000 Confederates. Among those who actually got into the fight on July 1, the South had about a 3–2 numerical advantage.[2]

Combined, more than a third of the men who got into the fight on July 1 became casualties, with roughly 9,000 Union soldiers and 6,800 Confederates killed, wounded, or missing. The first day at Gettysburg was the war's twelfth costliest in lives, with more casualties than those at the battles of First Manassas and Franklin, Tennessee, combined. Two more days of killing would push the Gettysburg casualty toll to over 46,000, making it the deadliest battle of the Civil War.[3] The 11th Corps artillery lost sixty-nine officers and enlisted men, and ninety-eight horses, over three days of fighting.[4]

In the aftermath, only the heroics of non-combatants saved some of the wounded. Others could not be saved, irrespective of equally heroic actions by their families. Stories of men who fell, wounded, in the hour that Bayard Wilkeson also did, were often too much to believe or too much to bear.

John Benton Callis, a Union lieutenant colonel, was part of Solomon Meredith's division of the famous Iron Brigade. That July 1 morning, their ranks decimated by point-blank rifle and artillery barrages, the black-hatted Wisconsin men fixed bayonets and drove a Confederate brigade under General Archer across a gash in the fields called Willoughby's Run, capturing hundreds of Confederates, including Archer.

Callis was slightly wounded by buckshot in that attack, but he pressed on. By mid-afternoon, as Bayard Wilkeson's men were desperately trying to hold on about a mile to the northeast, Callis's Black Hats were being pressed from three directions in Herbst's Woods about three-fourths of a mile west of Gettysburg's Lutheran Seminary. The close-quarters fighting was so intense that some of Callis's men were shotgunned in the back by Union artillery canister. It was so loud that his men could not hear Callis's order to retreat to the seminary. Callis was shot through the side by a Confederate rifleman, the ball lodging in Callis's lung. Left to die in a field of fragrant clover, he watched as the Confederates literally jumped over him to push his men into a disorganized retreat. A few Rebels stopped to pilfer Callis's pockets of $200 in cash, but a Confederate officer who came to check on Callis learned of the pillaging and ordered the men to return the money. They gave all but $20 back. One of Callis's would-be robbers, perhaps to make amends, gave him a shot of whiskey, telling Callis "it would be better for me than cold water."[5]

Eventually, while Callis lay wounded on the field, the bluecoats were pushed off Seminary Ridge on a final assault by Pender's men about 4:00 p.m., about the same time Bayard Wilkeson's guns and the surviving infantry on the Union right wing were being pushed back through Gettysburg itself. But Pender's men, stepping over and around hundreds of dead and wounded Union soldiers, then themselves paid a terrible price. Charging directly into the face of eighteen Union cannons situated almost wheel to wheel, five regiments of North Carolinians—about 1,400 men—were reduced to roughly 500 left standing in a matter of minutes. One regiment, the 13th North Carolina, lost 150 of 180 men.[6] Seventeen days later, Pender himself would die from wounds he suffered on the second day at Gettysburg.

But not Callis. Years later, Callis ran into Meade, who told Callis that his actions on the first day—including the suicidal charge into Archer's brigade where Callis was first wounded—helped win the battle. "It was a very hazardous movement," Meade told Callis, "but it was the most fortunate hazard of the day in this, it stopped the Confederate advance and gave me time to dispose of my troops on Cemetery Ridge, Culp's Hill and Round Top, the impregnable points where the battle was won."[7]

After the battle, the 11th Corps's Commander Howard would say precisely the same thing about Bayard Wilkeson and the men under his command. In fact, although eventually overrun and pushed back, the delaying actions of the 1st and 11th Corps facing odds that looked futile and impossible on Day One at Gettysburg were as important to the Union victory as the more famous and penultimate clash of thousands of men on Cemetery Ridge that the correspondent Sam Wilkeson would witness two days later.

Others would be told those reassuring lines as they died. Union sergeant Alex Stewart was mortally wounded in fighting near McPherson's farm west of town. His "Bucktail Brigade," roughly 450 men of the 149th Pennsylvania, suffered 75 percent casualties. But as the Union lines broke, what was left of the brigade held for twenty ferocious minutes under direct orders from Gen. Abner Doubleday, and it, too, helped cover the Yankee retreat to Cemetery Ridge.[8] This also happened as Bayard Wilkeson's guns desperately fired point-blank canister into the oncoming men in gray as Battery G retreated.

Sallie Myers, the young schoolteacher who had handed out cups of cool water to Union soldiers as they marched to the battle, would care for Stewart as he languished and died in the aftermath at Gettysburg.

The battle's shock waves were reverberating far beyond Gettysburg. Lt. Andrew Gregg Tucker fell about the same time that Bayard did on a different part of the field. His 142nd Pennsylvania had gone into the battle with 336 men and suffered 211 casualties, including 31 dead or mortally wounded, while holding on until finally broken on the Union left near the Lutheran Theological Seminary.[9] Tucker's mother, like Sam Wilkeson, got word of her son's wounding early the next day. She set off immediately to the battlefield to find him.

For much of the day, deadly accurate Union artillery had helped beat back several Confederate assaults. As a result, as the newest Union battery on the field, Bayard and his men had been prime targets for Confederate cannons and sharpshooters the minute they emerged onto the battlefield.

CHAPTER 29

"I Have Spiked the Gun for Them"

EVEN THE LOWLIEST PRIVATE IN LIEUTENANT WILKESON'S COMMAND could easily see the dangerous position they were ordered to hold on Barlow's Knoll. On top of the obvious threats from the north and northwest, including the thousands of men arriving down Mummasburg Pike that Fischer had looked upon with fear and awe, Union scouts were returning with news that Early was arriving in force from the northeast down the Harrisburg Pike. And the 11th Corps's strength north of the town had been lessened when Howard decided to leave about 1,600 men on Cemetery Hill as a fallback position should the 1st and 11th need to retreat. It would turn out to be a fortuitous move, but one questioned by officers during the rapidly deteriorating Union tactical situation who were clamoring for reinforcements north of town.

Wilkeson's route to Barlow's Knoll took him and his men behind the already engaged six-gun battery commanded by fellow 11th Corps artillery Capt. Hubert Dilger, the Medal of Honor recipient at Chancellorsville. Dilger's guns were among the first 11th Corps elements to arrive on the battlefield, about 12:30 p.m., and were furiously exchanging fire with about a dozen Confederate Napoleons and rifled cannons around Oak Hill when Wilkeson arrived with his battery. Despite being outnumbered, Dilger's skillful gun-and-run action on the Union right was creating havoc among Confederate infantry and artillery arriving piecemeal to the battlefield.

Dilger was an outsized character—mercenary, robust and fearless, an artillery craftsman with a noble pedigree. German-born and professionally trained as an artillerist, Dilger had needed the permission of his employer, the Grand Duke of Baden, to come across the ocean and serve in the Union army. Capt. Dilger was the kind of leader that younger Union officers like Bayard Wilkeson aspired to be. By the time Wilkeson's battery joined Dilger's on the Gettysburg battlefield, Dilger had again shown his courage and expertise in one of the most remarkable feats of marksmanship of the entire war.

Dilger had been ordered to position part of his battery facing north-northwest on a slight rise between the roads to Carlisle and Mummasburg, about a quarter mile northwest of Gettysburg's outskirts. Almost immediately, his two guns (and soon the remaining four he hastily called in from reserve) became the target of Confederate Napoleons at the base of Oak Hill. [1] As infantry troops on both sides looked on, a fierce artillery duel commenced at 1,000 yards, and both sides were producing ghastly, accurate results. Rifled Confederate cannons on Oak Hill were shredding with deadly accuracy the hastily forming 11th Corps lines.

The first return shot out of Dilger's battery may have been fired too quickly, and it sailed high over the Confederate lines. A soldier of the 157th New York, deployed nearby, said that "the Rebels were jubilant and yelled in derision."

That only got Dilger's dander up. With Confederate shells whistling overhead and plowing up the earth all around him, he took personal control of one cannon.

"Captain Dilger now sighted the gun himself and fired it," the 157th New Yorker reported. "The shot dismounted a Rebel gun and killed the horses. Captain Dilger tried a second shot, sighting and firing the gun. No effect being visible with the naked eye, (Dilger was asked), 'What effect, Captain Dilger?' Captain, after looking through his glass, replied, 'I have spiked the gun for them, plugging it at the muzzle.'" Dilger's shell had hit a Rebel cannon directly in the barrel.[2] J. M. Silliman of the 17th Connecticut, whose regiment was then rushing to deploy with Wilkeson's battery about a half mile to the northeast of Dilger's guns on the far slope of Barlow's Knoll, three days later saw the "rebel cannon that had been struck in its mouth by one of our shots and flattened out."[3]

During early-afternoon fighting, as Wilkeson's guns were approaching the field, Dilger's cannons held off attacks from two Confederate infantry regiments for about a half hour. He knocked out five Rebel cannons while losing one of his own. Supported by another Union battery under Lt. William Wheeler, they conducted frantic run-and-gun theatrics across hundreds of yards of open battlefield, to great effect. Dilger's canister and grape temporarily stopped an Alabama brigade crashing toward the thin Union right flank, buying more time for Wilkeson to set up on the knoll.

Later, remnants of Dilger's, Wheeler's, and Wilkeson's batteries displayed similar effectiveness covering a hectic Union retreat through Gettysburg, at times firing into charging Confederates just yards in their front.

Dilger's guns "changed position several times, and did so with excellent results and in the best possible manner, Captain Dilger using much judgment in the selection of his several positions," wrote Osborn, the 11th's artillery brigade commander, in his after-action report. "They did not leave their immediate locality until the corps was ordered by the commanding general to fall back to Cemetery Hill."

Dilger believed he would have done more damage if his ammunition that day had not been so defective. Fused shot, he reported, had a tendency to go off just after being fired, spraying friendly fire over his own side's troops.[4]

As Dilger wreaked his deadly harvest, Barlow sent elements of the 54th and 68th New York and the 153rd Pennsylvania under von Gilsa to sweep disorganized Confederates off the knoll. The riflemen set up a thin line of defense in wheat fields and woods to the front of where Wilkeson was setting up four of his six guns on the knoll itself. His guns faced north and northeast on the plump knoll roughly 250 yards on the west side of Rock Creek. Picket lines were sent out to deploy closer to the creek. Ames's 107th and 25th Ohio and 75th Ohio, and the 17th Connecticut were deployed all around Wilkeson, with four companies of the 17th assigned to head for the farm of Josiah Benner, east of Rock Creek, thereby becoming the extreme point of the Union right. The two

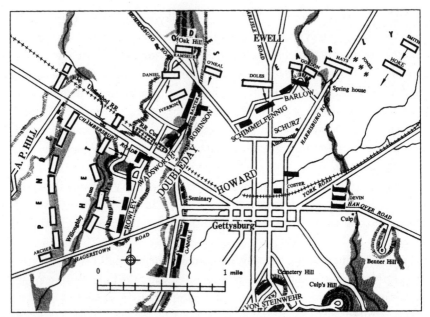

Gettysburg, afternoon of July 1. Wilkeson's battery was with Barlow's division north of town.

Ohio regiments, about to be decimated, would two days later be ordered to clear Gettysburg itself on the morning of July 4.

The Yankees deploying around the knoll were instantly met with heavy rifle and cannon fire from lead elements of Early's and Rodes's divisions. Immediately on Wilkeson's left flank more than 1,300 more Confederates under Robert Doles were positioned scarcely 350 yards away. Overall, with other elements of the 11th and the 1st Corps holding out against disjointed and uncoordinated Confederate assaults to the west and northwest, the federals were not badly outnumbered on the entire battlefield at that moment. But the 11th had arrived piecemeal, and their stretched lines made their right flank ripe for a rollup. The Confederates reveled in their luck. As happened at Chancellorsville, the 11th was about to again be overlapped and outflanked by Early's larger force.[5]

Emerging out of Gettysburg, Wilkeson had placed two of his guns near the Almshouse, and put Lt. Christopher F. Merkle in charge.

Merkle would be held in reserve there and be in a position to fight off further flanking attempts by Early's brigades.[6] As Barlow's remaining four guns set up on the knoll, von Gilsa's and Ames's men began taking the onslaught on his front, right, and rear, facing to the north and northeast. There was little cover on the rolling ground, and Confederate sharpshooters and big guns were raking them with deadly result, with shot and shell piling on from Confederate guns on Oak Hill further distanced to their left and rear. Confederate rifled artillery just across Rock Creek, some of the guns barely 300 yards in Wilkeson's front, was just starting to plow shells throughout the ranks of Barlow's two brigades and Wilkeson's guns.[7]

Barlow would become so gravely wounded in the fighting to follow that he did not write a post-battle official report, but he never backed down from his decision to deploy Wilkeson and the infantry where he did. History would be an unkind judge.

CHAPTER 30

"A Terrible but Incredibly Fascinating Scene"

UNLIKE MANY OF THE BATTLES OF THE CIVIL WAR, WHERE THOUSANDS of men at a time could wander into or surprise one another in forests or swamps, the men caught in a tightening pincer at Gettysburg could see what was happening. Those pressing on them or fighting from a distance could also glance over and see what was happening with rare clarity. Lieutenant Fischer, the Missourian assigned to clear fences and other obstacles for Wilkeson's men and the infantry regiments rushing to the field, said Gettysburg's first-day fighting took place on "the most remarkably open and one of the most stubbornly contested fields" of the entire war. He described the fighting as a "terrible but incredibly fascinating scene."[1]

The peril was obvious as well. If the Confederates could exploit this weak junction between the now-dead Reynolds's Union 1st Corps and Howard's (and now Schurz's) 11th Corps, the Confederates could destroy two Union corps before Meade could get the rest of his army up to help. The Yankees faced a potential defeat even more devastating than Chancellorsville, and Howard again was in command. Fortune seemed to again be cruelly conspiring to exploit every Yankee mistake.

But uncoordinated and poorly executed Confederate attacks under Rodes typified the confusion and disjointed action that reigned over the field that day. A feisty Virginian, Rodes had left the Virginia Military Institute before the war after losing out on a full professorship to Stonewall Jackson. He, like the Union's General Howard, had been wounded at Seven Pines the year before. Although not all Rodes's fault, the attacks he ordered had come piecemeal and not with the full vigor he expected from subordinates, and this gave the arriving Union 11th Corps enough time to set up for a brutal delaying fight to follow. The Cemetery Ridge redoubt Howard had ordered occupied on Gettysburg's southern edge was still available for the two battered Union corps if they weren't totally destroyed north of town. Ultimately, on that high ground, the remnants of the 1st and 11th Corps would that night be reinforced by enough fresh troops from Meade's army to hold the weary Confederates at bay. Both sides were flailing about. Reynolds's death had also created a ripple effect in the Union high command that resulted in disjointed and confusing actions on the North's side, too.

Mostly, the Confederates benefitted from fortunate timing. While Rodes was pressing the tenuous junction between the Union 11th and 1st Corps, Jubal Early's division of 5,500 Confederates of Ewell's corps arrived at the federal right flank, as if they had planned it just this way. His men called the short-tempered, profane Early "Old Jube." Lee knew him as "Bad Old Man." The closer Early got to Gettysburg, the more he could barely believe his luck. There, in front of him, the Yankees were assembling in thin and exposed lines against another Rebel thrust, presenting a target ripe for a flank attack from the very direction he was approaching. It had an eerie, almost otherworldly, familiarity. Some of Early's men had fought in the late Stonewall Jackson's rout of the Union right at Chancellorsville. Bayard's battery had not been involved in that rout, but von Gilsa's brigade had been among the first men hit by Jackson's men on the right flank of the Union army at Chancellorsville.

As Wilkeson's battery unlimbered and began firing from the knoll, the tempestuous Early rushed twelve Rebel cannons to an open field along the Harrisburg Road on the other side of Rock Creek. The two batteries were scarcely 300 yards apart, virtual point-blank range for artillery. Under the command of Virginian Hilary P. Jones, the Rebel gunners soon began killing and maiming federals at a ghastly rate. The rebel shells had "considerable effect" on the Yankees, Early reported.[2] With targets all over the field, the Rebel guns alternated from ripping into infantry ranks and then to Wilkeson's guns, back and forth, a murderous turkey shoot.

In his immediate front alone, Lt. Bayard Wilkeson was outgunned by a ratio of 3–1 in cannons, and the Union infantry brigades under von Gilsa and Ames were about to be hit head-on and on both flanks by Confederate forces more than twice their numbers.

To make matters worse, Barlow did not trust in his men's abilities, starting with the officers directly beneath him. During the march to Gettysburg the rigid Barlow had disciplined von Gilsa, sending him to the rear of his column for allowing too many men to break ranks to fetch water in the overwhelming heat and humidity. Only as they approached the battlefield did Barlow reinstate von Gilsa, a move that sent rolls of cheering through the ranks.[3] After the battle, Barlow would complain bitterly about his men's lack of courage, including how von Gilsa's men ran again at Gettysburg, just as they had crumbled at Chancellorsville.[4] But Barlow would also dish out some credit, including to Bayard Wilkeson.

Howard was not blind to Barlow's bad reputation among his men. He knew that Barlow, "indefatigable in camp and on drill" was "not popular with those whom discipline galled." Howard felt those negatives were outweighed by Barlow's "remarkable coolness and self-possession" when the fighting got hottest.[5] Whether it was the right decision or not to occupy the knoll, Howard had the right man in the job on the badly exposed Union right flank.

But Barlow's self-possession was not enough to overcome his tactical decision this day. Ames's men, mostly from Connecticut and Ohio, could see the terrifying mismatch they were being placed in. They did not have time to send out skirmishers to clear the way or probe the enemy's strength. The Confederates who watched Barlow's men deploy admired the precision at which Wilkeson's battery and Barlow's infantry moved into place, but knew they were marching to certain destruction. "These troops marched in perfect order, but they had not sent out scouts," Confederate major general Isaac Trimble said.[6]

Men and horses were panting in the heat. Lt. Eugene Bancroft, Wilkeson's second in command, said the battery "immediately" went into action, taking no time to catch their breath after the 12-mile march to the battlefield. Lead elements of the 11th Corps arrived on the southern edge of Gettysburg around 12:30 p.m., but because of the clogged street in the town itself, it was probably close to ninety minutes later before Wilkeson's battery fired its first shots.

To make matters worse, Barlow's division was undersized because he had left some men behind in Maryland to scout for Confederates or to keep refugees from fleeing to Confederate lines and giving away Union positions. As a result, scores of men under his command did not make the battlefield that day.[7]

If heroism and action alone could avert a total disaster, Barlow was the right choice. A twenty-nine-year-old Harvard-educated lawyer and staunch abolitionist, his demeanor seemed perpetually intended to convince subordinates he was tougher than his boyish appearance would suggest. "His men at first gazed at him wondering how such a boy could be put at the head of regiments of men," his superior, Schurz, thought. "But they soon discovered him to be a strict disciplinarian, and one of the coolest and bravest in action. In both respects he was inclined to carry his virtues to excess."[8]

Unlike Lieutenant Wilkeson's desires to make a name, Barlow had nothing left to prove about personal heroism or manhood. He was still recovering from the severe groin wound suffered while leading a brigade of the Union's 2nd Corps in grisly fighting at the Sunken Road at Antietam the previous September. His heroism that day had eventually gotten him promoted to brigadier general, and his reputation as a disciplinarian had gotten him transferred into the troubled 11th Corps. But like many of his fellow newcomers, including Bayard Wilkeson, he worried that he would be tainted by the association with the discredited corps. "I am busy occupied with these miserable creatures and get very little time to do anything," Barlow wrote his mother three weeks before the battle, a letter in which he said he had been discussing moving back to the 2nd Corps under John Gibbon.[9]

But redemption was another thing. Having survived the hand-to-hand savagery of Antietam, having been decorated for a decisive move that captured 300 Confederates in that fight, and mindful of the 11th Corps's capitulation on the right flank at Chancellorsville, Barlow had ample motivation for bold action at Gettysburg. Fortune had given the

11th Corps a second chance. He and Howard could avenge Chancellors-ville with redemptive work at Gettysburg. As much as any tactical choice before him that day, these impulses, fears, and memories must be placed in the context of Barlow's decision to order Wilkeson's battery and the supporting infantry to the knoll that was about to be named after him.

Schurz, who had taken control of the 11th Corps upon Reynolds's death and Howard's elevation to overall command on the field, main-tained for the rest of his life that he had not intended for Barlow to occupy the knoll. Barlow, Schurz said, had either badly misunderstood him or was simply overcome by "ardor" in the heat of battle.[10]

In Barlow's defense, the knoll was familiar to Otis Howard. At about 12:30 p.m., as Wilkeson and the rest of Barlow's 1st Division were approaching the town from the south, Barlow rode out ahead and joined Howard for a quick reconnaissance ride over that ground. Early's columns were not yet in sight. In that ride, Barlow may have intimated from Howard that his superior valued taking and holding what high ground there was at that end of the field. That Howard-Barlow scouting ride had produced one of the day's many surreal moments. As the two blue-coat commanders rode toward the knoll under fire from Confed-erates still some distance off, a woman stood on the porch of a house, ignoring the flying metal and bravely waving her handkerchief in support of the two Union commanders. She kept it up as Wilkeson's guns and follow-up columns of infantry came streaming by on their way to the battlefield. The men cheered her. "It was indeed a patriotic stimulus," Howard recalled later.[11]

Howard always maintained that he wanted Barlow to deploy "near the upper waters of Rock Creek."[12] To Schurz, that meant a position south from the exposed salient that Wilkeson and the men under von Gilsa and Ames eventually created, closer to the Almshouse and more concentrated and coupled to the stressed 1st Corps.[13] There, the combi-nation of the two corps would have been less stretched and exposed, bet-ter able to move men in reserve where needed, and not leave thousands in the air to the eventual pincer of Rodes and Early.

For a bit, that is what Barlow appeared to be doing. His men moved out of town and paused for a few minutes around the Almshouse. But they had stopped only momentarily to dump knapsacks and other extra gear to be held under guard, as was customary before a big fight. Had they deployed there and stretched their lines west to link with the 11th Corps Third Division, under Brig. Gen. Alexander Schimmelfennig, another Prussian-born Union commander, it would have been closer to what Schurz later said he was expecting.[14] Had that happened, roughly 5,000 men then would have held a quarter-mile section of the Union right.

It may not have been a strong enough flank to hold out for good against the two-pronged assaults of more than 13,000 men under Rodes and Early, but it also would not have extended by hundreds of yards the smaller force in blue. As it was, with the 1st Corps inexorably being pushed back, Barlow's decision to send his men to the knoll created an overall configuration of two Union corps resembling a left hand, the fingers being pushed back in an ever-tightening clinch, but with the thumb extended and exposed to grievous injury from a superior force on three sides.

When Wilkeson's men fired their first shots at Early's oncoming brigades and artillery, the 2,450 men that Barlow had committed to the knoll and surrounding fields were immediately confronting more than 3,100 men to their front under Early and Rodes, with another 2,400 in follow-up brigades preparing to circle behind Early and flank the federals on their right. To make matters worse for the Yankees, Alabama sharpshooters had regrouped and advanced with Rodes to within a few hundred yards of Ames's men, and they were piercing the ranks with deadly sniper fire on the exposed Yankee lines.

Meanwhile, more than 6,300 of Rodes's men were in a fierce struggle with a roughly equal force of Yankees at the juncture between the 1st and 11th Corps less than a mile to the west of Barlow's Knoll. A mile and a half to the southwest, the remnants of the Confederate and Union forces that had first clashed that morning were in a monumental struggle in which the Union troops would be first pushed off McPherson's Ridge, then Seminary Ridge, and then sent on a full-bore retreat to Cemetery Hill.[15]

While Schurz blamed Barlow's "ardor" or a misunderstanding, Barlow never admitted that occupying the knoll was tactically unsound or dangerous. Instead, he blamed his men for running.[16] In his defense, command decisions throughout the first day at Gettysburg were heavily defined by a race to, and defense of, precious high ground, both north and south of the town. Barlow also would have heard and witnessed what Dilger's guns had done in blunting previous Confederate attacks while firing from open and exposed positions, and the reputation that Bayard Wilkeson's Battery G had gained over the previous month could have played into the decision to place Bayard in such a challenging position. The "ardor" that Schurz talked about may have led Barlow to conclude that the slight rise of Barlow's Knoll was the last, best strategic high ground to stand and fight the Confederates and prevent another Chancellorsville. An 11th Corps with something to prove, with artillery that had already demonstrated its deadly effectiveness, might this time hold on. But only if properly led.

No matter the reasoning behind Barlow's decision, by the time that Bayard's cannons began banging away at the oncoming Confederates, any hope of a Union victory north of Gettysburg had turned into a desperate struggle for survival for the 11th and 1st Corps.

In his memoir, Howard said he originally hoped Schurz had enough strength to take and keep Oak Hill. But Howard said that he soon received "alarming intelligence" that "Early's division of Ewell's corps was at hand" on his right flank. Barlow's—and Bayard Wilkeson's—exposure on the knoll made any further thought of the federal troops going on the offensive impossible. For all practical purposes, from the moment he came onto the field, Wilkeson was on the defensive and simply fighting for time.

"Barlow against a shower of bullets made a strong effort to advance his lines, but as soon as I heard of the approach of Ewell and saw that nothing could prevent the turning of my right flank if Barlow advanced, the order [(to take Oak Hill)] was countermanded except to press out a skirmish line," Howard wrote after the war.

Within minutes, Howard wrote, "the firing, growing worse and worse, showed me that the front lines could not hold out much longer."[17]

Despite the odds, Howard said that he had made a decision to stand and fight and wait for the rest of Meade's army to come up.

"It seemed almost hopeless that Meade, the 6th Corps (commanded by the steady, heavy-set John Sedgwick, known as "Uncle John" to his men) being over 30 miles away, should gather his widely separated troops in time to promise success to our arms, but from a sudden resolution which entered my heart I exclaimed, 'But, God helping us, we will stay here till the army comes,'" Howard wrote in the *Atlantic Monthly* in 1876.

He added, in a passage that advanced the theory that Howard always saw the 1st and 11th Corps's heavy losses as a down payment on holding the cemetery: "I immediately determined to hold the front line as long as possible; and when compelled to retreat from the Seminary line, as I felt I would be, to dispute the ground obstinately; but to have all the time a strong position at the Cemetery and one that I could hold until at least (Henry) Slocum and (Dan) Sickles (commanders of the 12th and 6th Corps, respectively), with their 18,000 reinforcements, could reach the battlefield; and possibly until the arrival of Meade and the whole army."[18]

Speaking to veterans in 1888, Howard said that "a Napoleon would have given special recognition to the first day at Gettysburg. To have lost so little ground, and with an inferior force to have taken and secured the strong position which gave us the most important victory of the war, ought not be passed over and set aside merely as 'a defeat.'"[19]

"Reynolds and myself followed the plain instructions of strategy," Howard continued, in a letter commemorating the dedication of the 119th New York Regiment's monument at Gettysburg twenty-five years after the battle. "Namely, that an advance guard of the main army should meet the enemy boldly, dispute the ground foot-by-foot, till the army behind it can be concentrated and prepared for effective resistance."[20]

Foot-by-foot, the toll was horrendous. Barlow was severely wounded while trying to rally his routed division, one reason why he never wrote an after-action report. But in a letter to his mother written from a Union hospital 3 miles east of Gettysburg right after the battle, he defended his orders and said that only the cowardice of his men prevented him from holding on. "I had an admirable position," he wrote his mother. "The country was an open one for a long distance around and could be swept by our artillery."[21]

He added: "I had my entire force at the very point where the attack (of Early) was made. But the enemies (sic) skirmishers had hardly attacked us before my men began to run. No fight at all was made."[22]

Some of his men did run. But Barlow's blanket condemnation was unfair to the many that did not, including Bayard and his gunners. Many stood and fought heroically, the memory of the humiliation at Chancellorsville fresh on their minds.

Once he got his orders, Wilkeson—the brash, young officer who had worried he would never see a fight hot enough to give him a name—rushed off to almost certain failure. It might as well have been called Barlow's Island. Surrounded and outgunned, it was an "unequal contest" from the beginning, Brig. Gen. Henry Hunt, the Army's chief of artillery, said in his official report.[23]

Schurz, surveying the threat to Barlow from the roof of a house near the edge of town, ordered troops to the west of the knoll to stretch their lines to link up with Barlow's position. He also pleaded for more reinforcements, sending "one staff officer after another" asking Howard to draw from the reserves on Cemetery Hill, but by then it was too late.[24] Howard kept the 11th Corps brigades he'd originally deployed there in place. It was now only a matter of how badly the retreat to that redoubt would turn out for the two endangered Union corps. And whether they'd have enough strength to hold there with whatever survived the rout north of town.

Across Rock Creek, Confederate lieutenant general John Brown Gordon's all-Georgian brigade of Early's division led the charge that eventually pushed Wilkeson's battery and the surrounding infantry off the knoll. He and Barlow were similar, and they had a recent history. Just thirty years old, Gordon was a year older than Francis Barlow. Like Barlow, Gordon was a lawyer. Like Barlow, Gordon had fought and been wounded at the Bloody Lane at Antietam. Like Barlow, Gordon's wife, Fanny, was credited for saving his life after Antietam. Gordon had been shot five times at the Bloody Lane, the last leaving him face down, unconscious, drowning in his own blood. Only a bullet hole in his cap allowed the blood to drain, saving him from drowning and his wife, who was traveling with the army, nursed him back to health with a diet of beef broth and brandy.

Gordon was handsome, proper, and revered by the Georgians serving under him. He personified the pageantry of the Southern war culture in 1863. At Gettysburg, Gordon rode a magnificent black stallion that his men had captured for him in fighting at Winchester, Virginia, a few days earlier. His striking presence on the field that day stuck with men on both sides forever.

"I never saw a horse's neck so arched, his eye so fierce, his nostril so dilated," recalled Confederate artillery major Robert Stiles. "He followed in a trot, close upon the heels of the battle line, his head right in among the slanting barrels and bayonets, the reins loose upon his neck, his rider standing in his stirrups, bareheaded, hat in hand, arms extended, and, in a voice like a trumpet, exhorting his men. It was superb; absolutely thrilling." A private in Gordon's brigade called Gordon "the most prettiest thing you ever did see on a field of fight. It'd put a fight into a whipped chicken just to look at him."[25]

While Barlow came away from their fight convinced his Union soldiers had failed him, Gordon came to the opposite conclusion about Barlow's division from the other side. The Confederate commander credited Barlow's men for holding on just long enough to sow doubt and hesitancy in the ranks above him, preventing Lee's first-day vanguard from pressing the fight long enough, and hard enough, to push the Yankees completely off the heights at the Cemetery.

In two of the most important words of the war, Lee messaged Ewell to try to take the heights on Cemetery Hill and nearby Culp's Hill "if practicable." Apparently it was not. Gordon forever blamed Ewell for missing out on a chance to win the battle, and possibly, the war, had they used the momentum of overrunning Wilkeson and the rest of Barlow's Division to keep pushing the retreating 1st and 11th Corps off Cemetery Ridge and other high ground during the late afternoon of July 1. Gordon maintained that had Stonewall Jackson been in charge of the Confederate forces that attacked Wilkeson's guns and Barlow's infantry brigades, that the audacious Jackson would have exhorted his men to push harder, not stop to take stock and rest as they momentarily did. After the war, Gordon claimed that he briefly considered disobeying Ewell's orders. But he did not.

"No soldier in a great crisis ever wished more ardently for a deliverer's hand than I wished for one hour of Jackson when I was ordered to halt" after overrunning Barlow's Knoll, Gordon wrote after the war. "Had he been there, his quick eye would have caught at a glance the entire situation, and instead of halting me he would have urged me forward and have pressed the advantage to the utmost, simply notifying General Lee that the battle was on and he had decided to occupy the heights. Had General Lee himself been present this would undoubtedly have been done."[26]

Gordon viewed the decision to not keep pressing more vigorously after the success on Barlow's Knoll as a "fatal mistake."[27]

Gordon's claim is unprovable, and in any case, the blame cannot be solely laid upon Ewell. Jackson was almost two months' dead at Gettysburg, and Lee, accustomed to Jackson's initiative, had gotten in the habit of suggesting rather than ordering. The resistance that Wilkeson's guns and Barlow's infantry put up might even have given Jackson pause. Gordon had benefited from lucky timing to achieve the advantage he had. "A more timely arrival never occurred," Gordon later reported, describing his men's fortuitous appearance on the Yankee flank.[28] But he also watched those men pay a dear price for pressing that advantage.

That advantage terrified Schurz, as he watched the attack on his right wing commence from that rooftop. A friend of Abraham Lincoln who had been ambassador to Spain before the war, Schurz never shook the memory of Gordon's division and the rest of Early's force pouring down the Harrisburg road and out of woods abutting it, heading straight for Wilkeson's guns and the exposed and extended Union infantry thinly fanned around it. For gut-wrenching minutes, Schurz thought his 11th Corps faced destruction before survivors could retreat to Howard's fallback position on the heights south of town.[29]

"I had hardly deployed my two divisions. . . . on the north side of Gettysburg, when the action very perceptibly changed its character," he wrote after the war. He blamed Howard's cold feet and Barlow's tactical blunder for the trap. Schurz believed that had not Howard rescinded the objective to take Oak Hill, that he might have been able to deal a crippling blow on disorganized Confederates before Early had a chance to strike and before Rodes's men were firmly in control of those heights. Summarizing what went wrong after the battle, Schurz blamed it on a lack of bold action before Wilkeson even arrived on the field, and then on a tactical blunder by the subordinate Barlow that placed Wilkeson and supporting infantry in an untenable position.

According to Schurz, "the 1st Corps had been driving before it a comparatively small force of the enemy, taking many prisoners, among them the rebel general Archer with almost his whole brigade. My line, too, advanced, but presently I received an order from General Howard to halt where I was, and to push forward only a strong force of skirmishers. This I did, and my skirmishers, too, captured prisoners in considerable number. But then the enemy began to show greater strength and tenacity. He planted two batteries on a hillside, one above the other, opposite my left, enfilading part of the First Corps.

"Captain Dilger, whose battery was attached to my Third Division, answered promptly, dismounted four (actually five) of the enemy's guns, as we observed through our field-glasses, and drove away two rebel regiments supporting them. In the meantime the infantry firing on my left and on the right of the 1st Corps grew much in volume. It became evident that the enemy's line had been heavily reinforced, and was pressing upon us with constantly increasing vigor. I went up to the roof of a house behind my skirmish line to get a better view of the situation, and observed that my right and center were not only confronted by largely superior forces, but also that my right was becoming seriously overlapped.

"I had ordered General Barlow to refuse his right wing, that is to place his right brigade, Colonel (von) Gilsa's, a little in the right rear of his other brigade, in order to use it against a possible flanking movement by the enemy.

"But I now noticed that Barlow, be it that he had misunderstood my order, or that he was carried away by the ardor of the conflict, had advanced his whole line and lost connection with my Third Division on his left, and in addition to this, he had, instead of refusing, pushed forward his right brigade, so that it formed a projecting angle with the rest of the line. At the same time I saw the enemy (Early) emerging from the belt of woods on my right with one battery after another and one column of infantry after another, threatening to envelop my right flank and to cut me off from the town and the position on Cemetery Hill behind.

"I immediately gave orders to the Third Division (Schimmelfennig's) to re-establish its connection with the First, although this made still thinner a line already too thin, and hurried one staff officer after another to General Howard with the urgent request for one of his two reserve brigades to protect my right against the impending flank attack by the enemy.

"Our situation," Schurz noted with horror and foreboding, "became critical."[30]

CHAPTER 31

"The Marvel Is That Any of Them Escaped"

N<small>O SITUATION HAD BECOME MORE CRITICAL THAN</small> L<small>T.</small> B<small>AYARD</small> W<small>IL-</small>keson's. Although his guns were sleeting iron to deadly effect on Jones's cannons and Gordon's advancing infantry, the Confederates' artillery superiority allowed the Rebels to pour shot after shot on the knoll and into the thinly deployed regiments around it. In his official report, the Confederate gunner Jones said his guns did terrible damage to the Union forces in front of them but he also credited Wilkeson's marksmanship for holding back the Confederate onslaught for a time. His men furiously loading and firing, Bayard's guns in short order knocked out four of Jones's. "Our fire was very effective upon their infantry, presenting as they did large bodies in easy range of us," Jones reported. "In this engagement I had three guns temporarily disabled and one permanently so."[1]

Of Wilkeson's artillery and Barlow's infantry in his front, Gordon concluded, the "the marvel is that any of them escaped."[2]

Although some Confederate officers later claimed the Yankees put up little resistance once Early's advance reached full throttle, the Rebels up front actually doing the fighting saw a different, stubborn foe. "Our brigade (Gordon's) and the rest of Early's division formed in line of battle and advanced," recalled Confederate private G. W. Nichols. "We attacked them immediately but had a hard time in moving them. We advanced with our accustomed yell, but they stood firm until we got near them. They then began to retreat in fine order, shooting at us as they retreated.

They were harder to drive than we had ever known them before. Men were being mown down in great numbers on both sides."

The Yankees, Nichols said, regrouped at a fence line for a volley, then, swept backward beyond the knoll, made a final, "desperate stand" at the Almshouse, before skedaddling piecemeal through the town and back toward the heights south of it.[3]

Some of von Gilsa's troops positioned along Rock Creek did take flight in the face of Gordon's advancing men. General Ames, who during Reconstruction after the war would become provisional governor and a senator from Louisiana, later complained that von Gilsa's men were "creating considerable confusion" as they streamed back through his lines.[4] Von Gilsa disputed that. Ten days after the battle, speaking in German, he told his men that they had fought well that first day and throughout the battle of Gettysburg, and that they could "rightly claim a large part of the outcome there."[5]

As Gordon's line of infantry advanced, with Wilkeson's guns shredding away at almost point-blank range, Col. Douglas Fowler of the 17th Connecticut, who had advanced to the east side of the creek, ordered his men to fix bayonets and charge into the oncoming gray, and brutal hand-to-hand fighting broke out. Within yards of Wilkeson, Fowler sat conspicuously on a white horse, brandished his sword and urging his men to hold on. But he was soon killed with a shot to the head, his brains splattering his aide, Lt. Whitney Chatfield. Chatfield's hat and sleeve were slashed by bullets, his Revolutionary War sword was shattered, and his horse was killed underneath him. Another Connecticut soldier on the knoll, Capt. James V. Moore, had had a premonition the night before, telling his men he would soon be "at rest." He was killed with two shots to the head.[6]

Although just as desperate, the fighting on Barlow's Knoll was different from Chancellorsville because the Yankees could see what was coming. At Chancellorsville, where Private Nichols had participated in the rout of Howard's 11th Corps, there had been "carelessness" and an "ease" among Howard's men. "Never was an army more completely surprised, more absolutely overwhelmed," than the 11th Corps had been at Chancellorsville, Nichols recalled.[7]

There was no surprise at Gettysburg. Barlow's men were giving ground more grudgingly, but the masses of Gordon to the northeast and Rodes to the north were simply too much. As Gordon pressed the 11th Corps on the right flank, the Union 1st Corps to the west and southwest was also starting to collapse under pressure from Pender and others. The Union's Lieutenant Fischer, by then having climbed a light post near Gettysburg College to catch a better view, saw it unravel across a 2-mile front.

"A foreboding of the coming massacre kept me riveted to the spot, here and there artillery and musketry fire opening at intervals of a few seconds, then the volley from, an entire regiment on our extreme right likely the 17th Conn., when all along the lines of the Eleventh and the First Corps the demon of battle is turned loose without stint or favor."[8]

It was a turning point that might have also saved the Confederates from disaster. Gordon always maintained that Early's arrival on the Union right not only gave it a perfect shot at Barlow's exposed men, but that it relieved potentially unsustainable pressure from the Union 1st Corps on Rodes's and Heth's men. They were "almost overwhelmed" before Early slammed into the Union right, Gordon maintained.

But now, with momentum and numerical advantages, the Rebels under Gordon came on with their high-pitched yells. "We charged the heavy line of the enemy & had a desperate fight," the Confederate commander said. "I consider the action of the Brigade as brilliant as any charge of the war. . . . We captured a great many prisoners & routed the enemy in our front. The movements of the brigade gave great relief on the whole line. We drove them before us in perfect confusion; but night came on and they fell back to a strong position & fortified themselves— received also very heavy reinforcements."[9]

Even the Union's big guns, as effective as they had been throughout the day, could no longer stem the gray tide. "When I reached the ground I found it unfortunately near the enemy's line of infantry, with which they were engaged, as well as two of his batteries, the concentrated fire of which no battery could sustain," Osborn, the 11th Corps's top artillery officer, wrote in his official report four weeks later.[10]

He galloped to the knoll, where Wilkeson's gunners were blazing away as fast as they could, and he immediately felt the nakedness of the position. "The lines of battle were in the open field and very close together," Osborn recalled. "The enemy's line overlapped ours to a considerable extent on both flanks." Wilkeson's battery, he said, was "doing good work," but "I knew that the two divisions must soon fall back or would be drawn back."[11] Osborn galloped off the knoll to check the condition of four remaining 11th Corps batteries, including Dilger's, who was delivering hellfire into oncoming Confederate infantry that was threatening to totally envelop Wilkeson's big guns and Barlow's infantry still trying to hold the knoll. Even as the trap was closing, Wilkeson's cannons delivered deadly accurate fire on the Confederates.

As Early sat with officers on his horse on a rise east of Rock Creek, one of Wilkeson's shots killed the horse of Maj. Peter Hairston of Early's staff and ripped off the tail of Hairston's coat, leaving him dazed but unscathed. Confederate officer John Warwick Daniel was sitting on his horse between Hairston and Early, scanning Wilkeson's guns with binoculars, when he saw the flash of the barrel and recoil of the gun as the shell that hit Hairston was fired. In an instant, Hairston was down, and Daniel immediately urged Early to move. "That gunner yonder is shooting a cannon like a pistol," Daniel told Early, referring to Wilkeson's battery. "If I were a Confederate Major-General I think I would save my bacon." The two men quickly rode off the hill. In the hail of shell and shot, Ewell's wooden leg—he had lost a leg at the Battle of Groveton—was shattered, and he replaced it with a second one mid-battle.[12]

But it was not enough. Osborn had scarcely vacated the knoll when the first of Gordon's men came crashing over it.

Maj. Gen. Henry Hunt, who had been named chief of Union artillery just three days earlier, explained what happened next.

"On the east of Rock Creek, Jones's artillery battalion, within easy range, enfiladed its whole line and took it in reverse, while the brigades of Gordon, Hays, and Avery in line, with Smith's in reserve, advanced . . . upon Barlow's position (with a brigade under George) Doles, of Rodes's division, connecting with Gordon. An obstinate and bloody contest ensued, in which Barlow was desperately wounded . . . and the whole corps forced back to its original line, on which, with the aid of Coster's brigade and Heckman's battery, drawn from Cemetery Hill, Schurz endeavored to rally it and cover the town. The fighting here was well sustained, but the Confederate force was overpowering in numbers, and the troops retreated to Cemetery Hill, Ewell entering the town about 4:30 p.m. These retrograde movements had uncovered the flank of the First Corps and made its right untenable."[13]

It was some of the most brutal fighting of the war.

The Confederate charge and artillery fire on the Union right was "one of the most warlike and animated spectacles I ever witnessed," said Confederate major Campbell Brown, Dick Ewell's aide and stepson, who was at the rear of Gordon's furious charge.[14] The artillery and rifle fire on and around Barlow's Knoll had been so intense that it unnerved veterans as well as rookies. Adding to the confusion, smoke was swirling over the battlefield from the Benner farmhouse, which had been repeatedly hit by artillery fire. As Jones's shells landed with repetitive fury among them, a 17th Connecticut officer sensed his men losing their nerve. "Dodge the big ones, boys," he called out.[15]

That was becoming harder and harder to do. Lt. Clyde Miller of the 153rd Pennsylvania had been ordered to set up a defensive line about 200 yards in front of Wilkeson's booming guns at Blocher's Woods, a band of trees rimming Rock Creek's western banks. As Miller urged his men to dig in as best they could, a Rebel cannonball flew so closely to his head that the fuse brushed his cheek. Every man could see the dangerous fix they were in. "Accidentally we had gotten into an angle," Miller recalled, of Early's men directly in their front and the second-wind pushes from Rodes's men to their left.[16]

Sgt. W. R. Kiefer informed Miller that "the woods in front of us were being massed with men behind the thicket for a charge." At first he couldn't see what the sergeant did, but, getting down on hands and knees, he could see thousands of legs in bramble and trees in front of them. "By crouching down, I could see their legs up to their knees," Miller said. "I did so, and I saw their force was a large one."

With rifle fire intensifying on his men and shells aimed at Wilkeson's battery whooshing just above their heads, Miller hurried back to warn a superior officer of the gathering threat in the woods. That officer drew his sword. "Go back and hold our line at all hazards," he shouted.

Miller responded that the situation was "useless, as the force massing in front of us was a large one."

When the officer hesitated, Miller pressed further. "Where is the battle line?" he asked the officer. The man scanned the knoll and the ground around it and relented. "It's gone," he responded. "Get yourselves out the best you can and report at Cemetery Hill." Upon those orders, Miller said, "we surely got."[17]

But not before exacting a deadly toll on the oncoming Southerners. Private Ruch, still recovering from typhus that had so beleaguered him on the march north, was in a line of men deployed in scattered woods about 20 yards from Rock Creek. Shots from Wilkeson's guns aimed at Early's advancing lines whizzed so closely over Ruch's head that he could feel their heat. The men in his vicinity were so tired that when they first got to the position, some of the men had lain down, "more dead than alive." But now they were standing in rifle range so intimate they could pick out features of the men they were shooting.[18]

Dilger, his guns stopping to shoot and then retreating toward Gettysburg at Wilkeson's left and rear, lost twenty-four horses killed by artillery fire. This was becoming a problem for all artillery units. Wilkeson's battery would lose thirty-one horses in the three-day battle, most in these first crucial hours.[19] Men in both batteries were going down at an alarming rate. Some fourteen in Dilger's battery were wounded, killed, or captured, fifteen in Wilkeson's battery, as Confederate cannons on Oak Hill to the northwest and Jones's guns to the east alternately turned their guns on the federal cannon and the lines of infantry around them, before turning them back on Wilkeson and the infantry near him.[20]

Howard claimed after the battle that holding the ground north of town was not the ultimate Day One goal. He was focused, he wrote afterward, "throughout the first day of the battle" on holding Cemetery Hill as the crucial fallback point for his 11th and the late Reynolds's 1st Corps.[21] There has long been debate about who was most responsible for holding the heights south of town—Howard, Reynolds, or Winfield Scott Hancock. But no matter, it was the ground from which the Union army would fight and defend for the next two days, leading to the most important Northern victory of the war.

One of Howard's initial defenses of his actions on Day One at Gettysburg came in a letter to Sam Wilkeson, one in which he claimed that Bayard's actions and that of the rest of the 11th Corps had courageously held out against odds and bought enough time to allow the Union army to occupy and hold the eventual high ground they used to win the battle.

Howard in his memoirs took great pains to argue that it was his decision alone to choose Cemetery Ridge as a fallback and that he helped steady the remnants of two shattered Union corps as they were pushed back from the fields north and west of the town.

"After observing the whole sweep of the country," Howard wrote in his autobiography, he concluded that he would "use that Cemetery Ridge as the best defensive position within sight." Refuting the claims of an aide to the late Reynolds that it was Reynolds who first suggested Cemetery Ridge as the best place to fight the battle, Howard declared that, "the testimony, both direct and indirect, points all one way"—that "I chose the position and used it throughout the first day of the battle."[22]

Years later, Howard even solicited his messenger at Gettysburg to issue a statement saying that he had never heard Reynolds declare that Cemetery Ridge was the logical place to make the stand. Capt. Daniel Hall claimed that Howard had chosen Cemetery Ridge the first moment he saw it late in the morning of July 1, when he and Howard were galloping along the Emmitsburg Road south of the town late, the battle's roar intensifying north and west of the town.

"I remembered that as we passed along the road at its base, you pointed to the crest of the Cemetery Ridge on (our) right, and said, 'there's the place to fight this battle,' or words to that effect," Hall wrote Howard in 1882.[23]

Irrespective of who chose the ground, the narrative of the beleaguered 11th Corps staving off disaster, and earning redemption from the loss at Chancellorsville, set in even as the battle raged. The *Cleveland Morning Leader* reported on July 4 that "the 11th Corps, which has felt the stigma of retreat at Chancellorsville, had an important part to play in this contest, and nobly retrieved its reputation. It showed signs of wavering at first, but General Howard shouted, 'Remember Chancellorsville,' and the whole corps hurled itself against the enemy, men fighting like infuriated demons and driving the enemy before them."[24]

Hyperbole aside the Union army was able to hold onto the crucial heights south of town, and the 11th Corps's 3,801 casualties[25] at Gettysburg were testament to the demonic fighting it engaged in, and the salvation of an army and a cause it helped bring forth.

Accepting Howard's claim that he always saw the heights around the cemetery as the best place for the Union army to fight a battle, and coupling that with his orders to pull back from trying to take Oak Hill at a crucial moment, the placement of Bayard Wilkeson's guns and Barlow's infantry on Barlow's Knoll can only be seen as sacrificial. The fog of war, the misunderstanding between Schurz and Barlow, the arguable tactical decision by Barlow to occupy the exposed high ground, does not cloud that central truth.

Congress added to the Howard-Hancock controversy in January of 1864 when it passed a joint resolution singling out Howard, Meade, and Hooker for their roles at Gettysburg and the march leading to it. But that congressional resolution conspicuously left out Hancock. He had arrived on the field late in the afternoon—he estimated about 4:00 p.m.—with orders from Meade to take control of all Union forces then at Gettysburg. After a short and uncomfortable chain-of-command discussion with Howard, he did just that. According to Brevet Gen. E. P. Halstead, an aide to Reynolds, who witnessed the exchange, Howard initially protested, then acquiesced with the proviso that Hancock issued no orders in front of him. Honor, even in the fury of battle, could not be ignored.

According to Halstead, Hancock said the following: "Very well, General Howard I will second any order that you have to give, but General Meade has also directed me to select a field on which to fight this battle in rear of Pipe Creek," referring to the original location, miles away, that Meade had wanted to lure Lee into. Looking at the field, from Culp's Hill to the northeast to the two round-top heights to the south, Hancock then declared, according to Halstead: "But I think this the strongest position by nature upon which to fight a battle that I ever saw, and if it meets your approbation I will select this as the battlefield." According to

Halstead, Howard responded, "I think it a very strong position, General Hancock. A very strong position!"

"Very well, sir, I select this as the battlefield," Hancock then said, according to Halstead.[26]

A year after the war Hancock finally received his own congressional resolution praising his actions at Gettysburg. But during the war his omission in the first congressional citation after Gettysburg caused friction between Hancock and Howard. Howard viewed the commendation as part of the politics of the 1864 presidential campaign, in which Lincoln eventually defeated his former commanding general, McClellan. Howard was known as a staunch supporter of Lincoln. Hancock was nominally a Democrat, although it was reported that he voted for Lincoln in 1864.[27]

"I do consider that an act of injustice was done by Congress, in singling out any Corps commander at Gettysburg for his services there, and I do not consider that any one receiving the thanks of Congress was impelled by motive to decline such an honor, even if it were proper for him to do so," Hancock wrote Howard after Howard had complained about press reports denying him the credit he thought he deserved by recognizing the advantage of Cemetery Ridge.

Hancock wrote that "I have my own views concerning the battle of Gettysburg, but I have not yet put them in print," and that "I have seen many things in print which I consider unjust, but I do not think it wise to reply to them." It was a thinly disguised slap at the politicking that Howard had undertaken to defend his actions almost as soon as the battle ended.

Hancock continued: "I thought myself the act of Congress might have been induced by a desire on the part of the Administration to make you prominent, to have an effect in case it should be thought wise or advisable to use your name and reputation in the coming Presidential or Vice Presidential Campaign."

Some Union officers were convinced that Howard, and his corps, had almost cost the Union another shattering defeat on July 1. Hancock's inspector general, Lt. Col. Charles H. Morgan, credited Buford's cavalry more than Howard's corps for the position on Cemetery Ridge. Furthermore, he said, Howard's 11th Corps was "unreliable and quite unmanageable," by the time that Hancock arrived, that Howard "was despondent," and that Howard's aide and brother, Maj. Charles Howard, "could not restrain his mortification at the behavior of the corps."[28]

Men who fought with Lieutenant Wilkeson that day, the men most invested to make a judgment on their superiors, remained bitter about the decision to occupy that ground. The 82nd Ohio, which sustained 181 casualties among its 258 men, including 18 killed and 85 wounded, was positioned west and south of the knoll, to the rear of Wilkeson's batteries, when Early's forces slammed it. Pvt. Arthur T. Lee wrote that the advance to the knoll was "unspeakable folly" and that "instead of advancing, we should have fallen back, as soon as the approach of the enemy from the right was developed, and should have reformed, and barricaded the line with our right well refused upon the time, and our left connecting, as well as it might be, with the right of the 1st Corps.

"I don't know who is responsible for the advance, but whoever ordered it deserves the severest censure," Lee wrote twenty-five years after the battle.[29]

Lt. Louis Fischer said the threat of impending doom he saw should have been just as readily apparent to commanding officers, and he wondered why reserves were not committed. "That a repulse was inevitable must have been apparent to the Commanding General, as the enemy's regiments were plainly visible to him," Fischer said. "No; my poor comrades had to be sacrificed, just as they were sacrificed at Chancellorsville two months previous."[30]

All the post-battle second-guessing, blame-passing, and credit-taking would have meant nothing to the nineteen-year old Lt. Bayard Wilkeson. Outnumbered, outgunned, and outflanked, he followed orders until the end.

Chapter 32

"The Ground Shook"

Bayard Wilkeson's position had become untenable, and indefensible, and within minutes of setting up his guns, he was hauled off the knoll to the Almshouse, gravely wounded. But the training he had drilled into his men temporarily paid off. Bancroft, now in charge of the guns, held firm for a crucial half hour, even as the knoll began crawling with waves of Rebel-yelling Confederates, and his superior—Wilkeson—was now out of action altogether.[1] The ground in front of the battery was soon striped by long lines of wounded and dead men who had fallen in volleys from Gordon's men. Sensing the danger before he was wounded, Wilkeson had immediately called for Merkle and his two guns to be rushed up from the reserve near the Almshouse to augment the four guns already banging away from the knoll.

On the Confederate side, with Jones's cannons covering them, the broad front of Old Jube's men threatened to surround Barlow's. Early recorded that a "great slaughter" commenced within minutes, and he had the Yankees retreating in "great confusion" toward Gettysburg.[2]

Still, even after he was wounded, and even after he was carried off the field, Wilkeson's guns kept banging away. Ruch, the Pennsylvania private, saw cannon fire shred and temporarily halt a Rebel charge to his left just before a second wave hit his part of the line. "We could see balls plowing up the ground along the rear of the line, and if ever Johnnies ran for cover those fellows did," Ruch said. "Shortly after this they made another charge near the center of our line, but to the left of us. I think it was a feint, their object being to keep us in our position until they got ready. As soon as they fell back I told some of the boys near me that we would get a chance next."[3]

He was right. The Rebels that Miller had seen assembling in the shelter of the woods along Rock Creek moved forward in full-throated fury. Trilling the Rebel Yell, they slammed head-on into Ruch's section of the line. Men on either side were shot simultaneously. While ramrodding another ball into his barrel, Ruch fixated on the face of one of the men as the soldier died. Four or five volleys later, the order to fall back was shouted along the Union line; Ruch's last shot in this stand caught a man climbing over a fence, sending him toppling no more than 30 yards away. Ruch had spared a flag bearer, moving from that target to the man on the fence because he had a gun. It was a tableau of individual epics, hand-to-hand, man-to-man. The fighting became so close quarters that flag bearers for Gordon's Georgians and the 25th Ohio under Lt. Col. Jeremiah Williams stabbed wildly at one another, flags flying wildly with the deadly thrusts.[4] The Union lines were disintegrating. "Our line was broken in the left and our right was attacked in flank," Ruch said. "There was nothing left for us to do but to retire or surrender."[5]

Retreating about 30 yards up Barlow's Knoll, Ruch turned to fire once more and saw a "windrow of human dead" in front marking the line of where an initial stand had taken place. "There was a regular swath of blue coats, as far as I could see along the line. They were piled up in every shape, some on their backs, some on their faces, and others turned and twisted in every imaginable shape."[6]

"The Johnnies were coming and coming fast," remembered Pvt. William Southerton of the 75th Ohio. "The ground shook," from Wilkeson's guns and the remaining infantry around him. It was point-blank killing.

"Confederates were closing on all sides, and fast," Southerton said. "The infantry held their fire until the Johnnies were well within range, then let loose. What a horrible roar of battle! Fumes thick and acrid. One could barely see the comrade beside him. Casualties were terrible."

Pressured and without its commander, Wilkeson's battery limbered up and began pulling off the knoll, and organized retreat soon turned to panic. Just south of Wilkeson's guns, the 75th Ohio's Col. Andrew Harris, wounded, struggled to keep a semblance of a fighting force. "We were much like a parcel of schoolboys turned loose," Private Southerton wrote.[7]

As the 11th Corps collapsed and fell back past the Almshouse and into the town, individual acts of heroism slowed and bloodied the Confederate advance. A Union private named Trombower was shot in the shoulder; standing behind a tree, he coolly reloaded and shifted to his good, left shoulder.[8]

One private in the 119th New York, his leg shattered so he could not stand, kept loading and firing and yelling at his fellow soldiers to get out of the way lest he shoot them in the back.[9]

Barlow knew he was in trouble when an aide, 1st Lt. Edward Culp, returned from delivering an order and saw Gordon's men massing in the woods near Rock Creek. Culp hurried back to warn Barlow, and the two officers galloped toward the knoll, where Wilkeson's guns were still blasting away. "One glance showed that I was correct," Culp recalled. "Thousands of fresh troops were hurled against our weakened lines."[10]

Pvt. David Knauss, of Company D, 153rd Pennsylvania, said he knew the odds were stacked against Barlow's division even before he and his mates set up a thin defensive position in Wilkeson's immediate front. "The first day of Gettysburg, it seems to me, the Rebels were bound to get the town," he said. When the lines began breaking, he joined his mates in a chaotic retreat, stopping to pick up discarded rifles, reload, and return fire. "I kept loading and firing back on my own measure," he said. His treasured pocket Bible fell out of his pocket as the combat continued through the town. More than fifty-five years later, a Virginia minister, given the Bible by a South Carolinian who had picked it up as he chased Yankees through the town, returned it to Knauss.[11]

Although wounded in both knees from shots off his flanks, Private Ruch made it back to the Almshouse compound, where General von Gilsa was trying to rally the remnants of his division. Under fire so heavy it felt that a sideways hailstorm was coming at them, a captain and a lieutenant helped boost Ruch over a fence on the edge of the poorhouse compound. One of the two men helping him was already wounded and the other was shot as they headed for cover in the poorhouse barn. Still, the Confederates kept coming.

By then, Bayard Wilkeson already lay wounded in the basement of the main house of the compound. The Almshouse was rapidly filling with wounded men from both sides; Ruch, sensing it was about to be captured, kept moving until he could go no more, taking temporary rest in a doorway. There, Ruch saw a cannon being pulled down the street, flying high in the air as its wheels went over a 2-foot wall. Stopping momentarily in front of him, the gunners swung the barrel toward the rear and let loose a thunderous blast of canister into a mass of Rebels rushing down the street toward them. "They were warming the rebels in great shape," Ruch said.[12]

As at Chancellorsville, artillery had helped avert an even greater rout. Wilkeson, Merkle, and Bancroft of Bayard's battery, joined by Dilger and Wheeler, Capt. Louis Heckman of the 1st Ohio, and Capt. Michael Wiedrich of the 1st New York, were all singled out for heroism. "The batteries of the Eleventh Corps did all that could possibly be expected of them, given the false positions they were compelled by circumstances to

Artist Alfred R. Waud's depiction of Bayard Wilkeson leading his battery at Gettysburg
ART AND PICTURE COLLECTION, THE NEW YORK PUBLIC LIBRARY

select," said Union colonel James P. Scott, who fought at Gettysburg and later wrote extensively about the battle.[13]

The artillery's rearguard action allowed men like Ruch more time to retreat. Von Gilsa passed by Ruch, who was unable to go further, lying in a street. The general shouted that Ruch either needed to find a hospital or he would be shot. Ruch got lucky; nearby, wounded men were being hauled into a church that was being turned into a hospital. He crawled in and found a "slaughter-house," with at least ten operating tables at work. Doctors with blood up to their shoulders ignored the fighting outside. Ruch crawled to the second floor, where fresh amputees were being placed. Ruch destroyed his remaining ammunition just before the church was overrun and captured by the Confederates. From the window, he saw fleeing remnants of the 1st and 11th Corps trying to regroup on Cemetery Hill. Ruch divided the last of his hardtack with wounded men from both armies lying near him.[14]

Other wounded 11th Corps men got luckier. Corp. Michael O'Brien of the 153rd Pennsylvania, which had 40 percent losses, was shot in the back near Barlow's Knoll, the ball passing through his body and shattering his right elbow. He was one of five Union soldiers who hid throughout the battle in the home of the parents of Tillie Pierce Alleman. O'Brien, who hid under a sofa when Rebel soldiers searched the house, returned twenty-five years later to thank Tillie's family for saving him.[15]

The 153rd Pennsylvania that deployed in Wilkeson's front suffered 23 killed, 142 wounded, and 46 captured out of 545 men. The 107th Ohio lost 23 killed, 111 wounded, and 77 captured. They were two of the twenty most damaged regiments at Gettysburg.[16]

In truth, there was nothing they could have done but delay. Even the Confederates noted it.

"That protecting Union line once broken left my command not only on the right flank, but obliquely in rear of it," the Confederate Gordon, who was elected to the Senate from Georgia after the war, and who was said to have been an organizer of the Ku Klux Klan, wrote in his memoirs. "Any troops that were ever marshalled would, under like conditions, have been as surely and swiftly shattered. There was no alternative for

Howard's men except to break and fly, or to throw down their arms and surrender."[17]

Decades after the war, Gordon told a Pennsylvania college audience that his Confederates "were thrown squarely on the right flank of Meade's army" and that "every man who was in that war on either side knows exactly what that meant.

"The fact that that portion of Meade's army melted was no disparagement of his courage, for the Old Guard of Napoleon himself would have been as surely and swiftly shattered," he said.[18]

The Union's General Howard, writing for the dedication of the 119th New York's monument in 1888, said that "Napoleon would have given special recognition to the first day at Gettysburg. To have lost so little ground, and with an inferior force to have taken and secured the strong position which gave us the most important victory of the war, ought not to be passed over and set aside merely as 'a defeat.'"[19]

CHAPTER 33

"There Was Neither Vanity nor Bravado"

Lt. Bayard Wilkeson was one of the most conspicuous targets on the field north of Gettysburg on that sweltering afternoon of July 1, 1863. Given the effectiveness of the run-and-gun maneuvers of Dilger's and Wheeler's batteries before he arrived, a fresh set of Union cannons immediately became Target Number One of any Rebel gun, large or small, within range.

On horseback and clearly in command of the guns, Bayard made sure he was visible and conspicuous. He did it to calm his jittery men. To get to their position, they had dodged cannon and rifle shot as they moved across nearly a mile of open fields. As his men set up four guns on the knoll and prepared to fire, Wilkeson brandished a revolver, purposefully walking his horse back and forth behind and within his men's hurried preparations. He leaned down and spoke individually and evenly to several of his men as they positioned the wheeled guns and began priming and pounding the barrels with powder and shell. Bayard seemed to focus on the greenest men. When the first shot was loaded and ready, he coaxed his horse "in front of his guns and ordered fire on Ewell's advancing corps," according to one eyewitness account. "There was neither vanity nor bravado in the young officer's selection of his position. He distrusted untried men. He knew that the fire on his battery would be very trying. He could see but one way to hold his men to their ground without flinching, and that was to sit still on his horse in their front, and to direct the fire . . . from his saddle."[1]

Experienced Union gunners could load and fire two shots per minute.[2] Artillery, effectively used, was a man and morale killer in advancing infantry. But the lethality that Wilkeson's battery began hurling at Early's men drew even more intense return fire. There was no natural protection, beyond slight elevation, to incoming 12-pound metal balls that screamed deadly paths through men or fused explosive shells that shredded flesh, or the canister or grapeshot that spewed an arc of lead that could leave men in heaps with a single shot.

As Wilkeson's guns continued to hit targets among the assembling Confederates, some claimed Gordon singled him out as he walked his horse slowly amidst his furiously working men. After "finding it impossible to advance his division in the face of Wilkeson's fire," the Confederate general, one anonymous account of the action said, "directed two batteries of his company to train every gun on him." Gordon does not mention this in his report or in his memoirs.[3]

Whether he was specifically targeted or not, five minutes after the beginning of his barrage a solid shot from one of Jones's guns ripped through Bayard's horse, killing the animal instantly and badly mangling the young lieutenant's right leg. Man and beast went down in a tangled heap of blood and flesh.[4]

Several of Lieutenant Wilkeson's men rushed to him and dragged him away from the dying horse. What happened next is disputed, subject to the haze and frantic action of battle. Some said Bayard's leg was already gone by then, a bloody stump of tendon, muscle, and nerve, and that Wilkeson calmly staunched the bleeding by using his pocketknife to tighten a tourniquet on his remaining stump made from his uniform sash. Others claimed that Wilkeson used the knife to cut tissue, bone, and tendon still holding the leg before applying the tourniquet. In his seminal New York Times account of the battle five days later, Sam Wilkeson did not report that Bayard had self-amputated his leg, although the father may have been the source of later accounts that maintained that, indeed, it had happened.

No matter the source or the truth, the self-amputation claim became part of the myth of Lt. Bayard Wilkeson's stand on Barlow's Knoll and the 11th Corps's doomed but sacrificial heroism. Enough order and individual acts of heroism scattered across the battlefield slowed the Confederates enough, it wearied them enough, it cost them enough in men and material, and it threw enough confusion and hesitation into the advance, that it gave the rest of the Union army just enough time to hold the high ground of Cemetery Ridge and Culp's Hill on the other side of the village.

Eyewitnesses reported that even after being wounded, the gravely injured Wilkeson instructed his men to sit him between two of his guns, where—propped up against the knee of a bugler, he continued to direct the fire of his guns. But with Wilkeson's grievous wound soon sapping his energy and focus—he almost certainly was in deep shock—Eugene Bancroft took command of the guns. Battery G's predicament was getting more precarious by the minute. With shells and rifle fire screaming over the knoll, four of Wilkeson's men placed him on a dirty blanket and began carrying him to the Almshouse, roughly a quarter mile to the south of the knoll.

Boston Journal correspondent Charlie Coffin, who days earlier had accurately predicted in his newspaper that the armies would clash at Gettysburg, pieced together one of the most vivid descriptions of Lieutenant Wilkeson's wounding.

"The only battery which could be spared on the Union side for the right line was G, Fourth United States, commanded by the Lt. Wilkeson, who had placed four of his light 12-pounders on a knoll overlooking a wide reach of fields on both sides of Rock Creek, and two pieces nearer the town, by the Almshouse, under Lieutenant Merkle.

"Von Gilsa, along Rock Creek, must hold this flank. The artillery duel began between Wilkeson, with four pieces, and twelve guns on the part of the Confederates. Wilkeson was supported by the 17th Connecticut regiment.

"It was a trying situation for the cannoneers of the Union battery. Their commander, to encourage them, to inspire them with his own lofty spirit, sat upon a horse a conspicuous figure, calmly directing the fire of the pieces. He rode from piece to piece, his horse upon the walk. Shells were bursting amid the guns, shot from rifled cannon cut the air or ploughed the ground, from cannon not a half mile away, upon a hill much higher than what he occupied. This young lieutenant bore an hon-ored name—Bayard Wilkeson—a family name, given him, in part, also, by his parents out of an admiration for the great Chevalier of France, the knight of other days, whose character was without a stain, whose life was above reproach.

"The self-possessed lieutenant from New York, accentuated by unquenchable patriotism, became a soldier at sixteen (actually 17), received his commission when he was but seventeen (18), and was not yet nineteen (he had just turned 19). For six months he had been com-mander—his captain engaged elsewhere. So admirable the discipline and efficient the battery under the instruction of the boy lieutenant that it had been accorded the post of honor—the right of the line. It is a brave spirit that can look out responsibly in a contest so unequal, but his guns are fired with precision and effect."[5]

Then Coffin described Bayard's wounding: "A rifled cannon shot strikes his right leg, crushing the bones and mangling the flesh. His sol-diers lay him upon the ground. With composure he ties his handkerchief around it, twists it in a tourniquet to stop the flow of blood, then with his own hand and knife severs the cords and tendons, and sitting there, tells his cannoneers to go on with their fire—a bravery unsurpassed even by that of the Chevalier of France.

"Faint and thirsty, he sends a soldier to fill (a canteen) at the Alms-house well. When the man returns a wounded infantry man whose life is ebbing away, beholding the canteen, exclaims, 'Oh that I could have but a swallow.' . . . 'Drink comrade, your necessities are greater than mine,' so Bayard Wilkeson, with like unselfishness, courtesy, and benevolence replies. 'Drink, comrade, I can wait.' In the coming thirst and fever of approaching death, the infantry man drains the canteen of its contents."[6]

Coffin concluded: "When it was seen that the line must retire, Wil-keson allowed himself to be carried to the Almshouse hospital, which a few minutes later, was within the advancing lines of the Confederates."[7]

Coffin employed dramatic license, but the basic story line of Bayard being badly wounded and eventually carried off the field to the Alms-house was confirmed by eyewitnesses, including some of Wilkeson's own men. The story of the self-amputation appears nowhere in any official

Army account, and the eyewitness account of a sergeant in his battery does not mention it. Another correspondent, writing in the *Washington Chronicle* a week after the battle, reported that Wilkeson "was shot from his horse by a cannon ball, which instantly killed his horse and cut off the right leg of the rider."[8] According to other accounts, the shared canteen episode happened, but it occurred at the Almshouse after Bayard's men had carried him there, not on the knoll as Coffin had described it.

Coffin, who gave more than 2,000 speeches in the decades after the war, often repeated the story that the young lieutenant cut off his own leg. There is no record of Sam Wilkeson trying to correct him.[9]

Whatever the truth is, over the decades that followed, the self-amputation story became embedded in the heroic folklore surrounding the young lieutenant. Commemorating the battle twenty-five years later, a veteran from the Union army, George L. Kilmer, wrote that Wilkeson had used his belt as a tourniquet and "with his own hand and a common knife he completed the amputation of the leg."[10] A century and a half later, official displays and monuments at the Gettysburg National Military Park continued to state the self-amputation as fact.

Truthfully, the fighting was so intense around Barlow's Knoll that two witnesses could have glimpsed the same thing and come to different conclusions. Eyewitnesses may have mistaken Bayard's use of his pocket-knife to twist and tighten a hastily applied tourniquet for actually cutting off the leg. But officially, Bancroft, the officer who took over the battery after Bayard went down; Osborn, the 11th Corps artillery commander; and Henry Hunt, the chief of all Union artillery at Gettysburg, did not mention self-amputation in their after-action reports, or in postwar correspondence, even though they went into detail on other matters. Hunt said only that Bayard was "wounded, and was carried from the field."[11] Howard also merely said that the "young officer of exceeding promise" had been wounded.[12] Bancroft, who took over for Bayard and fought heroically in the retreat to Cemetery Ridge, reported that Wilkeson was "struck in the right leg and . . . wounded."[13]

Ultimately, it does not matter. The known truth is dramatic enough. Even his enemies across Rock Creek recognized that someone of great promise had fallen.

From behind the advancing Confederate lines, Maj. Campbell Brown, an aide to Early, reported seeing a Confederate shell land among a "knot of horsemen" on the knoll. Shortly, he saw a man carried off. Brown said he knew it was an important officer "from the consternation plainly caused by his fall."[14] Brown had almost certainly witnessed Wilkeson's wounding, and litter bearers subsequently carrying him off the field.

As the young officer was being carried off the field, the blanket soon became saturated with the lieutenant's blood, leaving a dripping trail. It took probably ten minutes to traverse ground in which men were firing and retreating, and enemy shot and shell was increasingly concentrated. Just before they arrived at the poorhouse gates, the litter bearers ran into Osborn, the 11th Corps artillery chief. Recognizing Wilkeson, Osborn was so overcome with emotion that he could not speak. He had noticed and promoted the young man. Although by now in severe pain, it was the nineteen-year-old lieutenant who tried to buck up his senior officer.

"He spoke to me and was cheerful and hopeful," Osborn said.[15] Bayard, he said, was "very young, less than twenty years of age, and of remarkable promise." Sgt. Joseph Creed, one of the four men carrying him, said Wilkeson greeted Osborn with a matter-of-fact, "Hello major, here we are."[16]

Wilkeson appeared to be going into shock from the catastrophic injury. At one moment he "appeared to be very cheerful," recalled Creed. Addressing another subordinate, a sergeant named Hunter, Lieutenant Wilkeson announced, "I am done for, Sergeant, in this world."[17]

The only hint of blame came when Wilkeson, his pain intensifying, blurted out that "it was a very poor place to plant a battery."[18]

One of the other litter bearers, bugler Charles A. Lockwood, who may have been the man who propped up the young lieutenant as Wilkeson directed fire for a few moments after his injury, was wracked with emotion when he looked back and saw the trail of blood from Wilkeson's blanket. "Lieutenant, I am very sorry to see you wounded," he said. The young Wilkeson replied: "It is only a leg. I will be with you again in a few days."[19]

Once inside the Almshouse gates, the litter bearers first headed for a barn, speculating that its openness and size would become the most logical place for surgeons to set up for the wounded men falling in great numbers on the field behind them. But an officer inside the compound told them that surgeons at that moment were heading for the main house on the property, another 100 yards farther on. One of his men asked Wilkeson if he could withstand the extra five score steps. "If it would not tire you, I can stand it," Bayard replied. They assured him it would not tire them.

They carried him to the house, and hauled him down some steps into the cool basement, where they placed the young lieutenant on the floor just inside the door. Corporal George Robynane asked to remain with his lieutenant, to make sure he was tended to. Wilkeson replied with an order for the bugler Lockwood to do that. "Take your men, corporal, and return immediately to your piece," he ordered Robynane.

Then, according to Creed, Wilkeson asked for a drink of water, and someone produced a canteen. "When he was about to drink it," Creed said, "a wounded man that lay by his side begged for God's sake to give him a drink of water. The Lieutenant, before he would drink himself, ordered the water to be passed to the wounded man."[20]

Combing the battlefield after the fighting, Bayard's Uncle John, who had headed to Gettysburg as soon as Sam had gotten word to him that Bayard had been wounded, reconstructed a story similar to Coffin's and Creed's. It is possible that John Wilkeson, now taking on the role of supportive brother that Sam had shouldered when John Wilkes was killed at Seven Pines, talked to Coffin and Creed and other witnesses after the battle, although there is no record of that.

"Bayard was on his horse in command of his battery giving special attention to the right section, a long shell struck the horse and passed through it and hit him on his right leg below the knee, crushing it shockingly," John Wilkeson wrote his daughter, Maria, three days after the battle. "When he fell, his men put him in a blanket and carried into the rear into a low damp basement room in the county poorhouse, as wretched a place as well can be imagined. At this time the house was filled with wounded. Bayard went off the field bright and cheerful, in answer to his Second Lieutenant's demand for instructions, he told him to take the command, use his own judgment."[21]

Within minutes after Bayard was taken to the Almshouse, furious action rolled over and around the compound, as the remnants of Barlow's division and other elements of the 11th Corps were pushed back through Gettysburg itself, where all order disintegrated.

The correspondent Whitelaw Reid, who had broken off with Sam Wilkeson earlier that morning and had been one of the first reporters at Gettysburg, reported that the 11th Corps did "not flee wildly from its old antagonists, as at their last meeting when Stonewall Jackson scattered them as if they had been pigmies, foolishly venturing in the war of the Titans." The corps, he said, put up "stout resistance for a little while," but soon succumbed to "advantage of position" and numbers. The retreat was orderly until the 11th reached the town, he reported, and then further hell broke loose when unit commanders, trying to shelter their retreating men from murderous enfilading fire down the narrow streets, led their men on zig-zag marches toward the high ground on Cemetery Ridge.[22] Soon, men began breaking and running. The Confederates took more than 1,000 prisoners. Bayard Wilkeson, lying gravely wounded in the basement of the Almshouse, had become one of them.

The training he had instilled in his men, though, had been put to effective use. Bancroft and the remaining men of Battery G successfully fought their way out of the trap. They had held their ground on Barlow's Knoll for about half an hour, then pulled a short distance off the knoll to regroup, firing spherical case and canister into Early's infantry, now swarming toward the Almshouse and the town.

Merkle, whose two pieces Bayard had called up from reserve, ran out of ammunition except for the shotgun-like canister, but that was just as well. The Confederates were barely beyond the barrels of his guns, anyway. It was a fight for survival at point-blank range.

"The enemy was then within canister range," Merkle said in his official after-action report. "At the same time, our infantry fell back rapidly and left me almost without support." Retreating toward and through the village, he stopped his guns several times to fire, and he and Bancroft finally got the remnants of Wilkeson's battery—five of the six guns—to high ground near the cemetery at about 5:00 p.m. It had been a defeat but not a total rout.[23] "During this engagement the battery was separated into actions of half batteries, and its struggle to maintain itself was very severe and persistent," reported Osborn, the 11th Corps artillery chief.

Pvt. Charles Hofer of Wilkeson's battery had been killed. Seven men, including Lieutenant Wilkeson, were badly wounded. Four members of Battery G, including the bugler Lockwood, were missing and presumed captured. Twelve horses had been killed, and one of the six cannons had been knocked out of action. Over the three days of the battle, Wilkeson's battery would shoot 1,380 shells, most of them on the afternoon of the first day, on Barlow's Knoll and in the hectic retreat through Gettysburg.[24]

The blame-game started quickly. Lieutenant Fischer, who had directed the clearing of fences to ease the way of Union artillery onto the field, lamented the strategy that had exposed the Union right to what he called "the coming massacre" by the "demon of battle" of Confederates that had crashed into their flank.

"Thus I see my comrades murdered without them having any show for their lives," Fischer recalled. "What else can I call it, when they have to fight equal numbers—nay superior—in front, and equal numbers in flank and rear?"[25]

Sam Wilkeson came to the same conclusion in his *New York Times* dispatch three days later. He reported that Bayard's battery had been needlessly exposed, that the 11th Corps had been largely sacrificed, its wounded men left to fend for themselves.[26]

But while the critics lined up to take fresh shots at commanders of the beleaguered 11th Corps, Howard began an almost immediate public relations campaign to defend his actions on July 1. As reporters buttonholed him on the field over the next two days, he maintained that the fight put up by the 11th and 1st Corps on July 1 had given Meade enough time and fresh intelligence to win the race to the high ground on Cemetery Ridge that gave the Union army a tactical advantage for the pivotal new two days of the battle. In a decree read to 11th Corps survivors after the battle, Howard wrote: "On the First Day of July, with the First Corps and Buford's Division of Cavalry, you held double your numbers in check from 12 (noon) until night, and thus opened the way for victory to follow."[27]

Five days after the battle, Howard wrote Sam Wilkeson that Bayard had "contributed more than his proportionate part" to the Union victory that would turn the war.[28]

Bayard had made his name on the first day at Gettysburg. But in anxious, angry days to follow, Sam Wilkeson did not know if his boy was dead or alive.

CHAPTER 34

"Whether Living Now or Dead He Could Not Tell"

TWO DAYS LATER, STILL UNSURE OF HIS SON'S FATE, THE COLLEAGUES sitting in the shade with Sam Wilkeson at Meade's headquarters in that late-morning lull spared the normal ribbing they might have heaped on *The New York Times* correspondent for arriving late to the fight. Even as he reported and observed the intense fighting of the second day, the correspondent could not hide his worry about his boy. Whitelaw Reid was especially worried about his friend.

"His son, a gallant lieutenant of regular artillery," had been wounded "in Wednesday's disastrous fight," Reid wrote, "and whether living now or dead he could not tell—he was a prisoner (or a corpse) in Gettysburg."[1]

Wilkeson immersed himself in his work to keep the anxiety at bay. As he sat in the shade at the Leister house, he quietly made notes of the troops spread in the fields and up the slope to Cemetery Ridge. For a long time he fixated on a young private quietly brewing coffee a few dozen yards away. The boy looked to be about Bayard's age. The young private's deliberative focus on the mundane task was oddly comforting, a simple human action on a larger stage that repulsed humanity.[2]

Men in filthy blue uniforms, some of them stripped down to grimy undershirts, tended to their equipment or tried to catch naps. Some rested against a short stone wall that ran north and south along the top of the ridge and took a sharp-angled turn to the east. Teamsters kept coming back and forth at the Leister House to pick up bags of oats stacked along one outer wall. The smell of campfires and bacon cooking on iron pans began adding to stifling July air, but it also mercifully masked the putrid odor of decaying flesh from the bodies of men and the carcasses of horses. From Little Round Top, roughly a mile to the south, to the fields north and west of Gettysburg, bodies that had not yet been buried were bloating in the July heat. A mile to the west, Lee's center was stirring, but not yet visible on Cemetery Ridge.

"Our army cooked, ate and slumbered," Wilkeson noted of those hours. Within minutes that respite would go away with the songs from the bird in the peach tree.[3]

Even then, in a distance far beyond the battlefield but inexorably approaching, thousands were already on journeys to the shattered cross-roads to come to the aid of broken brothers, sons, and fathers. Gettysburg had already become the greatest human-made disaster in American history. In a few hours, Sam Wilkeson himself would join that aftermath. But the killing was not yet over.

As they watched the army stir, Reid and Wilkeson exchanged mental notes and speculated about what they might see next. Joined by other correspondents and a few officers, they debated whether the 100,000 militia that Lincoln had called up from towns in Pennsylvania and neighboring states would do much good if Lee pushed through to another victory this day and marched on to Harrisburg or Philadelphia or Washington, DC.

"We walked around to the east of the little house and lay down on the grass," Reid recalled. "Others were there; there was much comparison of views, talk of probabilities, gossip of the arrival of militia from Harrisburg."[4]

Gallows humor crept in. When a stray rifle shot zipped uncomfortably close overhead, Wilkeson said dryly: "That is a muffled howl; that's the exact phrase to describe it." The group of newspapermen chuckled. That is exactly how Reid described the shot in his battle dispatch.

About 20 yards from the house, Wilkeson watched as teamsters fed and watered sixteen horses tied to a rickety fence. Mounts of messengers and aides milling around the headquarters, they were lathered in sweat and gaunt from dehydration, wearing hard use of the previous two days.[5]

The widow Leister had lost her husband two years earlier, and she and six children struggled to live off the peaches and wheat they produced. She and her children had fled on the morning of Day One as the 11th Corps had rushed by her front door and through her fields. By this third day, her fences had been burned for cooking, her wheat fields trampled down to pulp, her peach orchard stripped and destroyed.[6]

Inside that house was Meade, protected outside by a ring of infantry and cavalry that encircled the tiny farm yard, a line of riflemen lying along a broken-up fence line that ran south along Taneytown Road from the Leister House. Those soldiers' faces were gray from dust and weariness. North of the house, dismounted cavalry soldiers gathered in small clusters, their mounts tied up nearby. The horse soldiers smoked hand-rolled tobacco and talked in low tones. An occasional ammunition wagon or messenger on horseback passed on the Taneytown Road 15 yards east of the widow Leister's front door. The road had been pounded hard and muddy with two days of heat, occasional showers, and the pounding of thousands of feet and horses' hooves.[7]

Clustered as it was here, the Union army's high command was also a fat target for Rebel cannons that could shoot nearly a mile with fairly reasonable accuracy. That thought was not lost on the small group of correspondents in the shade, either. But by then, veteran soldiers and correspondents had reached a fatalistic acceptance of the weariness, sickness, and death that had followed them, an ever-present shadow, across the landscape.

Lt. Frank Haskell, an aide to Union major general John Gibbon, and a superb writer and observer of human nature, made note of the soldiers' indifference on Cemetery Ridge that morning. Like Wilkeson, he marveled about how they simply rested or went on with the mundane tasks during such ominous hours.

"Men who had volunteered to fight the battles of the country," he wrote a few days later, "had met the enemy in many battles, and had been constantly before them, as had the Army of the Potomac, were too old soldiers, and too long ago had well weighed chances and probabilities, to be disturbed now."[8]

Some Union officers thought the men were more somber than usual. Some thought the workaday way that the men went about their business in the morning of July 3 was almost as disconcerting as the horrific fighting that followed.

"There was something ominous, something uncanny, in these strange, unexpected hours of profound silence so sharply contrasting with the bloody horrors which had preceded, and which were sure to follow them," recalled Schurz, the Union officer who had passed on the orders to Barlow on July 1. "Even the light-hearted soldiers, who would ordinarily never lose an opportunity for some outbreak of an hilarious mood, even in a short moment of respite in a fight, seemed to feel the oppression.

"Some sat silently on the ground munching their hard-tack, while others stretched themselves out seeking sleep, which they probably would have found more readily had the cannon been thundering at a distance," Schurz observed. "The officers stood together in little groups discussing with evident concern what this long-continued calm might mean. Could it be that Lee, whose artillery in long rows of batteries had been silently frowning at us all the morning, had given up his intention to make another great attack? If not, why had he not begun it at an earlier hour, which unquestionably would have been more advantageous to him?"[9]

The disquiet flowed from a general awareness of the stakes. Charlie Coffin, the *Boston Journal* correspondent who had ridden into Gettysburg with the Union 5th Corps, said that on the eve of the battle it had felt like "two storm clouds" approaching one another, two unstoppable forces of nature about to collide and create something unwanted, unprecedented and, in a morbid way, necessary to keep moving this war to an inevitable, but unknowable, end.[10]

Even the normally composed Lee had provided windows into worry and brittleness. Two days before the battle a Pennsylvania doctor who approached Lee about reparations for a horse he said that Lee's men had stolen said that "never have I seen so much emotion depicted upon a human being.

"With his hand at times clutching his hair, and with contracted brow, he would walk with rapid strides for a few rods, and then, as if he bethought himself of his actions, he would, with a sudden jerk, produce an entire change in his features," the doctor said.[11]

Twelve hours before Sam Wilkeson and his colleagues sought the shade of the Leister House, Meade had called his corps commanders and staff officers to a council to decide whether to fight on, or to retreat. Union troops would have been excused for betting on a withdrawal and retreat. Past commanders might have ordered a more defensive retreat to head off any possible Lee flanking motions toward Washington, DC, 90 miles to the south of Gettysburg; or Harrisburg, 40 miles to the northeast; or Philadelphia, 130 miles to the east.

Time after time in the previous two years, Yankee generals had chosen to break off or not pursue after hard fighting, deflating morale in the ranks. The Army of the Potomac was on its fourth commander in ten months. But at a dramatic consultation with his corps commanders the night before, Meade was convinced to stay and fight. The night produced an anxious morning.

Gen. Alfred Pleasanton, the head of the Union cavalry, "neat and trim in dress and person, with a riding whip tucked into his cavalry boots, was walking about uneasily," recalled Charlie Coffin. Nearby, Gen. Henry Hunt, Meade's top artillery commander, was sitting quietly under a peach tree. Gen. Gouvernor K. Warren, who the previous day had saved the exposed Union left by rushing in reinforcements to cover Dan Sickles's 3rd Corps's dangerous advance off Cemetery Ridge, arrived at headquarters appearing "calm, absorbed, earnest as ever."[12]

Then the calm was shattered.

Chapter 35

"Death Was in Every One of Them"

It began with a single Rebel artillery shell landing in the yard near the headquarters, close enough to rattle the veteran correspondents in the shade of the Leister house. "Jove, those fellows on the left have the range of headquarters exactly," one of Wilkeson's colleagues muttered disquietly.[1] Another shell exploded nearby, and in seconds one shot after another screamed toward their position or onto the men and wagons and guns on the slope toward Cemetery Ridge. Some shells were landing in the cemetery to the rear of the Leister House. Some of the shots were solid balls that could knock men down like bowling pins; some were fused explosives that splintered fences or buildings or the bodies of men.

Shells arced with deadly intention over a copse of trees up on the ridge, passing over the lines of men now hugging the right-angled stone wall on the heights. They landed among troops and artillery pieces on the eastern slope of the ridge, the same men who the correspondents had just watched napping or brewing coffee or attending to bedrolls or knapsacks. It was a predicate for the charge of 12,000 men under Pickett, a 120-gun Confederate artillery barrage designed to shred infantry defenses and silence Union cannons at the center of Meade's line. But those federal cannons began booming back. The fire was so furiously repetitive and overlapping that it was heard in York, 30 miles away.[2]

The two giant storm clouds that Coffin had described in the lead-up of the battle had finally come together. Haskell described the unnatural fury in similarly natural terms. Meade's headquarters, he said, felt like multiple thunderstorms had converged overhead, a feeling that was simultaneously "remote, near, deafening, ear-piercing, astounding."[3]

Wilkeson and a few colleagues scrambled to cover inside the Leister House with officers and orderlies, while others hugged the eastern side of the house, leeward of the incoming. "The air was full of the most complete artillery prelude that was ever exhibited," Wilkeson observed. "Every size and form of shell known to British and to American gunnery shrieked, whirled, moaned, whistled and wrathfully fluttered over our ground. As many as six in a second, constantly two in a second, bursting and screaming over and around the headquarters, made a very hell of fire that amazed the oldest officer."[4]

His colleague, Reid, said that "the air was alive with all mysterious sounds, and death was in every one of them." The shells arrived screaming their impending destruction, like "cries of warning or alarm."[5]

As the Union artillery on the slope of Cemetery Ridge banged back, men and metal took on devilish characteristics, in mechanically animate choreography that was simultaneously frightening, appalling, amazing, and awe-inspiring. As Confederate shells landed among them, the gunners, some of them stripped down to bare chests, became indistinguishable from the guns—cogs, like the iron and shot, of a singular killing machine. Mechanical hell on earth.

"These guns are great infuriate demons, not of the earth, whose mouths blaze with smoky tongues of living fire, and whose murky breath, sulphur-laden, rolls around them and along the ground, the smoke of Hades," Haskell, who would die leading a charge eleven months later at Cold Harbor, wrote. "These grimy men, rushing, shouting, their souls in frenzy, playing the dusky globes and the igniting spark, are in their league, and but their willing ministers. We thought that at the second Bull Run, at the Antietam and at Fredericksburg on the 11th of December, we had heard heavy cannonading. They were but holiday salutes compared with this."[6]

Amidst the hellfire, single actors and surreal images stood out. One salvo took out the entire line of horses that Wilkeson had noticed getting water and being wiped down just a few minutes before. The beasts fell in a line, some instantly killed, some badly mauled, mortally wounded, straining at their tied reins in unbridled terror in a final act of self-preservation. One officer ran out to kill his suffering mount while the shells were falling all around. Even amidst all the other death around them, the suffering of the animals was a sad sight.

Shells "burst in the yard—burst next to the fence on both sides, garnished as usual with the hitched horses of aides and orderlies," Wilkeson wrote. "The fastened animals reared and plunged with terror. Then one fell, then another—sixteen laid dead and mangled before the fire ceased. Still fastened by their halters, which gave the expression of their being wickedly tied up to die painfully, these brute victims of a cruel war touched all our hearts."[7]

A horse pulling an ambulance came rushing past Meade's headquarters, one of its hind legs missing, just now shot off at the hock. A frantic ambulance driver furiously whipped the horse, squeezing the last full measure of service out of the wounded animal. Wilkeson described it as a "marvelous spectacle" of sacrifice and terror.[8]

Confederate shells shredded Meade's headquarters, knocking down the pillars and collapsing the front porch. Two solid shots rifled completely through the house. One barely missed Army adjutant general Seth Williams, known and liked throughout the army. One explosive shell landed in the chimney, but it was a dud, to the relief of soldiers and correspondents hunkered down in the parlor.

Meade's inherited chief of staff, Gen. Dan Butterfield, was blown off his feet and temporarily put out of action; an assistant adjutant general had his wrist shattered. Nearby, another Meade aide was writhing on the ground, his arm ripped open and a bone exposed by shrapnel. Col. Joseph Dickinson of Meade's staff also was wounded.

Along Taneytown Pike and the ground around the Leister House more gruesome scenes unfolded as men sought any small semblance of cover. Some men, Wilkeson wrote, "were torn to pieces in the road and died with the peculiar yells that blend the extorted cry of pain and despair." He described it as a "tempest of orchestral death."[9]

Coffin rode out the barrage on the house's east wall. He saw one man hit directly by an artillery shell, his body "whirling in the air, a mangled mass of flesh, blood and bones." Another man, draped with canteens and walking resolutely through the fire and fury, had the knapsack blown off his back but was otherwise unhurt. It was not his time. He continued on toward the ridgeline, water vessels intact, momentarily noting his luck.[10]

"The soldier stopped and turned about in puzzled surprise, put up one hand to his back to assure himself that the knapsack was not there, and then walked slowly on again unharmed, with not even his coat torn," Haskell recorded. "Near us was a man crouching behind a small disintegrated stone, which was about the size of a common water bucket. He was bent up, with his face to the ground, in the attitude of a Pagan worshipper before his idol. It looked so absurd to see him thus, that I went and said to him, 'Do not lie there like a toad. Why not go to your regiment and be a man?' He turned up his face with a stupid, terrified look upon me, and then without a word turned his nose again to the ground. An orderly that was with me at the time, told me a few moments later, that a shot struck the stone, smashing it in a thousand fragments, but did not touch the man, though his head was not six inches from the stone."[11]

Some men died with memories of home literally in their grasp. A *New York World* reporter said the barrage began so suddenly and fiercely that it yanked men from "lazy siestas" leaving many "stricken in their rising with mortal wounds . . . some with cigars between their teeth, some with pieces of food in their fingers, and one at least—a pale young German from Pennsylvania—with a miniature of his sister in (his) hands."[12]

The bizarre became the commonplace, the terrifying the norm. A soldier in the 136th New York, 1st Lt. L. A. Smith, waited out the bombardment about a fourth of a mile northeast of Meade's headquarters in the cemetery where the 1st and 11th Corps had retreated on the first day. Some men who huddled behind a gravestone noted with irony that the stone was over a freshly dug grave of a Union sergeant killed at Seven Pines, in Virginia, the year before.[13] A correspondent embedded with the troops on that Cemetery Hill position said that before the barrage, Gettysburg itself had seemed "silent like a grave," with swarms of swallows and pigeons sweeping over the housetops.[14]

The death salvos ripped into the graveyard. One of the first shots landing was a jagged piece of railroad iron. Some men grasped for hope at its significance.[15] If the Confederates were down to shooting pieces of railroad track, maybe they were finally running out of ammunition.

The 136th infantry was stationed in front of Union cannons on the 505-foot-high Cemetery Hill when those cannons opened up against the Confederates on Seminary Ridge. Hugging ground behind a low stone wall or whatever other cover they could find, the infantrymen felt as if hell had ascended to the surface of the earth.

"If you laid down on the ground and put your fingers in your ears you got, in addition to the crash in the air, the full effect of the earth's tremor and its additional force as a conductor," Smith recalled of those terrifying minutes. "If you rolled over on your back and looked up into the heavens," the sky was "fairly black with missiles exploding continually and sending their broken fragments in every direction.

"If you sat with your back to the stone wall and looked over into the Cemetery," Smith continued, referring to the Union cannons blazing back at the Rebels, "you saw long, fiery tongues leaping toward you, thick clouds of sulphurous smoke settle down around you, blackening the countenance almost beyond recognition."[16]

A color guard in Smith's company was hit in the head and killed, and men all around him were ripped up by sleeting sheets of metal. Within days, one man in Smith's company lost all of his teeth, forever attributing it to the shaking he had gotten from the cannon concussions that afternoon of July 3 at Gettysburg. Men sweated entirely through their uniforms from the conspiracy of fear, nerves, and heat—but also a reminder one was still alive.

"Water rang from every pore in the skin like squeezing a wet sponge, and our clothes were ringing wet," Smith remembered. "It was nature's provision for our safety, as it prevented a total collapse of the nervous system, and the mind from going out in darkness."[17]

As the shelling intensified, Meade initially ignored pleas from his subordinates to move to a safer place behind the bombardment. He scoffed at men huddled on the east side of the house, downrange of the bombardment, telling a story about a man from the Mexican War who hid behind a wooden wagon, knowing it would not stop the shell if it was destined for him. But as the bombardment continued, he moved back to Henry Slocum's 12th Corps headquarters on Powers Hill, several hundred yards straight east of the house and Taneytown Road. Some correspondents moved back, too. But Sam Wilkeson and a *Times* colleague, Frank Henry, stayed and survived, shaken but ultimately untouched.[18]

After what Wilkeson recorded as one hundred minutes of continuous shelling, the bombardment stopped. There was death but no death-like stillness now. Screams and moans of the dying and shouts of the survivors pierced the air, and Henry and Wilkeson saw frantic stirring on the ridge above them. On the crest of Cemetery Ridge, men who had survived the bombardment behind the stone wall and other breastworks peered to the west as James Longstreet's Confederate corps, led by the colorful Pickett, came into view out of the woods on Seminary Ridge, ready to advance. The Confederate barrage had reaped destruction on the rear of the Union lines, but it had mostly overshot the front line of Union defenders. Shaken, they prepared for Pickett with grim anticipation.

With the afternoon sun descending toward the tree line behind them, Confederate lines a mile wide began walking, then trotting up the long slope toward the copse of trees and the angled stone wall. Wilkeson, Frank Henry, and other correspondents in the vicinity headed toward the higher ground up on the ridge to watch it unfold.

As the Confederate battle line moved ominously toward them, Union artillery, which had eventually been told to cease fire during the Confederate barrage to preserve ammunition, began ripping big gaps in the gray lines. As the line came to a fence astride on the Hagerstown Road 250 yards in front of the stone wall, Union riflemen knocked them down by the dozens in sleeting steel volleys. As the survivors got closer, federal batteries blazed away with grapeshot and canister, cutting twenty-men-wide swaths at a time.

Remnants of the Confederate line reached the stone wall, and desperate hand-to hand combat broke out. Wilkeson saw Union artillery captain Alonzo Cushing and a few of his men still prone push one of his guns down to the stone wall to fire point blank with intimate fury into men whose individual expressions were now noticeable. But Cushing was soon cut down and carried off the field, mortally wounded. Next to Cushing, five cannons commanded by Capt. Andrew Cowan were getting off shots as fast as his men could load and pull lanyards. Eventually, four of Cowan's five guns were put out of action, but he kept blasting away with the remaining one. "His service of grape and canister was awful," Wilkeson observed.[19] Cowan was barely firing over the heads of his own men, hurling backwards with deadly sprays Rebels that had drawn within 10 yards of the stone wall. Union artillery commander Henry Hunt, at Cowan's shoulder, emptied his pistol into the oncoming lines.

Cowan found himself face to face with a young Confederate officer, whose last words were, "Take the gun." Cowan answered with a double load of canister, and the young Rebel officer and men two and three deep around him went down with him. Cowan turned to give orders to a subordinate feet away, and the man was shot through a lung and fell on Cowan's feet.[20]

Parts of the Union lines began to give. When infantrymen in front of Cowan began to run, one of Cowan's gunners, a Vermonter named James Plunkett, hit one of the retreating Union riflemen over the head with a cooking pot so hard that the bottom broke, sending the man fleeing to the rear with a pot over his head.[21]

General Gibbon was wounded, and his men began wavering and some began running. Hancock, conspicuous in trying to rally his men from his horse, was severely wounded in the thigh. His friend, the Confederate general Lew Armistead, led a small group of Confederate infantrymen about 50 yards beyond the stone wall, near the angle. Armistead fell mortally wounded a short distance from where Hancock had fallen. Haskell, himself slightly wounded, rallied Gibbons' fleeing men, with what he described as "a great, magnificent passion" that overcame him. Striking some men with the flat of his saber, Haskell reformed the skeedaddlers a few dozen yards behind the original Union line, some of them, Haskell recalled, looking upon him as if he were a "destroying angel." At Haskell's command, Gibbons's re-formed line poured another murderous volley into what was left of the Confederates on the ridge. Pickett's Charge began a final disintegration from that sheet of fire on, but not before further destruction. "The jostling, swaying line on either side boiled and roared, two hostile billows of a fiery ocean," Haskell wrote. They were all of one, opposite sides together.[22]

"Individuality is drowned in a sea of clamor, and timid men, breathing the breath of the multitude, are brave," Haskell recounted. "The frequent dead and wounded lie where they stagger and fall; there is no humanity for them. The men do not cheer or shout; they growl, and over that uneasy sea, heard with a roar of musketry, sweeps the muttered thunder of a storm of growls."[23] He ordered a counterattack from the top of the ridge, and soon "pistols flashed with musket." Back toward the stone wall they rushed, a final "moment of thrusts, yells, blows, shots, an indistinguishable conflict, followed by a shout, universal, that make the welkin ring again."[24]

Many Confederates still alive who had made it to the stone wall were now on their hands and knees, either wounded or ready to surrender.

Sam Wilkeson, who saw this all unfold from behind the lines on the ridge, recorded it this way: "So terrible was our musketry and artillery fire that when Armistead's brigade was checked in its charge, and stood reeling, all of its men dropped their muskets and crawled on their hands and knees underneath the stream of shot till close to our troops, where they made signs of surrendering. They passed through our ranks scarcely noticed, and slowly went down the slope to the road in the rear. Before they got there, the grand charge . . . solemnly sworn and carefully prepared, had failed."[25]

Boston Herald Coffin reported that the Yankee guns on the ridge produced "a death tempest so pitiless that the brigades melted away as the snowflake in the running stream, the regiments breaking and disappearing. Officers tried to rally them, but in vain."[26]

The looks on men's faces were not recognizable in a normal world. Wilkeson's *New York Times* colleague L. L. Crounse said a second line of Confederates that reached the stone wall wore "expressions of fierce rage" before, they, too, were cut down or captured.[27]

The scene was at once too much to bear, yet too fascinating to turn from. The Union 2nd Corps, Coffin observed, had turned into a "thin blue ribbon." Seeing the line wavering, Howard yelled from the cemetery to "smash their supports," and that order unleashed a flame of fifty cannons into the attacking Confederates. Coffin, too, saw Hancock fall, shot from his horse. Unlike his friend Armistead, Hancock survived.

"Men fire into each other's faces, not five feet apart," Coffin reported in one of the most impressive combat descriptions of the war. From countless deadly movements the ridge became one massive, furtive, death clinch. Time both seemed to both speed up and stand. Wrote Coffin: "There are bayonet thrusts, sabre strokes, pistol shots; cool deliberate movements on the part of some,—hot, passionate, desperate efforts with others, hand-to-hand contests; reckless of life; tenacity of purpose, fiery determination, oaths, yells, curses, hurrahs, shoutings; men going down on their hands and knees, spinning around like tops, throwing out their arms, gulping up blood, falling; legless, armless, headless. There are ghastly heaps of dead men. Seconds are centuries; minutes, ages; but the thin line does not break!"[28]

More than 2,600 Confederates had been killed or wounded on their way up the slope. It was 5:00 p.m. Pickett's survivors retreated, rifle shots from the ridge cutting some down as they faded back toward the opposite ridge, where Lee sat on his horse, apologizing to crying, cursing men as they streamed past.

And now the moment of the great aftermath arrived.

In a quieting field, stunned survivors watched as litter bearers began combing for the wounded. In little time, civilians would come to give aid, gawk, or loot, but the immediate aftermath belonged to the combatants. Coffin walked along the stone wall. The field in front, he reported, "was very thickly strewn with prostrate forms—the dead of the second day's engagement, together with those that had gone down in the strife just ended. The wounded were calling for help, and already the hospital corps was upon the field, bringing Union and Confederate alike to the surgeons."[29]

Wilkeson sat down and wrote a 200-word dispatch for his paper and sent it off with a messenger with a promise to file more after he had had time to do more reporting. Writing near the stone wall, he described 360 degrees of utter destruction. "While I write the ground around me is covered thick with rebel dead, mingled with our own," he wrote. The enemy, he said, had been "magnificently repulsed." But it had come with a price. "The losses on both sides are heavy," he said, including the wounding of the indispensable Hancock and Gibbon.[30]

The aftermath would become even more gruesome in the coming hours and days. By nightfall, as Wilkeson and his fellow correspondents plied survivors for information before writing their dispatches, some men could hear hogs, cut loose from pens by the two clashing armies, gorging on bloated bodies.[31] In the fading light, a man missing an arm methodically carried water to dying men in both armies.[32]

About 11:00 p.m. that night, Meade sat on a boulder in a grove of trees northeast of the Leister House and took reports from officers who had been spread across the battlefield. Howard was there, and reporters noticed that, in his weariness, the empty right arm sleeve seemed more prominent. Meade took off his dirty slouch hat and leaned tiredly forward, trying to catch the gentle evening breeze. Fires lit up the shattered and gnarled trees around him. Incongruously, locusts and katydids sang "cheerily" in the night.[33]

Wilkeson and his colleagues tried to listen in to the reports Meade was getting. It was a Union victory, they felt, but how decisive, and at what cost? Would there be another day of fighting? Meade had stayed and fought and this time it was Lee who had been repelled and left the field, beaten. If Lee wanted a fourth day of killing, Meade was prepared to stay for it.

Meade suddenly stood up and yelled, "Bully! Bully! Bully!" He ordered up rations for another day and told Henry Hunt, the Union chief of artillery seated nearby, to gather all the artillery ammunition he could in anticipation of a continued fight on Independence Day. "Have your limbers filled," he told Hunt. "Lee may be up to something in the morning, and we must be ready for him."[34]

The moment turned surreal when, out of nowhere, a Union army band came marching up Taneytown Road, playing "Hail to the Chief."

"General Meade," Wilkeson shouted. "You're in a very great danger of being President of the United States."

An anonymous voice came ringing out: "No, finish this work so well begun, and the position you have is better and prouder than President."[35]

In reality, Lee's badly mauled army was already preparing for a tortured retreat back to Virginia. Over the coming days, Meade would offer only half-hearted pursuit, causing Lincoln to once again regret a missed opportunity to destroy the Army of Northern Virginia. The grim, and ultimately necessary, work of finishing off the rebellion, at the cost of tens of thousands more lives, would have to wait almost two more years.

As darkness came to July 3, despite all the shock and weariness of the day, Sam Wilkeson's real work was just beginning. He had already recorded the importance of the history he had witnessed, writing in his first dispatch that "the cannonading of Chancellorsville, Malvern and Manassas were pastime compared to this."[36]

He could gather bare facts and first impressions. But how could any mortal make people understand what humans had just done to one another? How could any mortal with a son lying somewhere on this bloody landscape keep focused on the challenges of describing the significance and scale of the fighting at Gettysburg? Lieutenant Haskell did not envy the correspondents' tasks. "Many things cannot be described by pen or pencil—such a fight is one," he wrote of Gettysburg. "Some hints and incidents may be given, but a description or picture never. From what is told the imagination may for itself construct the scene; otherwise he who never saw can have no adequate idea of what such a battle is."[37]

Yet somehow Sam Wilkeson would answer the challenge. His heart burdened with his known witness and the soul-searing unknown of his boy's fate, the war correspondent and father began that night composing one of the most compelling battlefield dispatches ever written. It would foreshadow Abraham Lincoln's famous Gettysburg Address, a little more than four months later, and a few hundred yards from where he now wrote. The images of redemption and consecration in Wilkeson's dispatch would be hauntingly similar to Lincoln's sparse words. Both passages would be transcendent, sorrowful, redemptive, and awe-inspired, and they would capture both the intimacy and enormity of these triumphant, tragic moments at Gettysburg.

More than 46,000 men in the two armies had been killed, wounded, or captured in three days. Lt. Bayard Wilkeson was among them. Now, in the swelling suffering of the aftermath, his father had to find him.

CHAPTER 36

"Pursuing His Duty as a Correspondent with a Heavy Heart"

As THE LIGHT OF JULY 3 FADED, SAM WILKESON PICKED HIS WAY through the stunned survivors and the dead and wounded on Cemetery Ridge. He was as diligent and probing as ever in his reporting, but it was apparent to the soldiers he ran into that something was distracting him.

Sporadic cannon fire and rifle shots rang out elsewhere on the battlefield, but Pickett's attack had spent the last reserves of Lee's army, and had brought final failure to the Southern army at Gettysburg. The aftermath was now the story, and the overwhelming challenges were only now becoming apparent on that evening of July 3, 1863. Sam's search for Bayard was one ripple in the rivers of suffering that were already flowing to and across the battlefield.

In the lingering heat of the evening, litter bearers and ambulances descended on the field to tend to thousands of wounded and dying men. Numb, in weary and mechanical movements, surviving Union troops picked through scattered equipment and retrieved rifles and ammunition from dead or wounded soldiers. Others checked the condition of still-hot cannons and their supply of ammunition. Percussive clanging of metal accompanied a disparate, pathetic chorus of wounded men strewn around the stone wall and in front of Cemetery Ridge. Despite what had just been done, preparations had to be made for more of it. There was no way of knowing if Lee would try one more time to break this part of the line. Follow-up charges after appalling slaughter had happened numerous times before. Many of the Yankees on Cemetery Ridge had lost brothers and colleagues in repeated attacks on the slopes at Fredericksburg less than seven months before.

In short order, Sam ran into Cowan, the artillery captain whose guns had poured deadly bursts of metal into the gray waves of Pickett's final assault. Cowan's battery had paid heavily for it. Four of his men had been killed, and another was mortally wounded in the leg and would die the next morning. Six more were wounded but would survive.[1] Artillery officers on either side of him had been killed, including Alonzo Cushing, who had been shot four times, and who would be posthumously honored with a Medal of Honor a century and a half later.

Cowan had survived without a scratch, although his uniform was riddled with bullet holes and his mind was grasping for anything normal at that moment.[2] Cowan immersed himself in the duty in front of him and he ordered his men to stay busy doing the same. Wilkeson ran into Cowan near the stone wall only moments after the climax on the ridge. Cowan's surviving men had already stripped to their undershirts and were gray with grime and sweat as they collected working guns and assessed what could be fixed. Some men were dealing with the dead and wounded. Cowan himself was pulling the harness off a dead horse when Wilkeson approached.

They instantly recognized one another. Wilkeson and Cowan had met under contentious circumstances fourteen months earlier at the Battle of Lee's Mills during the Union siege of Yorktown, Virginia. At midnight on April 16, 1862, in one of those lost nights of the Peninsula campaign, Sam had gotten disoriented in the dark and stumbled into Cowan's battery. The young lieutenant had taken Wilkeson for a spy, a potential hanging offense, and detained him overnight. Cowan had finally let Wilkeson go the next morning after being convinced that he was the man on his press pass. But that first meeting had not started or ended cordially.

And so much had happened since. John Wilkes Wilkeson was killed six weeks after the Cowan-Wilkeson contretemps. Antietam, Fredericksburg, Chancellorsville followed. And now, Cowan knew through the artillery grapevine that Lt. Bayard Wilkeson had been badly wounded two days before. It had all piled up toward this moment on the ridge at Gettysburg.

In the desultory wreckage on Cemetery Ridge, Wilkeson and Cowan found mutual solace in the simple offering of a human handshake. Wilkeson extended his hand and introduced himself, and they mutually consented to linger in the moment, appreciative of any genuine human connection. "Captain, we met at Lee's Mills before Yorktown when I stumbled into your battery," Wilkeson told him. Cowan indicated with a nod that he remembered, and the two men shook hands.[3]

Sam got right down to business. He wanted to know whether Cowan had heard anything about Bayard. He hoped that an artillery officer grapevine would bear news.

Cowan was sympathetic but of little help. He had no idea of Bayard's whereabouts. Lieutenant Wilkeson was attached to a different corps and had been wounded on the other side of the Gettysburg more than forty-eight hours earlier. Two miles of hostile ground stood between where they stood and where Bayard had been wounded. Cowan had just survived one of the war's most intense hours of killing, and now he was focused only on preparing for more of it. Yet in the aftermath, sensing the pain of a father, and despite their personal history, he suddenly realized he could help by consoling the older man.

"He was pursuing his duty as a correspondent with a heavy heart," Cowan recalled years later. "We stood there, with the dead and wounded covering the ground before our eyes, and the blazing sun beating on them mercilessly, while there was not a drop of drinking water to be had, the few wells in the vicinity having been pumped dry long before. The cries of the tortured men lying there, blue and gray mingled, were pitiful and harrowing. Wilkeson asked me to step down to the wall with him. There and beyond the dead and wounded covered the ground."[4]

The challenge of describing what he'd seen, knowing his son was in his horrible expanse of suffering someplace, would have ground down the most resolute soul.

Yet Cowan also sensed a resoluteness in Wilkeson, a feeling that the war correspondent fully realized that he had no choice but to do his job, that what had happened here demanded an accounting for the ages, no matter what he was confronting personally.

"I remember the scene and the man," Cowan recalled, "and I feel that he must have written under the inspiration of the wonderful scene he witnessed and feeling the great cost of life and the heroic courage by which that battle, the crisis of the Union cause, was won."[5]

In retrospect, Cowan's description of the butchery he had just participated in on Cemetery Ridge as "wonderful" seems inhuman, cavalier, detached from reality. But in the private letters of soldiers and the dispatches of the war correspondents, that was a common reaction. The hours were horrific and heroic. Gettysburg was one vast stage for the grandest and the most destructive acts of humans, the basest of human emotions soothed by the balm of human mercies. And it would now be defined by a magnitude of suffering none had seen before, and by the acts of ordinary people who were stepping into the darkness to confront it.

Wilkeson lingered with the captain as dusk drew closer, pitching in as Cowan and his men began burying some of the dead spread about the ridge. It took every last measure of resolve. Dead from both sides "lay in heaps" in front of his gun, and "no one will ever forget the sight," Cowan remarked. The young Union officer recognized the young Confederate officer who had yelled, "take the gun" and had been cut down on Cowan's command. Cowan ordered him buried with his own dead men, at that moment the best gesture of honor he could summon for a brave, fallen foe.[6]

Not yet twenty-two years old, an artillery officer of rising promise himself, Cowan was barely older than Bayard Wilkeson. Now, in the battle's aftermath, this young officer gave Sam Wilkeson a burst of hope. If an artillery officer could come through the deadly passage Cowan had just traversed, perhaps Bayard was still alive.

Within a half hour horse ride in any direction, roughly 20,000 wounded men were strewn about the fields and in homes, barns, shelters, and hospital tents. Scores of shallow, temporary graves already slashed the surrounding countryside. Fathers, brothers, mothers, and friends from all over the country were rushing toward the suddenly famous village. Sam Wilkeson was just one of thousands.

CHAPTER 37

"A Butcher's Pen"

SURVIVORS DESCRIBED THE NIGHT OF JULY 3 AT GETTYSBURG AS ONE OF the most ghoulish of the war. As Sam Wilkeson worked through the night on his dispatch, hoping to transmit it as soon as he could find a messenger or telegraph operator, constantly soliciting news of Bayard's whereabouts, nature conspired with the man-made disaster to create a dangerous, macabre, absurd darkness. Clouds rolled in and heavy showers fell at times. The darkness was filled with sounds of galloping horses and creaky ambulances, of men on foot carrying the wounded on litters or scavenging the battlefield, and of cries of wounded or dying men across the rocky fields calling for water, or their mothers.

Surreal detachment became the norm. As darkness descended, men of the 125th New York ate supper on Cemetery Ridge at the spot where they had just helped beat back Pickett's attack. It was a sight that would have killed a normal appetite, but not here, and not them. They were surrounded by bodies and wounded men, some crying, some praying—including Confederates who had just tried to kill them, some of whom had almost certainly been shot by the men now eating supper nearby. Two years of war had bleached away any unnecessary emotions, including hatred and fear. It had created a universal understanding of the mutual bargain with fate soldiers had made by that point. Both the fallen and the unscathed recognized it. Having walked through that door long ago, the survivors of the 125th New York simply sat and ate.

"In all those sickening things there was, I think, no hatred," Lt. Samuel Armstrong of the 125th remembered. "The malice and rascality engendered by war is near. There is a certain mutual respect among those who accept the wager of battle."[1]

Lt. L. A. Smith, the lieutenant of the 136th New York, said that as dusk descended that the fields in front of the stone wall looked as if a flock of sheep were lying in a pasture. But these were dead and wounded men in gray, some in "ghastly groups, so thickly bunched as to almost cover the ground," he recalled.

"Had fresh men, unaccustomed to such sights, been dropped down in our places they could not have endured such a night without danger of total collapse," he said. The survivors pushed through. Smith never forgot "the wails of the dying, the prayers and curses of the wounded, the agonizing cries everywhere for 'water, water.'"

Some men "in the delirium of pain were carried back to their childhood days," he said. The battlefield echoed with "the frequent call for mother."[2]

As Wilkeson and his colleagues interviewed survivors on the ridge, Union 5th Corps captain Robert G. Carter moved out with a small group of men to set up pickets about 500 yards ahead of the Union lines. Wounded and dead men from the previous day's fighting in the Devil's Den, wheat field, and peach orchard still littered the field. In the sticky air and fading light, it looked as if everything was covered in gauze. At midnight, Carter remembered, the air was "warm and muggy; the moon partially obscured by haze shed a dim and sickly light over the ground."

At times, Carter could reach with his rifle in any direction and touch a dead body, "many with their ghastly faces showing here and there by twos, threes and fours, or in clumps where they had gone down." The night sounds were punctuated "by the distressed and rattling breathing of a dying man, or the piteous appeals of the wounded scattered about everywhere." For quite some time in the middle of the night, Carter sat and quietly comforted a dying captain of the 5th Texas who, like Bayard Wilkeson had done a mile north of where he lay, had tried to stop the blood from a catastrophic leg wound with a tourniquet of cloth twisted with a bayonet. Carter shared watered-down, cold coffee in his canteen, and the Texan thanked him before dying.

When dawn mercifully came Carter led his men back to the Union lines on Cemetery Ridge. As far as they could see there was "the debris of battle—haversacks, caps, sombreros, blankets of every shade and hue, bayonets, cartridge-boxes, every conceivable part of the equipment of a soldier of the blue or gray, mingled with the bodies of Yankee and rebel, friends and foe, perchance father and son." There was a panoply of emotions in dead men's faces. Some had menacing looks and their fists were clenched, Carter noticed. Others had a "smile of peace."[3]

Between the peach orchard and wheat field, which had changed hands several times in horrific, hand-to-hand fighting on July 2, one dying man with at least twenty wounds was gasping and twitching on the ground. "Corpses strewed the ground at every step," Carter observed, "Arms, heads, legs and parts of dismembered bodies were scattered all about, and sticking among the rocks and against the trees, hair, brains, entrails and shreds of human flesh still hung, a disgusting, sickening, heart-rending spectacle to our young minds.

"It was indeed a charnel house, a butcher's pen," Carter remembered, "with man as the victim."[4]

Some wounded men sat quietly, waiting for whatever fate came to them. At dawn, Col. Birkett D. Fry of the 13th Alabama sat stoically smoking a pipe in a cluster of fallen Confederates near the stone wall on Cemetery Ridge. He sat in several inches of water that had pooled in the overnight rain. Union lieutenant colonel Charles C. H. Morgan, chief of staff for the severely wounded General Hancock, asked Fry where he was wounded. Fry pointed to a compound leg fracture but he did it with "so serene a satisfaction" that Morgan said he knew then that this officer, and Lee's army, was "not ready to give up the ghost yet, and was not surprised afterwards to hear of the Colonel's recovery."[5]

Fresh overnight additions in front of the stone wall added to the macabre scene in the early-morning light. Overnight, Union scavenger units had stuck hundreds of discarded Rebel rifles into the ground by their bayonets, "so that there were acres of muskets standing as thick as trees in a nursery," Morgan recalled.[6]

All of the Confederate bodies within sight had had their pockets turned inside out. Morgan came across two Union soldiers trying to get the ring off a finger of a dead Confederate. "Oh, damn it, cut the finger off," one of the men said.[7]

All across the battlefield, the calls of the wounded men fell into final bursts of desperation. Lieutenant Smith described them like final, fading volleys from the losing side, "more plaintive and intense as hopes gave away to despair."[8]

Sam Wilkeson spent that night of July 3 on the ridge, within earshot all night of the suffering pouring forth. Attempting to find the field where Bayard had fallen would have been a foolish, possibly fatal mission. Confederates still controlled the town, and whether or not Lee was using the night to reassemble for more fighting the next day was not yet clear. At daylight, after spending the stormy night at Meade's new temporary headquarters in the tree grove, he would set out to find his boy.

CHAPTER 38

"Hateful Ravages"

AT DAWN ON JULY 4, 1863, INDEPENDENCE DAY, THE SKIES WERE OVER-
cast and threatening more rain, which by early afternoon turned into a
downpour, adding to the misery of the wounded, the doctors and civilians
treating them, and of the family and friends and curious already descending on Gettysburg.

But this could not wash away the scourge of the three previous days.
Men lay near makeshift hospitals, and swaths of dead and dying men
marked the pressure point on the fields of the three previous days. Spread
across 5 miles, dead and wounded men leaned solitarily against trees or
rocks, or lay together along streams, drawn there by thirst.

Rain swelled Plum Run, which flowed between Devil's Den and
Little Round Top, threatening Rebel and Yankee wounded lying along
it. Some men were saved at the last minute, literally pulled out of the
rising waters by the hair. But dozens of Confederate wounded were
swept along and presumably drowned.[1] By the time Sam Wilkeson set
out from Meade's headquarters after dawn, the river of humanity in the
battle's aftermath was swelling, too. It would make it all that harder to
find the boy. The mercy givers and the plunderers were now carrying the
day. Typical of the former was the Reverend W. F. Watkins, a pastor in
Brooklyn, New York, who arrived on the battlefield that morning to link
up with the Sanitary Commission medical group that treated 692 men
on July 4, including 77 who had limbs amputated. About 10 percent of
the amputees died, which Reverend Watkins's hometown newspaper
called "the average ratio of deaths from that cause."[2]

This was the scene that confronted Sam Wilkeson at daylight as he began his search for his boy. Burial parties had been working all night, but after three days of fighting thousands remained unburied, and the stench of dead men and horses was so overwhelming that Gettysburg residents could not open their windows, even in July's heavy air. In the ensuing days, residents and visitors would combat the gagging aroma by rubbing the leaves of fragrant plants, often peppermint or pennyroyal, beneath their noses.[3]

Gettysburg was still a dangerous place, as Sam Wilkeson soon found out. Even as word of Lee's pullback filtered back through the Union lines, Confederate snipers were covering the retreat, and civilians in Gettysburg became targets. It prevented Sam, or anyone in blue, from immediately getting to the fields of the first day's fighting, including Barlow's Knoll.

At 5:00 a.m. two decimated Ohio brigades, the 25th and 75th, were ordered into Gettysburg to flush out whatever Rebels remained. The 25th had been placed along Rock Creek in front of Lieutenant Wilkeson's battery, the 75th had set up just yards north of the young lieutenant's guns, and both had suffered horribly. Combined, the two brigades had gone into the fighting alongside Wilkeson's battery on July 1 with 489 men; on this Independence Day morning, barely 130 answered the call. The 25th was on its third commanding officer in three days; the original had been captured on July 1, and his replacement was wounded and put out of action. But none of them, at that moment, could tell Sam Wilkeson what had happened to Bayard.[4]

As the Ohioans moved cautiously into eerily quiet streets of Gettysburg, the hue of dawn just starting to show itself, the Ohio boys could hear the sounds of digging and low voices from the direction of Culp's Hill, east of town. Union soldiers on that deadly slope who had spent three days digging trenches for protection had now shifted to digging trenches for their dead.[5]

Fixing bayonets, the Ohio boys had no idea what they would run into, although their commanders had been told there were signs the Confederates were withdrawing from the town. The 25th and 75th initially advanced carefully, but finding little resistance, the men in the ranks soon began yelling like demons, one of their captains would later recall. They moved methodically in a northwesterly direction through streets and alleys littered with discarded life and equipment. Dead horses were swelled up like fleshy balloons, fences and gardens were trampled, and knapsacks and weapons were strewn along the line of the chaotic Union retreat from three days before. At first there was no sign of anyone in the houses and storefronts. But then one window opened briefly to the rank air, then more, and the few residents who had stayed home during the fighting began greeting the boys in blue with relieved cheers of their own.

Soon the familiar face of a lieutenant from the 25th Ohio peered out of one window. He had been severely wounded in the arm, and was one of six Union soldiers who had spent the battle hidden and nursed by a Gettysburg family named, ironically, Culp.[6] Sam Wilkeson, following in the Ohioans' wake, would have seen hope in the signs of survival in the houses.

The Ohioans pushed on, finally reaching the western and northern edges of Gettysburg as rain again began falling. "We went like a set of devils and (it was raining) as hard as it could pour down, and of all the waveing of handkerchiefs and smiling faces, you never saw the equal."[7] They took 300 Rebel prisoners, many of them wounded and also in the care of Gettysburg civilians.[8]

Follow-up Union units entered and by the afternoon were pushing over Barlow's Knoll and the other heights north of town. But it was still incredibly dangerous ground, with Confederate snipers covering Lee's retreat, zeroing in on any movement in the streets.

Mary McAllister, who operated a general store in town, dodged that fire to get bread and butter for a wounded man in her house. She took temporary refuge in another house, and while there Gettysburg Theological Seminary student Amos Moser Whetstone was shot through the leg by a Confederate sharpshooter.

For three days, Mary had cared for wounded men sheltered in a Lutheran church across from her home on Chambersburg Street. It had produced horrors beyond anything she previously imagined possible. Inside the church, one Union solder, with seven of his fingers mangled, had pleaded for her help, and she had just started to respond when a passing surgeon stopped, took a brief look, and said, "What is the use doing anything for them?" He wielded his scalpel and cut off all seven fingers.

"Well, I was so sorry," Mary wrote in her diary.[9]

Despite that lingering danger of snipers, civilians were already starting to comb the battlefield south of town. The first rivulets of family members and loved ones, members of the Christian Commission and other religious groups with medical supplies, ordinary citizens with wagonloads of food and medical supplies, preachers with Bibles and sermons at the ready, and casket makers, were starting to arrive. Looters joined the river of suffering, too.

John Wilkeson had immediately headed south when he learned of Bayard's wounding. Switching trains at Baltimore, he arrived the next day, July 5. When John arrived on a train packed with worried family members and aid givers, the only solace would have been that the Wilkesons were not alone in their search for Bayard. Thousands were on their way to Gettysburg desperately hoping for life.[10]

The stories were never-ending and heartbreaking. After learning that her son, 1st Lt. Andrew Gregg Tucker of the 142nd Pennsylvania Volunteers, had been wounded on the first day's fighting—he fell about the same time Bayard had—Margery Tucker of Lewisburg, Pennsylvania, set out for the battlefield, 105 miles away. Her party left home early on the morning of July 2. It included her pastor, the Reverend Steven H. Mirick; Bucknell University president Justin Loomis; and professor George Bliss, all of whom had come to help find Andrew, a star Bucknell student before the war. Like Bayard Wilkeson, Lieutenant Tucker was a very young officer of great promise. His mother's party had a dangerous and exhausting journey to Gettysburg, which included a precarious rowboat ride across the rain-swollen Susquehanna River near Wrightsville, Pennsylvania, on July 4, because federal troops had knocked out the bridge there.

Tucker died just hours before his mother arrived at Gettysburg the next day. He had suffered for four days, and in his last hour he told a nurse: "I would like to see my mother and sisters, but I never will." His mother's party found him buried in a shallow hole near a pile of amputated limbs. She took his body home for burial on a peaceful Lewisburg Cemetery slope.[11]

On Independence Day, Mattie Burnett Callis of Lancaster, Wisconsin, was nearing the end of an 800-mile rail journey to Gettysburg. After receiving a telegram that her husband, Union colonel John Benton Callis, had been wounded in the battle's opening hours—he was the Iron Brigade commander who was left for dead on the field—Mattie had immediately set out for Gettysburg.

Mattie's long journey from Wisconsin to Gettysburg ended with the incredible news that her husband was still alive, although in grave condition. John Benton had lain for forty-three hours on the battlefield before being taken to a field hospital and given up for dead. His life had been saved by a black servant of a Confederate officer, who had sat with Callis and nursed him through four days and three nights on the battlefield. "The burning sun, the flies, and death (were) staring me in the face," Callis said years later. John Callis was eventually carried to the home of Fannie Buehler, the wife of postmaster D. A. Buehler, who—fearing capture—had himself fled before the Rebel armies arrived. Fannie stayed, and for weeks after the battle she and her husband cared for several wounded Union soldiers.[12] "We gave his wife the freedom of the house, and did all we could do to make her and her husband comfortable, free of expense," Fannie later recalled. "Indeed, we charged no one for anything they ate or drank."[13]

Colonel Callis occupied a third story bedroom in the Buehler home for six weeks before he and Mattie left for Wisconsin against doctors' advice. They told him he'd die if the bullet in his lung worked loose. He survived, and contributed as much to preserving his country after the war as he had during it.

As the armies slowly withdrew, Gettysburg's people focused on any act that could be construed as healing and recovery. As the Ohio brigades cleared one street that July 4 morning, a woman named Horner was already out scraping mud and blood off her front step.[14] Later, a Union regimental band tried to bring notes of normality by playing at the square at Baltimore Street. The musicians had to scramble for cover when Confederate sharpshooters began shooting at them, too. As litter bearers and ambulances traversed the streets, the band resumed later in the afternoon, playing the "Star Spangled Banner," "Tramp, Tramp, Tramp, The Boys

Are Marching," and "Rally Around the Flag Boys." In ensuing days, regimental bands took turns playing in the square and around the makeshift
hospitals, in part to drown out the cries of wounded men.[15]

Pure curiosity brought some of the first civilians onto the battlefield that July 4. Teenager Jacob Taughenbaugh living with his family in
Hunterstown, 5 miles northeast of Gettysburg. Old Jube Early's corps
had passed through that hamlet three days earlier on their way to smashing into Bayard Wilkeson's position on July 1.[16]

Early on July 4, with only the sound of an occasional sniper shot
or rattling wagon coming from the direction of the horizon that had
stormed with man-made thunder for three days, Jacob Taughenbaugh,
sixteen, and two other boys snuck away toward Gettysburg. On the
outskirts of Gettysburg they walked through what was an orchard, but
now was only a landscape of head-high, woody stumps chopped down
by the hail of shot and shell. The boys came to a Confederate trench that
stretched like a long, tattered ribbon of discarded war material.

There were "caps, worn-out shoes, damaged canteens, broken rifles
and pistols, bayonets, all jumbled in confusion," remembered the young
Taughenbaugh, who would live until one hundred, past World War
II. "The whole place looked as if a hurricane had passed over it."[17] He
and his friends grabbed pistols as souvenirs, hoping that Union troops
guarding the fields would not catch them. The word had already gotten
out that scavengers and looters would be severely punished and that
anything left on the fields—especially serviceable weapons—was government property. By the following week, nearly 28,000 rifles—some
of them jammed with up to a dozen balls by frightened soldiers who
had forgotten to shoot during the mayhem—would be piled up in
alleyways and temporary warehouses in Gettysburg.[18] About the same
time Taughenbaugh and his buddies were picking through the remains
of the battlefield, another teenager took a similar journey through the
destruction south of town.

Thirteen-year-old Lydia Ziegler and her family—her father, Eman-
uel, was steward of the edifice of the Lutheran Theological Seminary—
had fled their Gettysburg home as Bayard Wilkeson's corps was rushing
through the village on July 1. As they were leaving they saw Union troops

knocking down a big fence around their garden to clear the way for artillery caissons like Wilkeson's.[19]

The Zieglers had sheltered during the battle at a farmer friend's house a few miles south of the town. Lydia never forgot the anxious faces of men running toward the sound of guns on that first day of the battle. Now, on this July 4 of her thirteenth year, she would never forget the face of the suffering left behind.

Early on July 4, the Zieglers' friend took the family by wagon as far as Big Round Top at the southern edge of the battlefield. The Zieglers were carrying six loaves of freshly baked bread. Lydia, her parents, and her brother began walking north toward their home, directly through the center of the battlefield. It would take the Zieglers all day to go about 3 miles.

Past the rocky outcroppings that still sheltered dead and wounded, through fields of grass and wheat that had been pounded to greasy pulp by thousands of feet, and ripped in long gashes by cannonballs, the landscape did not seem of this world. The Zieglers' trip home turned into an immediate mission of mercy.

"The dying and the dead were all around us—men and beasts," Lydia recalled. "We could count as high as twenty dead horses lying side by side. Imagine, if you will, the stench of one dead animal lying in the hot sun for days. Here they were by the hundreds. All day long we ministered to the suffering, and it was night when we reached home, or what had been home, only to find the house filled with wounded soldiers."[20]

Lydia spent most of the day carrying water to wounded men using whatever containers she could find or devise, including cupped leaves. The six loaves of bread, in Sermon on the Mount symbolism, were dispensed morsel by morsel. "My father and mother," Lydia recalled, "stood by these wounded men, father with his pocket knife cutting off pieces of the bread which my mother would have to put into the mouths of some who were too weak even to lift the bread to their lips, or take the water which we children carried from the little streams or springs nearby in cups made by fastening leaves together."

For a thirteen-year-old, it was hideously overwhelming, but she summoned a maturity beyond her years. A week after the battle, Lydia comforted an old couple sitting wearily in front of her family's home. The woman, looking faint, was resting her head on her husband's shoulder. They had walked 21 miles over the mountains from Chambersburg, seeking their wounded son, Charlie. Lydia helped them find him, on the third floor of the Lutheran Seminary, where Charlie lay dying. "The cries of the mother as she bent over the body of her boy were heartbreaking," Lydia remembered. She knew no one could ever recover from that shock.[21]

Sallie Myers, the young schoolteacher who had passed out cup after cup of cool water on the battle's first day, had become a nurse by necessity. The day after the battle, a half dozen wounded Union soldiers were brought to her house, including three mortally wounded men: Amos Sweet, Wilson Race, and Alexander Stewart. Family members of all three would soon arrive in Gettysburg.[22]

Wilson Race, shot in the chest, lingered for twenty-two days, and his father came to be with him, Sallie Myers offering quiet comfort as she could. The elder Race had another son, who survived, fighting at Vicksburg at the same time as Gettysburg. "He never recovered from the shock" of losing Wilson, Sallie said of the father.[23]

Alexander Stewart, partially paralyzed with a shot through the spine, died on Tuesday, July 7, four days after the battle. His brother-in-law came to spend his last hours with him. Not long after the Ohio boys swept through the town on July 4, Sallie Myers went to a nearby makeshift hospital and brought a friend of Stewart's, Andrew Crooks, to her home to help comfort Alexander in his final hours. Crooks had been wounded carrying Alexander Stewart off the battlefield and had had his right leg amputated.

Stewart's father arrived within a week to take his boy's body home, and he was accompanied by a man named Baldwin, who also had come to find his son's body. The elder Stewart "is a poor, weak old man," Sallie Myers lamented. "He is very much distressed about his son." The elder Stewart arrived as Amos Sweet was in his last hours. Despite his own inconsolable sorrow at having lost his own son, Mr. Stewart lingered to help comfort Amos Sweet into his death. The dying Amos Sweet told Mr. Stewart and Sallie: "Tell my wife I am going home." When Amos Sweet died, the elder Stewart cried as if Amos had been his own son. He told Sallie, "Oh had it been but God's will that I could have stood by my son's death bed."[24]

Amos Sweet's widow arrived within hours after his death, expecting to see her husband still alive, having received only one encouraging letter from a doctor saying her husband had a good chance of recovery. That was the worst moment of all for Sallie Myers, and she nearly broke down after the relentless procession of "broken hearts and blighted hopes of such as she."[25]

By afternoon, with rain mercifully quenching thirsts while adding to the misery of men still on the ground, Sam Wilkeson could only learn that Bayard was not in the poorhouse where he had been taken. Ambulance driver Jacob Smith of the 107th Ohio had been among the first Yankees to reach it that July 4 morning. What he saw there and in other seized shelters for wounded men appalled him.

"The badly wounded of the first day's fight fell into the hands of the enemy when our forces retreated back to the line on Cemetery Hill," Smith recalled. "They had all been put into buildings, but no care or attention had been given them at all, and their wounds had begun to gangrene, thus rendering their recovery far more doubtful than if attention had been given them when first wounded. The Fourth of July we spent in moving these wounded who had fallen into the enemy's hands, and a very busy day we had of it before our work was completed there."[26]

Bayard Wilkeson was not there. He could have been anywhere by that point, dead or alive.

CHAPTER 39

"They Came by the Thousands"

IT LOOKED LIKE IT WOULD BE NEARLY IMPOSSIBLE TO FIND HIM. SAM Wilkeson had learned in the early morning of July 4 that surgeons from both armies had been working on wounded men all night in barns and houses scattered for miles. Many had been going non-stop on amputations. There were far too many wounded for the available number of doctors, and care often came through whim or pure luck. Many men simply died without any attention at all. As the two armies pulled out of Gettysburg, they left behind roughly 200 surgeons, about half from each army, to tend to more than 20,350 wounded.[1] As he moved cautiously through Gettysburg itself, he could only hope Bayard had gotten the attention he needed.

The next two days unfolded like nothing from a known world.

Sam joined a flow of civilian medical volunteers and family members that were arriving by the scores, to macabre scenes that they could barely describe. On Independence Day, J. Howard Wert, a young Gettysburg resident who helped guide Reynolds's 1st Corps to the battlefield on July 1, saw bodies being eaten at Willoughby's Run by "swine reveling in the remains in a manner horrible to contemplate."[2] Lt. Barzilia J. Inman of the 118th Pennsylvania, known as the Corn Exchange Regiment, was gravely wounded and lay on the northern edge of John Rose's wheat field for two days before being rescued on the morning of July 4. He told doctors that he had spent all of the previous night fending off hogs that were "rooting and tearing at the dead men around me." Several pigs came upon him and he jammed his sword in the belly of the largest, which "made him set up a prolonged, sharp cry," Inman said. "By constant vigilance and keeping from sleeping I contrived to fight the monsters off 'til daylight."[3] Pvt. Charles Drake of Bristol, New Hampshire, had his leg amputated and watched as a hog ate the discarded limb.[4]

Those ungodly scenes aside, amputation often saved a man from bleeding out or from gangrenous suffering and death. But that could happen only if the doctors could get there on time, and that prospect was getting worse, not better, in the battle's aftermath. The Union army's liberation of Gettysburg on July 4 only added to the overworked surgeons' patient lists, as wounded Union captain Alfred Lee from the 82nd Ohio discovered. At 7:00 a.m., as Gettysburg was still being cleared by the Ohio regiments, Lee was among a group of wounded soldiers from both armies moved from John Crawford's rambling house near the Almshouse, to a field hospital that had been set up in a barn about a mile outside of town. About 1,500 wounded Union troops were lying on the ground outside the barn, "begrimed, swollen and bloody," some barely alive, some just dead. Captain Lee, who had been shot Day One near Dilger's blazing guns west of Barlow's Knoll, was put down just inside the barn door. It was a scene he could not put out of his mind for the rest of his life.[5]

"In the center of the barn stood an amputating table, around which two or three surgeons were busily performing their dreadful offices. A handsome young German captain, whose leg had been shattered by a musket ball, was placed upon the table and chloroformed. After the operation of removing his injured limb was complete, he was brought to where I lay and placed beside me. The pallor of his face betokened great loss of blood and extreme weakness. After some minutes, he opened his eyes, and, turning languidly toward me, inquired, 'Is my leg off?' Being told that it was, he gazed intently at his hand, and, observing that a ring had been removed from his finger, he remarked, 'I would not care for this, were it not for a little friend I have down there at Philadelphia.' He could not say much more, for his remaining vitality was fast ebbing away. In a few hours it was gone." The wounded Alfred Lee survived, returning home a few days later to learn that his obituary had been printed in his hometown newspaper.[6]

Sam Wilkeson's sorrowful search became a grim process of elimination. Lt. Bayard Wilkeson was not among the mass of wounded and dead removed from the Crawford House, nor was he among the 1,500 wounded men in the barn with Captain Lee. Sam would also discover that Bayard had been moved from that basement in the Almshouse. At that moment, the thought would have occurred that Bayard was on his way to a Confederate prison. If he had died, Sam might never find him.

Mass burials were underway, and individual soldiers were being buried anonymously, and without any order or record, and in graves that might never be found.

Oliver Benner witnessed this up close. In his late teens, Oliver lived with his family in a small stone house near the base of Culp's Hill. The Benners' ripening wheat and oats fields had been flattened and left littered with discarded war detritus. Their house had been ransacked.[7]

Venturing out after the shooting stopped, Oliver discovered a dead Confederate sniper hanging by his belt in a neighbor's tree. He watched as Union troops cut down the dead sniper and buried him, without any attempt to identify him, in a hastily dug hole in the neighbor's field. Later that day, Benner and his father discovered another dead Confederate soldier in the same neighbor's field. The man had crawled to the hollow of an old tree to die. Oliver and his father buried him. Given how quickly the dead Rebel had decomposed, Oliver doubted the remains of this man would ever be identified by the people who loved him.

By this time in the war, Sam Wilkeson was accustomed to the assault on decency and sensibility in post-battle scenes. But civilians combing the battlefield with him that day were appalled at the detached, cavalier way some Union burial parties were going about their business. Philadelphian Augustus Steffan, who rushed by train and by foot to Gettysburg in search of his two Union army brothers—John had been killed, Edward wounded—entered the town past a long row of hospital tents. He stopped and asked for his brothers at every tent. At one, Augustus Steffan found thirty or forty dead men piled outside, and after gazing at each man's face, he gave quiet thanks that John was not in that heap. Soon Steffan came upon a small group of Union soldiers carrying a wounded man. Steffan talked with the litter bearers as they sat for a short rest. While doing that, the man they were carrying died. Steffan was struck by how the men took it as an everyday occurrence. In truth, it was.

"Around him stood his fellow soldiers laughing and talking, wholly unimpressed by the scene," Steffan wrote later. "It is surprising how this bloody & unnatural war brutalizes all the finer feelings of a man—most of the men who have been in service any time seem totally void of any such traits of humanity which are natural and proper in a civilized being." Steffan finally found a surgeon in his brother's regiment, and the doctor directed him to where John had been buried.[8]

Near the Benner home, a large Union burial party began digging long trenches and filling them with dead men. The methodical, mechanical geometrical efficiency in the grave diggers' work fascinated Oliver. Sweating soldiers dug long trenches 2 feet deep and a man wide, then the body-haulers followed, systematically stacking one man's torso on the legs of another, corduroying them to maximize the number of men that could go in a burial trench. When the dirt was thrown on the graves it left fresh, long gashes in the earth.

Before the bodies were covered, Benner noticed one universal thing: "All the pockets of the dead men were turned out." He wondered how any of these dead boys, their bodies stripped of earthly possessions, would ever be identified.[9]

Gruesome as the landscape was, it did nothing to slow the floods of outsiders that by the end of July 4 had burst into a second great invasion, this of the aftermath armies of mercy and exploitation. The Reverend Leonard Marsden Gardner first knew he was approaching the battlefield on the afternoon of July 4 from the stench of death. A Lutheran minister from Clearfield, Pennsylvania, 170 miles away, Gardner had set out on his horse about a week before the battle. His sick father lived 15 miles northeast of Gettysburg, but he had arrived too late to evacuate him. By then, he had been swept up in events beyond his control as he struggled against a tide of refugees fleeing Gettysburg and surrounding towns. He decided to keep on toward Gettysburg to see what he could do to help.[10]

Through York, Carlisle, and other towns where armies were advancing, farmers had hidden horses and cattle in woods. Roads were clogged with families hauling wagons full of grain and household goods, and herding cattle and sheep. "The last week of June one steady procession passed through Carlisle from early morning until late at night," Gardner remembered.

Nearing York Springs while the battle was in full force 10 miles away, Gardner stumbled upon a Union officer hiding from roving Confederate cavalry. Learning that Gardner had grown up near Gettysburg, the officer convinced the minister to guide him safely to the Union lines, although neither man knew where those lines were. Arriving on the day after the battle, they came to the knoll where Bayard's guns had been placed three days before. Bodies still littered the landscape. One dead Southern boy stood out to Gardner, a soldier with "a beautiful face, jet black hair, and skin as white as marble."[11] The description could have been that of Bayard Wilkeson, except this boy wore gray.

The preacher "could not help thinking of the anxiety of some Southern mother about that same boy, who would wait and hope to hear that he had escaped the scourge of battle, only to be plunged in grief at last to hear that she would see his face no more."[12]

Gardner came across one of the most horrific scenes in the aftermath, one that instantly converted the preacher from spiritual caretaker to one of the flesh. Leaving his horse in town early on July 5, he walked toward the Lutheran Theological Seminary, still overflowing with wounded. Continuing west on the Chambersburg Pike, the preacher came to a large stone barn roughly a mile southwest of where Bayard had been wounded.

As the preacher drew close to the barn, he heard a voice calling and saw a wounded Union soldier lying in a pig sty. "For God's sake, Chaplain, come and help us; there's no one here to do it," the wounded man said. Inside the pig pen, two men, each wounded in an arm, were teaming up to work a hand water pump with their good arms. Dozens of wounded men were in the barn, and dozens more were lying in a wagon shed and in a tenant house nearby. Others were in the open in the barnyards. Some of the men had been lying unattended for days.

Gardner immediately began hauling water to thirsty men in any available vessel he could find. He was surprised at his ability to fight the gag reflex over the repulsive odors and sights of festering wounds. About midday on that Sabbath, a single Union surgeon and two assistants arrived. Reverend Gardner helped build a makeshift operating table that consisted of a few boards laid on rough sawhorses. Inside a wagon shed, the assembly line began. The preacher was enlisted to hold limbs to be amputated so the surgeon could saw more cleanly.

A detached resolve came over him. There was no one else to help, and he realized that these men needed physical, more than spiritual, attention. "I would hold the limb until it was separated from the body," Gardner said. "During all this time I suffered no nausea from the offensive smell or ghastly sight of bloody limbs that lay at my side. In due time the ambulances came and all of these wounded men were removed to the hospital in town." For the rest of his life he remembered that day on that farm—possibly that of Lincoln's friend Edward McPherson's, although Gardner did not identify it—as his best Sunday work.[13]

Initially, people like Gardner were arriving on foot or via wagon because both armies had destroyed rail tracks and bridges leading into Gettysburg. By Sunday, July 5, trains were starting to arrive in the town, crammed with incoming visitors. Outgoing trains began hauling ambulatory wounded men to hospitals in Baltimore, Philadelphia, and Washington. By Monday, July 6, "hundreds of wagons and carriages from every direction filled the place," Gardner recorded.[14]

The Christian Commission and the government's Sanitary Commission set up temporary hospital tents. The Union army's main hospital, dozens of big tents in a grove of trees along the York Pike about a mile east of town, would operate through the summer, men from North and South sometimes being treated side-by-side.

By July 27, U.S. medical inspectors E. P. Vollum and John Cuyler would report that 16,125 wounded men had been moved out of Gettysburg by rail, but that thousands more were still in the large temporary hospital or spread out in homes and farm buildings as far away as Hagerstown, Maryland, 32 miles away. Cuyler lauded the "immense aid afforded by the Sanitary and Christian Commission" that "doubtless helped to save the lives of many."[15]

Among those who had come to help evacuate the wounded was Capt. John B. Linn of the 51st Pennsylvania, who had been recuperating from wounds of his own and on leave in Buffalo Grove, Pennsylvania. Anxious about the fate of men under his command, he joined a stream of refugees and others flowing back into Gettysburg on July 4. Roads and riverbanks were crowded with refugees on his journey into the town. His journey typified the lengths people were taking to get to the battlefield. Captain Linn had gotten to Carlisle via train, and then he and six other men hired a butcher at $1.37 a man to haul them by wagon as far as York. From there they walked for several miles, until they hitched a ride with an old man hauling medical supplies for the wounded. The old man's wagon was pulled by a blind horse that would stop every 200 or so yards, falling to its knees in exhaustion. Two miles outside of Gettysburg, convinced the horse would not make it all the way, Linn and his companions began walking again, this time through a scene that was even difficult for a veteran soldier to describe.[16]

Like Reverend Gardner, Linn also passed over the knoll where Lt. Bayard Wilkeson had been wounded.

Everywhere he looked he saw hastily dug graves, scattered contents of knapsacks, busted cannon caissons, and dead horses. He could not get "the smell of putrefied blood" out of his nostrils. Linn stopped for a grave marked crudely as "W.P.D. 2nd Louisiana." The dead soldier's "little tin bucket, carriage box (and) contents of his haversack" were lying nearby, and the cannonball that might have killed him was on the ground near a fence a few feet away. Death seemed so neatly contained in that one scene. Arriving in Gettysburg, Captain Linn came to a hospital in a Catholic church filled with wounded, including one man he knew who had been shot twice in the leg but was still awaiting treatment three days after the battle ended. The attending doctor seemed to have gone mad, Linn thought, "smoking and cursing, and paying no attention whatever to the frequent appeals made to him." One soldier in great agony was screaming and had been left unattended; a newly arrived civilian surgeon finally ripped off his shirt, to find a maggot-infested gunshot wound to his shoulder.[17]

As these horrific scenes played out from the wreckage-littered fields north of the town, through the splintered and burn-streaked homes in the village, to the pocked and bloodied slopes of Little Round Top more than 2 miles to the south, Sam Wilkeson's unsuccessful search continued, past the Globe Inn on York Street, where Union troops on the way to the battlefield on July 1 had begged for whiskey as they passed by. Beginning that night and lasting for days the hotel was jammed in every available space—including hallways and parlors and corners rarely used. "Citizens were coming in from all sections of the country," said John Wills, whose father owned the inn. The hotel had become an unofficial headquarters for outsiders seeking brothers, husbands, or fathers. They traded in rumors, snippets of information, overheard conversations, and they made plaintive appeals for help from strangers. Most of the visitors were women, the unlucky of which roamed the town at night because they had no place to stay.

"Train after train day and night came in loaded to their full capacity from every Northern state from Maine to California," Wills remembered. "The majority being women who came to look after their friends, the sick and wounded, to have them cared for and when it was possible to have them taken home and also to have their dead taken up and the bodies embalmed preparatory to shipping them home."[18]

By July 21, the *Adams Sentinel* was reporting that local carpenters had made at least 600–700 coffins and that "we expect this mournful business will be kept up for some time yet."[19]

Over the coming days, grief-stricken searchers sought any night shelter they could find, then headed out for often futile daylight searches. Some slept in the haylofts of stables or wandered all night through the streets. Visiting women filled every bed in the Globe Inn, and "we placed blanket and pillows on the carpets in the Parlor and reception room and they were occupied by women," Wills recalled.[20]

"The town was crowded with . . . friends and relatives (who) came to find those that had been wounded or killed," Reverend Gardner remembered. "The dead were being coffined to be taken to their homes for burial among their kindred. The wounded were being cheered by their friends or being furloughed for the time and placed in the hands of their loved one. This greatly relieved the pressure on surgeons, nurses and the volunteer helpers that were at work among the immense number of helpless soldiers of both armies."[21]

Misery and devastation lingered. Days after the battle, Mary McAllister—she who also had passed out cool water to troops jogging to the fight on Day One—saw a woman leaning against a tree, crying, that morning. Mary invited her in for a meal and soon learned that the woman had gotten a telegram saying her husband had been wounded. "I came here last night and every place was shut up and I could not get in, everything was so full, and they knew nothing about my husband," the woman told her. Later, she learned he had died and had been buried in a mass trench. Shortly thereafter, Mary again ran into the woman, still wandering aimlessly. Out of money, she "sobbed and cried." Finally, the destitute and devastated woman ran into wounded men who knew her husband, and they directed her to the trench where he had been buried. With help, the woman found her husband's body. "Employees around the depot paid her way back," Mary wrote.[22]

"They came by the thousands—from far Wisconsin, from the hills of Maine—from the prairie and the lakes—from the granite cliffs of New England—all torn by the same agonizing feeling of doubt, which too soon dissolved in the certainty of despair," the civilian scout Wert remembered. "They came to search for their dead, to minister to their wounded. Some were successful, some failed. Some exhumed hundreds of bodies but never found the dead for whom they searched. God grant our nation may never behold another field of fraternal slaughter."[23]

He said the saddest cases in the "vortex of destruction" after the battle were loved ones who exhumed "hundreds of bodies but never found the dead for whom they sought."[24]

Some in the aftermath also came to profit, and some Gettysburg residents found a commercial windfall. The town's carriage makers converted to coffin builders. Exhumation details made good money from distraught family and friends. The sale of whiskey soared to help dull the senses of those doing that grim work.

"At that time a number of our citizens made quite a good thing out of this gruesome business, of taking up the dead for those people and assisting them in preparing them for shipment to their homes," Wills said. "Men who were engaged in this work bought whiskies in large quantities, to prevent sickness in their work."[25]

There were reports that men with wagons were charging wounded soldiers exorbitant amounts for food, milk, and rides to the train station for journeys home or to big-city federal hospitals.

C. P. Cole, an editor from the Cortland, New York, newspaper, took an arduous, four-day journey to Gettysburg to retrieve the body of a friend. He walked the last 30 miles. Along the way, hungry, he stopped at a farmhouse and a farmer charged him $2.85—an outrageous sum—for a small loaf of bread, 3 ounces of rank-smelling ham, and a drink of water. "I have come hundreds of miles in search of the remains of an officer who fell while defending your homes and bread source from pillage, and you have the meanness to make this demand of me," Cole told the man. The farmer retorted: "Well, if you succeed in getting the remains of your friend, the bread and meat is worth that, ain't it."[26]

Looting occurred.

"The battlefield is visited daily by thousands of people from all sections of the country," one of Sam Wilkeson's *Times* colleagues reported. "Many come in quest of those who have fallen in battle, while most of them come through sheer curiosity. Thousands of dollars' worth of guns and other military valuables, are carried away by them from the field, notwithstanding the pretended vigilance of those charged with the duty of preventing such offenses, and the ground for miles, in all directions is still thickly strewn with all manner of such articles."[27]

Reporter Tom Knox saw on one small square of the battlefield a "countryman engaged in cutting the harness of one of the dead battery horses," a man carrying a dozen blankets dropped by soldiers in the heat of battle, and a third man carrying "three of the best muskets he can find." Nearby, was a dead officer, lying on his back, his right arm "extended as if to grasp the hand of a friend."[28]

Wilkeson's *Times* colleague Lorenzo Crounse was so disgusted that in one dispatch shortly after the battle he accused some Gettysburg citizens of "dishonor and craven-hearted meanness.

"I do not speak hastily I but write the unanimous sentiments of the whole army—an army which now feels that the doors from which they drove a host of robbers, thieves and cut throats, were not worthy of being defended." He accused Gettysburg citizens of charging exorbitant prices for milk (15 cents a quart), hotels ($2.50 a day), bread ($1.50 a loaf), and even 20 cents for a bandage.[29]

Crounse's piece, while undoubtedly capturing the cravenness of some, was unfair to others acting heroically and selflessly, often at great financial and emotional cost. Twenty outside ministers and doctors who had traveled to Gettysburg to give aid after the battle responded in a letter to the *Times* on July 11, accusing Crounse of a "slanderous and libelous tirade."[30]

Their letter read: "Imagine those who have been stripped of everything, and have sacrificed their all, who have divided with friend and foe their last morsel of bread and their last cup of water, whose children are crying with hunger, and are sent from home to sleep in order to make room for wounded soldiers, those who are worn out with days, aye, almost weeks of watching and nursing over the wounded warriors—imagine such, reading. . . . this courteous, refined and patriotic letter from the pen of Mr. L.L. Crounse. What stimulus to action! What a reward for toil and sacrifice."[31] Two years later, Crounse would return to make amends, and while there were rumblings of violent payback, he came away unscathed.[32]

Such post-battle chaos made finding one person an unfathomable challenge, as Sam Wilkeson was discovering. Pvt. George Frysinger's 36th Regiment, Volunteer Pennsylvania militia, was brought in to stop looting, and he wondered how anyone could be found, dead or alive, with the thousands that had descended on it, and the thousands suffering around it. "Gettysburg cannot be called a town, but a large collection of hospitals," he wrote.[33]

Union captain Joseph Hopkins Twichell, an army chaplain, said the "scene of great sufferings" expanded outward from Gettysburg like ripples in a pond. He stayed behind when the army pulled out to help in an army hospital, and he prayed that the cost exacted here would bring the end of the war. "All the country around is a graveyard," Twichell wrote a friend, "not an acre for miles but has some mark of death left upon it, yet if it only brings the blessing, we will rejoice."[34]

Abraham Lincoln was intimately attuned to wartime loss of a loved one. Eleven-year-old Willy had died of typhus in the White House in 1862. The country was pouring its suffering on him in letters, recounting tales of searching battlefields for loved ones. George W. Demers, editor of the Troy, New York, *Daily Times*, found out that his brother, Pvt. Eugene L. Demers, had been wounded and had had a leg amputated. The brothers' aging father had rushed to the battlefield to nurse the boy back to health and stayed with him for several days. But what Demers called a "red-tape" Union hospital eventually barred the old man from visiting his son, and he unloaded his anger and frustration in a letter to Lincoln.

"All he asks is permission a few hours a day to sit beside his bed and cheer him," Demers wrote. "He will interfere with no one and cost nothing. My brother languishes without him and may die."[35]

There is no record of a Lincoln response, but the wounded Demers soldier survived and was discharged later in the year.[36]

Oliver Otis Howard, the 11th Corps commander and man ultimately responsible for Bayard's position north of Gettysburg on the first day, thought that if everyone could see "the terrible groupings and revolting lineaments" that he and his men saw as they pulled out of the town, perhaps it would never again come to this. It was important, he thought, to know what happened after the armies left.

"There is need of a faithful portraiture of what we may call the after-battle," Howard wrote, "which shows with fidelity the fields covered with dead men and horses; with the wounded, numerous and helpless, stretched on the ground in masses, each waiting his turn; the rough hospitals with hay and straw for bedding, saturated with blood and wet with the rain; houses torn into fragments; every species of property ruthlessly demolished or destroyed—these, which we can well exaggerate, and such as these, cry out against the horrors, the hateful ravages, and the countless expense of war."[37]

In this great wash of suffering, on Independence Day, 1863, Sam continued his search for Bayard in the wake of the hateful ravages at Gettysburg. The family prayed and hoped for the best news. After hearing Bayard had been wounded, his cousin, Samuel H., then billeted with his cavalry unit protecting Washington, DC, wrote his sister: "Poor Bayard I trust will not be ruined for active service."[38] Plenty of men had lost legs and continued to serve.

CHAPTER 40

"How Beautiful He Looked at Her Out of His Eyes"

THE BASEMENT OF THE HOME FOR THE POOR WHERE BAYARD WAS taken after he was wounded was "as wretched a place as you could imagine," his uncle John said after he saw it upon arriving in Gettysburg on July 5.[1] The suffering that Bayard endured on that dirt basement floor mocked the heroic story line that writers and illustrators were already building up around him. Post-battle newspaper reports glorified the young lieutenant's heroic stand on the knoll. Books did later, and at the twenty-fifth anniversary year of the battle, the artist Alfred Waud, and Sam Wilkeson friend, canonized Bayard in what would become a famous illustration. Waud depicted Bayard on his horse and defiantly lifting his sword to the heavens, standing his ground on the knoll while others lie prone around him. Bayard is forever shown holding the line—and metaphorically, saving the Union. He was victory embodied.[2]

Reality was not nearly so undefiled.

While he was depicted heroically in many battle accounts, in reality, Bayard Wilkeson, nineteen years and forty-five days old, died in that basement while crying for his mother and father.[3] He had suffered terribly for seven hours. Upon arriving at Gettysburg early on July 5, his uncle John saw the outline of Bayard's body in the boy's blood on the floor of the poorhouse basement.[4] John helped piece together the story of Bayard's death.

On the battle's first day, as Bayard and men around him lay dying in the poorhouse basement, two women, one black, one white, came to comfort and care for them. The identities of the two women will never be known, their identities the victims of the day's chaos and their status on a field of combatants. It will never be known if they were Gettysburg residents who risked moving through a live combat zone to come to the aid of the wounded men in the poorhouse basement. Were they part of the long tails of camp followers of one of the armies? Were they residents of the poorhouse, among the paupers living there?

Before the battle the Almshouse compound had been home to about sixty men, women, and children who were either indigent or disabled or declared unfit. In the 1860 Census, Almshouse residents were listed as "pauper," some "crippled," some "idiotic," "insane," or "consumptive." It was not a place that local residents visited much.[5] Census taker Aaron Sheely "saw a good deal of misery there" when he did a head count in June of 1860.[6]

The 1860 Census of the Almshouse listed two black adult female residents. Joana Craig, who would have been thirty-eight in 1863, was officially identified as "pauper—lame." Margaret Dewan, thirty-seven, was listed as "pauper," along with her six children, all under age nine. Several women with Irish last names were listed on the Census report. The oldest, Sarah Conor, seventy-five, had been born in Ireland. She, too, was a "pauper."

No matter who they were, the two women who attended to Bayard as he slowly died were heroes in that valley of the shadow of death. Given how blacks were being rounded up and sent into slavery by Confederate soldiers, the black angel in particular risked her own freedom to come to the aid of suffering men. Given how the Almshouse was a frequent target of Union artillery during the battle, it would have been dangerous for anyone who entered the grounds.

These two angels of mercy represented distinct pieces of a shattered America in 1863—the black American in an age of slavery and the Irish American of the recent immigrant class. The image of them quietly confronting suffering in that basement is as worthy of memory as any heroic battlefield depiction by Alfred Waud.

In Bayard's last hours, a stench overwhelmed the room as dead and dying men lay in the subterranean humidity. Bayard's situation became even lonelier, and more foreboding, when a man who had also lost a leg died next to him.[7]

Bayard died about 10:00 p.m. on July 1.[8] It can't be known whether prompt attention from a surgeon of either army would have saved him. Medical procedures at the time did not produce good odds for catastrophic injuries like the one he suffered. But by that time in the war, veteran soldiers could predict with morbid likelihood which wounded men would die and which might make it. Upon seeing the wounded Lieutenant Wilkeson as he was being carried to the Almshouse, the 11th Corps artillery commander Thomas W. Osborn said he "knew at a glance that the wound was fatal."[9] That explains why Osborn could say nothing after Bayard's cheerful "here we are" greeting to his colonel.

After piecing together Bayard's last hours as best he could, his uncle John concluded that the nephew died of "neglect, and bleeding to death."[10] The injury was catastrophic enough that shock would have hastened the end for a man even as fit as Bayard was.

His uncle John saw Bayard's body after it was exhumed from a shallow grave on the Almshouse ground on July 4. John said he saw only cotton bandages on the stump that remained of Bayard's leg. The bandages had been crudely tied, John Wilkeson noticed, "doubtless by his own hands in a vain hope of staunching the blood."

The uncle was overcome with grief, and pity. "The little room where the poor boy died was full of wounded and he had to lie just within the door and alongside of him was another poor fellow who had received just such a wound, and died," his uncle wrote. "How dreadful shocking was poor Bye's fate."[11]

Sometime between his death and July 4, Bayard's body had been removed to a field outside the Almshouse and buried in a shallow trench with several other bodies. Sometime on July 4, he never said exactly when, Sam found Bayard's body.[12] As he had at Seven Pines with his dead-soldier nephew, John Wilkes, Sam had to examine the faces of other dead men, also shallowly buried in the vicinity, as they were exhumed, one by one, until he recognized his own son.[13]

In his heart, Sam had to have known the odds of finding Bayard alive were not good. He knew from Bayard's subordinates that his son had suffered a catastrophic injury, and that the fighting was so intense on July 1 that Confederate doctors or captured Union surgeons would have been unable to keep up with the butchery. Sam had run into Lieutenant Bancroft, Bayard's second in command, on July 3, and Bancroft had told him the wound looked bad.[14]

Those who saw Sam during his search after the battle say he had the appearance of a devastated, depleted man. Martin Luther Stoever, a professor at Pennsylvania College, ran into Sam the afternoon of July 4, before Sam had discovered his boy's body. According to Wilkeson's colleague, Lorenzo Crounse, Stoever came across Sam searching for Bayard, and "overcame him wholly with his tender outpouring of sympathy and offers of service." Despite the fact that he already had a dozen wounded men in his home, Stoever told Sam that he would have a room for him as long as he stayed at Gettysburg.[15]

Wilkeson did not stay with Stoever that night. He spent the night of July 4 or the early hours of July 5 at the side of his son's body on the poorhouse grounds, and there he wrote his full dispatch to the *Times*. On July 5, Stoever ran into Sam again, and Wilkeson told him he was on his way to an embalmer's office. The *Times* correspondent by then had also filed the story to the paper, probably by messenger and telegraph, a story that would tell of his son's death and appear on the newspaper's front page the next day, July 6. Upon that second chance meeting with Stoever, Wilkeson looked so lost, so despondent, that Stoever posted his young daughter on the doorstep of their home to watch for Sam as he returned from the embalmers. When he did, Stoever "went out and tenderly forced him in and showed him a room prepared for his use," Crounse reported. That afternoon of Sunday, July 5, as the embalmer prepared Bayard's body for shipment home to Buffalo, Sam Wilkeson had tea in Stoever's parlor with five strangers, probably the loved ones of dead or wounded soldiers on the same mission as Sam was.[16]

This somber scene was far afield from the triumphant way that Bayard's death would eventually be framed by Sam's colleagues, Coffin and others. Heroic accounts in newspapers, and illustrations like Waud's of the boy-soldier's suicidal stand on Barlow's Knoll, filled a deep moral, religious, and cultural space in the nineteenth century's concept of the Good Death.

But in his heart, Sam Wilkeson knew that would not be enough. After his sister had died five years earlier, he had written his brother, John, that "philosophize as we may about Death, it is always unwelcome to those who survive the loss of loved ones.

"I know no consolations for these afflictions," he had written then. "I never attempt to give any. The wounds of the heart have one cure. That is time."[17]

CHAPTER 41

"I Would Rather Hear He Was Dead Than That He Had Disgraced Himself"[1]

BAYARD WILKESON'S DEATH IS RECORDED IN HISTORY THE WAY HIS contemporaries would have wanted it: as that of a young man with purpose, in a just cause, giving the ultimate, his life, for others. The journalism that arose around it, including some from his father, flowed in heavenly tones. Waud's later illustration fit perfectly the description and prediction of what has since been labeled the concept of Good Death[1] that infused American religion and culture in the nineteenth century.

Attitudes toward death during the nineteenth century would be unrecognizable in the twenty-first. A long and healthy life was not a given. One in five men of military age in the Confederacy died in the war; an estimated 2 percent of the population of North and South died from combat or disease related to it.[2] Mass casualties were not new to the war. Before the firing on Fort Sumter, epidemics, accidents, and childhood diseases easily treatable in ensuing decades, all had conspired to make death a frequent visitor. Lincoln's loss of Willy in the second year of the war was not unusual. Prewar epidemics had cut swaths through communities that rivaled the death tolls of the war's battles, and mass burial parties were nothing new. About 12,000 died from yellow fever in New Orleans in 1853 alone; in 1849, New York officials, overwhelmed by cholera deaths, had hundreds of bodies buried in trenches just below the surface on Randall Island, a grisly prelude to the death trenches of Gettysburg and other Civil War battlefields.[3]

Bayard's death would have been seen as a Good Death because, in 1863, it was better, even desirable, to die young and innocent in the name of a just cause than to die old after a purposeless life. Furthermore, if one was to die in battle, the Good Death demanded it be as a hero in a just cause. In the North, there could not have been a more meaningful, more heroic, more transcendent death than Bayard's. The righteousness of cause, the heroism he exhibited, even the suffering he endured, was part of the Christian belief of trial, rebirth, redemption, and eternal life that so dominated American culture of that age. It was no accidental gesture that, in his famous *New York Times* dispatch about the battle and his son's death, Sam Wilkeson described dead Union soldiers as Christ-like.

For the North, Gettysburg was a victory of such importance and cost that there seemed to be no real earthly way to describe it. The expectations put upon the men who had fought there were immense, and intimate. Not long after leaving Gettysburg, the *Boston Journal*'s Coffin—who in his battle dispatches compared the dead Bayard to a shining knight—ran into a mother whose son had been captured the year before and then had been wounded at Gettysburg. Her boy had fought in fifteen battles. She, like thousands of others, had rushed to the battlefield, and there she was relieved to find he would survive. But she was more proud than relieved in what she had heard from her boy's captain about how hard her soldier boy had fought. "I told him, when he went away, that I would rather hear he was dead than that he had disgraced himself," the mother told Coffin.

Coffin told the mother that he thought the boy had done his part— fifteen battles and wounded—and that certainly she believed it was time for him to come home.

No, the mother responded, her son had re-enlisted even while lying wounded at Gettysburg. And she was happy about that. "I rather want him to help give the crushing blow," she told Coffin.

"There were," Coffin wrote, "thousands of such mothers in the land."[4]

Cate Cady Wilkeson was one of them. Given her confession that she had felt she had already given Bayard up to the fates of war long before Gettysburg, his death at Gettysburg would have come as a shock, but not surprise. Outwardly at least, she had surrendered to the same fateful hopes that Coffin's travel companion had. It was really only one expectation. "When my boy left me I gave him up to death, and hope if a soldier he will prove a brave one, better to die than live a coward," Cate Cady Wilkeson had written her sister-in-law.[5]

The ideal of the Good Death gave power to and at least a fleeting understanding of Waud's heroic image. Waud depicted the gallant young lieutenant as whole and in the prime of youth and standing firmly in the face of certain death. Bayard's myth had grown as Coffin and others told and re-told the stories of giving up the canteen for another dying man; of staying on his horse and talking calmly to frightened subordinates older than he; of the cheery front he tried to put up for the men carrying him from the field; and, finally, the severing of his own limb as a final act of defiance and courage. Were they all true? We can never know. Are they the whole truth? That search continues.

The awful reality of Bayard's final, suffering hours are also part of that truth. So are the sometime angry exchanges that followed over the questionable tactical decisions that led to Bayard's death.

Central to the never-ending and intimate search for Bayard Wilkeson's truth, this we know: This nineteen-year-old went forth onto a field where his training and experience would have immediately told him that the chances of him dying were very high. He had written in the abstract that a cause greater than he—abolition—could exact this price, and that his youthful craving for fame and eternal honor was part of that price. This, too, is part of Bayard Wilkeson's truth for the ages.

Ironically, it may have been Sam Wilkeson himself who fed the story of Bayard's self-amputation to help burnish Bayard's heroic, Good Death. In *Eyewitness to Gettysburg*, Coffin's book about the battle, Coffin footnoted his account of Bayard self-amputating with the notation, "Samuel Wilkeson to author."[6] It's possible that Sam or his brother John were told the story of the self-amputation by witnesses but found it too gory or personal to make it public themselves, or even that they doubted its accuracy. Sam's *Times* piece did not go into the details of Bayard's death. It only briefly, but deeply, mentioned his own suffering he endured after discovering Bayard's body in that shallow grave on the poorhouse grounds.

But John Wilkeson did note Sam's suffering. By the time he arrived a day after the battle, he saw in Sam the same catatonic anguish that Stoever had tried to ease by inviting him into his house for tea. "What a picture of grief and despair he presents," John wrote. "The loss of this noble, brave boy is a very hard thing to bear. Bayard was very dear to him, and in every way worthy of such a lasting love."[7]

If there was any consolation in Bayard's death, it was that he did not have to endure the even more prolonged suffering that some of his wounded colleagues did. Many brought to the Almshouse lingered for days in horrific conditions before dying or seeing a doctor.

Early's Confederates overran the Almshouse within minutes of Bayard's men carrying him there. By the evening of July 1, the basement and the two above-ground levels of the house were filled with wounded men from both sides, and the grounds outside the house were rapidly being covered with wounded and dead men.

John K. Rush, a private in Company K of the 153rd Pennsylvania, who had been deployed just yards in front of Wilkeson's guns, was shot in the left arm and in the right shoulder, the latter wound shattering his shoulder blade. Captured, by the time he was taken to the Almshouse it was already full, and men were being dumped outside. The house was "full of wounded, and the latecomer had to wait till some poor fellows died before he could get a bed," Rush said. He finally was taken to the upper level and for three days he saw no doctor. He cleansed his own wounds by pouring pitchers of water over them. A badly wounded Confederate soldier, shot in the head, offered to give up his bed "saying he had no right there as came there as an enemy." Rush turned him down, figuring the man was worse off than he was.

"Having more wounded of their own than they could take care of, they left me alone," Rush said of the Rebel doctors. He watched men die while deliriously crying. He was rescued by Union troops on July 4. Rush recorded no memory of seeing Bayard, even though they had fought yards apart on Barlow's Knoll and ended in the same hell hole in its aftermath.[8]

One of Rush's fellow 153rd privates, Levi Walter, lay wounded with a severe leg injury near Barlow's Knoll until the second day of the battle, when Confederate litter bearers finally hauled him to the Almshouse. He spent the rest of the battle lying outdoors on the grounds of the poorhouse, exposed to the heat and occasional shelling by Union artillery. He watched a steady stream of bodies being carried out to be buried on the grounds. On the third day, the Almshouse became a target of Union artillery when a Confederate signal corps soldier climbed on the roof to wave his flags. Union batteries took notice and soon federal shells began falling all over the poorhouse grounds, exacting fresh killing and wounding, and churning up freshly dug graves. An angry young Confederate officer—"his face flushed with shame at the actions of his comrade in arms"—drew his pistol and under the threat of death, ordered the signal corps man off the roof. But the brief burst of incoming federal shells had added more misery to the sufferers.

"Judging from the effect on the writer's own wound—each crash was like singeing the leg with a hot iron—the suffering of the wounded in the poor house must have been terrible," Walters recalled.[9]

As the postwar history was written and re-told through the Age of Chautauqua, Bayard Wilkeson's death was turned into a symbol of sacrifice and freedom. In an 1875 speech, Howard, Bayard's 11th Corps commander, told a Portland, Oregon, audience, that every day he was "reminded of (Bayard) not only by the devoted service he rendered even to the pouring out of his life-blood, but as an example of the costly sacrifice we gave."[10]

In Howard's rationalization, Bayard's death was a necessary price of winning the war. The young lieutenant had become the knight of Chevalier—young, brash, whole in memory—but most importantly, a willing participant in his own death for a cause greater than he. However he had suffered, however horrible the aftermath of Gettysburg had been for those who survived, men had to die to bear forth the necessary end of the war and slavery, and preserve the Union.

But what ultimately should give Bayard's death meaning also flows from the anonymous compassion and courage of the two women by his side in his final hours. As life flowed from the young lieutenant, they mopped his brow, they offered soothing words of comfort. "He became weak and suffered dreadful pains moaning and groaning and calling loudly upon his father and his mother, writhing in tortures most horrible and so continued till about 10 o'clock when he died," they told John Wilkeson.[11]

Toward the very end Bayard drew quiet. "He looked to be in a stupor but he could answer every question—simply waiting for the end," remembered another aid-giver, possibly another resident of the poorhouse. "A strong silent one, that one."[12]

As he faded, the women looked kindly into Bayard's eyes, and he returned their gaze. "The Irish woman told how when she wiped the blood off his face and gave him water, how beautiful he looked at her out of his eyes," John Wilkeson wrote. "The Negro woman said she knew he was a gentleman (that) he was gentle in his ways, and it was, she thought so bad to leave him unburied out of doors."[13]

They wrapped the dead boy in a blanket and he was eventually buried, although his body must have lain for some time above ground to prompt the regret of his overwhelmed caretakers. On his body when it was unearthed was a pocket-sized manual, "Evolutions of Field Artillery," issued to Union artillery officers. Sam gave it to John for safekeeping. John Wilkeson inscribed in it, "Given to John Wilkeson by Samuel Wilkeson," and, "died at 10 p.m., alone, uncared for in the basement room of the County Poor House. God bless him."[14]

In his last letter to his mother, Bayard had written Cate: "The Chief of Artillery of this corps has promised me the post of honor in the next battle, and we will win a name for our battery, even at the expense of half of its members."[15]

He was gone. His mother's fatalistic surrender of her son to the war devil had become real. In the worst hour of his life, an angry, grief-stricken Sam Wilkeson, sitting at the side of his dead son, somehow had to make sense of it all to the readers of *The New York Times.*

CHAPTER 42

"Who Can Write the History?"

THE WORDS WERE THE ONLY THING THAT SAM WILKESON COULD CONtrol. Sitting next to Bayard's body on the poorhouse grounds, with civilians and soldiers all around him picking through the aftermath of Gettysburg, he might have given up.

He did not. The words were catharsis and power. He rose, and the words flowed.

Gettysburg had become a passage for him and the nation. He had long preached for the necessary sacrifices that now tore at his soul. He had witnessed killing that had made the hardest men turn away. Yet somehow in those hours he composed one of the greatest battlefield dispatches ever written. It was another of Gettysburg's heroic acts.

After the battle, Sam would retreat for months into deep sorrow and seclusion, but on this day he did not surrender to his grief. As he wrote in longhand, perhaps he did it out of duty to his profession and fealty to a cause. Perhaps he did it as a minimal tribute a father could give his fallen son and all fallen sons on the bloodied fields around him. Whatever drove him, Wilkeson wrote an account "which ranks amongst the strongest descriptive word paintings of the English language," said J. Howard Wert, the young Gettysburg man who helped lead Reynolds's men onto the field, and who later became a scholar on the battle of Gettysburg.[1]

Sam's dispatch that ran in *The New York Times* on Monday, July 6, began with a confession. Like the father Holmes after Antietam, Wilkeson readily acknowledged that in that moment, he felt inadequate as a father and a correspondent. In a single lead sentence Sam confessed to that inadequacy, acknowledged his all-consuming grief, and condemned those whose blunders he said had caused Bayard's death.

"Who can write the history of a battle whose eyes are immovably fastened upon a central figure of transcendingly absorbing interest—the dead body of an oldest born son, crushed by a shell in a position where a battery should never been sent, and abandoned to death in a building where surgeons dare not to stay?"[2]

Bayard had become the source of inspiration and sorrow so deep that his father could not bear to write his son's name. In a dispatch that covered a column and a half of the *Times* front page, he never mentioned Bayard by name. But the boy would live forever in the father's words. Their transcendent sacrifice was what would be remembered.

Despite his professed anger at the blunders of Bayard's commanders, Sam Wilkeson sought to reassure his readers that death of their boys on this battlefield in the cause of the Union had not been in vain. "Young and bold blood," he wrote, had purchased "a second birth of freedom" at Gettysburg.

Those five words were a foreshadowing of Lincoln's consecrated "new birth of freedom" less than five months later. Did Lincoln draw that from Sam Wilkeson's dispatch? We will never know. What is known is that Lincoln was an insatiable consumer of war news, that he knew Wilkeson and Wilkeson knew him, and that the *Times* was a powerful voice in the country.

Writing vividly, passionately, and concisely under the deadline pressures of war is journalism's ultimate challenge. Having to meet it at the side of his dead son, after what he had witnessed in the slaughter on Cemetery Hill and in his sorrowful search for Bayard, was unworldly, cruelly unfair, but necessary.

"My pen is heavy," Wilkeson wrote, a confession of how his professional duty was being crushed by the weight on his heart. Yet what followed soared in detail, context, and historical sweep.

This hard-edged, hawkish war correspondent, the man who publicly proclaimed that the war demanded "whatever sacrifice necessary" to abolish slavery and preserve the Union, had now seen how great that price could be. He did not surrender to the despair or anger washing over him. He seamlessly wove the anguish that thousands of American families were enduring with lyrical descriptions of battlefield drama and hard-eyed analysis of the history-changing events he had just witnessed.

If anything, his heavy pen bore down to make the suffering universal, the history personal.

Wilkeson's earthy description of the desperate fighting on Culp's Hill at daybreak on July 3 was dispensed in a few phrases. "Out of its leafy darkness arose the smoke" of battle, he wrote, the sounds progressing from "intermittent to continuous and crushing."

The analysis of the fighting on Cemetery Ridge was concise, and it drew on the experience of two years of seeing such fighting. "Only a perfect infantry and an artillery educated in the midst of charges of hostile brigades could possibly have sustained" the defenses that turned back Pickett, Wilkeson wrote. The peril of the hour was made vivid and clear. The Union 2nd Corps, he wrote, repelled an attack "on which the fate of the invasion of Pennsylvania was fully put at stake." The conflicting emotions between utter repulsion and utter fascination came through. The "ghastly and shocking" numbers of dead and wounded men, Wilkeson wrote, were "more marvelous to me than anything I have ever seen in war."

In his final lines, he invoked Jesus Christ and redemption, paean to the Good Death and the religious and social mores of his age. It would have been familiar to his readers. Sam described Jesus Christ looming over the battlefield, "His right hand open to the gates of Paradise—with his left he beckons to those mutilated, bloody, swollen forms to ascend."

Wilkeson's *Times* dispatch was reprinted in newspapers across the country and published later as a pamphlet.[3] Given the wide circulation of Wilkeson's *Times* piece, Lincoln almost certainly was aware of its existence as the most powerful account of the battle of Gettysburg. By that time in the war, Lincoln's assistants were compiling a daily account of what was in the papers. Wilkeson's expansive account would have been at the top of any list.

Although there are strong, common threads in Wilkeson's dispatch and Lincoln's Gettysburg Address, historians and language scholars have predominantly identified other sources of inspiration for Lincoln's famous speech. They've ranged from Pericles's funeral oration from the Peloponnesian War, to the speeches of the great orator Daniel Webster, to the King James Bible.[4] Lincoln wasn't even the featured speaker for that ceremony on November 19, 1863. Lincoln wrote much of the speech on the train ride to Gettysburg and the night before its delivery.[5]

There also is no record of Lincoln and Wilkeson meeting to discuss the aftermath of Gettysburg. Sam went into seclusion and mourning shortly after and even his extended family had little contact with him until several months later. The closest intersection between Lincoln and Wilkeson before the Gettysburg Address may have come on November 2, 1863, when Sam, just back to work, ran into Lincoln's private secretary, John Hay, on the steps of the Treasury Department next to the White House. According to Hay, they talked mostly about politics, specifically Lincoln's 1864 re-election prospects. The impending dedication of the cemetery at Gettysburg did not come up, at least according to Hay's notes. Wilkeson, either trying to work beyond his sorrow or mask it, had humped back into political intrigue about the next year's presidential election.

Wilkeson told Hay that he had just "assisted at a formal conference of political people" whose conclusion was that Lincoln must reorganize his cabinet to get re-elected. Wilkeson and Hay had an awkward parting, as if Wilkeson was about to say something else, but decided not to. "He laid his finger mysteriously on his lips and flitted like an elderly owl into the Treasury Department," Hay remembered.[6]

But there is compelling evidence that in the immediate aftermath of the battle, that Wilkeson and Lincoln thought very similarly about its significance and meaning. The evidence is in a second Lincoln speech.

On the night of July 7, the day after Wilkeson's dispatch appeared in *The New York Times*, Lincoln spoke spontaneously to a crowd and to a band that had gathered outside the White House to serenade the Union victories at Gettysburg and Vicksburg. That July 7 speech and the Gettysburg Address were the only two times in Lincoln's presidency that he publicly spoke the phrase, "all men are created equal."[7]

In the July 7 address from the White House balcony, Lincoln spoke for about two minutes, about the same amount of time he spoke at

Gettysburg four months later. In the July 7 speech, Lincoln tried to be optimistic and to portray the two great battle victories as turning points, although he did note that they were in "trying conditions, not only in success, but for lack of success."[8]

Lincoln had reason to temper his enthusiasm. It was just four days after the battle but already Lincoln was seething about Meade's inability or unwillingness to pursue and destroy Lee's retreating army. "The president said this morning with a countenance indicating sadness and despondency, that Meade still lingered at Gettysburg, when he should have been at Hagerstown or near the Potomac, to cut off the retreating army of Lee," Navy Secretary Gideon Welles wrote in his diary that day. "While unwilling to complain and willing and anxious to give all praise to the general and army for the great battle and victory, he feared the old idea of driving the Rebels out of Pennsylvania and Maryland, instead of capturing them, was still prevalent among the officers."[9]

Publicly, however, Lincoln was already thinking in the "four score and seven years" sweep of history that he would so eloquently cite in the opening line of the Gettysburg Address.

"How long ago is it—eighty odd years—since on the Fourth of July for the first time in the history of the world a nation by its representatives, assembled and declared as a self-evident truth that 'all men are created equal?'" he asked the serenading crowd at the White House on July 7.[10] At Gettysburg on November 19, Lincoln portrayed the historical sweep similarly: "Four score and seven years ago, our fathers brought forth on this continent, a new nation, conceived in Liberty, and dedicated to the proposition that all men are created equal."

Wilkeson's dispatch, written while the wounded were still being tended to on the field, did not have that eloquent phraseology or direct connection to the Founding Fathers, but it does include the transcendently powerful phrase, "second birth of freedom."

Other common threads run through Wilkeson's July 6 *Times* dispatches, Lincoln's July 7 speech, and Lincoln's November 19 Gettysburg Address. Wilkeson wrote that the dead at Gettysburg are "to be envied" for their sacrifice, but he felt unprepared to sufficiently honor them. The next day, Lincoln told the serenading crowd outside the White House that sacrifice for freedom and equality "is a glorious theme, and the occasion for a speech, but I am not prepared to make one worthy of the occasion." In the Gettysburg Address, the president took that theme to a more eloquent, and shared, place: "We can not dedicate—we can not consecrate—we can not hallow—this ground. The brave men, living and dead, who struggled here, have consecrated it, far above our poor power to add or detract." Both Wilkeson and Lincoln keenly felt their own mortality and shortcomings in trying to explain the events and meaning of Gettysburg.

Themes of individual death leading to national rebirth on the battlefield at Gettysburg course through Wilkeson's dispatch and Lincoln's two speeches. The similarities are most obvious between Wilkeson's declaration that the men who died at Gettysburg had brought forth a "second birth of Freedom in America" and Lincoln's "new birth of freedom" in the Gettysburg Address. Less obvious, but still evident, are words indicating Lincoln was also thinking about birth and death in his July 7 speech. The President noted the "peculiar recognitions" that he had heard of the great victories in Gettysburg and Vicksburg on July 4, the eighty-seventh anniversary of the birth of the nation, and also the anniversary of the deaths of two of its founders. Lincoln took special note of two of the creators of the United States—Thomas Jefferson and John Adams—who had died on July 4, 1826, exactly fifty years after the signing of the Declaration of Independence. Now, on an Independence Day just thirty-seven years later, a new birth of freedom had taken place at Gettysburg.[11]

But even without the historical linkage to Lincoln's most famous words, Wilkeson's battlefield descriptions and analysis alone make it a powerful work of journalism. The *Times* soberly and perfunctorily headlined the dispatch, "Details from Our Special Correspondent."[12] There was no need to step on the narrative that followed. As one of the first comprehensive accounts of the battle that many Americans would read, it was a masterful summation of tactics, actions, and meaning.

Wilkeson framed the battle's first day, the day his son was killed, as a fortuitous blunder for the Union army. "I am told that it commenced on the 1st of July, a mile north of the town, between two weak brigades of infantry and some doomed artillery and the whole force of the rebel army," Wilkeson wrote, referencing again his anger at the tactics he believed led to Bayard's death. "Among other costs of this error was the death of Reynolds. Its value was priceless, however, though priceless was the young and the old blood with which it was bought.

"The error put us on the defensive," Wilkeson continued, "and gave us the choice of position.

"From the moment that our artillery and infantry rolled back through the main street of Gettysburg and rolled out of the town to the circle of eminence south of it, we were not to attack but to be attacked. The risks, the difficulties, and the disadvantages of the coming battle were the enemy's. Ours were the heights for artillery; ours the short, inside lines for maneuvering and reinforcing; ours the cover of stonewalls, fences and the crests of hills."

In fewer than 160 words, he had explained the first day's chaos, defined the strategies of the two armies in the subsequent two days, and dissected how the landscape and the respective armies' positions on it contributed to the Union victory.

Union battle lines, Wilkeson wrote, looked like "an elongated and somewhat sharpened horse shoe, with the toe in Gettysburg and the heel to the south." From there, the descriptions and analysis further poured forth. Hancock's 2nd Corps, he said, "will ever have the distinction of breaking the pride and power of the rebel invasion" on Cemetery Ridge. But what a price it was.

"The marvelous outspread upon the board of death of dead soldiers and dead animals—of dead soldiers in blue, and dead soldiers in gray—more marvelous to me than anything I have ever seen in war—are a ghastly and shocking testimony to the terrible fighting" on Cemetery Ridge.

How can something so ghastly also be marvelous? Wilkeson answers with his descriptions of Pickett's Charge.

Men, horses, material, were torn apart by the "howling and whirling" of the "infernal missiles" of cannon fire. Pickett's men, he wrote, came on "with war cries and a savage insolence as yet untutored by defeat.

"But they met men who were their equals in spirit, and their superiors in tenacity," Wilkeson wrote. Once that "grand charge" was repulsed, the two deadly hosts "straggled" until swallowed by the darkness of July 3.

The grieving father left readers with the figurative image of him embracing the body of his dead son. "I rise from a grave whose wet clay I have passionately kissed," he said.[13]

Sam put down his pen and prepared to bring Bayard's body home to Buffalo. On July 6, Sam's *Times* dispatch anchored a front page that was entirely devoted to the Union victories at Gettysburg and Vicksburg. Wilkeson's story prompted an immediate outpouring of sympathy.

The author Eunice White Beecher, the wife of the famous abolitionist Congregational minister Henry Ward Beecher, wrote Sam on July 7 from Peekskill, New York, that she was "very much grieved" to learn of Lieutenant Wilkeson's death. Wilkeson was a personal friend of her husband's, although their relationship would be tested after the war. Eunice Beecher saw in Bayard's death the sorrows of a nation.

"I could not leave you to the daily torture of an aching heart and broken shattered hopes without telling you that you and your kindness and your sorrows truly mourned are not forgotten," she wrote.

She lamented not being nearer to Cate Wilkeson. "If only I could comfort her." Then, echoing Sam Wilkeson's own professed inadequacy in finding words for the occasion, she, too, reached for meaning in a greater cause. "Words are so idle!" she wrote. "In these cruel times that try fathers' souls and crush mothers' hearts, at most the only comfort I can imagine in the first weeks of sorrow is the thought our dear country had need of these precious ones and for her sake they gave their lives."

Beecher praised Wilkeson's "glorious" *Times* reporting as a comfort for families across a divided nation.

"Throughout this great country how many families are there left that have not an aching heart in their midst!" she wrote. "Garments rolled in blood are the ghastly memorials that are to be found everywhere. When will the end be!"[14]

Poet, former war correspondent, and *New York World* editor Edmund Stedman wrote from Washington, DC, on July 6 that he had read Wilkeson's dispatch with a "wet eye." He addressed the letter to "My poor, dear Friend." Stedman included a poem.

"The sod that covers the grave of those we have given to fame, smells not of the hateful mould, but of roses and dewy ferns, and marvelous immortelles twine in beauty above, and their graces give us joy."

Bayard "fell in the most glorious victory of our cause," Stedman wrote. "For you, its historic vista must be forever suffused with rare and sacred light."[15]

But the most unexpected and most controversial letter came from Howard, the 11th Corps commander who Sam had implicitly criticized in the piece. It began decades of dialogue, some of it painful to read even centuries later.

Howard began his letter by referring to how the two men had run into one another shortly after the battle. It is obvious from the letter that the chance encounter came before Sam had learned of Bayard's death. The general said he was grieved to later learn that the young artillery officer with so much promise had died. Bayard's "conduct was so marked," Howard wrote, that his superiors spoke of him only in the "brightest terms."[16]

Then Howard pivoted to Sam's lead-paragraph condemnation of him and other Union commanders. Howard blamed Barlow, a skulking of responsibility that would have raised even more anger in a grieving father. Pleading a case he made for the rest of his life, Howard told Sam that irrespective of the decisions that led Bayard and his battery to Barlow's Knoll, Howard would never believe that the teenaged lieutenant died from a tragic mistake. Heroes had stood strong on Barlow's Knoll, he wrote, their steadfastness, as fleeting as it was, purchasing the precious time that made possible the most important Union victory of the war.

"Your son has spilt his blood for a noble cause," Howard wrote to Sam. "Oh, do not think it was in vain."[17]

There is no surviving record of Wilkeson's return correspondence. But years later, Howard noted that after that letter Sam Wilkeson had "complained strongly of my want of interest in and care for the Lieutenant," and that Sam had "alleged that neither I nor any of my subordinates gave him help in his time of need.[18]

"At first I was surprised and indignant," Howard said. "Could not Mr. Wilkeson see that I was not present with the battery; that I was responsible only for the general dispositions?"

Over time Howard eventually put himself in Sam Wilkeson's place and realized he was dealing with a "sore heart, a father's wounded spirit."[19] Still, bad blood between the grieving father and the commander on the battlefield would go on.

Two months later, Sam received another letter from another of Bayard's superior officers.

The tone of the September 15, 1863, letter from Brig. Gen. John Peck, Bayard's commander at the Battle of Deserted House, implied that the Union command had learned of the deep sorrow that descended upon Sam after Gettysburg. Letters between family members later in the summer of 1863 also expressed worry about Sam's mental state.[20]

General Peck's letter, written from his headquarters in Newbern, North Carolina, that September ostensibly was to inform Bayard's parents that their son had been posthumously promoted to lieutenant colonel for his service at Gettysburg and Deserted House.[21]

Peck, too, tried to assure a grieving father that his son had not died without meaning. Peck invoked the ideal of the Good Death. "He died as all would prefer in the service of his country, battling for her sacred rights and for the preservation of the finest institutions ever vouchsafed to man," Peck wrote.

Turning more personal, the general continued: "When your brother's son was slain at Fair Oaks (Seven Pines), you mourned bitterly for the lad, more as a parent than as a relative, and I have feared that the loss of Bayard would completely overwhelm you."

Peck tried to assure the grieving father that he should not despair.

"Your country demanded this sacrifice upon her holy altar at Gettysburg where the fearful and formidable tide of the rebellion was at its highest flood," Peck wrote. "That tide was only stemmed and turned back upon accursed rebeldom by an ocean of this nation's blood. Who can say that without young Bayards, victory could have settled upon the torn and shattered standard of the republic?"[22]

Whether these words reassured Sam is unknowable. He returned to reporting that fall, the contentious, cantankerous nature slowly coming back, but not as deeply, and not for good. He was different, and he had new worries. Mourning Bayard's death, his younger brother, Frank, also had been captured by the war devil. Frank would soon march off to war himself.

CHAPTER 43

"The Blood of a Brave Son Printing Upon His Tortured Heart"

IN THE LATE WINTER OF 1863, FRANK WILKESON, WHO HAD JUST turned sixteen, ran away from home to join the Union army. Brash, daring, sardonic, a gifted writer like his father, Frank eventually turned his experiences as a Union artillery private into one of the best personal books of the Civil War. Unlike much of the grandiose imagery shaped around his brother's death, Frank had an unusual gift of seeing war's cold despair and heroism on equal planes, and from the bottom, where it was felt the most.

Witnessing Bayard's funeral, and the outpouring of support for the family in Buffalo, left a deep and lasting impression. The suffering he saw in his parents, the overwhelming response his brother's memory invoked when his body was returned to Buffalo, would have imprinted impulses of revenge on any teenager's heart.

On July 8, 1863, a *Buffalo Morning Express* correspondent, referring to the *Times* dispatch as "Sam Wilkeson's Thrilling Word Picture of Gettysburg," wrote that "no wonder that the writer wrote as no historian of battle has ever written before, with the blood of a brave son printing upon his tortured heart its terrible impression of the scene."[1]

Bayard's body arrived in Buffalo from Gettysburg on the morning of July 10, nine days after his death, where preparations had been made to bury him alongside his famous grandfather and his cousin, John Wilkes Wilkeson. Their graves were on a gentle knoll in the family's section of historic Forest Lawn Cemetery. The city was draped in mourning bunting. The Buffalo newspapers called for a day of commemoration.

"Lt. Wilkeson is the second of his family who have come home in this sad yet glorious way, and it behooves the city which will henceforth claim their dust as its own, to render fitting honor to this latest traveler in the quiet of Forest Lawn," the *Buffalo Commercial Advertiser* opined on July 9. "Let the military organizations remaining in the city see to it that this matter is promptly attended to."[2]

The *Buffalo Morning Express* excerpted a story from one of Sam's *Times* colleagues, who wrote that Sam had obtained "the remains and effects of his eldest son, the gallant Bayard, who was mortally wounded Wednesday, left on the field, and dying finally, after ten hours suffering. . . . His death adds another noble soul to the holocaust of this terrible war."[3]

Veterans and active duty soldiers flocked to the funeral. Henry W. Rogers, commander of the Union Continentals and Capt. William T. Wardwell of the Buffalo Tigers organized a detail and the ceremony that received the coffin when it arrived at Buffalo's train station.[4]

For whatever reason, be it grief or a detour to accompany Cate and Bayard's siblings to Buffalo for funeral services, Sam was not with Bayard's body when it arrived in Buffalo the morning of July 10. Sam arrived on the 5:00 p.m. train. At 7:30 p.m. a flag-draped hearse, led by Union troops under Capt. R. M. Taylor and accompanied by a military cornet band, took the body on a 20-block procession through the heart of Buffalo, passing through the streets Bayard's grandfather had helped build. The *Buffalo Commercial Advertiser* reported: "The procession moved up Exchange Street to Main, up Main to Mohawk, down Mohawk to Genesee, down Genesee to Niagara, up Niagara to Main, down Main to Erie, down Erie to Pearl and to St. Paul's Church." Five men from the 21st New York Volunteers and two men from the regular U.S. Army served as pallbearers at the funeral, which was held the evening of July 11, a week after Sam had discovered Bayard buried in that shallow grave at the Almshouse.[5]

A *Buffalo Daily Courier* correspondent captured the mood as Bayard's coffin was taken to the church: "As the procession took up its line of march, and with reversed arms and solemn step, moved to the funeral music of the Cornet Band, we could not but feel that the exactions of this terrible war, were almost more than could be borne."[6]

It was a sad day, foreshadowing an even sadder one. On the night of Bayard's funeral, an exciting young actor, performing as Shakespeare's evil and ambitious Macbeth, starred onstage at Buffalo's Metropolitan Theatre. A review of the play in the *Courier*, printed adjacent to the story of Bayard's funeral, praised the work of the young actor.

His name was John Wilkes Booth.[7]

CHAPTER 44

"More Than His Proportionate Part"

THERE WERE NO EPIC, DRAWN-OUT PUBLIC BATTLES WITH THE GENERals of Gettysburg for Sam Wilkeson. Unlike his very public fight with Gen. David Birney after John Wilkeson's death at Seven Pines the year before, Sam let the lead paragraph of his *Times* piece stand for his feelings about Bayard's death: "Crushed by a shell in a position where a battery should never have been sent," he wrote, "and abandoned to death in a building where surgeons dared to not stay."[1] Retreating for the rest of the summer to the farm in upstate New York, Sam and Cate mourned in seclusion. Death was no stranger, but it was still a shock.

When their sister, Elizabeth, had died years earlier, Sam had written his brother John that death "comes to all with surprising speed. Few are on guard at the time, expectant."[2]

Cate Cady Wilkeson had spoken of heaven after her sister-in-law had died. Elizabeth, she said, had gone to a place where she could be "happy with those she loved so much on earth."[3]

The extended Wilkeson family felt helpless to assuage Sam's and Cate's grief.

Two weeks after the battle of Gettysburg, Sam Wilkeson's *New York Times* colleague Frank Henry reached out to Sam's nephew to inquire about his colleague's condition and whereabouts. "But I could give him no information," the cavalry officer Samuel H. Wilkeson wrote.[4]

While Sam went into mourning seclusion, officers responsible for placing Bayard's unit on Barlow's Knoll on July 1 were not silent. Publicly and privately, they began building a defense. Howard, the 11th Corps commander, did it both publicly—in official reports and in a letter to Lincoln—and in private letters. Francis Channing Barlow, the division commander whose orders placed Bayard on that exposed knoll, laid down a bitter defense in private letters to family and friends.

Howard filed detailed post-action reports and attached copies of the dispatches he sent to Meade and Meade's staff officers during the battle. Howard defended not only his own command of the 1st Corps and the 11th Corps throughout the afternoon of July 1, but he firmed up his claim that he was most responsible for the decision to occupy the Cemetery Hill high ground that afforded the Union army its strategic advantage for a great victory. He also defended Meade's post-battle actions, arguing that the Army of the Potomac's inability to finish off Lee was due more to the weariness and losses in the federal army than to any lack of will or initiative by Meade. It is unknowable whether Howard truly believed the Union army was too spent after the battle to pursue Lee, or whether Howard was soliciting an ally in Meade for the post-battle assessments. Retrospectively, the former certainly appears to be plausible. In defending Meade, Howard went to the highest possible office to begin his own defense of his decisions on the first day of the fighting at Gettysburg.

On July 14, Howard wrote Lincoln that it was the consensus of the officers under Meade that the Union army was incapable of heading off Lee in time to destroy the Army of Northern Virginia before it crossed the Potomac upon the retreat from Gettysburg. Writing from the 11th Corps's camp near Harpers Ferry, Howard told Lincoln he wished to correct "certain statements . . . which I deem (are) calculated to convey a wrong impression to your mind."

Howard told Lincoln that Meade instinctually "was in favor of an immediate attack, but with the evident difficulties in our way, the uncertainty of a success, and the strong conviction of the best military minds against the risk, I must say that I think the general acted wisely."[5]

More telling, Howard's letter to Lincoln included a subtle, but ingenious, self-defense of his decision on July 1. Howard told the president that he believed the Union army triumphed at Gettysburg because of Meade's timely reinforcements throughout the three days, starting with the arrival of the Union 12th Corps under Henry Slocum that lengthened and strengthened the Union line at Cemetery Ridge after the first day's fighting. Embedded in Howard's claims was the argument that Slocum's arrival would have meant nothing if the battered 1st and 11th Corps, under Howard's direction, had not held out long enough to hold the vital high ground on Cemetery Ridge.

Lincoln responded immediately. Initially, he was "deeply mortified" by Lee's escape, Lincoln wrote, because "the substantial destruction of his army would have ended the war." The Army of the Potomac, he said, "had expended all the skill, and toil, and blood, up to the ripe harvest, and then let the crop go to waste."

But Lincoln also acknowledged that "I am now profoundly grateful for what was won, without criticism, for what was not won." Meade, Lincoln said, still had his confidence. There was no mention of Howard's role in the battle.[6]

Meade gave only begrudging credit to Howard. In his official report, the commander of the Army of the Potomac noted that Howard had been outflanked by Early's superior forces, and that Howard "deemed it prudent to withdraw these two corps to the Cemetery Ridge." The Old Snapping Turtle also noted that the retreat through Gettysburg exacted "considerable loss" on the 11th and 1st Corps, in part because of "confusion" of "portions of both corps passing through the town." Meade was damning Howard with faint praise.[7]

Meade mostly credited Winfield Scott Hancock, who had taken command of all Union forces on the field late in the afternoon of July 1, for steadying the Union lines that first day. "In conjunction with Major-General Howard," Meade wrote in that official report, "General Hancock proceeded to post the troops on Cemetery Ridge, and to repel an attack that the enemy made on our right flank." But Meade also admitted that he did not decide to "give battle" on this ground until after Slocum's 12th Corps and part of Dan Sickles's 3rd Corps arrived. So, ultimately, the decision to stay and fight on Cemetery Ridge was his decision.[8]

The argument never ended. Later, in his memoirs, Howard firmed up his claim that, without him and the delaying actions of the men under his command on July 1, Meade would not have had the opportunity to stand at Cemetery Ridge.

"The First and Eleventh Corps and General Buford's cavalry did their duty that first day at Gettysburg—fought themselves into a good defensive position for the army, especially good when the whole Army of the Potomac came up to occupy Cemetery Ridge," Howard wrote.[9]

Howard had made that exact argument in the private letter to Sam Wilkeson right after the battle. But Howard was also trying to have it both ways, by implicitly blaming Barlow for the precarious position of the Union right while arguing that Barlow's orders that cost Bayard his life had, nonetheless, been a key to the victory. The stand on Barlow's Knoll had bought time, and time had saved the Union.

Howard tried to make it personal with Sam. He had grieved over Bayard's death, he said, ever since the two men had run into one another on the battlefield right after the fighting had stopped.

"I hope nobody has added to your affliction by asserting that the battery was doing no good," Howard wrote from Middletown, Maryland, where the 11th was encamped. "General Barlow may have pushed the battery too far to the front, but it did us noble service where it was. Ours was the contest of an advanced guard when we were obliged to hold in check a large force. These are the circumstances. The 1st and 11th Corps did all that they could have done from 10 a.m., to 4 p.m. . . . Your son contributed more than his proportionate part to this result."

Concluding, Howard declared that if the fallen Reynolds had not decided to make a stand north and west of town on the morning of July 1, and had the 1st and 11th not held out as long as they did, "the Battle of Gettysburg would not have been fought."[10]

That is a highly debatable claim, given that columns of two massive armies that had been stalking one another in the neighborhood of a village where ten roads crisscrossed all rushed toward it after the opening shots. Meade had specifically directed the two Union corps under Howard and Reynolds to march to Gettysburg on July 1. Lee, too, had sent his scattered corps in the town's direction. Neither general was prepared for a full-scale battle at Gettysburg on July 1. But from the moment that lead elements of Buford's cavalry engaged Heth's arriving

Confederates, commanders on the field on both sides put out urgent appeals for reinforcement to hurry to Gettysburg. The battle may have turned out differently had Reynolds decided not to make his stand west of town on Seminary Ridge and instead immediately retreated back to Cemetery Ridge or another location to await the arrival of the rest of Meade's army. But it is difficult to believe that, once the lead units of the two armies exchanged shots, that an all-out battle would not have been fought in the vicinity of Gettysburg.

In the letter to Sam, Howard admitted to initially having doubts about Reynolds's decision to stay and fight where he initially did. But in retrospect, Howard argued, the arrival of the 11th Corps, including Bayard's battery, had saved the destruction of the 1st Corps in the nick of time.

"At first I felt sorry that (Reynolds) pushed beyond Seminary Ridge," when the battle began, Howard wrote, "but now I think it was necessary to meet the enemy just as he did, and the position of my (11th) Corps on his right was a fleeting sequence. Ewell's column would have cut him off had mine not been placed there."

The devout Howard ended his letter with an assertion that God was in control the day Bayard died. "Criticism is easy," he wrote Sam. "All officers offer it but the more you look at the Battle of Gettysburg the more you will see the hand of a Guiding Providence."[11]

Wilkeson responded, but the letter did not survive. Howard would later refer to it as the correspondence of an anguished father. For over a decade, Howard would ponder, despair, and hope over its meaning. But the two men broke off their correspondence, at least for now.

The proud, prickly Frank Barlow was not about to ascribe events to God's hand or to take the blame. As he lay seriously wounded at Gettysburg, with doctors telling him he probably would not live, he wrote two angry letters to his mother, each defending his decisions and blaming his troops. After it was clear he would survive his wounds, Barlow later that summer wrote a similar letter to a friend.

Barlow had been as lucky as he was stubborn. The bullet that felled him on Barlow's Knoll just missed his intestines, avoiding the peritonitis that was usually a death warrant for gut-shot soldiers in the Civil War.

Confederate and Yankee surgeons, initially thinking Barlow's bowels had been perforated, had determined Barlow was not worth operating on and told him to be prepared to die.[12] So if the end was indeed inevitable, Barlow was going to leave a defense for the critics he sensed were already lining up against him. The day after Sam's piece condemning the tactics that he blamed for Bayard's death had appeared in *The New York Times*, Barlow wrote his mother that his men had put up "no fight" against Gordon's attack. Barlow also made the inflammatory claim that the Confederates as a whole had better fighters than all but the staunchest fellow abolitionists in his own army.

"They are more heroic, more modest & more in earnest than we are," Barlow wrote. "Their whole tone is much finer than ours. Except among those on our side who are fighting this war upon antislavery grounds, there is not much earnestness, nor are there many noble feelings & sentiments involved."[13]

The way he matter-of-factly described to his mother his own experience on July 1 bespoke of his stern outer countenance. After being shot, he had dismounted from his horse, and tried to rally his routed division, bullets whizzing past. "Everybody was then running to the rear and the enemy was approaching rapidly," he wrote. Two men grabbed his shoulders and tried to help him, but one of them was soon shot and fell to the ground. Barlow then fell himself, sitting and yelling orders as men fought, hand-to-hand, on all sides. He had the presence to destroy abolitionist correspondence in his pocket; being captured with the letters might have resulted in a firing squad. A prone officer was a fat target. A shot hit him in the back, but it must have ricocheted off something else and did not break his skin. Another ball whistled through his hat, and a third grazed the forefinger of his right hand. Eventually, a Confederate officer saw him on the field and ordered two men to carry him into a stand of trees. The men left him some water before turning to push on against Barlow's fleeing men. Barlow had expected to die there.[14] The Confederate commander Gordon, whose men by then were overrunning the Almshouse grounds, eventually claimed he was the officer who saved Barlow. Doubts were raised in Gordon's postwar telling, but the Barlow-Gordon story is deeply embedded in history books.

Some of his own men, by then Confederate prisoners, eventually carried Barlow to a house, where three Confederate surgeons saw him at about dusk on July 1. They gave him chloroform, probed his wound, pronounced it fatal, and moved on to the next wounded man.

Defying surgeons' predictions, Barlow gradually got better while recuperating in a temporary hospital near Gettysburg for several weeks, and then later that summer at hospitals in Baltimore and Sommerville, New Jersey.[15]

His wife, Arabella, may have again saved his life in one of the most courageous acts during the battle of Gettysburg. She had long followed the army as a volunteer nurse. Arabella had been a valuable consoler for Howard as the 11th Corps commander recovered from losing his arm at Seven Pines the year before. Some Union officers, Howard thought, believed that her "unremitting care" had saved Barlow after her husband's serious groin wound at Antietam the previous fall. Now, upon hearing her husband had been wounded again, she did the same at Gettysburg. She twice tried to go through the lines under a white flag to get to her husband while the battle was still raging, and eventually she got through late on July 2. Her "fearlessness and fidelity" saved her husband's life a second time, Howard maintained.[16]

Gordon credited Arabella, too. The Confederate officer told an interviewer after the war that, supposing Barlow was dying, he sent a man with a white flag to Union lines to summon Mrs. Barlow. She was 17 miles from the front, but was rushed up. "I had no idea she would find him alive," Gordon said.[17]

The ball lodged in Barlow's abdomen was removed about a month after the battle. Despite ongoing pain from the wound, he continued his letter-writing defense, lacing a subsequent letter with bitter criticism of the "Dutch" (German-speaking) soldiers in his division. He told friends and family that they should not believe critics who were claiming that Barlow had made critical tactical errors in occupying the exposed knoll.

Writing August 12, 1863, to his Harvard classmate, Robert Treat Paine, a Boston lawyer, philanthropist, and grandson of a signer of the Declaration of Independence, Barlow maintained that he had been "seduced" into taking the 11th Corps division he commanded at Gettysburg. Howard, he said, had enticed him "to see if I could introduce any discipline."

"But these Dutch won't fight," Barlow complained to Paine, no relation to the legendary pamphleteer of the American Revolution, Thomas Paine. "Their officers say so & they say so themselves & they ruin all with whom they come in contact."[18]

In a previous letter to Barlow, Paine must have alluded to allegations Barlow had been personally and tactically reckless at Gettysburg on July 1. "Where did you hear this nonsense about my going ahead of my skirmishers?" he asked Paine. "How could you suppose I was such a damned fool? It was not so. We had been under fire an hour before I was hit & it was not until the Division had fallen back. I stayed to rally them as long as it was of any use & just as I turned my horse to get back I was hit, the fight being about over. I wish you would correct the impression that I went ahead of my skirmishers."[19]

In his defense, Barlow did not condemn all of his men for lacking courage. Indeed, he singled out Lt. Bayard Wilkeson. "The Capt. of my battery had one leg carried away; one gun disabled and several horses killed, but still kept in position," Barlow wrote his mother, getting Bayard Wilkeson's day-of-battle rank wrong.[20] (Bayard was a lieutenant at the time and was promoted posthumously.)

Barlow's bitter criticism of his men's lack of courage belies the observations of General Gordon and his subordinates. Many of them observed that the Union troops in front of them fought as hard as could be expected from an indefensible position.

And Barlow's complaints to Paine about the cowardice of the "Dutch" belied even some of Barlow's own observations right after the battle. Writing on July 4 to an unknown friend, Barlow gave begrudging credit to brigade commanders Ames and von Gilsa, the latter whom Barlow described as "personally brave." "Some of the German officers behaved well," Barlow admitted.[21]

Barlow may not have penned an official after-action report because of his health, or because he feared his critics would simply use it against him. He never explained why. He had seen the criticism heaped on the 11th Corps after Chancellorsville and he may have viewed any defense of the 11th Corps's fight at Gettysburg as futile. "I do not want to have anything to do with the disputes in which the Corps will probably indulge as after Chancellorsville," he wrote to Paine.[22]

Robert Paine was no ordinary audience. His family, like the Wilkesons, was reeling from the loss of a teenaged son and brother at Gettysburg. Robert Paine did not serve in the Civil War, and after the war he helped organize international peace conferences. But Paine did have three brothers in the Union army. One of those brothers—eighteen-year-old Lt. Sumner Paine—was killed at Gettysburg while fighting in the 20th Massachusetts on Cemetery Ridge. "I am glad he died so bravely," Barlow wrote, trying to console his friend.[23]

Like Sam Wilkeson, Sumner Paine's father had also initially sought someone to blame for his son's death. The anguished father wrote his boy's commanding officer asking about reports that the young lieutenant had not received medical assistance and had been left to die after being shot. Lieutenant Sumner's commander, Capt. Henry Livermore Abbot, was sympathetic but at a loss as to how to console the grieving father. Truth was, he did not know how the boy had died in that savage fury that Sam Wilkeson, and others, had witnessed on Cemetery Ridge. "In the hurry and excitement of a charge at a moment when one sees nothing but the enemy, there is no time to note particulars," Captain Abbot wrote. "A man remembers certain phrases or acts, with a blank on each side, just as he does from a dream."[24]

As a testament to the challenges facing Sam Wilkeson and the many scores like him who came to the field to find loved ones, Sumner Paine's body was never returned to Boston. A lieutenant colonel in the 20th Massachusetts wrote Paine's father to say that the body "was so torn and disfigured it was impossible to recover his remains."

That may not have been entirely true. The reality was there were so many bodies, the action so furious, the aftermath so chaotic, that Sumner Paine was buried in one of the mass graves, and he remains in the cemetery there. Lt. Lansing E. Hibbard wrote the elder Paine that "as unnatural as it may seem, a Soldier, an Officer especially cannot stop during an engagement even if his own brother should fall by his side. . . . Therefore, you must not think hard of me because I did not stop to see your son where he fell."[25]

Despite Barlow's reassurance that Sumner had died "bravely," Robert Treat Paine eventually viewed all war deaths as needless sacrifice. Thirty years almost to the day that Frank Barlow wrote him from the hospital, Paine addressed an international peace conference. "We must cleanse the human mind of a great deal of the debris that has come down in it," he said in Paris on August 19, 1893. "We want to change the schools, the colleges, the whole system of instruction, that it may no longer be taught to boys and girls in their tender years that war is the glory of life."[26]

CHAPTER 45

"You Will Almost Want to Kill Him"

BAYARD'S YOUNGER BROTHER, FRANK, WAS SEEKING REVENGE AS MUCH as glory when he enlisted in the Union army late in early 1864. Bayard had inspired him, but he was mostly overcome with an unfocused rage over his brother's death. Unlike his brother, he never professed a desire to make a name and prove himself in battle. But Frank had made up his mind to enlist whether his grieving parents approved or not. "The war fever seized me in 1863," he wrote in 1887 in *Turned Inside Out: Recollections of a Private Soldier in the Army of the Potomac.* "All the summer and fall I had fretted, and burned to be off."[1]

He told enlistment officers he was eighteen and a farmer. He was immediately assigned as a private in the 11th Battery of the New York Light Artillery. For Frank, life in the Union army had no resemblance to the heroic, dashing brother-in-arms fraternity that Waud had immortalized in his painting, and that Charlie Coffin had exalted in his tribute to Bayard.

The unit Frank joined was in reality a "a den of murderers and thieves," he recalled, a regiment filled with bounty jumpers who went from state to state to enlist to collect bonuses, then desert and move on to the next bonus.[2] Older enlistees beat Frank and robbed him of his only possessions, a pocketknife, tobacco, and a pipe. When the regiment was finally shipped out of Albany to head to the front, 400 of the 1,000 recruits who had showed up in Albany to enlist were left behind as either suspected bounty jumpers or deemed unfit for duty.[3]

On a steamboat from Albany to New York City, some of the new enlistees, fortified with whiskey and seeking an opportunity to go AWOL for another bonus enlistment, jumped overboard. Four men were shot to death trying to desert. In the barracks as they were being rounded up and shipped out, men hid in mattresses, latrines, and under beds. Frank saw one man jump into a rancid compost pile, a "water tight swill box" into which "we threw our waste food and coffee slops." The man "was fished out, covered with coffee grounds and bits of bread and shreds of meat, and kicked downstairs and out of the building."[4]

In his book, Frank does not mention Bayard, but he does include a significant reference that suggests a healing that the family had undergone in the years after the war. *Recollections of a Private Soldier* is fundamentally an anti-war book, but it is not about resentment or condemnation, nor does it come across as envious of his hero brother, or condemning of the men who ordered Bayard to Barlow's Knoll. Frank's book draws a wider circle around the Wilkeson family's Civil War story. In descriptive, straight prose he lets the reader determine the ultimate depravity, or glory, in war. In his post-battle *New York Times* dispatch, Sam Wilkeson made Bayard's death a metaphor for sacrifice and redemption and the higher purposes of those who die in war. In his book, Frank completed the equation by showing that beneath the myth-making and the crowning of heroes there is a degrading, destructive and base reality. Most of the men he served with were not heroes, he wrote, had no aspirations to be so, and he detested the pious pronouncements of the politicians who would exhort them to be so.

"False history and dishonest congressmen who desire to seek re-election by gifts of public money and property to voters, say they were brave Northern youth going to the defense of their country," Frank wrote. "I, who know, say they were as arrant a gang of cowards, thieves, murderers, and blacklegs who were ever gathered inside the walls of (the prisons) Newgate or Sing Sing."[5]

Frank had become increasingly fed up with the fame-seekers and embellishers of dubious reputations. All the generals were writing books, why not he? On top of that, Frank had inherited Sam's love of causes, gift for a finely turned phrase, and never-ending capacity for outrage. He had seen too much, in his brother's death and in the self-aggrandizing accounts of the war, to let it go unanswered.

"Most of this war history has been written to repair damaged or wholly ruined military reputations," Frank wrote. But the true history of the Civil War, he said, could only be written by "the men who carried the muskets, served the guns, and rode in the saddle."

Frank's enlistment as a lowly private in a dubious unit had sent his family into a frantic search to bring him home. Frank's uncle, William Wilkeson, finally caught up with the young enlistee in March of 1864. Frank refused to come home, even after his father revealed to his commanders that they had enlisted a sixteen-year-old. Sam called in chits and got Frank transferred to Bayard's old artillery regiment. But Cate and Sam Wilkeson constantly worried they would lose a second son in the war.

By the summer of 1864, Sam mended his differences with Greeley and returned to the *Tribune*. Sam poured anew his worries about his soldier boy, to his old friend and editor, Sidney Howard Gay, shortly after Frank had turned sixteen. He did not know what to do with the boy, Sam wrote. "Sydney, don't have a boy 16 years and 21 days old," he wrote. "He will go and enlist as a private soldier within a year after his older brother was killed in the front of battle. And he will hide in a city you don't know of—& will conceal the name and number of the Battery into which he has fled. . . . And thence will write you letters upon the patriotic duty of letting sons of pith and vim fight for their bleeding country.

"And," Sam wrote to Gay, "you will almost want to kill him."[6]

Sam pulled strings for Frank, just as he had done for Bayard. On May 5, 1864, Sam wrote Brig. Gen. Seth Williams, the well-regarded Army chief of staff who had barely survived the bombardment at Gettysburg at the Leister House with Sam. Seeking to "trespass on your time and on your kindness," Sam asked Williams to expedite Frank's transfer to Bayard's 4th Artillery regiment.[7]

Frank survived the war in that unit. The second son of Sam and Cate Wilkeson saw some of the most brutal fighting of the war. He fought under Ulysses S. Grant in the bloody Overland campaign in May and

June of 1864. By then, Grant was on a campaign of purposeful, constant attrition, of weeks leading to months of constant fighting, a campaign designed more to leave just one army standing than to lead to glorious victory of one and honorable surrender of the other. Grant, unlike the Union generals ahead of him, had determined by then that only the destruction of the South's ability to wage war would end it.

Grant's armies spent nearly a year in a deadly clinch with the depleted, starving ranks of Lee's and other Confederate armies. Some of the most unholy slaughters of the war occurred in the 1864 campaign, at the Wilderness, Spotsylvania, and Cold Harbor. After three years of fighting, with Confederate battle victories holding Northern material superiority to a draw, with both sides threatening the other's capitals but yet unable to punch through, Grant had made personal peace with the cold calculation that the side most able and willing to endure loss would be the side that won. Even then, even with his superiority in men and material, Grant knew it would take a year to finish the war.

"The campaign now begun was destined to result in heavier losses, in both armies, in a given time, than any previously suffered," Grant wrote in his memoirs. "But the carnage was to be limited to a single year, and to accomplish all that had been anticipated or desired at the beginning in that time. We had to have hard fighting to achieve this. The two armies had been confronting each other so long, without any decisive result, that they hardly knew which could whip."[8]

Frank Wilkeson saw the results of that butcher's bargain from the ground up. At the battle of the Wilderness in early May of 1864, which produced nearly 30,000 combined casualties, Frank's regiment marched over ground strewn with human bones left over from the Confederate victory at Chancellorsville the year before. Shallow graves had been no match for hard rain and marauding predators, and human remains were scattered all over the battlefield. Now this new fighting was adding a fresh layer of flesh and bone. Camping there that night, Frank cooked supper from a freshly killed man's knapsack and slept under the cover of the same dead man's blanket.[9] At Cold Harbor three weeks later, he stumbled in the night and fell on the body of a dead cavalryman covered with insects.[10]

Frank's letters home were his catharsis. The teenager sometimes did see mercy rise above of the relentless, massive, sense of loss. On May 8 in the Wilderness, the Rebel lines in front of Frank's battery suddenly were adorned with white flags. Thinking that a Confederate surrender was imminent, the Union officers relented to a ceasefire, but soon discovered that the Confederates merely wanted a truce to bury the piles of dead men between the army's two lines. They needed to clear the air to fight some more, an irony that did not escape the young soldier. "The wind blew over them and as they had been there 5 or 6 days the smell of dead men almost drove them out of the works," Frank wrote home.

So under the white flag, men on both sides gathered between the lines to bury the dead just so they could settle the air to fight some more. Mortal enemies dug side-by-side graves because their comrades had fallen that way. "Rebs and our men mixed up together," Frank wrote of the dead. "You could not tell who any of them were except for what was in their pockets." The Union burial parties traded coffee for tobacco with some Mississippi boys, and as they went back to their earthworks soldiers on both sides warned soldiers on the other to keep their heads down because they were obligated to shoot if they got too conspicuous.

"They are a fine set of men," Frank wrote of the Mississippians, "large strong fellows, but a little down in the mouth about being driven back so far. I don't think they will fight as well as they did." He was right. Later that night, the Rebels they had just engaged with in a burial party came out of their trenches on a half-hearted charge, then soon retreated after a few half-hearted Yankee volleys. Neither side had the appetite for more killing that night.[11]

Fresh recruits were treated with maudlin derision, as if their very presence was evidence that the war would go on and on. During the battle of Spotsylvania, which exacted another 30,000 combined casualties in late May 1864, a grimy and ill-tempered Frank watched as an artillery unit fresh from the Washington defenses arrived on the field in spotless uniforms, marching in a precision that annoyed him and his fellow battery mates. The fresh troops were led into the line of battle by a military band playing patriotic songs. They were heckled and mocked by the veterans they had come to reinforce.

To get to the front lines the replacements had to pass what Frank morbidly described as a "double hedgerow of death"—a half-mile-long line of wounded and dying men waiting for ambulances and burial parties. Some wounded men taunted the clean-faced newcomers. One man pointed to his shattered leg and yelled out, "This is what you will catch up yonder in the woods." Another group of wounded men kept covering and uncovering the horribly contorted face of a dead man as the green troops marched by. The newcomers blanched and kept marching.[12]

At the Wilderness, Frank's battery mates sat around a campfire, the bones of the Chancellorsville dead strewn all about them. One veteran went into great detail about how wounded men at Chancellorsville were burned to death in the dense woods around them. As the soldier finished his story, another veteran rolled a skull in front of them near the fire and said in a deep voice, "This is what you are all coming to, and some of you will start toward it tomorrow."[13] And that horror did recur for some of the wounded men at the Wilderness.

After Spotsylvania, Frank's regiment moved on to a new fight at the North Anna River, which piled on another 3,500 casualties. On the way the federals passed through once-picturesque Virginia towns showing the wear and tear of three years of war. The federals marched by in seemingly endless columns of blue, sometimes taunting women standing by the edge of the road. Women and children glared back. Frank remembered passing through the town of Bowling Green, Virginia, "where many pretty girls stood at cottage windows or doors, and even as close to the despised Yankees as their garden gates, and looked scornfully as we marched through the pretty town to kill their fathers and brothers."[14]

He got a taste of what men of his father's profession faced as Union army embeds. At Cold Harbor, Frank saw the *Philadelphia Inquirer*'s Ed Cropsey forced onto a mule and paraded in front of Union troops, within range of enemy guns, bearing the sign "libeler of the press" affixed to his back. Cropsey's alleged transgression? Reporting that Army sources had told him that Meade had urged Grant to retreat during the nasty Wilderness fighting. Meade, denying it, retaliated by running Cropsey out of camp.[15]

Cropsey had written a "libelous statement," Meade charged, "calculated to impair the confidence in the army in their commanding officer." Meade held Cropsey out as an example to the rest of the correspondents following the Union armies.[16]

"The Commanding General trusts that this example will deter others from committing like offense, and he takes this occasion to notify the representatives of the public press, that, while he is ready at all times to extend them every facility for acquiring facts, and giving circulation to the truth, he will not hesitate to punish with the utmost rigor all instances like the above, where individuals take advantage of the privileges awarded them to circulate falsehood," Meade wrote.[17]

Frank Wilkeson described Meade's revenge, and Cropsey's humiliation, this way: "He was howled at, and the wish to tear him limb from limb and strew him over the ground was fiercely expressed."

Later in the war, Frank ran into Cropsey on a Washington, DC, street. "He told me that he was a newspaper war correspondent, and his offense was in writing, as he thought, truthfully, that General Meade advised General Grant to retreat north of the Rapidan after the battle of the Wilderness."[18]

Meade, the hero of Gettysburg, had become a hater of the press. The press hated back. By the time he punished Cropsey, he was being virtually written out of accounts of many battles, through an informal agreement between Northern correspondents to mention his command only as "Grant's army."[19] Aside from Sherman, he developed one of the rockiest relationships with journalists covering the last two years of the war.

But Meade's humiliation of Cropsey did not deter Sam Wilkeson from criticizing him, or other Union commanders. The next barrage came at the Battle of the Crater, during the siege of Petersburg, just weeks after Meade's humiliation of Cropsey.

Meade had signed off on an elaborate tunneling operation and explosion that resulted in initial success but soon capitulated into failure, costing the Union another 3,800 casualties, many of them newly enlisted black troops. They were among Union troops that charged into the crater left by the explosion, only to be trapped and slaughtered from point-blank range by Confederates on the rim. Some newspapers reported it favorably as an audacious attempt to break the Petersburg stalemate that had led to minor, but temporary, gains of territory. Wilkeson ripped back at those competitors. "Why, O Swindled People!" he wrote in the *Tribune*, to which he had returned. "The ink that made the lie that gave the false journalism in New York its last sensation, was not yet fully spread on the types, while every drummer-boy and mule-driver of the Army of the Potomac knew that a crowning disaster, and a crowning disgrace had happened to it, and the number of our killed, wounded, and missing was whispered among them to be five thousands."

Sam mocked one headline in a rival paper with a familiar biblical reference: "'Three tiers of earthworks carried!' Aye, carried as Pharaoh's cavalry and war charioteers carried the Red Sea—carried precisely in that way."[20]

The old scold was back. Wilkeson then turned on the goat of Fredericksburg, Burnside. Wilkeson reported that after ordering his men into the crater, after a delay of forty-five minutes, Burnside "did not accompany the troops" on the suicide mission he had sent them on. The newly formed bomb hole, a rectangular cleavage 30 feet deep, 170 feet long, and 60 feet wide, became "a solid mass of wriggling, heaving, twisting, crawling, helpless soldiers, black and white, that, inextricably intermingled, defied all attempts to tactically extricate them," Wilkeson wrote.[21]

Wilkeson's criticism of Burnside was as tough as any he delivered during the war, and it might have gotten a correspondent of lesser stature sent out of camp backwards on a mule. But the *Tribune* went with the story because of Sam Wilkeson's reputation. The indefatigable Charlie Page—he of the watermelons and whiskey and great quip to Greeley that "early news is expensive news"—wrote Sidney Gay that "every word" of Wilkeson's dispatch from the Crater disaster was authentic. Alluding to Wilkeson's stature, Page told Gay that "I could not state it so sweepingly without being expelled, but *he* may."[22]

Frank Wilkeson inherited that gift of sweep from his father. At Petersburg, where trench warfare was a foreshadowing of the butchery of France in World War I, he wrote with uncommon insight into what drove men in the army. Frank decried the "coffee boilers," men who snuck off into the woods and brewed coffee when the action got hot. Some of these coffee boilers were not much better than murderers in his mind, sneaking out at night to kill wounded men. Hundreds of them were at Petersburg. "They plundered houses. They frightened women and little children. They burned dwellings. To call a soldier of the Army of the Potomac a 'coffee burner' was an insult to be promptly resented."[23]

The faces of dead men in battle should never be trusted, Frank Wilkeson declared. He'd seen enough die to know that some look peaceful in death, and some look to be in pain or in a rage or fearful. But he had come to the realization that their expressions had nothing to do with the way they died, and anyone who sought meaning in them was naive or delusional. Death masks come from pure physiology, Frank concluded, so why make it into something meaningful or transcendent or mythological?

It's just death.

Not a Good Death or an angry death or an heroic one.

Just death.

"The face is plastic after death," Frank wrote, "and as the facial muscles cool and contract, they draw the face into many shapes. Sometime the dead smile, again they stare with glassy eyes, and lolling tongues, and dreadfully distorted visages at you. It goes for nothing. One death was as painless as the next one."[24]

Frank's most revelatory passage is near the end of the book, as he declares that rank-and-file soldiers separated their officers into two groups: those that fought from the front, and those that didn't. Two generals stood out as front-fighters.

"It is true the regulars, typified by Major General (Charles) Griffin of the Fifth Corps, and volunteers by Major-General Francis C. Barlow of the Second Corps, commanded the universal respect of the enlisted men," Frank wrote. "We knew the fighting generals and we respected them, and we knew the cowards and despised them."[25]

After the war, Griffin ran the Department of Texas for the Union army and engendered much controversy by registering blacks to vote and removing Confederate supporters from public jobs.[26] He built a stellar reputation in war and peace, and his mention in Wilkeson's book would not have been a surprise to anyone. But it was Frank's mention of Frank Barlow that marked significance for the Wilkeson family.

It showed that there were no lingering resentments for Barlow's order to send Bayard to that deadly knoll on July 1, 1863. The animus that Sam had expressed in his *New York Times* dispatch from Gettysburg had been tempered by the time Frank published his book twenty-four years later. Perhaps Frank Wilkeson admired Barlow's defiance, his steadfast unwillingness to declare he had done anything wrong or explain his actions in an attempt to assuage the family members who blamed him for the death of their soldiers. Unlike General Howard, Barlow had never tried to reassure the Wilkesons that Bayard had not died in vain. Barlow had not pled for their understanding, nor sought reconciliation, as Howard had done repeatedly. In the end, Frank Barlow was just a fighter, a man willing to do everything he demanded of others. And that was enough for Bayard Wilkeson's brother.

CHAPTER 46

"Bone of Our Bone and Flesh of Our Flesh"

SAM WILKESON'S POSTWAR LIFE WAS FULL OF INTRIGUE, IRONY, ADVENture, and more controversy. He lived out his former editor Greeley's "Go West" exhortation by spending the last twenty-five years of his life helping to build the Northern Pacific Railroad and boosting the settlement of the Pacific Northwest. In some of these endeavors, he was joined by Frank Wilkeson, who blossomed into a nineteenth century renaissance man, dabbling in journalism, mining, Kansas cattle, and wheat farming. Cate Wilkeson spent those same years immersed in family. She remained mostly a private figure until her death in 1899.[1]

Oliver Otis Howard and Frank Barlow, the two generals at Gettysburg most responsible for ordering Bayard to his fateful position on the knoll, immersed themselves in public service following the war. Each left lasting imprints on their age's politics and civic life. More significantly, Howard's and Sam Wilkeson's paths crossed again, to a final reconciliation that neither might have deemed possible in the immediate and bitter aftermath of Gettysburg.

Going back on his pre-Gettysburg promise to Sidney Howard Gay that he would never again work for the *Tribune*, Sam reconciled with Greeley several months after Gettysburg. By the spring of 1864, Wilkeson was back writing for the *Tribune* with the old spark, as his fiery reporting out of the Wilderness illustrated. He and Greeley healed the old divisions enough that in early 1865 Sam told Greeley he thought that the veteran editor's just-released history of the war, *American Conflict: A History of the Great Rebellion in America*, was Greeley's finest work. "These two volumes of yours are going to be your monument—not the New York Tribune," Wilkeson wrote. No other work on the war "has the right to claim a place on the same shelf as yours," he said.[2]

Sam had left the *Times* on good terms, telling Gay that he had "almost rather taken a flogging than write that letter" of resignation to the courtly Henry Raymond.[3]

Wilkeson had shown the first public signs that he was still healing from Bayard's death when he spoke at a dinner at the Willard Hotel honoring the new Speaker of the House, Schuyler Colfax, in December of 1863. Colfax was an ex-newspaper editor from Indiana and would be elected vice president as Grant's running mate in 1868. He was well-liked by fellow journalists, and it didn't hurt to have a newspaperman in such a key position with the government censoring dispatches and throwing journalists in jail, as Lincoln's administration did off and on throughout the war.

Wilkeson toasted Colfax that night at the Willard Hotel as "bone of our bone and flesh of our flesh." During a speech introducing Colfax, Sam made what appeared to be oblique reference to the deaths of Bayard and John Wilkes. He said that in "that journalist's life that lives in the present, current day, and is denied retrospect and memory, two events only permanently abide with me, in the distinctness and freshness of their happening."[4]

Quoting Colfax from their first meeting, in Indiana, years before, Sam said: "I consider that day wasted in which I have not done some good to some human being, or added to someone's happiness." It was a poignant toast that said volumes about Wilkeson's state of mind six months after discovering his dead son in the wet clay of Gettysburg.[5]

After Lincoln's re-election in the fall of 1864, Wilkeson spent time in Washington, plying sources and feeding Greeley fresh insider information on who would be up and down in the new administration. In December, after Lincoln defeated his challenger and one-time commander McClellan, Wilkeson wrote Greeley a lengthy letter detailing the likely contours of the cabinet in Lincoln's second term. "Stanton is supremely strong in his place in the Cabinet," Wilkeson wrote. "He can't be shaken any more than Gibraltar can be."[6]

Within four months, Stanton would prove that steadfastness by holding an all-night vigil at the bedside of a dying Lincoln after Booth shot the President at Ford's Theatre. "Now he belongs to the ages," Stanton would declare.

As usual, the reporting with Grant's army during 1864 had made Sam Wilkeson ill again. He complained to Greeley that he was still recovering from "inflammatory rheumatism," which made it hard to walk from room to room.[7]

He never gave up his resistance to wartime censorship. In January of 1865, after censors three times refused to transmit his scoop on the dismissal of a Union general, Sam filed a petition to the House of Representatives complaining that "a censorship has been established without law and exercised without authority," and he urged Congress to pass a law declaring "the telegraph as accessible as the trains."[8] But Colfax's House of Representatives, then debating the Thirteenth Amendment's ban on slavery, was too busy for that.

After Grant's attritional Overland campaign of 1864, Sam and Cate were relieved when they heard that Pvt. Frank Wilkeson had been transferred to a post near Elmira, New York, where he served out the war's final winter, writing his parents to say he was happy to have a stove in his tent.

Young Frank was already thinking about the end of the war. In the spring of 1865, he again gave his parents fits by telling them that he was thinking of joining an expedition to Mexico to fight French emperor Napoleon III's attempts to establish a client state for Maximillian, the Archduke of Austria. To Sam's and Cate's relief, Frank did not follow through.[9]

By early 1865, Sam Wilkeson was also thinking about the end of the war and his next step. He finally quit reporting, although he called himself a journalist and wrote until he died. As Grant and Sherman squeezed the last life out of the Confederacy, Wilkeson went to work selling war bonds for the financier Jay Cooke, who had helped bankroll the Union war effort.

One of Wilkeson's first promotional works for Cooke was a pamphlet, published in the summer of 1865, entitled, "How Our National Debt May Be a National Blessing." In it he describes Cooke as the "general subscription agent of the government loans." Wilkeson defended the nation's burgeoning debt on financial and moral grounds. The war, he said, was leaving many children fatherless and wives without husbands. An expanding, healing nation had both the resources and the obligation to take care of them, he argued, and should do so by borrowing.

"The debt is public wealth," Sam wrote, necessary for "political union, protection of industry, secure basis for national currency, the Orphans' and Widows' Savings Fund."[10] The pamphlet was not universally praised and it became more controversial when the collapse of Cooke's bank eight years later sparked the financial Panic of 1873 and forced a temporary halt in the construction of the Northern Pacific Railroad.

Wilkeson and Cooke forged a relationship as close to the one that Sam had had with his former *Tribune* editor, Sidney Howard Gay. Wilkeson became Cooke's public face, writing articles boosting the railroad or heralding the resources and beauty of the Pacific Northwest at the railroad's prospective terminus in Tacoma, Washington.

Controversy and conflict followed Sam Wilkeson. In 1868, he testified in the impeachment of President Andrew Johnson. Keeping with his insider reputation, Wilkeson testified about a private conversation he had had at the Willard Hotel with Lorenzo Thomas, the same adjutant general whose leaked report Wilkeson had used to scoop the world on the Fremont-Sherman trip at the beginning of the Civil War. Johnson had wanted Thomas to replace Stanton as secretary of war. Sam told the impeachment committee that Thomas had broached the possibility of Johnson calling up troops to enforce Stanton's removal.[11] Johnson barely survived the impeachment. The war hero Grant was elected to replace him that fall.

In June of 1869, despite the health woes he often complained about during the Civil War, fifty-one-year-old Sam Wilkeson joined an expedition commissioned by Cooke to explore possible rail routes to the Pacific Northwest. His series of letters, published as "Wilkeson's notes" by the railroad, boasted of the lumber and coal resources and the temperate weather in the region.[12] It was vintage railroad industry boosterism of the late nineteenth century, hyperbolic, and sounding too-good-to-be-true—because it was.

The trip completed a circle for Sam Wilkeson. Cooke had sent out two parties to explore a possible route west; Wilkeson went along on one as an "historian" with a group headed by an engineer named Milnor Roberts. They were accompanied to as far as present-day Wyoming by Seward, the former secretary of state and senator, for whom Sam had ghost-written speeches about western rail routes some fifteen years earlier.[13] The irony could not have been lost on either man.

While Sam was on that journey, Frank Wilkeson married Mollie Crouse in Johnstown, Pennsylvania, one day after the sixth anniversary of his brother Bayard's death.[14]

Three days later, Sam Wilkeson's Northern Pacific exploration party arrived in Portland, Oregon, on Independence Day. It was six years to the day from when Sam found Bayard's body. The trip west had included constant threats of attacks from Indians and constantly threatening weather. Wilkeson wrote Cooke a letter demonstrating his propaganda skills. "There is nothing on the American continent equal to it," he wrote, describing the Puget Sound. "Such timber—such soil—such orchard—such fish—such climate—such coals—such harbors—such rivers. And the whole of it is but the western terminus of our railroad. The empire of the Pacific coast is to be enthroned on Puget Sound. . . . Salmon are not caught here, they are pitchforked out of the streams. Jay, we have got the biggest thing on earth. Our enterprise is an inexhaustible gold mine."[15]

Not everyone bought it. Wilkeson was so over-the-top in praise of the Pacific Northwest's climate and resources that critics soon derisively began referring to the Puget Sound region as "Jay Cooke's banana belt."[16]

Returning to New York after that trip, Sam became the railroad's secretary and promoter, jobs he would hold for most of the next two decades before his death in New York City in 1889.

He was widely recognized as a pioneer in this second profession. Years later, the *Wall Street Journal* described Sam Wilkeson as the "first of Wall Street's officially revealed press crusade agents," a pioneer of the "public relations engineers" who wrote glowingly, if not always accurately, of the prosperity that railroads would bring to the unsettled West.[17]

More circles were completed. In 1879, Wilkeson's old colleague and brief sparring partner, Henry Villard, took over ownership of the railroad and he steered it through the finish of transcontinental construction in 1883.

Wilkeson had once described Villard as a "coarse brute" but the two men got along in their later years and reversed roles.[18] They shared too many interests. After the war Villard became a pacifist and, like Wilkeson, married into a suffragette family when he wed the activist Helen Frances Garrison. Villard also retained his journalist's interests. The man who had come to the United States as a penniless teenager before the Civil War bought the *New York Evening Post* and the *Nation* magazine in the 1880s.[19]

In 1875, Sam was a reluctant witness in one of the most sensational trials of the century. The Reverend Henry Ward Beecher, the most famous Protestant minister of his age, and the husband of the woman who had so emotionally consoled Sam in the letter right after Bayard's death, was sued for adultery by one of his former publishing business associates and top Republican operative, Theodore Tilton. A former editor of the *Independent,* Tilton was a man of standing himself, having organized Lincoln's speech at New York's Cooper Union in the spring of 1860 that launched Lincoln to the Republican nomination and presidency.

Testifying on March 12, 1875, Sam said he was living on 40th Street in New York. He described himself as a journalist of thirty-five years who also happened to be secretary of the Northern Pacific Railroad.[20]

Ultimately, Beecher, the brother of *Uncle Tom's Cabin* author Harriet Beecher Stowe, was found not guilty both in civil trials and church disciplinary proceedings, but the trial exposed the underside of upper-class New York society and the city's publishing industry. On the witness stand, Sam was asked about rumored payoffs of newspapers to suppress the allegations against Henry Beecher, but he testified he knew of none. The trial briefly put him at odds with his feminist sister-in-law, Elizabeth Cady Stanton, when he testified that he had heard fellow suffragette Susan B. Anthony referred to as a "morbid old maid."[21] But there was never any evidence of lasting friction from the trial, and Elizabeth Cady Stanton later would describe her brother-in-law favorably as a man of "fine presence, liberal education, moral character, and marked ability."[22] While Wilkeson's old colleague, Villard, joined him in the railroad business, other former journalism colleagues looked askance at his conversion to public relations. Ridiculing his work for Cooke in selling war bonds and defending the national debt, the *Chicago Tribune* in 1872 referred to Wilkeson as "pamphleteer-in-ordinary."[23]

But he lived an extraordinary life.

CHAPTER 47

"Stood at My Side"

THE BOY CAME BACK TO HIM IN A DREAM. EIGHT MONTHS AFTER Gettysburg, Sam saw Bayard standing clearly before him. The young soldier had no wounds, his spirit was intact, and his determination and youth preserved.

"Do you believe in spiritualism?" Sam wrote Sidney Howard Gay in March of 1864. "By Jove I do know that I talked with my slain artillery man this morning—that the boy with the grand yet modest carriage, his piercing good looks, his wonderful intelligence, and his silent yet awful determination, stood at my side, and answered my questions. I do know it."[1]

Sam underlined three times the "I do know" and the "I do know it" to leave no misunderstanding of what he had felt in the dream. They are hard, bold lines, the kind made as much to one's self as to a recipient. They underlined a certainty that had been absent in Sam's *New York Times* piece after the battle, the one that had declared a divine role for the fallen at Gettysburg, while still wondering whether Bayard had been needlessly sacrificed in that cause.

In the *Times* piece, Sam had described Bayard as broken and buried, his boy's body "crushed" and buried in the "wet clay" of a shallow Pennsylvania grave. In the hours after the battle, he wrote, Bayard had been "abandoned to death" by fate and incompetent superiors.[2]

In Sam's dream a year later Bayard was whole again and very much in his father's embrace. Something, probably a combination of things— time, forgiveness, the realization that the Wilkesons were not nearly alone in the crushing sacrifices that the country had endured during the Civil War—had made Bayard whole again. Sam had noted in his Gettysburg dispatch that he wrote next to his son's prone body at Gettysburg. In his dream a year later, Bayard "stood at my side," upright, and full of life.

"All his extraordinary beauty was unimpaired," Sam wrote Gay, "and his craving for action and great responsibilities was unchanged—and he was yet but nineteen."[3]

In memory, history, and mythology, Bayard Wilkeson will forever be nineteen, and with all of the promise and devotion of an American hero.

The description about Bayard came in an otherwise businesslike letter to Gay. As the war was drawing to a close, Sam was coming to a broader and different understanding of its toll. He still leveled the same criticism of commanders on the battlefields when he felt they deserved it, but he was paying more and more attention to the war's great aftermath. What he did after the reporting on the Crater was illustrative.

Meade had girded for a court-martial over the "newspaper abuse" he was getting over the Crater disaster. "My conscience is clear," he wrote his wife, Margaretta.[4] He never expected what would come next.

Not long after dreaming of Bayard, Sam Wilkeson showed up at Meade's headquarters. The commander of Gettysburg was perplexed. Wilkeson had been "one of my most bitter vilifiers," Meade said, but now the veteran correspondent had come to apologize.

Although maintaining his criticism of the Crater stood, Wilkeson told Meade he had been "deceived" into many other criticisms. Wilkeson had come "to express the most friendly feelings for me," a flabbergasted Meade wrote his wife.

"I received his apologies as if nothing had ever taken place, and he left me quite pleased," Meade wrote.[5]

If all the old fire was not gone in Wilkeson, as the war fired through its fourth summer, it was freshly accompanied by a deepening sensibility toward those left behind in the great war's great aftermath, and those who were stepping up to help them. It was increasingly evident in Wilkeson's reporting as 1864 moved along. In a tacit tribute to Bayard's suffering, Wilkeson was spending less time at the front, more in hospitals and surgeons' tents.

During the Wilderness fighting, as his artilleryman son, Frank, camped among the skulls and bones, Sam spent several days in the war-battered town of Fredericksburg, Virginia. Like Frederick, Maryland, it had been turned into one vast hospital. One late spring day, Sam walked down the streets of the town, where wounded men had been sheltered by the score in abandoned buildings or with whatever family or establishment would have them, some left for three days without food or medical care. Wilkeson's dispatch raged with condemnation of those in charge, and it ached for the sufferers.[6]

Awakening the next morning to a chorus of noisy martins, he fixated upon them as he had on the songbird at Gettysburg before Pickett's Charge. Once again, he searched for something normal, placid, and sweet, in the misery around him. Good and bad were in a struggle over sights and sound. The morning air was filled with "operatic songs and bird-talk," Wilkeson reported, while the streets were filled with a line of ambulances pulled by "mules and harness hid with mud" and filled with men "who groan, and call for cold water."[7]

Yet, above it all, the birds still sang, just as they had at Gettysburg before the final fury. The birds sang, Wilkeson wrote, "with infinite variety of love talk," despite the death beneath them—or maybe because of it. He fantasized that it was a chorus acknowledging the selflessness of the endless sacrifices of the war's long years.

"There is harmony, unquestionably, between the noisy happiness of the songsters and the establishment of freedom upon the destruction of Slavery by revolution and war," Wilkeson wrote. "The freedom of a happy civilization and the freedom of birds are not of wide apart kinship—and civilization comes not, save through blood, and wounds and death."[8]

He pondered, as he had at Gettysburg, the meaning of all the suffering. The certainty of redemption and rebirth that he had expressed at Gettysburg was not as apparent. Anger, futility—the "nameless horror and suffering"—was part of the war's eternal aftermath, too. He seemed ready for his own personal surrender, despite how stirred up he had become in witnessing the suffering all over again.

"What is all this?" Wilkeson asked. "Shall it be baptized the inevitable accident of war, and let to slide into the unremembered? I have done more than my share of warfare upon official persons, and have grown weary.

"If I were not weary of strife I would search for one of those pens whose strokes draw blood and empty offices, and, so help me God! I would never let up upon the officials responsible for the criminal want of preparation at Fredericksburg for the wounded from Grant's battles in the Wilderness, until they were out of place forever, and forever under the feet of the vengeful friends and relatives of this army of neglected sufferers."[9]

He wrote this on what would have been Bayard's twentieth birthday.

The war would drag on for another year of butchery and attrition. The country had crossed into a realm of weary acceptance that things would get worse before they could get better. Wilkeson could witness it in the faces of the wounded men lying in the filth of Fredericksburg.

"There was resignation and acceptance of the fate of war in their faces as they looked up from their bloody and dirty blankets," he wrote.[10]

For years after the war, peace would be declared but not practiced. Lincoln's assassination would rob the nation of a tested and forgiving hand over Reconstruction. In a country shocked by four years of war, the preservation of a Union that Wilkeson had declared saved by the sacrifices of his boy at Gettysburg and the thousands like him, and etched into those faces at Fredericksburg, would not come just with surrender at Appomattox.

In all his attributes and shortcomings, in all that he had witnessed and illuminated and provoked, Sam Wilkeson epitomized this flawed, expansive, adventurous nation as much as any American over the last half of the nineteenth century.

He died in New York on December 2, 1889, four days before the death of Confederate president Jefferson Davis. Sam was seventy-two.

The *Wall Street Journal*, ever vigilant of its interests, declared that Wilkeson's greatest achievement was the reconnaissance of the route for the Northern Pacific and "subsequent writings to protect and promote the enterprise."[11]

The *Journal* got it wrong. Sam Wilkeson's Gettysburg account, written in the hours of his deepest despair, was his finest and most enduring act. He had run with the captains of industry, but it was his homage to the nineteen-year-old lieutenant, his flesh and blood, and his witness to the last full measures of devotion of those who died with his son, that was most worthy of remembering.

Sam Wilkeson's funeral attracted leaders of business, the arts and letters. His old employer, *The New York Times*, reported that the funeral was at the family home at 8 West 40th Street in Manhattan, where he and Cate lived after the war. About 200 people attended, including Villard and nearly a dozen other top Northern Pacific executives: Thomas Oakes, who was president of the railroad at the time; F. K. Billings; E. L. Colby; William L. Bull; Colgate Hoyt; R. G. Rolston; Henry Stanton; George S. Baxter; Robert Lenox Belknap; J. A. Baxter; George H. Riddle; and L. R. Kidder. A few were about to have western towns named after them.[12]

Other attendees reflected the broad and adventurous life that Sam had led. There was his old colleague, Ed Stedman, who had written the poetry about Bayard that appeared in the *New York World* right after the battle of Gettysburg. There was the Wall Street broker and financier J. C. Reiff, an intimate of J. P. Morgan. There was Harry C. Fahnestock, a longtime president and vice president of the Bank of New York, and a close associate of Jay Cooke's. And there was Thomas C. Acton, abolitionist, New York Republican Party founder, anti–Tammany Hall Crusader, and acting chair of the Board of Police Commissioners during the 1863 New York draft riots scarcely a week after the battle of Gettysburg.[13]

The funeral service was conducted by the Reverend Henry Van Dyke, minister of the Brick Presbyterian Church. Van Dyke would later chair the committee that wrote the first Presbyterian printed liturgy, *The Book of Common Worship*. He would also later pen the lyrics to the Christian song, "Joyful, Joyful We Adore Thee," set to Beethoven's "Ode to Joy." Reverend Van Dyke's closing funeral prayer, the *Times* wrote, "made cordial and fitting references to the public services of Mr. Wilkeson, to his devotion to the interests with which he was connected, and to his great love of his country." Family members in attendance included Elizabeth Cady Stanton's son and Bayard's cousin, Daniel, the boy whose grammar was corrected by Bayard's grandfather a half century earlier.

Sam Wilkeson would have taken great delight in the *Tribune's* edition in which his funeral was reported. Like great newspapers aspired to be, it contained the broad strokes and telling details of life that day—the quirks and conflicts, the eclectic facts and tales of history's first drafts. There was optimism and adventure mixed with the mundane transgressions or calamities of humans. A lengthy front-page story described the latest thrilling African exploration of the British journalist and adventurer, Sir Henry Morton Stanley. There was a story about the nomination of a Supreme Court justice, about the transfer of the U.S. Weather Bureau to the Agriculture Department, about a murder in a New York tenement house filled with Italian immigrants, and about a boat that caught fire on the Hudson River. There were stories about weddings and divorces, and ironically, in the late Greeley's paper—he of "Go West, Young Man"—a cautionary story about whether the United States could support a projected population of 100 million people by 1910.[14]

The West had "already showed its boundaries," the late Greeley's *Tribune* proclaimed in this edition, predicting that by 1910, the country "will have developed the neglected South, re-peopled the abandoned farms of the Eastern and Middle States, and will be eating all the food they raise" rather than selling it overseas.

Tucked in one corner was a two-paragraph letter-to-the editor about the temperance fight that would build to a crescendo three decades later. "Every day we let loose 50,000 lunatics upon New York, like the man who struck down John J. Devine," C. C. McCabe wrote. "The rum traffic is at the bottom of all these murderous assaults."

The same edition of the *Tribune* that carried the story of Sam's funeral contained ads selling banjos, pocket watches, and real estate, and an announcement by Tiffany's that it would remain open late into the evenings on every day until Christmas. And there was a story on the latest communications technology, the typewriter.

"Don't laugh," the article said, "even love letters are written in this mechanical age."[15]

Sam's body was taken that day to Buffalo, where he was buried in the family plot on the knoll with his father, his son Bayard, and his nephew, John Wilkes Wilkeson.

Cate, who lived out the rest of her life in quietude, died ten years later. She did not publicly reveal how her oldest son's death at Gettysburg affected her.

Wilkeson, Washington, a railroad town tucked in the foothills of the Cascade mountain range, was named for Sam, and it was officially incorporated twenty years after Sam died in New York. At one time it had more than 3,000 people, but it soon shrunk to roughly an eighth that size when the timber and mineral boom wore off. Sam and Cate Wilkeson's third son, Samuel Gansevoort, invested in lumber and coal mining near the town named for the family. Samuel G. Wilkeson had followed his father west, first arriving in Tacoma, Washington, in 1873, the year that town was chosen as the terminus for the railroad his father was helping to build.[16]

Two years after his father died, Frank Wilkeson opened a store for gold miners on Bridge Creek, near the town of Stehekin. For a time the store was run by Frank's oldest son.

His name was Bayard.

Frank Wilkeson died in Washington in April of 1913, a year before the outbreak of World War I, the "War to end all Wars." His two sons, Sam and Bayard, were at his side when he died.[17]

Maggie Wilkeson, Bayard's older sister, the young woman who accompanied her parents to that 1862 Washington party in which her father began discerning General McClellan's downfall, married a young doctor after the Civil War. Dr. Ellwood M. Corson was a surgeon for the 69th Regiment, Pennsylvania Volunteers, and he nearly died from typhus contracted at Antietam. He and Maggie settled in Norristown, Pennsylvania, they had three children, and they also named their oldest son Bayard Wilkeson Corson.[18]

CHAPTER 48

"I Know What I Saw Distinctly with My Own Eyes"

FRANK BARLOW, THE STUBBORN BRIGADIER GENERAL WHO ORDERED Bayard Wilkeson and his battery to the deadly knoll at Gettysburg, became an anti-corruption crusader after the Civil War. He barely survived the war himself. Based on descriptions of his condition later in the war, he was almost certainly suffering from PTSD. After being nursed back to health by his wife after Gettysburg, Barlow rejoined the army as a division commander in a newly reorganized 2nd Corps in the spring of 1864. He was sullen and pessimistic. After 15,000 Confederates under Jubal Early pushed through Union resistance in the battle of Monocacy and threatened Washington, DC, itself, Barlow wrote his mother on July 15, 1864: "I am utterly disgusted with the craven spirit of our people. I wish the enemy had burned Baltimore + Washington + hope they will yet."[1]

But more horrific fighting was ahead of him. Serving under Grant, Barlow led a frontal assault at Cold Harbor in Virginia that would cost the Union 3,000 men in seventy-five minutes and haunt Grant more than any decision he made in the war. "I have always regretted that the last assault at Cold Harbor was ever made," Grant wrote in his memoirs. "No advantage whatever was gained to compensate for the heavy loss we sustained."[2]

Eight weeks after Cold Harbor, Barlow's wife, Arabella, who had nursed him back from death's edge after grievous wounds at Antietam and Gettysburg, got typhus serving in a Union hospital and died. His

friend, Lt. Col. Theodore Lyman, said Barlow became "entirely incapac-
itated by this sudden grief."[3]

After her death on July 28, 1864, Barlow left the siege of Petersburg
to bury her. Devastated, his physical and emotional health deteriorated,
and the rest of the war Barlow was in and out of hospitals, once having to
be carried from his headquarters to a hospital on a stretcher. He traveled
solitarily through Europe to regain his health, and slowly, his life and
spirit returned. He returned home as the war was ending, determined to
not let it define him. It didn't.[4]

Frank Barlow, a survivor above all else, was elected secretary of
state of New York less than seven months after the end of the war. He
re-opened his law office in New York.

In 1866, he remarried, this time to Ellen Shaw, the sister of Col.
Robert Shaw, the white officer who was killed leading a brigade of black
soldiers on the assault of Fort Wagner in South Carolina, fifteen days
after the Battle of Gettysburg. Fort Wagner became a celebrated battle
that proved the heroism of newly enlisted black Union army soldiers.

Barlow was elected New York attorney general in 1870. He prosecuted members of the corrupt Tweed Ring that ran New York politics.
He was a founding member of the National Bar Association.

Barlow is forever memorialized in Winslow Homer's 1866 painting,
Prisoners from the Front, which depicts the man they called "Boy General"
gazing at three Confederate prisoners captured at Petersburg in 1864.
Homer and Barlow were friends, and Homer had often visited Barlow
during the war. A half century after the war, the painting was given to
New York's Metropolitan Museum of Art, where it was hung on permanent display.[5]

Barlow did little publicly to defend his actions at Gettysburg, but
he never strayed from the defenses he put up in the private letters while
lying in the hospital right after the battle. Twenty years later, Barlow
wrote the tireless Gettysburg chronicler, John Badger Bachelder, that
"I know what I saw distinctly with my own eyes, and nothing will ever
convince me to the contrary."[6]

In 1889, Barlow wrote Bachelder again, applauding Bachelder's
diligence in double-checking the accounts of Civil War veterans. It was

important, Barlow wrote, "to prevent people from getting credit for things which they did not do."[7] Frank Barlow died in 1896 and is buried in his family's tomb in Brookline, Massachusetts.[8]

Carl Schurz, the division commander who passed on Barlow's orders that exposed Bayard Wilkeson's battery on July 1, became a U.S. senator from Missouri and, later, secretary of the interior. He led a Liberal Republican revolt against President U. S. Grant in the 1872 election that resulted in Greeley's nomination to oppose Grant. Joseph Pulitzer, the restive journalist who published the *St. Louis Post-Dispatch*, once described Schurz as "the most industrious and the least energetic man I have ever worked with."[9] Grant described Schurz in 1872 as "an ungrateful man, a disorganizer by nature."[10]

Sallie Myers, the young schoolteacher who had offered cool cups of water on that hot afternoon at Gettysburg, who had opened her home to wounded and dying men, was anything but ungrateful.

Gettysburg did not totally define her, either. The battle began for her a long and emotional journey of sorrow, redemption, and more sorrow. The death of one of the young men in Sallie Myers's care became the beginning of another story. The Myers and Stewart families had forged a deep bond over her care of Alexander Stewart. On July 29, Sallie received a "splendid letter and coming from a grateful heart" from Alexander Stewart's younger brother, Henry. A long-range romance began, and they were married in 1867.[11]

But Sallie Myers Stewart's sorrows returned. Henry Stewart died a year after the wedding, and Sallie gave birth to their only son ten days later.

The boy eventually became a doctor, and Sallie Myers Stewart, steeled in Gettysburg's great aftermath, went on to become treasurer of the National Association of Army Nurses. She never remarried.[12]

CHAPTER 49

"He Would Have Rather Died That Way Than Any Other"

HORACE GREELEY RAN FOR PRESIDENT AND LOST TO GRANT IN A LAND-slide in the election of 1872. Greeley died twenty-four days later, on November 29, 1872, devastated by the death of his wife shortly before the election. His restlessness, his civic-mindedness, his often emotional and sometimes changing positions on issues, his belief in newspapers as clarions for the common citizen, all helped define an age of ascendant journalism in America. Greeley may have been the Perfect American because his great passions and his great flaws were so true to the imperfect, changing, always aspiring mosaic of nineteenth century America.

The Reverend Theodore Cuyler, a leading Presbyterian minister and writer, connected Greeley with Lincoln in a memorial tribute after the editor's death. "Abraham Lincoln and Horace Greeley were the most thorough(ly) American of all our leading characters in this generation," Cuyler wrote. "Both sprang from obscurity; both were cradled in poverty; both worked their way up by sheer brain-work; both were excessively simple, democratic, and homespun in their manner and dress; both were awkward in gait; both abounded in quaint dry humor."[1]

Oliver Otis Howard, the "Christian general," commanded in Sherman's army as it cut a swath of destruction across Georgia and the Carolinas in the winter of 1864 and 1865. Howard would become controversial once more during the burning of Columbia, South Carolina, in February of 1865. Howard blamed retreating Confederates, escaped penitentiary prisoners, and "army followers," among others for setting massive fires that destroyed vast swaths of the city. Howard ordered his men to fight the fires, but by then it was too late. "The very heavens at times appeared on fire," he wrote in his memoirs.[2] Sherman would later deny any culpability, saying that had he decided to do it, "I would have burnt it with no more feeling than I would a common prairie dog village."[3] But Howard's men, Sherman said, did not do it.

It was saying something for all he had gone through, but the one-armed general described that night in Columbia as his worst of the war. Some of his men drank themselves into a stupor and then burned to death themselves.[4]

He responded with whatever mercies he could summon. As Sherman was preparing to move his army out of Columbia, the distressed city's mayor approached Sherman and asked who would feed the suddenly homeless. "Go to Howard," Sherman responded. "He runs the religion of this army."[5]

Howard ordered half the army's rations and half its beef herd left behind for the citizens.[6]

Four month later, a month after the war ended, Howard was named the first and only commissioner of the Freedmen's Bureau, a government agency set up to help the estimated four million recently freed slaves assimilate into new lives in a hostile culture. Besides confronting the immediate crisis of blacks left suddenly homeless, jobless, and penniless, the bureau attempted to set up schools for children of freed slaves.

Howard's deputy was John Benton Callis, the Iron Brigade commander who had been given up for dead and languished for forty-three hours on the battlefield, only to be nursed back to health by Fannie Buehler and Mattie Benton Callis. John Benton Callis carried the slug from Gettysburg in his lung for the rest of his life. At the Freedmen's Bureau, he helped Northern charitable organizations build schools for children of freed slaves. John and Mattie Callis moved to Alabama and, despite his record as a Union army officer, John Callis was elected to Congress from Alabama's 5th District, from where he fought the rising Ku Klux Klan. Gettysburg had wounded and scarred John Benton Callis, but it did not defeat him.[7]

Howard's Freedmen's Bureau's challenge was daunting and dangerous. Teachers who came from the North to teach in Southern schools for blacks faced constant death threats on a scale that Civil Rights workers would a century later. Legions of the former slaves wandered the countryside, homeless and facing starvation, vulnerable to random or organized violence. In his autobiography, Howard wrote that the years 1865–1867 were scarred by the "baser classes. . . . In all parts of the South" who "burned school buildings and churches used as schools, flogged teachers or drove them away, and in some instances murdered them."[8]

Although the Freedmen's Bureau was wracked by corruption, Howard was not widely blamed for it, perhaps because he was among the first national figures to stand up against the Klan. The Klan turned into a "monster terrible beyond question," Howard wrote in his memoirs, and "in some parts of the South came to rival the Nihilistic assassins of Russia or the inner chamber of the old Spanish Inquisition."[9]

Ironically, Gordon, whose men overran Barlow's Knoll on the first day at Gettysburg, was reputed to be an early supporter of the Klan in Georgia. After the war, Gordon became a U.S. senator from Georgia, then that state's governor, and was the first president of the Confederate Veterans of America. He traveled the country giving speeches for years.[10]

In 1867, Howard founded one of the nation's most prestigious historically black universities. Howard University in Washington, DC, bears his name. Howard later served as the superintendent at West Point, and retired from the Army in 1894. A year before his retirement, he was awarded the Medal of Honor for bravery at Seven Pines, the 1862 battle in which he had lost his right arm and John Wilkes Wilkeson lost his life.

In retirement, Howard traveled through Europe and the Middle East, wrote two volumes of his lengthy memoirs, lectured and, in the late 1890s, helped co-found and raise money for the establishment of Lincoln Memorial University in Tennessee. He told fellow organizers that he had promised to establish a university in Tennessee in his last private meeting with Lincoln in the fall of 1863.

And then Howard confronted the same soul-searing loss that Sam Wilkeson had.

In 1899, General Howard's son, Guy, a colonel in the U.S. Army, was killed in the Philippines during the Spanish-American War. The pain stayed with him. "This is the heaviest blow our family had," he wrote in his memoirs.

Howard's daughter, Bessie, tried to console the old general by summoning the rationale of the Good Death. "Father," she told him, "he would have rather died that way than any other."[11]

Oliver Otis Howard died ten years later at age seventy-eight. He was buried in his hometown of Burlington, Vermont.[12]

CHAPTER 50

"The Sorrowful Joy and the Profound Gratitude"

THE CIVIL WAR ENDED IN 1875 FOR SAM WILKESON. THE IMPETUS FOR a personal peace came from a newspaper report about the speech that Howard had given in Portland, Oregon, that winter, the one in which the aging general told the story of Bayard Wilkeson as an "example of the costly sacrifice we gave."

Sam began his peace offering with a letter.

"I hear from Portland you have delivered publicly a lecture on the Battle of Gettysburg, in which you complimentarily mention the dear boy and the brave officer, my son, who was killed in your first day's fight," Sam began his letter of March 1, 1875. It was written on the letterhead of the Northern Pacific Railroad Company, 23 Fifth Avenue, in New York City.[1]

One can only wonder what the deeply religious Howard, who had made such earnest appeals for Sam's sympathy and understanding in the days after the battle only to be rebuffed, was thinking after that opening paragraph. Was this a cease and desist demand from a still-grieving father to stop using his boy's name?

It turned out to be anything but that.

"I cannot express to you the sorrowful joy and the profound gratitude kindled in my heart by this public honor of my son by his distinguished commander," Sam wrote.[2]

He asked for a copy of the speech. Sam hoped it was not given extemporaneously, so that a true copy could be procured. No doubt recalling the wide circulation of his own piece after Gettysburg, Sam suggested that Howard have the speech published in pamphlet form "or in the columns of a great newspaper." Whatever Howard could say about that first day at Gettysburg, Sam wrote, "should constitute part of our country's history."

Wilkeson signed the letter, "most respectfully and gracefully yours."

Howard responded eighteen days later.

He had just received Wilkeson's "kind letter," he wrote, and although the Portland speech had been given extemporaneously, he would happily write it down from memory, much as Lincoln did after the Gettysburg Address. Howard did just that, enclosing "excerpts" from the Portland speech.[3]

In the address, Howard had singled out two artillery officers—Hubert Dilger and Bayard Wilkeson—for their heroism at Gettysburg. Bayard, "a gallant young officer," was "desperately wounded and left in the hands of the enemy during the sudden and enforced retreat that I have previously described as beginning between three and four o'clock in the afternoon," Howard wrote.[4]

"I am reminded of him not only by the devoted service he rendered even to the pouring out of his lifeblood, but as an example of the costly sacrifice we gave," Howard declared. "His father (Mr. Samuel Wilkeson, the writer) wrote in a letter calling me to account for wasting his son's life. I read it carefully and perceived the language of a true father's heart in anguish at the loss of his dearly beloved son.[5]

"I then wrote the stricken father as good a letter as I knew how, explaining the sincere stress of the battle and the retreat. Very soon I had a beautiful reply. It said in substance I could not know fully how his father and mother could know how good—how true—how affectionate—how self-sacrificing—how manly—how noble a boy he was!"[6]

Despite its bitterness and raw emotion, Howard said he'd viewed that letter from Wilkeson shortly after the battle of Gettysburg as "the strongest and sweetest expression of a father's love I ever received. It is suggestive of the deep sorrow that filled thousands of homes after that single battle of Gettysburg."[7]

The one-armed general and Sam Wilkeson kept corresponding after that 1875 rapprochement. Sam offered to help Howard get articles published about the war. Howard did, in the *Atlantic Monthly*, in the *National Tribune*, and elsewhere. Bayard's death was always mentioned.

"I have thought that the death of Wilkeson in the very bloom and freshness of youth, with it echoing sorrow, had its counterpart in many thousands of precious, loving households," Howard wrote twenty years after the war. "If, then, liberty and Union have been purchased at the cost of blooming youth, and bleeding, broken hearts behind them, the sacrifice is very sacred and calls for eternal fidelity to liberty and Union. Let not our children or children's children forget it."[8]

By then, Sam Wilkeson had declared an armistice with his own bitterness. On January 27, 1877, Sam wrote Howard what could only be seen as a letter of final and total forgiveness.

"I shall always hold you tenderly and gratefully in my heart for your generous and appreciative mention of my brave boy," Sam wrote. "He had rare qualities."[9]

Acknowledgments

Writing a book is like planning a trip where you have only a vague sense of the destination and no idea of the detours that you will take on the journey there. Many people helped on the road to this book's publication.

To my agent Victoria Skurnick, thanks for steering through the baffling, mystifying, frustrating, exhilarating world of book publication. You have it figured out better than anyone.

Henry Pogodzinksi, a passionate Buffalo historian, was encouraging and accommodating over three years of correspondence. I will be forever grateful for his hospitality when we toured the Wilkeson gravesite at Buffalo's stately Forest Lawn Cemetery. That visit to a place that shelters so many important stories convinced me that this one needed to be written.

Henry arranged for me to have access to the files of his long-time friend, the late Ben Maryniak. Ben's collection of Wilkeson family history was helpful in confirming many details in this book. I regret never knowing Ben, who died in 2009. He was a president of the Buffalo Civil War Round Table for many years, authored two books on Civil War chaplains, and played bass guitar when he was not working or researching. Thank you to his wife Catherine for making Ben's files available.

Cynthia Van Ness, director of library and archives at the Buffalo History Museum and her staff were incredibly helpful in accessing the library's Wilkeson collection.

Special thanks to Ann D. Gordon, who went extra miles to help locate relevant documents and material on Catherine Cady Wilkeson, who was far more private than her famous sister, Elizabeth Cady Stanton. Ann is editor of the *Papers of Elizabeth Cady Stanton and Susan B.*

Anthony and Research Professor in the Department of History at Rutgers University and, even when under the weather, she was cheerful and responsive to my frequent questions.

John Heiser and his colleagues at Gettysburg National Military Park Library were professional and patient with pesky researchers. What a vital resource that library is.

Thanks, too, to the staff and volunteers at the Adams County Historical Society, whose impressive collection helps preserve the history and memory of the most important battle in American history.

The staff at Columbia University's Butler Library was helpful in providing access to the Sidney Howard Gay collection in its possession.

Americans do not know what a treasure their Library of Congress and National Archives are. Nor are they appreciative enough of the yeoman's work being done to provide online access to vital historical records. Transparency and access should apply to historical records as well as contemporaneous ones, and it is a battle worth fighting to constantly push back on government's insatiable appetite for secrecy. The digitalization of the official records of the Civil War at Cornell University will help researchers forever. Thankfully, the Union and Confederate armies were inveterate record keepers, and Americans in the mid-nineteenth century were consummate letter writers. We are losing these traditions and skills in an era of 140-character "communication."

The Clark family of Addison, VT, and I were destined to meet. I am convinced of that. Erwin, Janet, and their son, Bradley, and I crossed paths on Little Round Top when I was reporting a 150th anniversary story on the Battle of Gettysburg for *USA TODAY*. That they so treasured a preciously held diary of a family member, Pvt. Myron Clark, who was killed on the battle's final day, was an epiphany: The aftermath of Gettysburg is never-ending.

Many friends were encouraging along the way. Ruth Kane, John Runyan, Michelle and Apostolos Deimendes—Candle Club forever! Chris and Jeff Stinson—the world could not have created better friends. Keith White, Marsha Mercer, and the Civil War hiking club—you know who you are. Thanks for the inspiration and sorry for that 7-miler on Gettysburg's first day. Dave, Rob, Tim, Ruth, Kim, Kate, all you Argus folks; our beloved John and the Cover Story Gang; the professionals at GNS, *USA TODAY*, and the *Post-Dispatch*—there's no better or more honorable or more vital passion in the world than the one we chose to follow.

My parents, Bob and Donna, imbued in me the curiosity and love of reading that is absolutely essential to a full life. Paul, Rose, Karen—let's pay it forward. Mark, we miss you.

To my son's, Sam and Will, your encouragement means more than you can know. You are good men and we are proud of you.

Finally, to my life and love, Sandy, the story is not nearly finished. Love you.

Endnotes

Introduction

1. *Atlantic Monthly,* November 1865.
2. Shane Mountjoy and Tim McNeese, *Technology and the Civil War* (New York: Chelsea House Publishers, 2009), 33.
3. David Hochfelder, *The Telegraph in America—1832–1920.* (Baltimore: Johns Hopkins University Press, 2012), 7.
4. U.S. Census Bureau, "Historical Statistics of the United States, 1789–1945," 1949, 200; and "Railroads and the Making of Modern America," digital report, University of Nebraska, http://railroads.unl.edu/resources/, accessed January 10, 2016.
5. Ibid.
6. Ulysses S. Grant, *The Autobiography of Ulysses S. Grant, Memoirs of the Civil War* (St. Petersburg, FL: Red and Black Publishers, 2008), 433.
7. Joseph G. C. Kennedy, U.S. Census Bureau, "Preliminary Report on the Eighth Census," Government Printing Office, Washington, DC, 1862, 102.
8. Ford Risley, *The Civil War: Primary Documents on Events, 1860–1865* (Westport, CT and London: Greenwood Press, 2004), 4.
9. Joseph G. Kennedy, "Preliminary Report on the Eighth Census," 102.
10. Ralph Waldo Emerson, *The Prose Works of Ralph Waldo Emerson, Volume II* (Boston: Fields, Osgood & Company, 1870), 455.
11. Mary Bedinger Mitchell, "A Woman's Recollection of Antietam," in *Battles and Leaders of the Civil War, Volume II,* Robert Underwood Johnson and Clarence Clough Buell, eds., based on "The *Century* war series" published from November 1884 to November 1887 in the *Century* magazine (New York: The Century Co., 1887–1888), 686–95. Hereafter known as *Battles and Leaders.*
12. Interviews with the author in May 2013, and in follow-up e-mail exchanges in July 2013 and November, 2015. The Clark family also electronically shared excerpts of the diary with the author.
13. Ibid.

Chapter 1

1. Accounts taken from letter from John Wilkeson to his daughter, Maria, July 6, 1863, Wilkeson Collection. Buffalo History Museum, Buffalo, NY. The Buffalo History Museum will hereafter be referenced as BHM.

Chapter 2

1. Sam Wilkeson, *The New York Times*, July 6, 1863.
2. *The New York Times*, July 6, 1863.
3. A. L. Long, ed, *Memoirs of Robert E. Lee* (Secacus, NH: The Blue and Gray Press, Secacus, N.J., 1983), 289.
4. Wilkeson, *The New York Times*, July 6, 1863.
5. *The New York Times*, July 6, 1863, drawn from accounts of several correspondents on that date.
6. Wilkeson, *The New York Times*, July 6, 1863.
7. *St. Louis Democrat*, July 10, 1863, from the archives of the Gettysburg National Military Park, hereafter referenced as GNMP.

Chapter 3

1. Allen C. Guelzo, *Gettysburg, The Last Invasion* (New York: Alfred A. Knopf, 2013), 105.
2. Observations by author drawn from extensive correspondence between Wilkeson and Sidney Howard Gay, in the files of the Sydney Howard Gay Papers, Rare Book & Manuscript Library, Columbia University, New York. Hereafter known as Gay Collection, Columbia University.
3. Description of Newspaper Row taken from Henry Villard, *Memoirs of Henry Villard, Journalist and Financier, 1835–1900, Volume 1* (Boston and New York: Houghton, Mifflin and Company, 1904), 338–39; and from William Russell, *My Diary North and South*, July 8, 1861 (London: T.O.H.P. Burnham, 1863), 393. Throughout this book some reference citations will be through online access at archive.org, a nonprofit library of books and other materials.
4. Louis M. Starr, *Bohemian Brigade, Civil War Newsmen in Action* (New York: Alfred A. Knopf, 1954), 74.

Chapter 4

1. John Wilkeson to his daughter, Maria, July 6, 1863, Wilkeson Collection, BHM, and from the files of Ben Maryniak, late historian of the Buffalo Historical Society, Buffalo, NY, hereafter known as the Maryniak Collection.
2. *Buffalo Morning Express*, July 6, 1869, Maryniak Collection.
3. John Wilkeson to his daughter, Maria, July 6, 1863, Wilkeson Collection, BHM.
4. *New York Tribune*, July 4, 1863.

Chapter 5

1. Descriptions of the Wilkeson family from the Maryniak Collection; from unpublished Wilkeson family biographical notes, possibly written by Sam Wilkeson, the newspaper correspondent, in the Wilkeson Collection at the BHM; and from a biographical family tree also in the Wilkeson Collection at the BHM.

2. Obituary of Sarah Wilkeson, *New York Evangelist*, April 30, 1836, Maryniak Collection.

3. Account of Sam Wilkeson's eulogy in Maryniak Collection.

4. Ibid., and biography of Wilkeson family, Wilkeson Collection, BHM.

5. Maryniak Collection, "1820s" entry in Wilkeson family timeline.

6. Cate Cady Wilkeson to Mary Swan Wilkeson, Wilkeson Collection, BHM. This letter was written just after the death of her husband's sister, Elizabeth Stagg, on September 5, 1858.

7. Sam Wilkeson to Sidney Howard Gay, July 29, 1862, Gay Collection, Columbia University.

8. Cate Wilkeson to sister-in-law, June 11, 1862, Wilkeson Collection, BHM, referenced in Maryniak Collection.

9. *New York Herald*, May 1, 1862. The rival newspaper reveled in Wilkeson's leaving town.

10. Ibid.

11. *Boston Liberator*, September 6, 1850, from the archives of the Stanton and Anthony Papers, Rutgers University, provided by Ann Gordon.

12. National Archives, copy provided by Ann Gordon of the Elizabeth Cady Stanton & Susan B. Anthony Papers Project, Rutgers University.

13. Elizabeth Cady Stanton, *Eighty Years and More, Reminisces 1815–1897* (New York: European Publishing Company, 1898), 4, https://archive.org/stream/cu31924032654315#page/n135/mode/2up/search/presence, accessed January 9, 2016.

14. Daniel Cady to Elizabeth Cady Stanton, June 23, 1842, Elizabeth Cady Stanton papers, Library of Congress.

15. *Elizabeth Cady Stanton and Susan B. Anthony, In the School of Anti-Slavery, 1840 to 1866*, Volume 1 of *The Selected Papers of Elizabeth Cady Stanton and Susan B. Anthony*, Ann D. Gordon, ed. (New Brunswick, NJ: Rutgers University Press, 1997), 188.

16. The Emma Willard Association of Troy Female Seminary, Troy, NY, questionnaire, circa 1890, provided by Ann Gordon of the Elizabeth Cady Stanton & Susan B. Anthony Papers Project, Rutgers University, via the Emma Willard School archives.

17. Description of Cady children's childhood in Elizabeth Cady Stanton, *Eighty Years and More*, 1–20.

18. Ibid., 20.

19. Ibid., 4.

20. Ibid., 19.

21. Ibid., 3.

22. "Wilkeson family biographical notes," Wilkeson Collection, BHM.

23. Sam Wilkeson to Sidney Howard Gay, March 7, 1863, Gay Collection, Columbia University.

24. Account of the election in a letter from Sam Wilkeson to a "cousin," November 23, 1842, in the files of the Adams County, PA, Historical Society, hereafter known as ACHS.

25. Ibid.

CHAPTER 6

1. Sam Wilkeson to "Gerrit," March 23, 1848, Transcript on file, ACHS. Gerrit Smith was a leading reformer, abolitionist, and Republican Party donor, and the nephew of Margaret Livingston, Cate Cady Wilkeson's grandmother.

2. Eugene Virgil Smalley, *History of the Northern Pacific Railroad* (New York: G.P. Putnam's Sons, 1883), 284.

3. *Albany Evening Journal*, October 5, 1855.

4. Weed comments in *Albany Evening Journal* cited in the *New York Tribune*, March 22, 1861.

5. *New York Tribune*, March 22, 1861.

6. Sam Wilkeson to Sidney Howard Gay, November 1862, Gay Collection, Columbia University.

CHAPTER 7

1. J. Cutler Andrews, author of *The North Reports the Civil War* (Pittsburgh: University of Pittsburgh Press, 1955), estimated that there were forty-five reporters at Gettysburg in a speech to the Pennsylvania Historical Association's annual convention, October 11, 1963. A copy of the speech is online at file:///C:/Users/Chuck/Downloads/23007 -22846-1-PB%20(11).pdf, accessed January 10, 2016.

2. *Atlanta Constitution*. "Men Who Wrote History in the Smoke of Battle in 1860–65," was reprinted in the *Sacramento Daily Union* and *Los Angeles Times*, September 27, 1896.

3. Starr, *Bohemian Brigade*, 61.

4. Sidney Kobre, *Development of American Journalism* (Dubuque, IA: Wm. C. Brown Company Publishers, 1969), 324.

5. Starr, *Bohemian Brigade*, 4–5.

6. *Brooklyn Eagle*, July 11, 1886.

7. Starr, *Bohemian Brigade*, 4.

8. Carl Sandburg, *Abraham Lincoln, the Prairie Years and the War Years* (New York: Galahad Books, 1954, originally published as separate books, 1926 and 1939), 254.

9. Starr, *Bohemian Brigade*, 4.

10. Preliminary Report on the Eighth Census, Washington, DC, Government Printing Office, 1862, 102.

11. *New York Herald*, June 27, 1864.

12. Harold Holzer, *Lincoln and the Power of the Press: The War for Public Opinion* (New York, London, Toronto, Sydney, and New Delhi: Simon & Schuster, 2014), 336.

13. Holzer, *Lincoln and the Power of the Press*, 432.

14. Ibid., 73.

15. James M. Perry, *A Bohemian Brigade* (New York: John Wiley and Sons, 2000), 32.

16. An example appeared in the *New York Tribune*, August 15, 1861. An article entitled, "The Magnetic Telegraph in California" begins: "The magnetic telegraph occupies a prominent position in the business of this state."

17. Sam Wilkeson to Sidney Howard Gay, undated letter, Gay Collection, Columbia University.

18. Andrews. *The North Reports the Civil War*, 343.

19. A lively description of how Hooker got his nickname was put together by History .com, at www.history.com/topics/american-civil-war/joseph-hooker.

20. Correspondence between Hooker and Halleck, in *The War of the Rebellion: a Compilation of the Official Records of the Union and Confederate Armies,* U.S. Government Printing Office. Series 1, Vol. 28, Part 1, 52. Heretofore known as *OR.*

21. Andrews, *The North Reports the Civil War*, 411.

22. *Plymouth* (IN) *Weekly Democrat*, April 3, 1862.

CHAPTER 8

1. Mathew Brady's portrait of Horace Greeley is included in the Prints and Photographs Division, Library of Congress, Washington, DC. Alexander Gardner's portrait of Sam Wilkeson hangs in the Smithsonian's National Portrait Gallery. Descriptions of the two men are drawn from them.

2. Champ Clark, *Gettysburg: The Confederate High Tide* (New York: Time-Life Books, 1985), 151.

3. Sandburg, *Abraham Lincoln: The Prairie Years and the War Years*, 254.

4. Ibid.

5. Janet E. Steele, *The Sun Shines for All: Journalism and Ideology in the Life of Charles A. Dana* (Syracuse, NY: Syracuse University Press, 1993), 40.

6. Andrews, *The North Reports the Civil War*, 60.

7. Don Nardo, *The Camera Is the Eye of History* (Rochester, NY: Enslow Publisher, 2009), 50–51.

8. *New York Tribune*, May 17, 1851.

9. Charles Keener, "United States Christian Commission, Second Report of the Committee of Maryland," Baltimore, James Young, 1864, 91–92, www.mocavo.com/United-States-Christian-Commission-Second-Report-of-the-Committee-of-Maryland -Volume-2/607942/93, accessed January 10, 2016.

10. David S. Heidler and Jeanne T. Heidler, eds., *Encyclopedia of the American Civil War: A Political, Social and Military History* (New York: W.W. Norton and Company, 2000), 806–7.

11. Starr, *Bohemian Brigade*, 49.

12. Ibid., 16.

13. Kobre, *Development of American Journalism*, 233; *New York Herald*, May 6, 1835.

14. Ibid., 236–41.

15. Ibid., 235.

16. Ibid., 256.

17. Oliver Wendell Holmes Sr. "My Hunt After the Captain," *Atlantic Monthly*, December 1862. Online *Atlantic* archives at www.theatlantic.com/magazine/archive/1862/12/my-hunt-after-the-captain/308750/, accessed January 10, 2016.

18. J. Thomas Scharf, *Atlanta Constitution,* reprinted in the *Los Angeles Times* and *Sacramento Union,* September 27, 1896.

19. *The New York Times*, October 2, 1862.

20. Starr, *Bohemian Brigade*, 61.

21. Whitelaw Reid and A. J. L. Fremantle, *Two Witnesses at Gettysburg: The Personal Accounts of Whitelaw Reid and A. J. L. Fremantle*, 2nd Edition, Gary W. Gallagher, ed. (Hoboken, NJ: Wiley-Blackwell, 2009), 8.

CHAPTER 9

1. Andrews, *The North Reports the Civil War*, 43.
2. William Harlan Hale, *Horace Greeley, Voice of the People* (New York: Harper & Brothers, 1950), 251.
3. Villard, *Memoirs, Volume 1*, 339.
4. Horace Greeley to Sam Wilkeson, December 9, 1862, Cited in Louis M. Starr, *Bohemian Brigade*, 53. The letter reminded Wilkeson of an earlier conversation.
5. Michael P. Roth, *Historical Dictionary of War Time Journalism* (Westport, CT: Greenwood Press, 1997), 39–40.
6. Thomas Butler Gunn diaries, Vol. 19, 176. Transcripts at the Missouri History Museum, at www.historyhappenshere.org/archives/tag/thomas-butler-gunn-diaries, accessed January 10, 2016.
7. Ibid.
8. Simon Cameron Papers, Library of Congress, cited in Starr, *Bohemian Brigade*, 68.
9. Sam Wilkeson to Sidney Howard Gay, September 5, 1861, Gay Collection, Columbia University.
10. Ibid.
11. *New York Herald*, March 23, 1862, cited in Louis M. Starr, *Bohemian Brigade*, 70.
12. Andrews, *The North Reports the Civil War*, 44.

CHAPTER 10

1. Andrew Rolle, *John Charles Fremont, Character as Destiny* (Norman: University of Oklahoma Press, 1991), 215.
2. Wilkeson to Greeley, October 15, 1861, copy of letter on microfilm at the BHM.
3. Ibid.
4. Ibid.
5. Ibid.
6. *New York Tribune*, October 30, 1861, excerpted, as are many newspaper cited in this book, from *Chronicling America: Historic American Newspapers*, Library of Congress, http://chroniclingamerica.loc.gov/lccn/sn83030213/1861-10-30/ed-1/seq-1.
7. Ibid.
8. *Boston Evening Transcript*, December 11, 1861.
9. Grant, *Autobiography*, 424–25.
10. William Tecumseh Sherman, *Sherman, The Memoirs of General W. T. Sherman*, Literary Classics of the United States (distributed by Viking Press, 1990), 218–19.
11. Ibid.
12. Ibid.
13. Ibid., 220.

14. Ibid.

15. Emmett Crozier, *Yankee Reporters, 1861–65* (New York: Oxford University Press, 1956), 176–78.

16. Ibid., 178.

17. Ibid., 225.

18. Ibid., 232–33.

19. Ibid., 223.

20. Ibid., 234.

CHAPTER 11

1. *New York Tribune*, October 28, 1861.

2. Ibid., May 30, 1861.

3. Ibid., June 28, 1861.

4. *The New York Times*, July 23, 1861.

5. *New York Tribune*, October 28, 1861.

6. Ibid.

7. Ibid.

8. *The New York Times*, October 29, 1861.

9. Ibid.

10. Ibid.

11. William Howard Russell, *My Diary North and South,* December 2, 1861, 581–82.

12. Ibid.

13. Ibid., 582.

14. Holzer, *Lincoln and the Power of the Press,* 367.

15. Sam Wilkeson to Horace Greeley, February 1, 1862, Wilkeson Collection, BHM.

16. Ibid.

17. Abraham Lincoln. "Executive Order—Special War Order No. 1," January 31, 1862, Gerhard Peters and John T. Woolley, eds., The American Presidency Project, www .presidency.ucsb.edu/ws/?pid=69788, accessed January 10, 2016.

18. George McClellan to Edwin Stanton, February 3, 1862, Report of Maj.-Gen. George B. McClellan, August 4, 1863, United States Adjutant-General's Office, Army of the Potomac, 103–12, https://books.google.com/books?id=rEsWAAAAYAAJ&pg =PA103&lpg=PA103&dq=McClellan+to+Stanton+Feb.+3,+1862+%E2%80%9Ca +mere+collection+of+regiments,+cowering+on+the+banks+of+the+Potomac%22&source =bl&ots=bkbsB3Cr6C&sig=AnH51FWuHv5r_bvMDYpLTlaymQU&hl=en&sa=X& ved=0ahUKEwiIkpOw_p_KAhWJ2T4KHRfLBgQQ6AEIJzAE#v=onepage&q= McClellan%20to%20Stanton%20Feb.%203%2C%201862%20%E2%80%9Ca%20 mere%20collection%20of%20regiments%2C%20cowering%20on%20the%20banks%20 of%20the%20Potomac%22&f=false, accessed January 10, 2016.

19. Ibid.

20. Ibid.

21. *New York Tribune*, February 5, 1862.

22. *New York Tribune*, February 11, 1862.

CHAPTER 12

1. Russell. *My Diary North and South*, July 9, 1861, 393.
2. Villard, *Memoirs*, 154–55.
3. Russell, *My Diary North and South*, July 13, 1861, 403.
4. Samuel H. Wilkeson to John Wilkeson, August 3, 1861, Wilkeson Collection, BHM.
5. Samuel H. Wilkeson to John Wilkeson, June 19, 1861, Wilkeson Collection, BHM.
6. Ibid.
7. Ibid.
8. Samuel H. Wilkeson to John Wilkeson, August 15, 1861, BHM.
9. Ibid.
10. *Buffalo Express*, November 29, 1914, Obituary of Samuel H. Wilkeson.

CHAPTER 13

1. Bayard Wilkeson letter to Gen. Lorenzo Thomas, October 22, 1861, files of ACHS and Maryniak Collection.
2. Handwritten description of Bayard Wilkeson, author unknown, ACHS and Maryniak Collection.
3. Cate Cady Wilkeson to her sister-in-law, Mary, June 11, 1862, Wilkeson Collection, BHM; transcript in Maryniak Collection.
4. Sam Wilkeson to brother, John, September 25, 1858, Wilkeson Collection, BHM.
5. Sam Wilkeson to John Wilkes Wilkeson, December 8, 1853, transcript in Maryniak Collection.
6. Sam Wilkeson to Samuel H. Wilkeson, October 22, 1851, Wilkeson Collection, BHM.
7. *The New York Times*, January 31, 1855.
8. Daniel Cady to Daniel Cady Stanton, July 3, 1850, Elizabeth Cady Stanton papers, Library of Congress.
9. Daniel Cady to Daniel Cady Stanton, December 2, 1858, Elizabeth Cady Stanton papers, Library of Congress.
10. Ibid.
11. John Wilkeson to Samuel H. Wilkeson, May 21, 1861, Wilkeson Collection, BHM.
12. Ibid.
13. John W. Forney. *Washington Chronicle*, July 11, 1863, files of GNMP.
14. Descriptions of Bayard Wilkeson from Forney, *Washington Chronicle*, July 11, 1863; from a portrait of Bayard Wilkeson, National Archives; from Bayard Wilkeson's letters to his father, Wilkeson Collection at BHM; from an undated, typewritten biography, ACHS; and from an undated 1862 letter from Sam Wilkeson to Gen. Egbert Viele, Wilkeson Collection, BHM.
15. Unpublished and handwritten biography of Bayard Wilkeson, Wilkeson Collection, BHM; and Maryniak Collection.
16. Ibid.

17. Unpublished Wilkeson typewritten family biography, Wilkeson collection, BHM.

18. Samuel H. Wilkeson to his brother, John Wilkes Wilkeson, November 26, 1861, Wilkeson Collection, BHM.

19. Sam Wilkeson to his brother, John, November 1862, Maryniak Collection.

20. Civil War Trust, FAQ, www.civilwar.org, accessed January 10, 2016.

21. Handwritten description of Bayard Wilkeson, Wilkeson Collection, BHM; Maryniak Collection.

22. Undated letter of Brig. Gen. John Peck to Sam Wilkeson, files of GNMP.

23. Ibid.

24. Bayard Wilkeson to Sam Wilkeson. Sam copied parts of Bayard's letter to Egbert L. Viele, July 31, 1862, Wilkeson Collection, BHM.

25. Ibid.

26. Sam Wilkeson to Egbert L. Viele, July 31, 1862, Wilkeson Collection, BHM.

27. Ibid.

28. Jack W. Melton Jr. "Basic Facts Concerning Artillery," civilwarartillery.com, accessed January 11, 2016.

29. History of Lieutenant Wilkeson's batteries drawn from Brig. Gen. Theo S. Rockenbogh and Maj. William L. Haskin, eds., *The Army of the United States Historical Sketches of Staff and Line with Portraits of Generals in Chief* (New York: Maynard, Merrill and Co., 1896), 366–67.

30. Whitman Archive, December 19, 1862. Part of an account of Whitman's trip to the battlefield at http://whitmanarchive.org/biography/correspondence/tei/duk.00528 .html.

31. "Clara Barton at Chatham," February 19, 1863, National Park Service, www.nps .gov/frsp/learn/historyculture/barton.htm, accessed January 11, 2016.

32. Walt Whitman, *Complete Prose Works* (Philadelphia: David McKay, 1892), entry dated December 21, 1862, accessed in 2005 at www.gutenberg.org/files/8813/8813-h/ 8813-h.htm#link2H_TOC; *Specimen Days—After First Fredericksburg*, December 23–31, 1862, www.bartleby.com/229/, accessed January 11, 2016.

CHAPTER 14

1. Gunn diaries, Vol. 19, 165.

2. *OR*, Series 1, Vol. 11, Part 1, 816.

3. Ibid., 890.

4. Wilkeson to Gay, June 6, 1862, Gay Collection, Columbia University.

5. A short and excellent biography of Oliver Otis Howard by the Civil War Trust is at www.civilwar.org/education/history/biographies/oliver-howard.html?referrer=https:// www.google.com/, accessed January 11, 2016.

6. Cate Cady Wilkeson to her sister-in-law, Mary, June, 11, 1862, excerpts typewritten in Maryniak Collection.

7. Ibid.

8. John Wilkes Wilkeson to Samuel H. Wilkeson, April 22, 1862, Wilkeson Collection, BHM.

9. Ibid.

10. John Wilkes Wilkeson to sister, May 31, 1862, Wilkeson Collection, BHM.

11. Ibid.

12. Ibid.

13. Accounts of Sam Wilkeson's search for John Wilkes Wilkeson's body are contained in a letter he wrote to his brother, Will, on June 6, 1862, Wilkeson Collection, BHM.

14. Ibid.

15. Ibid.

16. Cate Cady Wilkeson to sister-in-law, June 11, 1862, Maryniak Collection. A lengthy description of the letter and excerpts are in a Wilkeson family chronology, original letter location unknown.

17. Samuel H. Wilkeson to John Wilkeson, June 28, 1862, Wilkeson Collection, BHM; and Maryniak Collection.

18. Samuel H. Wilkeson to his sister, Maria, December 1, 1862, Wilkeson Collection, BHM; and Maryniak Collection.

19. Handwritten and unpublished description of John Wilkeson, Maryniak Collection.

20. Samuel H. Wilkeson to John Wilkes Wilkeson, May 24, 1861, Wilkeson Collection, BHM.

21. Benedict R. Maryniak, "John Wilkeson Diary of Travel with the Army of the Potomac on the York and James River Peninsula, April–May 1862," *The Civil War Courier*, September 1995, 45–61. Drawn from John Wilkeson diaries, Wilkeson Collection, BHM. Maryniak cites a history of the 100th New York for the observation about John Wilkeson.

22. Ibid.; John Wilkeson May 11, 1862, diary entry, diary transcripts also in the Wilkeson Collection, BHM.

23. Ibid., May 11, 1862.

24. Ibid.

25. Ibid. This conversation was recounted by John Wilkeson in his diary on May 13, 1862, cited both in the Wilkeson Collection, BHM, and by Benedict Maryniak in *The Civil War Courier*.

CHAPTER 15

1. Ibid., May 16, 1863.

2. Gunn diaries, Vol. 19, 160.

3. Adam-Max Tuchinsky, *Horace Greeley's New York Tribune: Civil War-era Socialism and the Crisis of Free Labor* (Cornell University Press, Ithaca, N.Y., 2009), 216.

4. Greeley to Sam Wilkeson, November 17, 1861, cited in Starr, *Bohemian Brigade*, 54; and Harry J. Maihafer, *The General and the Journalists, Ulysses S. Grant, Horace Greeley and Charles Dana* (Washington, DC: Brassey's Inc., 2001), 104.

5. Robert C. Williams, *Horace Greeley: Champion of American Freedom* (New York: New York University Press, 2006), 221.

6. Greeley to Lincoln, July 29, 1861, cited in Rose Strunky, *Abraham Lincoln* (New York: The MacMillan Company, 1914), 162.

7. Holzer. *Lincoln and the Power of the Press*, 331.

8. This description of John Wilkes Wilkeson is contained in an unsigned brief family biography in the Wilkeson Collection at BHM; judging from its content it was most likely written by Sam Wilkeson.

9. *New York Tribune*, May 5, 1862.

10. Gunn diaries, Vol. 19, 178.

11. Gunn diaries, Vol. 19, 174.

12. A clip of Wilkeson's *New York Tribune* file is contained in the Gunn diaries, Vol. 19, 183.

13. Ibid.

14. Ibid.

15. *New York Tribune*, July 3, 1862.

16. *New York Tribune*, July 4, 1862.

17. The Civil War Trust estimates McClellan's forces at a peak of 120,000, while history.net estimates Lee's at 92,000.

18. Wilkeson to Gay, September 10, 1862, Gay Collection, Columbia University.

19. Wilkeson to Gay, undated, September 1862, Gay Collection, Columbia University.

20. *The New York Times*, March 28, 1863.

21. Ibid.

22. Ibid.

23. Ibid.

24. *OR*, Series I, Vol. 11, 854.

25. *The New York Times*, March 28, 1863.

26. Ibid.

27. *The New York Times*, April 2, 1863.

28. Ibid.

29. Wilkeson to Gay, June 6, 1862, Gay Collection, Columbia University.

Chapter 16

1. Perry, *A Bohemian Brigade*, 33.

2. Wilkeson to Gay, May 12, 1862, Gay Collection, Columbia University.

3. Death from illness and combat estimates from the Civil War Trust, www.civilwar.org/education/civil-war-casualties.html?referrer=https://www.google.com/, accessed January 11, 2016.

4. Wilkeson to Gay, May 1, 1864, Gay Collection, Columbia University.

5. Wilkeson to Gay, undated, but from the content of the letter, was shortly after the Battle of Seven Pines in 1862. Gay Collection, Columbia University.

6. Ibid.

7. Wilkeson to Gay, June 26, 1862, Gay Collection, Columbia University.

8. Ibid.

9. Wilkeson to Gay, September 28, 1861, Gay Collection, Columbia University.

10. Starr, *Bohemian Brigade*, 99.

11. Wilkeson to Gay, undated 1861 letter, Gay Collection, Columbia University.

12. Wilkeson to Gay, undated 1862 letter, Gay Collection, Columbia University.

13. John William Jones, ed. *Personal Reminisces and Letters of General Robert E. Lee* (New York: D. Appleton and Company, 1875), 241.
14. Grant. *Autobiography*, 312–13.
15. Ibid., 412.
16. Ibid.
17. William T. Sherman, *Memoirs of William T. Sherman, Volume II* (New York: Charles L. Webster & Co., 1892), 408.
18. Ibid.
19. Kobre, *Development of American Journalism*, 335.
20. Wilkeson to Gay, March 7, 1863, Gay Collection, Columbia University.
21. Expenses contained in a document in Wilkeson Collection, BHM.
22. Wilkeson Collection, BHM.
23. Gunn diaries, Vol. 21, 7.
24. Gunn diaries, Vol. 19, 134.
25. Ibid.
26. Gunn diaries, Vol. 20, 17.
27. Ibid., Vol. 22, 23.
28. Ibid., Vol. 22, 25–26.
29. Ibid.
30. Ibid., Vol. 22, 8–9.
31. Ibid., Vol. 22, 39.
32. Ibid., Vol. 22, 40.

CHAPTER 17

1. J. Cutler Andrews, "The Press Reports the Battle of Gettysburg," *Pennsylvania History* 31 (2), April 1964.
2. Ibid., 176.
3. Ibid. Andrews, in 178–98, provides an excellent explanation of the reporters present at Gettysburg.
4. Byington's experiences at Gettysburg are best described in Andrews, *The North Reports the Civil War*, 427–28.
5. Ibid.
6. Ibid., 429.
7. Reid and Fremantle, *Two Witnesses*, 4.
8. Crozier, *Yankee Reporters*, 357.
9. Charles Carleton Coffin, *Boys of '61* (Boston: Estes & Lauriat, 1885), 296.
10. Ibid.
11. *Boston Journal*, July 6, 1863.

CHAPTER 18

1. Oliver Wendell Holmes Sr., "My Hunt After the Captain." The accounts in this chapter are based on the article, which is available through the *Atlantic Monthly* at: www.theatlantic.com/magazine/archive/1862/12/my-hunt-after-the-captain/308750/, accessed January 10, 2016.

CHAPTER 19

1. Villard, *Memoirs*, 385–91.
2. Villard, *Memoirs*, 389.
3. Villard. *Memoirs*, 390–91.
4. Andrews, *The North Reports the Civil War*, 336.

CHAPTER 20

1. Gary L. Shugar, "The 167th Pennsylvania: Civil War's Only All-Berks Regiment," Berks (Pa.) History Center. Article originally appeared in the summer 2000 issue of *The Historical Review of Berks County*, www.berkshistory.org/multimedia/articles/the-167th-pennsylvania/, accessed January 11, 2016.
2. Sgt. George Tipping, February 1, 1863, transcript of letter excerpt in Maryniak Collection.
3. *OR*, Series 1, Vol. 18, 134.
4. *The New York Times*, February 15, 1863.
5. *The New York Times*, November 29, 1864.
6. *OR*, Series 1, Vol. 18, 134.

CHAPTER 21

1. Wilkeson to Gay, March 7, 1863, Gay Collection, Columbia University.
2. Ibid.
3. *New York Tribune*, August 20, 1862.
4. *New York Tribune*, August 25, 1862.
5. James Roberts Gilmore, *Personal Recollections of Abraham Lincoln and the Civil War*, 84. L.C. Page and Company, Boston, 1898.
6. Ibid., 82.
7. Wilkeson to Gay, undated. Judging from content, probably sometime in the summer of 1862. Gay Collection, Columbia University.
8. Wilkeson to Gay, August 15, 1862, Gay Collection, Columbia University.
9. Wilkeson to Gay, December 13, 1862, Gay Collection, Columbia University.
10. Greeley's response was printed in the *New York Tribune*, January 30, 1863, and reprinted in *The New York Times*, February 5, 1863.
11. Ibid.
12. Wilkeson to Gay, January 28, 1863, Gay Collection, Columbia University.
13. Wilkeson to Gay, February 1863, Gay Collection, Columbia University.
14. Wilkeson to Gay, March 7, 1863, Gay Collection, Columbia University.

CHAPTER 22

1. Stephen W. Sears, *Chancellorsville* (Boston, New York: Houghton Mifflin Company, 1996), 277–78.
2. Stephen W. Sears, *On Campaign with the Army of the Potomac: The Civil War Journal of Theodore Ayrault Dodge* (New York: Cooper Square Press, 2001), 263.

3. Bert Barnett, "If Men Ever Stayed by Their Guns: Leadership in the 1st and 11th Corps Artillery on the First Day of the Battle of Gettysburg," National Park Service, History Online, NPS.gov, 82.

4. Sears, *On Campaign*, 262.

5. Bayard Wilkeson to Sam Wilkeson, June 22, 1863, transcript of letter at GNMP, Wilkeson Collection BHM, and Maryniak Collection.

6. Ibid.

7. Ibid.

8. Ibid.

9. Francis Channing Barlow to mother and brothers, May 8, 1863, GNMP. Originals of many of Barlow's letters, which have been widely published and cited, are held at the Massachusetts Historical Society, which also provided copies.

10. Ibid.

11. Ibid.

12. James A. Scrymser, *Personal Reminisces of James A. Scrymser in Times of Peace and War* (Easton, PA: Eschenbach Printing Company, 1915), 9.

13. Ibid., 10.

14. Bayard Wilkeson to Sam Wilkeson, June 22, 1863, GNMP, Wilkeson Collection at BHM, and Maryniak Collection.

15. Ibid.

CHAPTER 23

1. G. W. Nicols. *A Soldier's Story of His Regiment (61st Georgia)* (Cornell University Press, 1919), 115. Originally published by Continental Book Company, Kennesaw, GA, 1898. Subsequently published by the University of Alabama Press, Tuscaloosa, AL, 2011.

2. Lee, General Order 73, *Memoirs*, 272.

3. Joan E. Cashin, *The War Was You and Me: Civilians in the American Civil War* (Princeton, NJ: Princeton University Press, 2002), 212.

4. James C. Mohr, *The Cormany Diaries: A Northern Family in the Civil War* (Pittsburgh, PA: University of Pittsburgh Press, 1982), 212.

5. Rev. Phillip Schaff's account was printed as "The Gettysburg Week, a Diary of Mercersburg Methodist Minister Phillip Schaff" by *Scribner's Magazine*, July 1894, 21–30.

6. Ibid.

7. Ibid.

8. John B. Gordon to his wife, Fanny, July 7, 1863, archives of GNMP.

9. Schaff, *Scribner's*, 25.

10. Ibid., 26.

11. Ibid., 27–31.

12. Albertus McCreary's account was printed as "Gettysburg: A Boy's Experience of the Battle," in *McClure's* magazine, July 1909, 250–51.

13. *OR*, Series 1, Vol. 27, Part 1, 50–51.

CHAPTER 24

1. Overall descriptions of the 11th Corps's march to Gettysburg come from the letters or official reports of members of the Corps, including Howard, Bayard Wilkeson, and other soldiers cited elsewhere too numerous to mention. Howard's account is detailed in *Memoranda of the 11th Corps Movement*, signed July 25, 1863, a copy of which is in the archives of GNMP.

2. Two of the best accounts of Emmitsburg before the battle of Gettysburg are by John Allen Miller, "Cavalry Operations at Emmitsburg, 1863," and "Emmitsburg During the Pennsylvania Campaign of 1963." They are online at www.emmitsburg .net/archive_list/articles/history/civil_war/cavalry_battles_around_emmitsburg.htm and www.emmitsburg.net/archive_list/articles/history/civil_war/pennsylvania.htm.

3. Diary entry of Jacob Engelbrecht, March 31, 1863, *The Diary of Jacob Engelbrecht*. William R. Quynn, ed., published by the Historical Society of Frederick County, MD, 2001 (archives of the society in Frederick). Accounts of the weather over the previous fall and winter are interspersed throughout.

4. Sears, *On Campaign*, 283.

5. Maj. Gen. Oliver Otis Howard, *Autobiography of Oliver Otis Howard, Volume 1* (New York: Baker & Taylor, 1907), 389.

6. John T. McMahon, *John T. McMahon's Diary of the 136th New York, 1861–1864* (Shippensburg, PA: White Mane Company, 1993), 50.

7. The Reverend W. R. Kiefer, *History of the 153rd Pennsylvania Regiment* (Easton, PA: The Chemical Publishing Company, 1909), https://archive.org/stream/historyof onehund01kief#page/n7/mode/2up, accessed January 8, 2016, 195. Reverend Kiefer was a musician in the regiment.

8. Ibid., 193.

9. McMahon, *Diary of the 136th*, 49.

10. *Winona* (MN) *Daily Republican*, June 26, 1863.

11. Stone Sentinels, GNMP, First Minnesota Volunteer Regiment, www.Gettysburg .stonesentinels. The Stone Sentinels, like the monuments on the field, depict the actions of the multitude of units that fought at Gettysburg.

12. Kiefer, *History of the 153rd Pennsylvania*, 195.

13. Private William B. Southerton, *Memoir by Pvt. William B. Southerton*, William B. Southerton Papers, Ohio Historical Society, Columbus, 1. Undated, in the archives at GNMP.

14. McMahon, *Diary of the 136th*, 50.

15. Kiefer, *History of the 153rd Pennsylvania*, 205.

16. Ibid.

17. John W. Schildt, *Roads to Gettysburg* (Parsons, WV: McLain Printing Company, 1978), 362.

18. Ibid., 284–85.

19. Ibid.

20. Kiefer. *History of the 153rd Pennsylvania*, 206.

21. Southerton, *Memoir*, GNMP.

22. Ibid.

23. Schildt, *Roads to Gettysburg*, 294.

24. Harry W. Pfanz, *Gettysburg: The Second Day* (Chapel Hill and London: University of North Carolina Press, 1978), 20. A good overview of Early's men in Pennsylvania can also be found at http://explorepahistory.com/hmarker.php?markerId=1-A-1F8.

25. Col. William Christian's June 28, 1863 letter to his wife was posted (in transcript) on June 28, 2011 by the *Encyclopedia Virginia* blog for Civil war scholars, by the Virginia Foundation for the Humanities: http://blog.encyclopediavirginia.org/2011/06/28/this -day-all-in-good-fun-edition/, accessed January 16, 2016.

26. Ibid.

27. Ibid.

28. Schildt, *Roads to Gettysburg*, 294–95.

29. Southerton, *Memoir*, GNMP.

30. Quynn, *Diary of Jacob Engelbrecht*, 972.

31. Ibid.

32. Southerton, *Memoirs*, GNMP.

33. McMahon, *Diary of the 136th*, 53.

34. Guelzo, *Gettysburg*, 125.

35. Howard, *Autobiography, Volume 1*. 395.

36. Stephen W. Sears, *Gettysburg* (New York: Houghton-Mifflin, 2003), 189.

37. Guelzo, *Gettysburg*, 125.

38. Gunn diaries, June 2, 1862.

39. Richard F. Welch, *The Boy General: The Life and Careers of Francis Channing Barlow* (Kent, OH and London: Kent State University Press, 2003), 64.

40. Howard, *Autobiography, Volume 1*, 403.

41. Ibid.

42. Ibid., 404.

43. Ken Bandy and Florence Freeland, *The Gettysburg Papers, Volume 1* (Dayton, OH: Press of Morningside Bookshop, 1978), 313.

44. Ward Hill Lamon, *Recollections of Abraham Lincoln, 1847–1865* (Cambridge, MA: The Harvard University Press, 1911), 116.

45. Howard, *Autobiography, Volume 1*, 390.

46. Miller, Emmitsburg Area Historical Society, www.emmitsburg.net/archive_list/articles/history/civil_war/cavalry_battles_around_emmitsburg.htm, accessed January 2, 2016.

47. Schildt, *Roads to Gettysburg*, 363.

48. Kiefer, *History of the 153rd Pennsylvania*, 207.

49. Ibid., 139.

50. Howard, *Autobiography, Volume 1*, 386.

51. Bayard Wilkeson to Sam Wilkeson, June 22, 1863, GNMP.

CHAPTER 25

1. *OR*, Series 1, Vol. 27, Part 3, 398.

2. Description of Frederick before the battle of Gettysburg drawn from an interview by the author with George Wunderlich, executive director of the National Museum of Civil War Medicine, February 26, 2014.

3. Reid and Fremantle, *Two Witnesses*, 12.

4. Charles Coffin, "Antietam Scenes," in *Battles and Leaders, Volume II*, 682–85.

5. F. E. Pierce, "The Civil War Letters of F. E. Pierce," Rochester in the Civil War, Blake McKelvy, ed., Rochester Historical Society. Rochester, NY, 166–67. Copies of these two pages on file at ACHS.

6. Reid and Fremantle, *Two Witnesses*, 3.

7. Ibid., 5.

8. Ibid.

9. *Chicago Journal*, June 27, 1863. Reprinted on an undisclosed date in the *Janesville* (WI) *Daily Gazette*. Archives, GNMP.

10. Andrews, *The North Reports the Civil War*, 414.

11. *OR*, Series 1, Vol. 27, Part 3, 429.

12. *The New York Times*, July 1, 1863.

13. *Baltimore American*, June 30, 1863.

14. Ibid.

15. Reid and Fremantle, *Two Witnesses*, 7.

16. Library of Congress biography describing the Uriah H. Painter paper at the Chester, PA County Historical Society.

17. Reid and Fremantle, *Two Witnesses*, 7.

18. Ibid.

19. Ibid.

20. Ibid.

21. Ibid., 10.

22. Ibid.

CHAPTER 26

1. Eugene Bancroft to Lorenzo Thomas, July 10, 1863, ACHS.

2. Reid and Fremantle, *Two Witnesses*, 14.

3. Reid's account of his route to the battlefield covers pages 12–17 in *Two Witnesses*.

4. *The New York Times*, July 1, 1938.

5. Stephen W. Sears, *Gettysburg*, 192.

6. Kiefer, *History of the 153rd Pennsylvania*, 208.

7. Howard, *Autobiography, Volume 1*, 408–9.

8. Private William Clark's journal is online as part of the 17th Connecticut's history at http://seventeenthcvi.org/blog/the-soldiers-story/william-clark/. This excerpt is from page 4 of that journal, accessed January 11, 2016.

9. Howard, *Autobiography, Volume 1*, 408–9.

10. William Clark, Journal, 4.

11. Southerton, *Memoir*, GNMP.

12. Ibid.

13. Kiefer, *History of the 153rd Pennsylvania*, 184–85.

14. Henry Steele Commager, *The Blue and the Gray: The Story of the Civil War As Told By Participants* (New York: The Fairfax Press, 1982), 603.

15. Stephen W. Sears, *On Campaign*, 303.

16. Ibid., 313.

17. Ibid.

18. Ibid., 308.

19. Kiefer, *History of the 153rd Pennsylvania*, 209.

20. Ibid.

21. Carl Schurz, "The Reminisces of Carl Schurz," *Harper's Magazine*, July 1907, 274.

22. "The 11th Corps at Gettysburg," *National Tribune*, December 12, 1869, copy in archives of GNMP.

23. Kiefer, *History of the 153rd Pennsylvania*, 176.

24. Sears, *On Campaign*, 314.

25. Reid and Fremantle, *Two Witnesses*, 19.

26. *OR*, Series 1, Vol. 27, Part 1, 756–57.

27. Interview of Mary McAllister before her death in 1907, and published in the *Philadelphia Inquirer*, June 26–29, 1938 (upon the 75th anniversary of the battle), Archives, ACHS.

28. McCreary, "Gettysburg: A Boy's Experience of the Battle," *McClure's*, July 1909.

29. Kiefer, *History of the 153rd Pennsylvania*, 177.

30. Ibid.

31. *San Francisco Sunday Call*, August 16, 1903, Archives of ACHS.

32. Kiefer, *History of the 153rd Pennsylvania*, 209.

33. Glenn Brasher, "The Battle in Public: Newspaper Reports from Gettysburg," *Civil War Monitor*, www.civilwarmonitor.com/front-line/the-battle-in-public-newspaper-reports-from-gettysburg, accessed January 2, 2016.

34. *OR*, Series 1, Vol. 27, Part 1, 747.

CHAPTER 27

1. Sam Wilkeson to Samuel H. Wilkeson, May 8, 1865, Wilkeson Collection, BHM; and Maryniak Collection. In this case, illustrating his use of the word, the senior Wilkeson was using it to describe his second son, Frank's, desire to go to Mexico to fight there.

2. The Editors of Stackpole Books, *Gettysburg, The Story of the Battle With Maps* (Mechanicsburg, PA: Stackpole Books, 2013), 28, 30.

3. Scott L. Mingus, *The Louisiana Tigers in the Gettysburg Campaign June–July 1863* (Baton Rouge, Louisiana State University Press, 2009), 127.

4. *Gettysburg Compiler*, July 2, 1915.

5. Descriptions of battlefield movements come from myriad sources, including official reports of officers involved in *OR*. The author has also drawn insight from Harry W. Pfanz's *Gettysburg* trilogy; Allen C. Guelzo's *Gettysburg—The Last Invasion*; and Stephen W. Sears's *Gettysburg*, all cited earlier, along with David G. Martin's *Gettysburg, July 1* (Boston: Da Capo Press, 2003).

6. *National Tribune*, December 12, 1869.

CHAPTER 28

1. Sears, *Gettysburg*, 209–11.

2. Estimates of the size of the armies and the casualties at Gettysburg have varied through the decades. These estimates are based on a compilation from John Busey and

David G. Martin, *Regimental Strengths and Losses at Gettysburg* (Highstown, NJ: Longstreet House, 2005). Garry Adelman, an historian for the Civil War Trust, estimated in 2013 correspondence with the author that the actual number of soldiers engaged on July 1 was roughly 18,000 for the North, 28,000 for the South.

3. Estimates and comparisons drawn from the work of Garry Adelman and D. Scott Hartwig, former supervisory historian, GNMP, as well as official reports of those involved. John Heiser, GNMP historian, cites John Busey and David G. Martin, *Regimental Strengths and Losses*, which says 17,870 Union troops were engaged minus the brigade left on Cemetery Hill, while 29,043 in the two Confederate corps saw action.

4. James P. Scott, "The Artillery at Gettysburg," undated, Archives, GNMP.

5. David Ladd and Audrey Ladd, eds., "Report of Lt. Col. John Callis," *The Bachelder Papers, Volume 1* (Dayton, OH: Morningside Press, 1994), 141–43.

6. D. Scott Hartwig, "The Army of Northern Virginia in the Gettysburg Campaign, Never Have I Seen Such A Charge. Pender's Light Division at Gettysburg, July 1," paper published by the National Park Service, 49–50.

7. Ladd and Ladd, *Bachelder Papers, Volume 1*, 145.

8. Stone Sentinels, Monument to the 149th Volunteer Infantry Regiment, GNMP.

9. Stone Sentinels, Monument to the 142nd Pennsylvania Volunteer Infantry Regiment, GNMP.

CHAPTER 29

1. Dilger's Official Report was straight to the point, like his shooting. *OR*, Series 1, Vol. 27, 753–55.

2. Bertram Barnett, "I Ordered No Man to Go When I Would Not Go Myself: Leadership in the Campaign and Battle of Gettysburg," Papers of the Ninth Gettysburg National Military Park Seminar, 2002, GNMP.

3. Edward Marcus, ed. *A New Canaan Private in the Civil War: Letters of Justus M. Silliman, 17th Connecticut Volunteers* (New Canaan, CT: New Canaan Historical Society, 1984), 42.

4. *OR*, Series 1, Vol. 27, Part 1, 755.

5. Descriptions of movements of Wilkeson's battery and Ames's and von Gilsa's divisions drawn heavily from D. Scott Hartwig, "The 11th Corps on July 1, 1863," *Gettysburg Magazine*, Vol. 2, 1990, and the previously cited Barnett, "I Ordered No Man to Go When I Would Not Go Myself."

6. *OR*, Series 1, Vol. 27, Part 1, 757–58.

7. Ibid., 756–57.

CHAPTER 30

1. *National Tribune*, December 12, 1869.

2. *OR*, Series 1, Vol. 27, Part 1, 468.

3. Harry W. Pfanz, *Gettysburg—Culp's Hill and Cemetery Hill* (Chapel Hill: University of North Carolina Press, 1993), 29.

4. Barlow to his mother, July 7, 1863, in Christian G. Samito, ed., *Fear Was Not in Him—The Civil War Letters of Major General Francis C. Barlow, USA* (New York:

Fordham University Press, 2004). Originals on file at the Massachusetts Historical Society.

5. *National Tribune*, December 31, 1885.

6. Guelzo. *Gettysburg*, 182.

7. Martin, *Gettysburg, July 1*, 201.

8. Frederick Bancroft and William A. Dunning, *The Reminisces of Carl Schurz, Volume III* (London: John Murray, 1909), 7–9.

9. Samito. *Fear Was Not in Him*, 140.

10. Bancroft and Dunning, *The Reminisces of Carl Schurz, Volume III*, 9.

11. Howard, *Autobiography*, Vol. 1, 414.

12. Ibid.

13. Bancroft and Dunning, *The Reminisces of Carl Schurz, Volume III*, 9.

14. Martin, *Gettysburg*, July 1, 267.

15. Unit sizes drawn from *Busey and Martin, Regimental Strengths and Losses*; and *Gettysburg, The Story of the Battle with Maps*.

16. Samito, *Fear Was Not in Him*, 152–64.

17. Howard, *Autobiography, Volume 1*, 416–17.

18. Oliver Otis Howard, *Atlantic Monthly*, July–November 1876, transcript of the article in the files at GNMP.

19. Oliver Otis Howard, "Ceremonies and Address of the Dedication of a Monument—N.Y. State Vols," July 3, 1888. Copy of address at GNMP.

20. Ibid.

21. Samito. *Fear Was Not in Him*, 162.

22. Ibid.

23. *OR*, Series 1, Vol. 27, 230.

24. Bancroft and Dunning, *The Reminisces of Carl Schurz, Volume III*, 9.

25. Robert Stiles, *Four Years Under Marse Robert* (University of North Carolina Press, 1903, Chapel Hill), 210–11.

26. John B. Gordon, *Reminiscences of the Civil War* (New York, Atlanta: Charles Scribner and Sons, and The Martin and Hoyt Co., 1904), 154–55.

27. Ibid., 156.

28. Ibid., 150.

29. Bancroft and Dunning, *The Reminisces of Carl Schurz, Volume III*, 8.

30. Ibid.

CHAPTER 31

1. *OR*, Series 1, Vol. 27, Part 2, 496.

2. Gordon, *Reminiscences*, 151.

3. Private G. W. Nichols, *A Soldier's Story of His Regiment (61st Georgia)* (Cornell University Press, Ithaca, N.Y., 1919), 116–17. Originally published by Continental Book Company, Kennesaw, GA, 1898.

4. *OR*, Series 1, Vol. 27, Part 1, 712.

5. "Farewell Address of General Gilsa to the Officers and Soldiers of the 153d Pennsylvania, July 13, 1863," transcript translated from German, in the archives of GNMP.

6. Samito, *Fear Was Not in Him*, 157.

7. Nichols, *A Soldier's Story*, 98–99.

8. *National Tribune*, December 12, 1869.

9. Gordon to his wife, Fanny, July 7, 1863, GNMP.

10. *OR*, Series 1, Vol. 27, Part 1, 748.

11. Editors at Time-Life, *Gettysburg, Voices of the Civil War* (Alexandria, VA: Time-Life Books, 1996), 57.

12. John Warwick Daniel, "Early and P.W. Hairston at Rappahannock Bridge," and "Garber's Battery at Gettysburg," in Daniel Papers, University of Virginia, 1904–1908, copy in files of ACHS.

13. *Battles and Leaders, Volume 3*, 281.

14. Martin, *Gettysburg, July 1*, 277.

15. Ibid., 282.

16. Kiefer, *History of the 153rd Pennsylvania*, 140.

17. Ibid., 140–41.

18. Ibid., 211.

19. *OR*, Series 1, Vol. 27, Part 1, 751–54.

20. Ibid., 754, 756, 758.

21. Howard, *Autobiography, Volume 1*, 410.

22. Ibid.

23. Capt. Daniel Hall to Gen. O. O. Howard, May 20, 1882, transcript in the archives of GNMP.

24. *Cleveland Morning Leader*, July 4, 1863. This depiction could have come from Howard himself. There is evidence he talked to many correspondents, including Sam Wilkeson and Homer Byington, during the battle.

25. Stone Sentinels, 11th Corps Monument, GNMP.

26. Brevet Gen. E. P. Halstead, "The First Day of the Battle of Gettysburg," a paper read before the District of Columbia Commandery of the Military Order of the Loyal Legion of the United States, March 2, 1887, posted online in 2006 by the Military Order of the Loyal Legion of the United States, http://suvcw.org/mollus/warpapers/DCv1p3.htm, accessed January 3, 2016.

27. Biography of Hancock, Civil War Preservation Trust, "Civil War Figures as Examples of Character and Leadership," http://telegraph.civilwar.org/education/curriculum/Gifted%20and%20Talented/CWPT%20Gifted%20Curriculum%20-%20Winfield%20Scott%20Hancock.pdf, accessed January 11, 2016.

28. Ladd and Ladd, *The Bachelder Papers, Volume 3*, 1,350–51.

29. Ibid., 1,525.

30. *National Tribune*, December 12, 1869.

CHAPTER 32

1. *OR*, Series 1, Vol. 27, Part 1, 756

2. *OR*, Series 1, Vol. 27, Part 2, 469.

3. Kiefer, *History of the 153rd Pennsylvania*, 211.

4. Bradley M. Gottfried, *Brigades of Gettysburg: The Union and Confederate Brigades at the Battle of Gettysburg* (New York: Skyhorse Publishing, 2012), 312.

5. Kiefer, *History of the 153rd Pennsylvania*, 212.

6. Ibid., 213.

7. Southerton, *Memoir*, GNMP.

8. Kiefer, *History of the 153rd Pennsylvania*, 213–14.

9. Sears, *On Campaign*, 320.

10. Edward C. Culp, *Raising the Banner of Freedom: The 25th Ohio Volunteer Infantry in the War for the Union*, Tom Edwards, ed. (iUniverse LLC, 2003), https://books.google.com/books?id=9ESYIkpmHqgC&pg=PA87&lpg=PA87&dq=Thousands+of+fresh+troops+Edward+Culp&source=bl&ots=n5MJScg-8p&sig=NbZirmMSbgEIEr57Dr3rFKPHQGM&hl=en&sa=X&ved=0ahUKEwju_eiigpTKAhUGzz4KHf_7BUkQ6AEIHDAA#v=onepage&q=Thousands%20of%20fresh%20troops%20Edward%20Culp&f=false, 87, accessed January 5, 2016.

11. Kiefer, *History of the 153rd Pennsylvania*, 173.

12. Ibid., 216.

13. James P. Scott, "The Artillery at Gettysburg," undated, in the archives of the GNMP.

14. Kiefer, *History of the 153rd Pennsylvania*, 214–15.

15. Matilda "Tillie" Pierce Alleman, *At Gettysburg, or, What a Girl Saw and Heard of the Battle. A True Narrative* (New York: W. Lake Borland, 1889), 92.

16. Lt. Col. William F. Fox, *Regimental Losses in the Civil War* (Dayton, OH: Morningside Books, 1985), 439–40.

17. Gordon, *Reminiscences*, 151.

18. John B. Gordon, "The Last Days of the Confederacy," speech delivered at Keystone State Normal School, Kutztown, PA, October 24, 1896, archives of GNMP.

19. Oliver Otis Howard, "Ceremonies and Addresses at the Dedication of a Monument by the 119th Regiment, N.Y. State Volunteers, July 3, 1888," 18–19, archives of GNMP.

CHAPTER 33

1. Handwritten description of Bayard Wilkeson, author unknown, ACHS.

2. Donald Vaughn, *The Everything Civil War Book* (Avon, MA: Adams Media, 2000), 178.

3. *Battles and Leaders, Volume 3*, 281.

4. The description of Wilkeson's wounding is based on the official reports of Bancroft, Osborn, and Hunt, as well as myriad newspaper reports, as well as a July 11, 1863, letter from Sam Wilkeson's brother, John, to a daughter, on July 1863. A transcript of the letter is in the Maryniak Collection.

5. *Boston Journal*, July 6, 1863, reprinted in *Eyewitness to Gettysburg, Correspondent Charles Carleton Coffin*, introduction by John W. Schildt (Shippensburg, PA: Burd Street Press, 1997), 57–59.

6. Ibid.

7. Ibid.

8. *Washington Chronicle,* July 11, 1863.

9. Coffin, *Eyewitness to Gettysburg,* Introduction, x. A typical example: The *Wisconsin State Journal* reported on February 26, 1886, that Coffin had given a speech in Boston in which he said Bayard Wilkeson's "soul was on fire" to serve.

10. *Emporia* (KS) *Weekly News,* July 26, 1888.

11. *OR,* Series 1, Vol. 27, Part 1, 230.

12. Ibid., 706.

13. Ibid., 756.

14. Martin, *Gettysburg,* July 1, 282.

15. Bert Barnett. "If Ever Men Stayed by Their Guns. Leadership in the First and 11th Corps on the First Day of the Battle of Gettysburg," Gettysburg Seminar Papers, National Park Service, http://npshistory.com/series/symposia/gettysburg_seminars/9/contents.htm, accessed January 14, 2016.

16. Sgt. Joseph Creed, transcript of letter, undated, BHM.

17. Ibid.

18. Ibid.

19. Ibid.

20. Ibid.

21. John Wilkeson to his daughter, Maria Wilkeson, July 6, 1863. Copies of this letter are in both the Wilkeson Collection, BHM; and in the Maryniak Collection. This letter was one of several Wilkeson-related letters offered at auction by Raab Collection, 2013.

22. Reid and Fremantle, *Two Witnesses,* 33.

23. *OR,* Series 1, Vol. 27, Part 1, 757.

24. Ibid.

25. *National Tribune,* December 12, 1869.

26. *New York Times,* July 6, 1863.

27. Kiefer, *History of the 153rd Pennsylvania,* 84.

28. Oliver Otis Howard to Sam Wilkeson, July 8, 1863, Oliver O. Howard Collection, Bowdoin College, Brunswick, ME. Hereafter known as BCL.

CHAPTER 34

1. Reid and Fremantle, *Two Witnesses,* 59.

2. *The New York Times,* July 6, 1863.

3. Ibid.

4. Reid and Fremantle, *Two Witnesses,* 59.

5. *The New York Times,* July 6, 1863.

6. The description of the Leister House and surrounding soldiers during the battle is taken from the dispatches of Reid and Wilkeson; from Frank Haskell's *The Battle of Gettysburg,* Wisconsin History Commission, November 1908 (3,500 copies printed by the state printer, accessed at the University of California online library on January 4, 2016, at https://archive.org/stream/battlegettysburg00haskrich/battlegettysburg00haskrich_djvu .txt; and from post-battle photographs by Alexander Gardner, Library of Congress).

7. Ibid.

8. Haskell, *The Battle of Gettysburg,* 19.

9. Carl Schurz, *McCall's* magazine, July 1907.

10. Charles Carleton Coffin, *Stories of Our Soldiers* (Boston: Journal Publishing Company, 1893), 119.

11. Coffin, *Eyewitness to Gettysburg*, 32.

12. Coffin, *Boys of '61*, 292.

CHAPTER 35

1. *The New York Times*, July 6, 1863.

2. *Madison, Wis. State Journal*, July 6, 1863.

3. Haskell, *The Battle of Gettysburg*, 99.

4. *The New York Times*, July 6, 1863.

5. Reid and Fremantle, *Two Witnesses*, 61.

6. Haskell, *The Battle of Gettysburg*, 99.

7. *The New York Times*, July 6, 1863.

8. Ibid.

9. Ibid.

10. Coffin, *The Boys of '61*, 294.

11. Haskell, *The Battle of Gettysburg*, 101–2.

12. Andrews, *The North Reports the Civil War*, 425.

13. Bandy and Freeland, *The Gettysburg Papers, Volume 1*, 345–48.

14. *St. Louis Democrat*, July 10, 1863, GNMP.

15. Warren L. Goss, *Recollections of a Private* (New York: Thomas Y. Crowell and Co., 1890), 213, cited in "Artillery Employment at the Battle of Gettysburg," thesis by Army Maj. Mark A. Gilmore, Oregon State University, 1977.

16. Bandy and Freeland, *The Gettysburg Papers, Volume 1*, 345–48.

17. Ibid.

18. *The New York Times*, July 6, 1863.

19. Ibid.

20. *National Tribune*, November 12, 1908; Ladd and Ladd, *The Bachelder Papers, Volume 3*, 1,157.

21. Ibid.

22. Frank Haskell, *The Battle of Gettysburg*, 128.

23. Ibid., 127.

24. Ibid., 130.

25. *The New York Times*, July 6, 1863.

26. Coffin, *Eyewitness to Gettysburg*, 108.

27. *The New York Times*, July 8, 1863.

28. Coffin, *The Boys of '61*, 247.

29. Coffin, *Eyewitness to Gettysburg*, 116.

30. *The New York Times*, July 6, 1863. Wilkeson had two dispatches on the paper's front page that Monday, the one referenced here and dated July 3, and a more famous and detailed dispatch, dated Saturday night, July 4.

31. William A. Frassanito, *Early Photography at Gettysburg* (Gettysburg, PA: Thomas Publications, 1995), 340–41, ACHS.

32. *Portsmouth, N. H. Journal of Literature and Commerce*, July 18, 1863.
33. Coffin, *Boys of '61*, 299.
34. Ibid.
35. Reid and Fremantle, *Two Witnesses*, 68.
36. *The New York Times*, July 6, 1863.
37. Haskell, *The Battle of Gettysburg*, 130.

CHAPTER 36

1. *OR*, Series 1, Vol. 27, Part 1, 690.
2. *National Tribune*, November 12, 1908. The newspaper printed Cowan's extensive account of July 3 at Gettysburg, including his encounter on the ridge with Sam Wilkeson just after Pickett's Charge had been repelled.
3. Ibid.
4. Ibid.
5. Ibid.
6. Ibid.

CHAPTER 37

1. Ladd and Ladd, *The Bachelder Papers, Volume 2*, 1,000–1,002.
2. Bandy and Freeland, *The Gettysburg Papers, Volume 1*, 345–48.
3. Ibid., 732–35.
4. Ibid.
5. Ladd and Ladd, *Bachelder Papers, Volume 3*, 1,366.
6. Ibid., 1,366–67.
7. Ibid., 1367.
8. Bandy and Freeland, *The Gettysburg Papers, Volume 1*, 349.

CHAPTER 38

1. *Brooklyn Eagle*, July 22, 1863, in the archives of the ACHS.
2. Ibid.
3. McCreary, "Gettysburg: A Boy's Experience of the Battle," 251.
4. Stone Sentinels, GNMP, www.gettysburg.stonesentinels.com/OH/25-75OH .php.
5. Richard A. Baumgartner, *Buckeye Blood—Ohio at Gettysburg* (Huntington, WV: Blue Acorn Press, 2003), 167–69.
6. Ibid., 168.
7. Ibid., 167.
8. Ibid.
9. Mary McAllister, *Interview*, ACHS.
10. John Wilkeson to Maria Wilkeson, July 6, 1863, Wilkeson Collection, BHM. Also, files of ACHS.
11. Michael Dreese, *Bucknell World*, Spring 2008, files of ACHS.
12. Ladd and Ladd, *The Bachelder Papers, Volume 1*, 141–43.

13. Fannie Buehler, *Recollections of the Rebel Invasion and One Woman's Experience during the Battle of Gettysburg,* self-published, 27, files of ACHS.

14. Mary McCallister, *Interview,* ACHS.

15. Fannie Buehler, *The Rebel Invason and One Woman's Experience during the Battle of Gettysburg,* 26.

16. T. W. Herbert, "In Occupied Pennsylvania," *Georgia Review,* Summer 1950, 103–5, copy in files of ACHS.

17. Ibid.

18. *Gettysburg Star and Sentinel,* February 9, 1864, files of GNMP.

19. Lydia Ziegler, *An Account of the Battle of Gettysburg by Lydia Catherine Ziegler Clare,* self-published, about 1900, www.genealogystories.net/account_of_lydia_clare .html, accessed January 11, 2016.

20. Ibid.

21. Ibid.

22. Salome M. Stewart, *Reminisces of Gettysburg Hospitals,* files of the ACHS.

23. Ibid.

24. Ibid.

25. Ibid.

26. Baumgartner, *Buckeye Blood,* 170.

CHAPTER 39

1. Sears, *Gettysburg,* 508.

2. J. Howard Wert, *A Complete Hand-Book of the Monuments and Indications and Guide to the Positions on the Gettysburg Battlefield* (Harrisburg, PA: B.M. Sturgeon and Company, 1888), 156.

3. Lt. Barzilia J. Inman, *History of the Corn Exchange Regiment, 118th Pennsylvania Volunteers* (Philadelphia: J. L. Smith Publisher, 1888), 250, https://archive.org/details/ historyofcornexc01unit, accessed January 11, 2016.

4. Duane E. Schaffer, *Men of Granite—New Hampshire's Soldiers in the Civil War* (Columbia: University of South Carolina Press, 2006), 156.

5. Alfred Lee, "Reminisces of the Gettysburg Battle," *Lippincott's Magazine,* Vol. 32, July 1883, 60.

6. Ibid.

7. Clifton Johnson, *Battlefield Adventures* (New York: Houghton Mifflin, 1915), 166–75, excerpts in files of ACHS.

8. Transcript of Steffan diary, Vertical File 90, Special Collections & College Archives, Musselman Library, Gettysburg College, Gettysburg.

9. Johnson. *Battlefield Adventures,* 174.

10. Leonard Marsden Gardner. *Sunset Memories: A Retrospect of a Life Lived during the Last Seventy-five Years of the Nineteenth Century, 1831–1901.* First printed as a four-part series in the *Gettysburg Times and News,* beginning September 19, 1940. Later reprinted as a book by The Times and News Publishing Company, 1941. Excerpts in the files of the ACHS. Hereafter referenced as Gardner, *Sunset Memories.*

11. Ibid.

12. Ibid.

13. Ibid.

14. Ibid.

15. John M. Cuyler and Edward Vollum, July 27 and July 25, respectively, *OR.* Series 1, Vol. 27, Part 1, 24–27.

16. John B, Linn, "Journal of My Trip to the Battlefield at Gettysburg, July 1863," paper in collection of ACHS.

17. Ibid.

18. John Charles Wills, "Reminisces of the Three Days Battle of Gettysburg at the Globe Hotel," typewritten, 30–31, ACHS.

19. *Adams Sentinel,* July 21, 1863.

20. Ibid.

21. Gardner, *Sunset Memories.*

22. Mary McAllister, *Diary,* ACHS. Also, these salient portions have been transcribed and posted online at www.gdg.org/Research/Underground%20Railroad/mary mcallister.htm.

23. Wert, *A Complete Hand-Book of the Monuments and Indications and Guide to the Positions on the Gettysburg Battlefield,* 156.

24. J. Howard Wert, "In the Hospitals of Gettysburg," *Harrisburg* (PA) *Telegraph,* July 2, 1907.

25. Wills, "Reminisces of the Three Days Battle of Gettysburg at the Globe Hotel," 30–31, ACHS.

26. *Cortland* (NY) *Gazette and Banner,* July 16, 1863.

27. *The New York Times,* July 11, 1963.

28. Ibid., July 6, 1863.

29. Ibid., July 7, 1863.

30. Ibid., July 11, 1863.

31. Ibid.

32. *The New York Times,* July 10, 1865.

33. *Lewistown* (PA) *Gazette,* July 15, 1863, cited in paper, "36th Regiment, Volunteer Pennsylvania Militia," by Robert E. Nale and Jean A. Suloff, Mifflin County, PA Historical Society.

34. Joseph Hopkins Twichell, *The Civil War Letters of Joseph Hopkins Twichell,* Peter Messent and Steve Courtney, eds. (Athens: University of Georgia Press, 2006), 254.

35. George W. Demers to Abraham Lincoln, Friday, August 14, 1863, transcribed and annotated by the Lincoln Studies Center, Knox College, Galesburg, IL, available at Abraham Lincoln Papers at the Library of Congress, Manuscript Division (Washington, DC: American Memory Project, 2000–2002), https://memory.loc.gov/ammem/alhtml/malhome.html, accessed January 8, 2016.

36. Ezra D. Simons, *A Regimental History of the 125th New York State Volunteers,* 1888, self-published, https://archive.org/stream/cu31924030912038/cu31924030912038_djvu .txt, accessed January 8, 2016.

37. Oliver Otis Howard, *Autobiography,* 440.

38. Samuel H. Wilkeson to his sister, Maria, July 5, 1863, Wilkeson Collection, BHS.

CHAPTER 40

1. John Wilkeson to his daughter Maria Wilkeson, July 6, 1863, Wilkeson Collection, BHM.

2. An image of Waud's illustration is available in the New York Public Library's digital collection at http://digitalcollections.nypl.org/items/510d47e0-fa24-a3d9-e040 -e00a18064a99, viewed January 8, 2016.

3. John Wilkeson to his daughter, Maria Wilkeson, July 6, 1863.

4. Ibid.

5. Almshouse Census in files of ACHS.

6. Aaron Sheely diary, typewritten transcript, files of ACHS.

7. John Wilkeson to his daughter, Maria, July 6, 1863, Wilkeson Collection, BHM.

8. Ibid.

9. Bert Barnett. "If Ever Men Stayed by Their Guns: Leadership In the First and 11th Corps on the First Day of the Battle of Gettysburg," files of GNMP.

10. John Wilkeson to his daughter, Maria Wilkeson, July 6, 1863, BHM.

11. Ibid.

12. Sam Wilkeson dated his famous dispatch, which mentioned Bayard's death, Saturday night, July 4, 1863.

13. John Wilkeson to his daughter, Maria Wilkeson, July 6, 1863.

14. Handwritten letter from Lt. Eugene Bancroft to Gen. Lorenzo Thomas, July 10, 1863, transcript in ACHS.

15. *The New York Times*, July 9, 1863.

16. Ibid.

17. Sam Wilkeson to his brother, John Wilkeson, undated letter, probably 1858, Wilkeson Collection, BHM.

CHAPTER 41

1. Drew Gilpin Faust, *The Republic of Suffering—Death and the American Civil War* ((Thorndike Press, Detroit, New York, San Francisco, New Haven, Conn., Waterville, Me., London, 2008), 295. Faust's book deeply explores this concept. "The Good Death," she wrote, "was the foundation for the process of mourning carried on by survivors who used the last words and moments of the dead soldier as the basis for broader evaluation of his entire life."

2. Ibid., 14.

3. Mark S. Schantz, *Awaiting the Heavenly Country: The Civil War and America's Culture of Death* (Ithaca, NY: Cornell University Press, 2008), 14.

4. Coffin, *Boys of '61*, 301.

5. Cate Cady Wilkeson to her sister-in-law, Mary, June 11, 1862, Maryniak Collection.

6. Coffin, *Eyewitness to Gettysburg*, 127.

7. John Wilkeson to Maria Wilkeson, July 6, 1863, Wilkeson Collection, BHM.

8. Kiefer, *History of the 153rd Pennsylvania*, 252.

9. Ibid., 179.

10. Oliver O. Howard to Sam Wilkeson, March 19, 1875, Oliver Otis Howard Collection, Bowdoin College.

11. John Wilkeson to daughter, Maria Wilkeson, July 6, 1863, Wilkeson Collection, BHM.

12. Anonymous, "The Famous Long Ago," typewritten account of unknown date in the Maryniak Collection.

13. John Wilkeson to daughter, Maria Wilkeson, July 6, 1863, Wilkeson Collection, BHM.

14. Wilkeson Collection, BHM.

15. "Bayard Wilkeson last letter to his mother," typewritten excerpts, unknown date, Maryniak Collection.

CHAPTER 42

1. *Gettysburg Compiler*, September 28, 1907, ACHS.

2. *The New York Times*, July 6, 1863.

3. A copy is in the Library of Congress archives.

4. Martin P. Johnson, *Writing the Gettysburg Address* (Lawrence: University of Kansas Press, 2013), 239.

5. Ibid.

6. John Hay Papers 1783–1999, November 2, 1863, Manuscript Division, Library of Congress.

7. Johnson, *Writing the Gettysburg Address*, 56.

8. Accounts of Lincoln's July 7 speech were reported by the *New York Tribune*, *The New York Times*, and *New York Herald*, July 8, 1863. All are recounted in *Collected Works of Abraham Lincoln, Volume 6* (New Brunswick, NJ: Rutgers University Press, 1953), 320, http://quod.lib.umich.edu/l/lincoln?cginame=text-idx;id=navbar browselink;page=browse, accessed January 8, 2016.

9. Gideon Welles, *Diary of Gideon Welles, Secretary of the Navy Under Lincoln and Johnson, Volume 1* (Boston and New York: Houghton Mifflin Company, 1911), 363.

10. *Collected Works of Abraham Lincoln*, 320.

11. Ibid.

12. *The New York Times*, July 6, 1863.

13. Ibid.

14. Mrs. Henry Ward Beecher to Samuel Wilkeson, July 7, 1863, transcript. ACHS.

15. Edward C. Stedman to Sam Wilkeson, July 6, 1863, Maryniak Collection.

16. Oliver O. Howard to Sam Wilkeson, July 8, 1863, Wilkeson Collection, BHS.

17. Ibid.

18. *National Tribune*, December 31, 1885.

19. Ibid.

20. Samuel H. Wilkeson to his father, John, July 19, 1869, Wilkeson Collection, BHM.

21. John J. Peck to Sam Wilkeson, September 15, 1863, Wilkeson Collection, BHM, files of GNMP.

22. Ibid.

CHAPTER 43

1. *Buffalo Morning Express*, July 8, 1863. (Clips of the Buffalo newspapers' accounts are contained in the Maryniak Collection.)
2. *Buffalo Commercial Advertiser*, July 9, 1863.
3. *Buffalo Morning Express*, July 10, 1863.
4. Ibid.
5. *Buffalo Commercial Advertiser*, July 11, 1863, cited in Maryniak Collection.
6. *Buffalo Daily Courier*, July 11, 1863.
7. Ibid.

CHAPTER 44

1. *The New York Times*, July 6, 1863.
2. Samuel Wilkeson to his brother, John, after the death of their sister, Elizabeth, on September 5, 1858. Date of letter unknown. Wilkeson Collection, BHM.
3. Cate Cady Wilkeson to her sister-in-law.
4. Samuel H. Wilkeson to his father, John, July 19, 1863, Wilkeson Collection, BHM.
5. Oliver O. Howard to Abraham Lincoln, July 18, 1863, *Collected Works of Abraham Lincoln*, 341.
6. Abraham Lincoln to Oliver Otis Howard, July 21, 1863, *Collected Works of Abraham Lincoln*, 321.
7. George Gordon Meade, *OR*, Series 1, Vol. 27, Part 1, 115.
8. Ibid.
9. Oliver Otis Howard, *Autobiography*, 418–19.
10. Oliver Otis Howard to Sam Wilkeson, July 8, 1863, transcript in files of ACHS.
11. Ibid.
12. Samito, *Fear Was Not in Him*, 162–65.
13. Ibid., 164.
14. Ibid., 163.
15. Ibid., 163–65.
16. *National Tribune*, December 31, 1885, drawn from an article by Howard in that edition.
17. John B. Gordon, "The Last Days of the Confederacy," speech delivered at the Keystone State Normal School. Kutztown, PA, October 24, 1896. Files of GNMP.
18. Samito, *Fear Was Not in Him*, 168–69.
19. Ibid.
20. Ibid., 162.
21. Ibid.,165.
22. Ibid.
23. Ibid., 168.
24. Henry Livermore Abbot to Mr. Paine, *20th Massachusetts Regimental Collection of the Boston Public Library, Volume 2*, 41, http://people.virginia.edu/~mmd5f/abb2pain.htm#firstletter, accessed January 9, 2016.

25. Richard F. Miller, *Harvard's Civil War: A History of the Twentieth Volunteer Massachusetts Infantry* (Hanover and London: University Press of New England, 2005), 275.

26. Robert Treat Paine, transcript of speech in the *American Advocate of Peace*, Vol. 55, No. 12, December 1893, published online by the World Affairs Institute at http://www .jstor.org/stable/27899998, accessed January 9, 2016.

CHAPTER 45

1. Frank Wilkeson, *Turned Inside Out: Recollections of a Private Soldier in the Army of the Potomac* (New York and London: G.P. Putnam's Sons, 1887), 1.

2. Ibid., 2.

3. Ibid., 6.

4. Ibid., 7.

5. Ibid., 14.

6. Starr, *Bohemian Brigade*, 292.

7. Sam Wilkeson to Seth Williams, May 5, 1864, Maryniak Collection.

8. Grant, *Autobiography*, 255.

9. Frank Wilkeson, *Turned Inside Out*, 6.

10. Ibid., 126.

11. Frank Wilkeson to his father, Sam Wilkeson, May 8, 1864, BHM and ACHS.

12. Frank Wilkeson, *Turned Inside Out*, 85.

13. Ibid., 51.

14. Ibid., 104.

15. Curtis S. King, William G. Robertson, and Steven E. Clay, S*taff Ride Handbook for the Overland Campaign, Virginia, 4 May to 15 June, 1864* (Fort Leavenworth, KS: Combat Studies Institute Press, 2007), 315–16.

16. Ibid.

17. *The New York Times*, June 10, 1864.

18. Frank Wilkeson, *Turned Inside Out*, 146.

19. Ernest B. Furgurson, *Not War But Murder, Cold Harbor 1864* (New York: Alfred A. Knopf, 2000), 220–22.

20. *New York Tribune*, August 6, 1864.

21. Ibid.

22. Charles Page to Sydney Howard Gay, August 5 or 6, 1864, cited in Andrews, *The North Reports the Civil War*, 600.

23. Frank Wilkeson, *Turned Inside Out*, 189.

24. Ibid., 200.

25. Ibid., 185.

26. Biography of Charles Griffin online at the Texas State Historical Association at https://tshaonline.org/handbook/online/articles/fgr60, accessed January 9, 2016.

CHAPTER 46

1. *New York Tribune*, August 19, 1899.

2. Sam Wilkeson to Horace Greeley, January 4, 1865, Wilkeson Collection, BHM.

3. Starr, *Bohemian Brigade*, 291.

4. *Chicago Tribune*, December 24, 1863.

5. Ibid.

6. Sam Wilkeson to Horace Greeley, November 29, 1864. BHM.

7. Ibid.

8. *Newark* (NJ) *Daily Advertiser*, January 13, 1865.

9. Sam Wilkeson to Samuel H. Wilkeson, May 8, 1865, Wilkeson Collection, BHM.

10. Sam Wilkeson, *How Our National Debt May Be a National Blessing*, Issued by Jay Cooke, General Subscription Agent of the Public Loans (Philadelphia: McLaughlin Brothers, 1865), 4, https://archive.org/details/howournationalde00wilkrich, accessed January 11, 2016.

11. *Baltimore Sun*, March 3, 1868.

12. Sam Wilkeson, "Wilkeson's Notes on Puget Sound: Being extracts from notes by Samuel Wilkeson of a reconnaissance of the proposed route of the Northern Pacific Railroad made in the summer of 1869," Wilkeson Collection. BHM.

13. John Lubetkin, *Jay Cooke's Gamble: The Northern Pacific Railroad, the Sioux, and the Panic of 1873* (Norman: University of Oklahoma Press, 2006), 19–22.

14. "Marriage Index, *Cambria-Tribune* and *Johnstown-Tribune*, Johnstown, PA., 1853–1885." Accessed online March 23, 2016, at http://www.rootsweb.ancestry.com/~pacblack/interests/JTDMI1853_85.pdf.

15. Sam Wilkeson to Jay Cooke, July 11, 1869, Maryniak Collection.

16. From an introduction, "Northern Pacific Railway Company, Secretary's Department. Unregistered letters received and related records, undated and 1864–1876," http://www2.mnhs.org/library/findaids/m0459.pdf on January 9, 2016, original at Minnesota Historical Society, St. Paul, MN.

17. *Wall Street Journal*, March 4, 1932.

18. Starr, *Bohemian Brigade*, 358.

19. Ibid., 357.

20. Sam Wilkeson's testimony appears in *The New York Times*, March 13, 1875.

21. Ibid.

22. Stanton, *Eighty Years and More*, 111.

23. *Chicago Tribune*, February 25, 1872.

CHAPTER 47

1. Sam Wilkeson to Sidney Howard Gay, March 1864, date unknown, Gay Collection, Columbia University.

2. *The New York Times*, July 6, 1863.

3. Sam Wilkeson to Sidney Howard Gay, March, 1864, Gay Collection, Columbia University.

4. George Gordon Meade to his wife, August 6, 1864, in *The Life and Letters of George Gordon Meade, Major-General United States Army. Volume 6* (New York: Charles Scribner & Son, 1913), www.perseus.tufts.edu/hopper/text?doc=Perseus%3Atext%3A 2001.05.0134%3Achapter%3D6&force=y, accessed January 11, 2016.

5. Ibid.

6. *New York Tribune*, May 18, 1864.

7. Ibid.

8. Ibid.

9. Ibid.

10. Ibid.

11. *Wall Street Journal*, December 3, 1889.

12. *The New York Times*, December 3, 1889.

13. Description of the funeral taken from *New York Tribune* and *The New York Times*, both the issues of December 5, 1889.

14. *New York Tribune*, December 5, 1889.

15. Ibid.

16. *Skagit River* (WA) *Journal*, biography of Frank Wilkeson and his family, Neil V. Bourasaw, ed., www.skagitriverjournal.com/wa/library/wilkeson/wilkeson01-bio.html, journal, undated, accessed January 9, 2016.

17. Ibid.

18. *Biographical Annals of Montgomery County, Pennsylvania*. Elwood Roberts, ed. (New York and Chicago: T.S. Benham & Company, The Lewis Publishing Company, 1904), www .mygenealogyhound.com/pennsylvania-biographies/pennsylvania-montgomery-county -biographies/ellwood-maulsby-corson-genealogy-montgomery-county-pennsylvania -norristown-pa.html#, accessed January 9, 2016.

CHAPTER 48

1. Samito. *Fear Was Not in Him*, 209.

2. Ulysses S. Grant, *Personal Memoirs of U.S. Grant, Volume 2* (New York: Charles L. Webster & Co., 1886), 276.

3. Welch, *The Boy General*, 180.

4. Ibid., 197–98.

5. The painting can be viewed on the Metropolitan Museum of Art's website at www.metmuseum.org/toah/works-of-art/22.207.

6. Ladd and Ladd, *The Bachelder Papers, Volume 2*, 938.

7. Ibid., 1, 963.

8. At Barlow's funeral, a Harvard classmate, Edwin H. Abbott, said that Barlow "was incapable of fearing anything in any form. Fear was not in him." Cited in Samito, *Fear Was Not in Him*, 229.

9. H. W. Brands, *The Man Who Saved the Union: Ulysses S. Grant in War and Peace* (Doubleday, a division of Random House, New York, London, Toronto, Sydney, Auckland, 2012), 494.

10. Ibid., 492.

11. Salome M. Stewart. *Reminisces of Gettysburg Hospitals*, in the files of the ACHS.

12. *Gettysburg Times*, August 10, 2013.

CHAPTER 49

1. *The Temperance Record,* January 25, 1873.

2. Oliver Otis Howard, *Autobiography, Volume 2,* (Baker & Taylor Company, New York, 1904), 122.

3. December 11, 1872 deposition, Mixed Commission, XIV, 91, cited in Marion B. Lucas, *Sherman and the Burning of Columbia* (Columbia: University of South Carolina Press, 2000), 154.

4. Howard, *Autobiography, Volume 2,* 122.

5. Ibid., 124.

6. Ibid., 124–25.

7. An account of Callis's postwar life was written by Norman M. Shapiro for the Huntsville (AL) *Historical Review,* Spring-Summer 2004, 7–56, http://huntsvillehistory collection.org/hh/hhpics/pdf/hhr/Volume_29_2_Spring-Summer_2004.pdf, accessed January 9, 2016.

8. Howard. *Autobiography, Volume 2,* 375.

9. Ibid.

10. W. Todd Grace, Georgia Historical Society, December 10, 2004, online posting on *New Georgia Encyclopedia,* www.georgiaencyclopedia.org/articles/government-politics/john-b-gordon-1832-1904, accessed January 9, 2016.

11. Howard, *Autobiography, Volume 2,* 573.

12. An obituary of Howard said that while the 11th Corps was "surprised" and "put to flight" at Chancellorsville, "his corps redeemed this disaster" by seizing Cemetery Hill and holding it on the Battle of Gettysburg's first day. Files of GNMP, publication not identified.

CHAPTER 50

1. Sam Wilkeson to Oliver O. Howard, March 1, 1875, Oliver O. Howard Collection, BCL.

2. Ibid.

3. Oliver Otis Howard to Sam Wilkeson, March 19, 1875, BCL.

4. Ibid.

5. Ibid.

6. Ibid.

7. Ibid.

8. *National Tribune,* December 31, 1885.

9. Sam Wilkeson to Oliver Otis Howard, January 27, 1877, BCL.

INDEX